Into the Heart

of European

Poetry

By the same author:

Prose

The Presence of Things Past
Mysteries of the Body and the Mind
The World As It Is
Some Sort of Joy
The Apocalypse Tapestries

Criticism

Paths to Contemporary French Literature

Paths to Contemporary French Literature

Dimitris Souliotis

Selected Translations

Mary Koukoulès, *Loose-Tongued Greeks: A Miscellany of Neo-Hellenic Erotic Folklore*

Elias Papadimitrakopoulos, *Toothpaste with Chlorophyll* and *Maritime Hot Baths*

Elias Petropoulos, *Rebetika: Songs from the Old Greek Underworld*

Dominique Schnapper, *Providential Democracy: An Essay on Contemporary Equality*

Into the Heart of European Poetry

John Taylor

Transaction Publishers
New Brunswick (U.S.A.) and London (U.K.)

2-6-09

Library of Congress Catalog Number: 2008026872
ISBN: 978-1-4128-0797-5
Printed in the United States of America

Library of Congress Cataloging-in-Publication Data

Taylor, John, 1952 Sept. 30-
    Into the heart of European poetry / John Taylor.
        p. cm.
    Includes bibliographical references and index.
    ISBN 978-1-4128-0797-5 (alk. paper)
        1. European poetry--20th century--History and criticism. I. Title.

PN1271.T43 2008
809.1'034'094--dc22

PN
1271
.T43
2008

2008026872

Contents

Introduction

I like to think that this book somewhat resembles one that I had imagined and had hoped to find in the Des Moines Public Library, in the late 1960s. It was there and then that I had chanced upon *The Wasteland*; and after puzzling over that long poem and *Prufrock*, I entered *The Sacred Wood*. Eliot's essays, much more than Pound's (which I was also soon to read), opened the door to Europe and its classics. And if I write "door" here, and not "gate" or "gateway," it is because—if I may transform Eliot's sylvan metaphor—I had the impression of a wooden door in a high stone wall behind which—as I discovered when the door swung open—extended a teeming, multifarious garden, some parts of it rigorously yet strangely arranged, others blithely untended. From that moment on, I couldn't stroll often enough in that fascinating garden: European poetry. I was indeed especially drawn to Eliot's opinions about non-English poets, even though or perhaps because—as a product of the American public school system—I had studied not a single foreign language at the time, except a bit of Latin.

Nearly forty years have gone by. During more than the past three decades, after long stays in Germany and Greece, I have lived in France. During this time, I have often crossed the borders of my adopted country by car, train, airplane, and even more frequently by book, and thus temporarily left behind what has become my specialty: contemporary French literature. That is, I have continued to pursue a literary wanderlust sparked in Des Moines (a town in which, it must be said, such ignition was unlikely), to learn from unexpected mentors, to practice and dabble in languages, and to delight in far-reaching and deeply moving writing that is often scarcely known elsewhere. Whence this anthology of essays, articles, and reviews: a sort of Grand Tour of modern and contemporary European poetry, including stopovers at a few monuments of prose and at much unclassifiable "poetic prose"—a particularly fecund aspect of European writing, by the way. Because there are so many arresting European works "between genres," I no longer much believe in the standard distinction between prose and poetry, or fiction and poetry.

I have long observed that most European poets and writers have an exceedingly precise, yet nonpragmatic, approach to style; they each remain in a dynamic individual confrontation with an oft-ancient linguistic, stylistic, and literary heritage that may well (to reiterate a necessary cliché) resemble only slightly our own Anglo-American literary inheritance, not to mention the particular qualities and limitations of our language. Rhyme, meter, word order, and diction, let alone clarity, complexity, and poetic beauty, are perceived differently from language to language, from literary history to literary history. As this book progresses from poet to poet, from country to country (in a more or less counter-clockwise manner beginning and ending in France), one of my goals is to elucidate some of these differences so that certain foreign poetics can be more readily appreciated by English readers.

This intention presupposes the essential distinctness of national literatures. When dealing with European literature, the critic can never neglect this point, and I hope that I have not erred too often, propelled by enthusiasm, when analyzing particulars that I have not comprehended accurately enough in the appropriate national linguistic and literary context. Every European language possesses a rich and multifaceted literary tradition, and no national literature—despite occasional rumors to the contrary—has lost its vitality.

Yet some common denominators can be defined, and they have guided most of my choices here. If an intense concern with and knowledge of style and poetics are attributes linking European poets and writers to each other, then a second, even more important one, is constituted by the profound and extensive philosophical heritage that Europeans acquire from childhood onwards. I now know that this is the main reason why, via Eliot's own stimulating poetic and philosophical analyses, I was attracted to European poetry in the first place. This heritage is often said to commence with the pre-Socratic philosophers (who often voiced their ideas in mesmerizing verse), but the mysterious and moving volume *Waterlings*, by the Slovene poet Veno Taufer, rightfully sets the clock back much further, in prehistoric times, all the while pointing to the future. Not less importantly, the Old World, in its troubled and turbulent present, is intimately and inextricably interlaced with History; some of its contemporary poets indeed examine, even from unusual oblique angles, the import of this *donnée*. A common geography and the gruesome events that have often taken place in Europe also create thematic affinities between otherwise disparate poets. Poets featured here have faced up to the Second World War, the Shoah, Communism, the fall of the Berlin Wall, or the war that raged in many areas of ex-Yugoslavia. Other poets, in different places, have pondered the brutal destruction of landscapes and the disappearance of lifestyles that they had loved as children. And to this philosophical and historical backdrop can be added the equally deep and pervasive influences of Judaism, Christianity (in its Catholic, Protestant, and Orthodox variants), and occasionally Islam—as is brilliantly illustrated, to cite a little known example, in the novels of the classic Bosnian writer Meša Selimović.

These philosophical and religious foundations, even when essential aspects of them are violently rejected, can induce rather similar quests in poets who are otherwise at stylistic antipodes. Common pursuits include the exploration of the quotidian (not just its facts and routines, but its very essence), the search for the "thing-in-itself" (and the corresponding anxiety of being hopelessly separate from both the material world and imaginable transcendent realms), the grappling with such dichotomies as subjectivity and self-effacement, presence and absence, or negativity and affirmation, as well as the examination of "origin" and uprootedness as categories that are as ontological as they are geographical, historical, political, sociological, or cultural. The Polish poet Adam Zagajewski has notably asked: "Why is childhood our only origin, our only longing?" Such resonant questions, with all their philosophical implications, crop up repeatedly. It is difficult to read European poetry, be it written in Slovenia or Scandinavia, Russia or Spain, Italy or Holland, without simultaneously thinking of the metaphysical, ontological, and existential issues that have engaged Europeans for millennia.

Another Pole, Tadeusz Różewicz, observes: "from the crack / between me and the world / between me and the object / from the distance / between noun and pronoun / poetry struggles to emerge." Many modern European poets stare at these fundamental fissures, which are perceptible yet ineffable, at least until the poem begins to grapple with the break or gap and its corresponding ominous silence. The Hungarian Ágnes Nemes Nagy similarly argues that her work is situated in "a no-man's land of the nameless." It is an impressive phrase that indicates analogous aspirations in other key European poets. Recalling Rilke's remark about poets standing arrested at borders and grabbing at "nameless things," this image of an unclaimed or uninhabited land—ambiguous or indefinite in character and perhaps extending between opposing armies—provides a graphic way of thinking about how certain poets have lingered solitarily in zones ignored or avoided by others. Is this focus, not on empirical facts per se but rather on vague, indefinable, yet essential—as one is persuaded to agree—subject matter also perhaps preeminently European? In such cases, the very tools grasped or invented for the focusing become the poem, as it were.

Specialists of the national literatures represented here will spot oversights (and I would be happy to learn them), but my goal has never been exhaustiveness. I would rather draw readers into the heart of European poetry, hoping that they will be engaged by its authenticity and variety, and, above all, encouraged to seek out even more of the work of the poets who are presented sometimes in detail, sometimes—with regrets—only briefly. I wish that I had been able to include at least one piece on a poet from every country. (But there is no reason why my wanderlust should cease.) A few authors studied here were essential to my own development as a writer; others, equally important at various periods of my life, are missing because I have never written about them: the Hungarians Dezsö Kosztolányi and Imre Kertész come to mind, as does the Turkish short-prose writer, Sait Faik. Needless to say, the boundaries of this book do not quite correspond to current European boundaries, which are constantly debated, by the way. Even as I have included some Russians in this critical panorama of European poetry, so would I have gladly included a piece on Faik's subtle, melancholy, precisely observed short stories. And I was long tempted to add a few Irish and English poets to this anthology in order to determine what bridges or underwater tunnels might connect continental poetry to that of Eire and the Isles. This task I turn over to you, dear reader.

Peter Handke is also one of those lacunae. One short article about the translation of his novel *Die Abwendigkeit* is devoted to him here, but that is all. When I was studying literature and philosophy at the University of Hamburg in 1975-1976, a well-read German medical student pointed me toward Handke's play *Publikumsbeschimpfung*. I thereafter read all his early books. Some of his later writings—*Die Lehre der Sainte-Victoire*, the three *Versuche* (Essays), and indeed his long-poem, *Gedicht an die Dauer*—have been important to me. I have hunted down his own literary preferences, such as Nicolas Born and Gustav Januš. And our respective admirations certainly coincide in the poet Philippe Jaccottet, whose poems and prose texts, it seems to me, influenced Handke's own work during the 1990s. Because I have learned from and taken great pleasure in Handke's writing, I must add that I do not agree with some of the positions that he has taken on the Balkan War. His opinions and acts have been widely commented on; I will not enter into them here. This being said, it has become an almost routine exercise for English-language reviewers to impugn Handke's strictly literary work. The reasons given (his so-called alembicated sentences, vague characters, aimless plots, or narrative narcissism) actually represent some of the miscomprehensions that persist between English-language (and especially American) critics and certain kinds of European poets and writers. In these essays, I have tried to counter this tendency by delving into the pertinent stylistic, aesthetic, or philosophical backgrounds, and—I hope most of all—by reading foreign prose and poetry on its own terms. Enough said: I turn these pages over to you. In "Bread and Wine," Friedrich Hölderlin flatly asked: 'What good are poets in times of dearth?" This question, I am sure, is amply answered by many of the poets featured here.

Saint-Barthélemy d'Anjou
October 11, 2007

France

Exalting What Is
(Jacques Réda)

Born at No. 29, Twentieth Century, as he quips in *Le Vingtième me fatigue* (2004), the French poet Jacques Réda has fully blossomed in the twenty-first. He has produced, during the past three years especially, a variety of invigorating books: no less than two novels, a major collection of verse, a shorter second collection (*Moyens de transport*, 2003) unified by a favorite theme (motion and locomotion), as well as five gatherings of autobiographical prose interspersed with some adventuresome forays into short fiction. (And in these collections of short prose a few poems are usually thrown in as extras.) In addition, Jennie Feldman, an excellent late-blooming British poet who remains to be discovered (see her *The Lost Notebook*), has now vividly and resourcefully translated Réda's early verse in *Treading Lightly: Selected Poems 1961-1975*. It is a splendid selection of the poems that "anticipated," as Feldman points out in her introduction, "the 'new lyricism' [in French poetry] that was to gather momentum in the 1980s." Until now, all that we have had in English are Mark Treharne's equally fine rendering of Réda's best-known volume of prose poems, *The Ruins of Paris* (the French original dates back to 1977), and Dorothy Brown Aspinwall's long out-of-print translation of his second (1970) collection of poetry, *Récitatif / The Party is Over*. During the past several years, the American poet Andrew Shields has translated, for literary reviews, samplings of Réda's more recent verse; but despite the efforts of these four translators, most of the poems, stories, mini-essays, delightful prose memoirs, and lively critical writings produced by this essential European author still remain inaccessible in English. (As this book goes to press, Aaron Prevots's version of *Retour au calme* [1989] has welcomely been brought out by Host Publications.)

The time is ripe to discover him, all the more so because his prose and poetry should be particularly compelling for English-language readers. Focused, like other distinguished French poets of his generation, on both the immanence of the real world and the question of metaphysical transcendence, Réda is simultaneously playful and humorous—which is not the case with his colleagues. He is an astute practitioner of the classical French alexandrine, but he knows how to shake up the solemnity of this twelve-syllable line associated with Racine by adding or subtracting a syllable or two, by concocting audacious

3

rhymes, by employing several levels of diction all at once, and by taking on everyday themes spurned even by the more sociologically oriented among his contemporaries; at the same time, he knows how to use traditional meter and rhyme to achieve the kind of gracefully melancholic effects that have too often disappeared from French verse. In a striking afterword to his punningly entitled collection, *L'adoption du système métrique* (2004), he argues that "the so-called *constraints* of the *metrical system* [prosody] underlie its freedom."

Nearing him above all to Anglo-American sensibilities is his insatiable curiosity about facts, phenomena, and everyday events: he can be a realist and an empiricist of a kind rarely encountered in French poetry. An admirer of Robert Frost (whom he has translated), he constantly pinpoints riddles in the humblest features of reality, such as those "sacred spots"—mentioned in a text from *Les Cinq Points cardinaux* (2003)—that are no more than "a copse, a brook, or a simple fold in the earth, like the sole hexameter preserved from a vanished elegy." He may well prefer Paul Gauguin, Camille Pissarro, Nicolas Poussin, and Camille Corot to Pablo Picasso and his descendants, consider Le Corbusier to be "inept" (*Le Vingtième me fatigue*), deplore "the elimination of meaning" from the language of contemporary (French) poetry because of "metaphorical abuse, garbled syntax, and highly personal encoding" (*Les Cinq Points cardinaux*), yet no French poet has more free-spiritedly roamed the chaotic contemporary urban world—and conveyed that chaos so engagingly.

His position in French literature is assuredly complex. He has been nourished by several literary traditions, ranging from the ancient Greek and Roman poets, through the Romantics (with a particular liking for William Wordsworth), to modernists like Jorge Luis Borges (about whom he has penned a book-length study) and his cherished mentor, the Swiss writer Charles-Albert Cingria, whose unclassifiable writings Anglo-Americans would be wise to discover as well. Most French readers know that Réda has since 1963 worked as a sharp-eared music critic for *Jazz Magazine*; far fewer that he was interested, during the 1950s, in the theoretical implications of Alain Robbe-Grillet's first experimental novels. A second telling affinity is worth mentioning. Réda pays homage to Fernando Pessoa in the prose-cum-poetry volume *Europes* (2005), applauding in the process the municipal authorities of Lisbon for inscribing none of the names of "this poet with ten names who was literally 'nobody'" on his official statue.

At least with hindsight, it is not surprising that Réda has studied Robbe-Grillet's novelistic innovations and, more recently, been intrigued by Pessoa's heteronyms. Réda's own novels, *Nouvelles aventures de Pelby* (2003) and *L'affaire du* Ramsès III (2004) have brought into full daylight his longtime passion for narrative logic (and the parody thereof), not to mention the thorny question of personas in his ostensibly autobiographical writings. If the reader looks twice, such concerns have always informed his short prose, with its emphasis on the narrator-author's falling prey to obscure imbroglios fomented by outside forces or, more generally, what might be called "meta-events." Inclined to meditation and lyricism, Réda has always been equally fascinated by "events" and the way they link up or jumble disparately together. In his personal essay "Ce qui nous arrive" ("What Happens to Us"), published in *Les Cinq Points cardinaux*, he even posits that "in the final reckoning, there are only events." *L'affaire du Ramsès III* is a spoof on detective novels, and the first-person narrator has "often been invented by events." "The events" constitute a character of sorts, and they include "certain facts [about the narrator] in their plans." This list of Réda's contrasting affinities, idiosyncrasies, and talents could be continued.

If he has been prolific, especially since retiring as editor-in-chief of the *La Nouvelle Revue Française* (which he directed for Gallimard between 1987 and 1996), no line, rhyme, or turn of phrase in any of these new writings shows haste or waste. His work has long provided rare reading pleasures; these new books increase them and, in the case of *Ponts flottants* (2006), in which prose texts—genuine "floating bridges"—are constructed by means of successive (plank-like?) paragraphs each consisting of a single declarative sentence, Réda convincingly experiments with a formal scheme that he has never used before. A superb connoisseur of form in both poetry and prose, Réda experiments more often than French critics tend to perceive. Perhaps it could be asserted that this specific book even builds a "floating bridge" between the two genres that he practices with equal success. Grouped under section titles such as "Space Exercises," "Ruminated Moments," and "Presumptions as to Elements," the texts in *Ponts flottants* particularly impress with their half-in-jest, half-in-earnest speculations about time, space, mind, matter, and movement. Here as elsewhere, cosmological wonder and a few persistent metaphysical qualms inform the author's scrutiny of overlooked aspects of land-, city-, and—hardly least—sky-scapes.

Ever since his first books (Feldman has rendered about half of the poems included in *Amen* [1968], the aforementioned *Récitatif*, and *La Tourne* [1975]), Réda has always been an open-eyed describer of skies. Probably no other natural element better suits his literary sensibility, for he is an indefatigable contemplator of change, color, geometric shape, and atmosphere, any of which can spark his incorrigible penchant for metaphysical speculation. (The title of one poetry collection confesses to this little sin: *L'incorrigible*, 1995.) *Treading Lightly* comprises memorable lines about ephemeral configurations of clouds, reflections, seasons, and hues, notably this apperception that also reveals Réda's concern with how subjective observers and the outside world interact, even at times (almost) re-unite: "Barely a millimetre's water under the trees, but it catches / Convulsions in a sky that eases and deepens / Letting winter and its clouds be born between our steps." In the same book, "Autumn" is a French-style "Ode to the West Wind," beginning:

> Ah, I know that sound—autumn's wandering gust
> Here already, breeding its thunder silently
> Deep in forests and crippling overloaded orchards;

This solemn wind that's like us, speaking our language
Where disaster sings an undertone.

Interestingly, in his recent writings, Réda often devotes his descriptive talents to the sun, both rising and setting. The most synaesthetically extravagant among these evocations occurs in the story "Apples," from *Cléona et autres contes de voyageurs solitaires* (2005). There, a setting sun "sprawls out for a long time on brilliantly fringed bedding, a heap of cushions ranging in color from mystical pink to thick tars which, if diluted, would render an abstraction in azure or the emerald green of a theological virtue."

These new books continue to display his heady and sensual combination of the cosmic and the local, the abstract and the concrete, the structured and the chaotic, the wacky and the reasonable—mixtures that (it occurs to me) also define the verse, if not the prose, of Joseph Brodsky, whose philosophical inquisitiveness and insistence on the virtues of versification parallel the same qualities in his French peer. In *L'adoption du système métrique*, a "New Letter on the Universe"—Réda implicitly refers to his earlier *Lettre sur l'univers et autres discours en vers français* (1991)—initially recalls how breaking down matter into increasingly smaller particles implies that "if you descend into the depth of things, nothing exists." The poem then turns to the "shimmering surfaces" of matter that ever attract the attention of this stylistic hedonist: the sun, soil, oceans, wind, dust, and his beloved "lazy clouds." "All at once everything exists—and nothing," he finally concedes, before situating our existence and, implicitly, the quest of poetry, at this "crossroads." It is helpful to keep this crossroads in mind when reading him.

Here explicitly, elsewhere in passing, Réda appeals to philosophical concepts and, increasingly, scientific findings or theories. He tests them against the random serendipitous discoveries that he makes while he is wandering around Paris (and a few foreign towns), riding in train cars, on overcrowded city buses (though rarely in a Paris métro car), and in the occasional tramway (as a graphic evocation in *Europes* reveals), or—famously—touring the French countryside on "Xélos," his Vélo-Solex motorbike. As he recounts his half-haphazard itineraries ("half-," because he usually first heads somewhere specific), characteristic dichotomies take shape, collide: the straight line and the zigzagging detour, the quick, vivid image and the digressing rumination, the spontaneous exit and the unplanned prolonged delay, the clarity of reason and the amusing obscurities of unreason, indecision, self-doubt, yearning. For all of Réda's jocularity and self-ironic remove, sometimes quite intense emotions rise to the surface, especially in his poetry; stark contrasts obtain when strong feelings surge up within the strictures of a formal prosodic scheme. An illustration occurs in the opening lines of "L'écluse," from *Moyens de transport*, where the poet makes a surprising, though otherwise unelucidated, avowal: "The train had long followed the course of my sadness / (no: near terror—but scream in this compartment?) / when the sight of lock gates being maneuvered / on a canal brought me peace."

The new poems and stories involving the author's antiquated Vélo-Solex are particularly welcome in that Réda seemed to have abandoned this means of transportation. He has claimed that this change was forced upon him because the French National Train Company (SNCF) had stopped letting passengers take small motorbikes aboard, a privilege that the poet formerly took advantage of in order to arrive safely and speedily in provincial outposts, whose environs he would then investigate "astride Xélos." A Vélo-Solex such as Réda's is capable of a maximum speed of only about thirty miles per hour. (For the French, the Vélo-Solex, like the "2CV" car, immediately conjures up endearing images, as also does the Olympia typewriter, commemorated in *Ponts flottants*, which Réda still apparently uses for all his writing.) Moreover, being able to stow the Vélo-Solex on a train is crucial because the dangers of puttering out of the capital via speedy expressways are many; the perils of provincial thoroughfares are numerous enough. "Apples" opens with a classic scene: "After crossing a national highway blocked by a steady stream of Spanish semis (I had taken Xélos by the bridle and ventured across while reciting my act of contrition), I followed a country road which, escorted by two rows of increasingly small apple trees, attacked a long, gently rising slope." It is indeed the country road that is in motion, attacks the slope, is escorted; and the apple trees decrease in size.

Meditating on movement and how we perceive it is typical of Réda. More than once he alludes favorably to Heraclitus, for whom all was flux; relativity theory sneaks in, too. The author of *Le Sens de la marche* (1990)—another important prose-cum-poetry volume whose title puns on "facing forwards" and "the meaning of walking"—likes to inverse our habitual perceptions of objects as they and we move through space and time. At one point in *Ponts flottants*, Réda sums up his writerly vantage point as follows: "Thus, while moving, I explored the inert and abandoned myself, immobile, to the voluptuousness of movement." A typical voluptuous perception, this time from the vantage point of a very fast TGV train, sums up a rape (colza) field as a "splendor of incomprehensible yellow expressing no more than its utter jubilation, the extreme point of a thought that only color makes explicit." A thought? Whose thought? This is the kind of unexpected question that one ponders when reading Réda.

Another of his fascinations is architecture. It, too, is frequently associated with movement. While describing Ravenna in *Europes*, Réda points out that the town "engrosses one in details, but what I call detail can be an entire basilica. And thanks to the details of that detail, one senses more forcibly and voluptuously the kinesthesia typical of such noble architectural accomplishments, which always consist of a noble movement that has—to all appearances—been captured." In other words, appearances are deceiving: the basilica is still moving. Réda's descriptions often set stable objects into motion or, at least, suggest their internal dynamics. In a reminiscence about visiting the Escurial near Madrid, he similarly mentions a famous description by François-René de Chateaubriand, who contends that the Spanish monument is the exact architectural result of history and politics. Claiming ignorance of such matters (but his tongue is in his cheek), Réda observes that his own inductions are based merely on "brute phenomena," specifying, however, that "their considerable effects do not merely depend on their pure factuality." "The hidden causes of a phenomenon participate in our emotion," he adds. "The emotion I feel when spotting a mountain range...draws some of its force from the unfathomable depths of orogenesis." After this digression, he describes the impression that the Spanish monument makes on him.

Although Réda sports here with the magisterial Chateaubriand, the quotation is not to be taken lightly. It is hard to say what matters more to him: brute phenomena (whose sheer existence provokes wonder, jubilation) or what might lie behind them. A skilled, but no strict or full-fledged, realist, Réda is ever hunting for primum mobiles and trying to intimate mysterious long-term consequences. In a poem from *Moyens de transport*, he exalts the "ecstatic platitude" of flat country, the "vertigo of the horizontal on an endless plain." He adds that all directions disappear; all that remains is the "diffuse yet powerful magnetism of the expanse, drawing you in the right direction, / the only one, / bringing you more deeply, with every step, into the silent intimacy of Everything."

Like Frost, Réda is sensitive to place, to what certain places spontaneously express, without words, indeed point to beyond words. An early poem rendered by Feldman notably begins with the discovery of a dilapidated house near the Alsatian town of Schirmeck. "Towards Schirmeck tall trunks crowd steeply in mist," notes the poet, "Around a house without walls where breath / Lingers." Réda concludes:

> The abrupt and never-baptised earth entrenched
> In its irritability, digs in deeper towards Schirmeck
> And that's where the heart, stoved in by words, takes its rest.

Born not far away in the Lorraine town of Lunéville (which comes to life in his most moving prose memoir, *Aller aux mirabelles* [1991]), Réda has often set poems or prose texts in eastern France, a part of the country mostly overlooked by French writers. Family ties to and vacations spent in Burgundy have induced him to devote poems or narratives to lesser-known corners of that province as well. Now and then, the poet reminds us that one of his grandfathers was Italian, from the Piedmont. In Ravenna, for example, Réda spots a "barbaric coefficient" in the town's monuments, including the basilica; yet this initial impression is qualified by a typical self-ironic observation: "But I do not deny that my eye perhaps suffers from a certain barbarism, due to some ancient Lombard strain in me that is dumbfounded by oddities from Byzantium."

More characteristically, Réda relishes wandering around the outlying *arrondissements* of Paris (where he has lived since 1953) as well as the outskirts of the capital, seeking out "fugitive beauty in the faubourgs," as he puts it in a poem collected in the *L'adoption du système métrique*. He has always been attracted to the faubourgs, those intermediate, half-residential, half-industrialized districts lying beyond official city limits yet not quite so far as the genuine bucolic countryside. In another poem from the same collection, he remembers how, in his youth, the "white wind of the faubourgs" would call him back, either from distant fruit orchards or from the center of town, to a peripheral "gap" or "remove" ("écart" in French); throughout his work, such in-between settings become the locus of indefinable emotions (including amorous stirrings), spiritual intimations, or solitary discoveries. "Often I have revisited those same faubourgs," he adds in a third poem, "in other towns where I have wandered.../ Though without knowing that I was looking for them." Is not the scorned faubourg one telling emblem of our civilization?

Similar metaphors indicating spatial "in-betweenness" crop up in the work of other key twentieth-century French writers. Julien Gracq's early fiction often takes place near tense "borders"; the notion of "threshold" recurs in the poetry of Yves Bonnefoy, Philippe Jaccottet, Pierre-Albert Jourdan, and others. For Réda, who also evokes "thresholds" of various kinds, the ambivalence and indeterminacy of the faubourg sharpens his focus: the lackluster back street suddenly displays an architectural curiosity whose geometry invites cosmological or philosophical generalization; or the vacant lot has an acacia tree blooming ecstatically, unexpectedly. A third instance occurs in a café called at once "Le Gouleyant," which suggests a smooth and delicious wine, and "Chez Mahmoud," which reveals that its owner is Muslim. The author spots three old painted wall panels that recall "the first period" (he specifies) of the art of Maurice Denis. He photographs the panels, and at a later date brings copies back to the café to give them to the owner and show them around to the regular customers who, however, are not very interested because it is Ramadan, the sun has just set, and they can finally dig into a good meal. This latter scene takes place, not in an authentic faubourg, but in the twentieth *arrondissement*. With the growth of big-city *banlieues* and their high-rise low-cost apartment complexes, Réda has re-discovered "faubourgian" ambiences in the Belleville quarter of "Le Vingtième," where has been living for the past decade (after living for many years in the fifteenth *arrondissement*, which he also extensively memorialized). *Le Citadin* (1998) already includes vivid diary-like reports on what he has come across in and around Belleville; appended to *Le Vingtième me fatigue*, whose title implies that both the twentieth century and the twentieth *arrondissement* are wearing him down, is a *Supplement to a Lacunary Inventory of the Streets of the 20th Arrondissement of Paris* (the funny prose texts of which, incidentally, clarify the origins of poems in other collections). He declares that he searches for each street's peculiar "qualities." Often the details that he happens upon offer a flash of transient beauty or even a transcendent shimmer. Are these troubling signs mere mirages? Réda is more than aware of this possibility.

That he has applied this literary project, with all its philosophical resonance, to such unlikely places as the drabbest French faubourgs, the most ordinary Parisian streets, and the sleepiest provincial localities is a significant accomplishment. In his open-minded and, in fact, mind-liberating scrutiny of the here and now (absolutely wherever he finds himself), he always ends up finding something to celebrate, amid a few grumbles and amusing pet peeves of course. Contemporary art has become a favorite target; there is a hilarious text, in *Ponts flottants*, about an "installation" that actually consists of the equipment of housepainters who are repainting the inside walls of the apartment building in which the author lives. What this literary viewpoint more seriously indicates is that Réda pits the possibilities of affirmation, even hope, against despair and negativism wherever he wanders. Even his poems about death (there are several in *L'adoption du système métrique*) convey touching personal images, such as when, in "Elegy on the Pink Factory," he speculates that "the final image / passing through [him]" may be, not a face, but rather the pink wall of a brown-roofed factory at which he liked to look when he was living "for ten years of slight misfortune" in—once again—a faubourg. He adds that the pollution billowing out of the factory chimney had "an exotic stench of chocolate."

Réda has deepened and extended the great French tradition of the poet-*flaneur* who investigates and meditates on change and contemporaneity, an archetypal literary figure going back at least to Charles Baudelaire's pensive and solitary "stroller immersed in the moving / waves of the multitudes." For Réda, a daily "ration of asphalt is vital," as he confesses in *L'adoption du système métrique*. One certainly believes him. However, it is critically myopic to reduce his work to this strolling-poet tradition. The poetic and philosophical ramifications of his method are many. Comparing the early poems that Feldman has translated to Réda's work since the mid-1970s (with *The Ruins of Paris* as the turning point), I have the impression that the poet eventually, and perhaps quite consciously, allowed his initially more self-absorbed, sometimes more tormented, lyricism to give way, at least partly, to a more objective scrutiny of vibrant details amid the teeming reality in his midst. Perhaps it could be said that Réda resolved to acquire this new capability, to chart this new territory, as it were. The *hic et nunc* is ever uncharted, let alone pondered, as he shows so brilliantly. In her introduction, Feldman mentions Réda's love for Dante, which I was unaware of, but now that she has established the link it is hard not to think of "il gran rifiuto" (*Inferno*, III, 60) that also disturbed another favorite poet of Réda's, C. P. Cavafy. Perhaps Réda, at some point, made the decision to refuse "the great refusal." There is certainly a stripping away of the needlessly subjective and a turning to the positive in, say, this passage from *Les Cinq Points cardinaux*: "the meaning of music is inexpressible because it is excessive, and it is excessive because music, like the world, eloquently asserts that it *is*, outside of all questions of meaning." Here is a French poet and prose writer who eloquently exalts this "is," all the while meditating on what underlies it all.

Spain

The Chromatic Prose of Josep Pla's Gray Notebook

Thanks to a Barcelona bookseller, who intuitively grasped my literary tastes, bent down, and pulled a slightly damaged out-of-print French edition from a dusty bottom shelf, I have discovered the Catalan writer Josep Pla (1897-1981). The book is *Le Cahier gris*, that is Pascale Bardoulaud's vivid and enjoyable version of *El quadern gris* (1966), the magnum opus of Pla's vast and varied output. (In Catalan, Pla's *Obra Completa*, with *El quadern gris* as its first installment, runs to forty-six volumes.) It's always better to be late than never: *The Gray Notebook* deserves to be translated into English as soon as possible and studied as a classic of modern European literature. As far as I can tell, this absorbing and oft-funny tome of 612 finely printed pages otherwise exists only in Spanish, Dutch, and Serbian renderings. Apparently a German translator is about to tackle it. Purportedly a diary, it is much more than that. I have never read a book quite like it.

The impetus for Pla's project, which he initiated when he was only twenty-one years old, was the Spanish flu epidemic of 1918. A little-motivated law student at the time, he found himself relegated to an early and prolonged summer vacation because the University of Barcelona had closed down in accordance with a public health measure. The first diary entry is dated March 8th. Pla has returned home with his brother to live with their parents in Palafrugell, their native village. "I see my brother, who adores playing soccer—although he once broke an arm and then a leg while doing so—only at mealtimes," begins Pla. "He lives his own life. As for me, I get by as I can. I do not miss Barcelona, even less so the University. Life in the village, with my friends who live here, suits me fine."

What this disabused avowal already hints at is the birth of a writer—the central theme of the book. Because Pla is forced to flee the Spanish flu (and thus, gladly, his dismal law studies), he can finally give rein to his urge to write. In one early passage, dated April 12th, he reports his father telling him to take his textbooks up to the attic. "Whenever you want to study," his father suggests, "no one will bother you there." "After wandering around the whole house for a while," adds the author, "I ended up climbing the stairs." But instead of opening his textbooks, Pla contemplates the "gentle, sweet, mellow light" that is coming

13

from the skylight. He then describes the attic, complains about his mother's omnipresence in the house ("if she could, she would tidy up our feelings" as one puts a messy room back in order), evokes the hilly seaside landscape that he can spot from a window, and finally reflects on his Catholic upbringing. After this auspicious stint of writing, he concludes that the attic is too cold.

Little else will be heard about the attic and the textbooks. Pla thereafter spends most of his time outside. As the days go by, he scrutinizes everyday life in Palafrugell and, when summer comes, that of a nearby sea resort, Calella. He has little if anything to do except pass time with his sidekicks, hang out in cafés, sometimes get drunk ("I'm having lots of difficulties, and it is very unpleasant, trying to recover from a Pernod binge"), sharply observe the comings and goings of villagers, record and often satirize overheard conversations, poke fun at the local bourgeoisie and their facetious manners, read Catalan authors (such as the "affected, violinist-like" Xènius, the theoretician of *Noucentisme*, a national literary and philosophical movement), recall his childhood and its vicissitudes (the move to the new, chilly house has provoked a sort of permanent existential unease), think hard about the Catalan language (the ongoing grammatical and orthographic codification of which was a current topic), and think even harder about the personal literary style that he envisioned and was in fact already forging—and it differed significantly from the flowery academic idiom that was in vogue.

The idle law student, now a budding writer, thus actually has much to do in Palafrugell, especially as regards the perfecting of a style that was to become one of the finest in Catalan literature. As Pla explains several times in acute critical reaction to his literary elders, simplicity and clarity are his goals. But this is not all. As he rejects the temptations of stylistic ornamentation and seeks the most specific nouns and adjectives for his perceptions, he never neglects irony. It is masterfully applied in countless passages of *The Gray Notebook*. The epithet "realist," which is sometimes applied to Pla, is insufficient, at least by American standards. (Hemingway was by one year his exact contemporary.) So witty and subtly intricate are Pla's precisely crafted objective descriptions that *The Gray Notebook* is brilliantly chromatic throughout. It is emotionally colorful. It is also richly sensate, for Pla excels at transcribing physical sensations, especially those relating to temperature. The author's subjectivity is disclosed as often through carefully recorded details from the outside world as through his lively opinions, frank confessions, and sometimes rather brutal self-appraisals.

Pla, who revised and expanded his initial diary manuscript much later in adulthood and first brought it out nearly a half-century after the events recounted, structures the somewhat haphazard contents of a normal diary into narratives on several levels. Because he thinks back on and analyzes his childhood (which already seems remote and forever lost, even though he is sojourning in his hometown at the mere age of twenty one), the book sketches the broad lines of a coming-of-age novel. Because each entry is dated, the diary self-chronicles a work-in-progress, only later to be entitled *The Gray Notebook*. For the same reason, the notebook charts Pla's development as a writer; it is a literary logbook that includes probing passages on creativity, literary innovation, and the author's Catalan literary heritage. It offers the first chapters of his autobiography, in both anecdotal and intellectual senses of the genre.

The second part of the book traces the author's return, in January 1919, to Barcelona, where he resumes his law studies but is now convinced that his destiny lies elsewhere. His textbooks have "yellowed," he admits. "They look like old-fashioned things, like lifeless, useless objects. Things can indeed be ordinary; they can even possess a profound, massive, inherent ordinariness. But in this regard, there is nothing like textbooks."

Pla's satirical pen turns to the hypocrisies and pretensions of academic life. In the evenings, he delves into the literary and artistic life of the city. From these descriptions emerges still another narrative, that of Barcelona as an active locus of European modernism. Through these various story lines, which are discarded, then picked up again and set forth, the book displays much less heterogeneity than is commonly found in writer's journals. And bringing these different narrative strands together on a personal existential level is the deadly flu epidemic, an invisible leitmotiv in the first section. Arguably, the epidemic catalyses Pla's desire to write in the first place; it provokes him into summing up his young life. All along, he is writing and living intently because his days may be numbered.

Among other curiosities, the notebook comprises an extensive and somewhat unsettling description of Pla's physical appearance. This passage is ostensibly penned for one "Lola S.," though it is never sent to her because the author suffers from "an excessive feeling of ridiculousness." At the same time the diarist speculates on his ethnic origins, noting that his mother's maiden name, Casadevall, can often be found on lists of Jews burned at the stake during medieval pogroms. However, as Pla boasts to Lola about his seductive handsomeness, he claims that he has no "typical" Jewish nose or neck, let alone the "sad eyes of a begging, beaten dog." Instead, he has "very lively eyes" and his neck is shaped "like a well-composed melody." Although he is obviously being self-ironic here and, elsewhere, goes on to ridicule his facial appearance, these few sentences may strike readers as racist. All told, it is not that easy to determine what Pla intends, as irony is superposed on irony. Interestingly, he visited Tel Aviv in 1957, traveling from Marseille on a boat full of homeless Jews. His *Les escales de Llevant* (1969) comprises an important eyewitness account of Israel in those days.

Despite the respect that his style and literary sensibility immediately command, some aspects of Pla's life have disturbed Catalan and Spanish intellectuals. During the Civil War years, and especially in 1938-1939, his stance toward Franco showed political ambiguity, or at best revealed the writer's survival instincts. Although he hated the Caudillo's prohibition of the use of Catalan, a law that was strictly enforced during the Second World War and only somewhat mitigated during the 1950s and thereafter, Pla seems to have believed that, despite the dictatorship, democracy would gradually establish itself in Spain. His advocates refer to his "interior exile," as opposed to the genuine expatriation undertaken by countless Spaniards. Pla was no revolutionary, but instead a conservative skeptic. During the rigorous prohibition of Catalan, he turned to Spanish, writing the well-known *Viaje en autobús* (1942)—just one example of his passion for getting around by all conceivable means of transportation—and several other books. Throughout his career, he traveled far and wide, and produced an impressive amount of journalism. After Franco's death in 1975, which was followed by a democratic Constitution in 1978, left-wing Catalan writers held it against Pla for a while that he had initially supported, or at least tolerated, the dictator.

The Gray Notebook is, of course, also a notebook, that is a high-precision laboratory for literary experiments. A splendid instance consists of several long dialogues that take place between two young bourgeois lovers. These dialogues are inserted into the diary as trial runs for what resembles a projected satirical novel. The couple's conversations—earnest for them, hilarious for us—bring the young man (who, by the way, is a law student) and his fiancée fully to life on the page. Their remarks and perceptions also illustrate telltale aspects of the summer resort beach life that Pla has been investigating with his sharpshooter eyes, perfect-pitch ears, and hypersensitive epidermis. Whether he scrutinizes societal mores as in this case or turns inward and wonders who he is, Pla compels throughout this little-known, formally original Catalan masterpiece.

The Pursuit of Shimmering Instants
(Luis Cernuda)

Luis Cernuda (1902-63) was a member of the Spanish "Generation of 1927," which included other well-known poets such as Federico García Lorca (1899-1936), Rafael Alberti (1902-1999), Pedro Salinas (1892-1951), Jorge Guillén (1893-1984), and Vicente Aleixandre (1898-1984). Following upon a Sheep Meadow reissue, in 1999, of Cernuda's verse (in a translation by Reginald Gibbons), *Written in Water* groups together two prose collections, *Ocnos* and *Variations on a Mexican Theme*, each made up of sad, delicate, gently thought-provoking short texts. As to the former title, Ocnos is a Roman mythical figure who twisted reeds into ropes only to discover that his donkey methodically ate them. Yet he persisted in his efforts in order to "give himself something to do" and "perhaps learn something," as Goethe reports in his retelling of this fable, which moreover provides the perfect epigraph for *Written in Water*.

An Ocnos-like resolution (animated by a sentiment of futility) indeed forms the biographical and thematic backdrop of Cernuda's book. Two years after publishing the first edition of his collected verse (*Reality and Desire*, 1936), the poet was forced to leave Spain for good because of the Civil War. He moved to towns in England, Scotland, then the United States. Each subsequent city was a "prison...useless in your life except for work, parching and consuming what youth you had left." After teaching at Mount Holyoke College, he finally settled in Mexico in the early 1950s. *Ocnos* looks back to his lost childhood and homeland, whereas the Mexican texts of the second section extol the sunlight and sensuality of southern climes. For Cernuda, Mexico was a Paradise Briefly Regained.

Forming a diptych, the book gathers nearly a hundred short poetic meditations of a kind rare in American literature. For lack of a better term, these texts are "prose poems" because the author always maintains a "graceful hold on [his] material"—as was required, he avows, by his beloved rhetoric teacher (whose portrait is affectionately drawn here). Yet Cernuda is also more inquisitive, philosophically, than most poets and prose poets. He muses, but he is equally interested in the phenomenology of musing. He tries to sense himself thinking and feeling, because self-reflexive apperceptions deepen his understanding of what it means to be alive. He takes seriously not just ideas and sense perceptions, but also emotions, for they are precious indicators of an individual's relationship to Time. In "The Bells," he notably ponders why "there are emotions... whose effect is not concurrent with their cause, and have to pass through the most vast and dense regions inside us, until one day we feel them. But why just then, and not before, or later?"

This probing Proustian intellectuality, ever keen to generalize from particulars (and then sometimes to call into doubt his generalizations, as in the gravely moving "Light"), presides over Cernuda's short poetic prose. His rational impulse complements his otherwise passionate search for "harmony." Interestingly, the Spaniard equates harmony with *Gemüt*, a complex German notion that goes back to Meister Eckhart (whose mystical and philosophical writings Cernuda has clearly perused). The German Romantics later picked up on this term, which means "soul," "heart," "mood," "sensibility," and, for Cernuda, a "unity of feeling and consciousness." The poet first associates this desired unity with "entering another body in the act of love [and thereby obtaining] oneness with life by way of the lover's body." More generally, his aim is to "obliterat[e]... otherness," become "one with the world"—an aspiration later encouraging him to observe Mexicans and their mores with benevolence, though he remains apart from them, ever a stranger among this people who speak his language. And here and elsewhere, Cernuda points out that merging with these various othernesses can be achieved only in fleeting "perfect shimmering instant[s]," each of which is like "a pearl between its valves." The especial melancholy of his texts is thoroughly Ocnos-like. As he recalls loci of ephemeral harmony, increases his knowledge and self-knowledge, and crafts his ruminations, he hints that these introspective and poetic labors are all in vain. The donkey is already chewing the beautiful reed-woven rope.

This contradiction, or antagonism, deeply informs Cernuda's literary project. There is absolutely no artifice in his warm and candid writings, but they are, as it were, constantly aware of their artifice. Finding words for the mute torments of his sensibility, he considers himself to be "a sleepless voice calling who knows what or to whom in night's nameless immensity." A permanent tension consequently underlies the calm, if syntactically intricate, surface of his prose (which has been sensitively rendered by Stephen Kessler, who also provides an insightful preface). Tellingly, Cernuda's *élans* toward artistic or amorous rapture are restrained by cogitation, retrospection, and comparison, not to mention the very act of literary creation. In "Music," he exalts the "contemplative bliss" that music provides—its "pure pathless delight," as Mallarmé phrased it. Yet by explaining how he covets this purity, how he absorbs himself in music, how it is "like a wave that might lift us from life into death...toward the farthest edge of oblivion," Cernuda actually charts a path for what, ideally, should have remained pathless. He is already separated from his bliss. It is kept in sight as a goal, but now it is defined, delineated, mapped out.

Not surprisingly, Cernuda admires Keats, who struggled with the same limitations of the soul. A phrase from the latter's epitaph entitles both this two-in-one volume and its somber "coda." Befittingly, and somehow nobly, it is Cernuda's final transposition of the Ocnos myth:

...God does not exist. The dry leaf, crushed in passing, told me so. The dead bird told me, its broken wing rotting on the ground. Consciousness told me, knowing it too will be lost one day in the vastness of nonbeing. And if God doesn't exist, how could I? I don't exist even now, dragging myself like a shadow through a delirium of shadows, breathing these breathless words, absurd testimony (by whom and for whom?) of my existence.

A Spanish Penelope
(Francisca Aguirre)

The Spanish poet Francisca Aguirre (b. 1930) revives legendary Penelope in *Ithaca* (1972), which has now been accurately and fluidly translated by Ana Valverde Osan. Focusing on Penelope instead of the Homeric Ulysses "of many wiles," the book is a thematically unified sequence of both long and short poems portraying the woman, letting her speak, as well as using her both as a persona and an alter ego so that Aguirre can speak in her own right. Some poems are almost diary-like, while others open out onto more timeless, mythical evocations of the sea and the island of Ithaca. Ithaca is often used metaphorically, as in the line "Ithaca is within, or one may not reach it."

These various approaches to the solitude and despair of a woman who has remained behind on the island while her husband is fighting in the Trojan War (and malingering on his return voyage, to say the least) greatly increase the psychological complexity of Penelope with respect to Homer's original model. Even more importantly, Aguirre's portrait is dual in that autobiographical allusions are rare but not excluded. The book is divided into two sections, the more personal second part of which notably begins: "That childhood was mostly sad. / To be a child in forty-two seemed impossible." 1942 was the year in which the poet's father was murdered by Franco's regime. Yet even without this tragic information (provided by Osan's introduction), this and other poems juxtapose Aguirre's life with that of Penelope. The days of childhood, adds Aguirre with respect to the same fatal year, "wrinkled up..., / while we grew toward the grief that invades us today." In a poem dated 1963, Aguirre commemorates a "dragon tree" that "grows mysterious / justifying the world uselessly." After a few such allusions, one wishes that more autobiographical insights had been included.

Penelope's grief persists during monotonous, lonely days. Her weaving by day and unraveling by night is a stunning metaphor of this unbearable stasis, though Aguirre specifically associates the unraveling with the woman's perception of the passage of time, the "tender and decomposing disaster / in the final hours of this day / that has gone by like the others." As regards the few significant events that occur, Aguirre respects little if any linear chronology. Penelope's son Telemachus "keeps on growing" in "Sisyphus of the Cliffs"

(p. 29); Ulysses returns to Ithaca in "The Welcome" (p. 47); but in the second section, we find him returning again in "The Stranger" (p. 93). Through these shifting time patterns, different levels of Penelope's experience of sorrowful waiting are brought forth as so many overlapping states of consciousness, involving memory, daydreaming, and anticipation, as well as a few perceptions of present reality (though the factual present is more often a conspicuously absent backdrop to the heroine's self-analysis).

At the same time, an emotional evolution is discernable. Beginning with the second section especially, both poet and protagonist grapple with morbidity ("Penelope, / we should do something other than dying") as they realize that they are being forced into a "horrible autophagy." However, like tense opposites that cannot be resolved, increasing self-awareness and a growing sentiment of impossibility culminate in Penelope's suicidal wishes, thwarted at the last instant by a "wall" of "handkerchiefs / and...voices...lovingly protect[ing] her." The beautiful final piece provides a *dénouement* as the poet and Penelope speak to, indeed blend into, each other. The last line, "Francisca Aguirre, accompany yourself," gathers all the preceding suffering and soul-searching into the resolution of a woman who is going to take her destiny into her own hands.

This is admirable and original. In other take-offs on *The Odyssey*, Penelope often remains a shadowy figure. She has been depicted as a dampener of Ulysses' adventurous spirit and an obstacle to his continuing self-development. In Nikos Kazantzakis's *The Odyssey* (1938), for instance, once Odysseus has killed Penelope's suitors and pretenders to his throne, he rejects Penelope and leaves Ithaca forever. Some of this marital tension is also suggested by Aguirre:

> He has returned. He doesn't know very well why.
> For he fears old age more than death.
> He suspects peace and quiet as if they harbored a virus.
> I am for him something worse than a treason:
> I am as inexplicable as he is.

As opposed to amorous yearning and unrequited love, Penelope's inexplicability—more to herself than to an imputable partner—is the central theme here. She must untangle and understand what has been woven of her life.

Penelope is likewise absent in C. P. Cavafy's famous poem "Ithaca." In her introduction, Osan records Aguirre's shock at reading "Waiting for the Barbarians," if not specifically "Ithaca." Yet the latter piece must have similarly affected her. Cavafy's "Ithaca" emphasizes the wisdom that Odysseus will have acquired by the time he reaches Ithaca—at which point the island "will have nothing left" to give him. Cavafy's poem implicitly turns Penelope into a negative factor, and could thereby have provided a provocative stimulus for the Spanish poet. This being said, Aguirre does not always sufficiently distance herself from Cavafy's immediately recognizable style and narrative method, especially in the first section.

This leads to an additional criticism. *Ithaca* chronicles a depression—to use the contemporary term. Depression frequently implies withdrawal from the world's particulars, but from the poetic viewpoint should not more of Penelope's thoughts, desires, and illusions be tied to concrete images? It is a delicate question of equilibrium for any literary text staging introspection. The present world must be given a bit of substance alongside evocations of a mind refusing that substance. Homer gives the outside world a firm foundation in Penelope's "chair inlaid with ivory and silver spirals." In "The World as Meditation," Wallace Stevens sets Penelope in the here and now by mentioning her "cretonnes" and "pillow." Some of Aguirre's poems are moving avowals, but others, relying too heavily on abstractions, lack a striking detail or two which would have created more memorable pictures of Penelope struggling with her inner torment.

Italy

Haunting Absence, Intense Presence
(Eugenio Montale)

Eugenio Montale (1896-1981) composed poems as hermetic as any ever written in any language. For the 1975 Nobel prizewinner, however, this obscurity was by no means gratuitous. Montale's highly conscious private symbolism is as autobiographically specific as it is strangely applicable to our own experience, as cryptically singular as it is thematically multifaceted. It is, in brief, an exceedingly complex lyricism embodying a challenging—and perhaps to some readers, irritating—psychoanalytical and philosophical stance, at least throughout Jonathan Galassi's superb version and edition of the *Collected Poems 1920-1954*, which represents the three long volumes—*Cuttlefish Bones, The Occasions,* and *The Storm, Etc.*—produced during early and middle stages of his career. William Arrowsmith's rendering of *Satura 1962-1970*, which has also appeared in English (both editions are bilingual), shifts toward the terseness of the poet's old age, a style especially associated with the rather dismissingly entitled *Diary of '71 and '72* (1973), *Notebook of Four Years* (1977) and *Other and Uncollected Poems* (1981). The man's oeuvre is thus marked chronologically—though salient counterexamples exist—by a dichotomy opposing enigmatic, allegorical versifying and succinct, anti-poetic, diary-like notations.

As a direct inheritor of an exceptionally rich tradition of intellectual Italian love poetry (and prose), which goes back to Cavalcanti, to the Dante of *Vita nuova*, and to Petrarch, Montale's poems are often intricate emblems of the ever-fluctuating thoughts, feelings, memories, and aspirations linking him to beloved women. From the early poetic archetypes of "Arletta / Annetta" (a woman whom Montale first encountered in the mid-1920s) and "Clizia" (based mostly on an American Italian-scholar whom the poet met during the mid-1930s) to his final muse, Annalisa Cima (a young writer about whom the elderly poet kept a long-secret *Posthumous Diary,* 1996), Montale considered his lovers to be, at once, sensual companions and spiritual guides. Interestingly, these inspirers are not precisely separable into distinct temporal periods; the women reappear in his poetry, as they must have in his personal life as well, like "figureheads that resurface and bring me / something of you."

Moreover, since these composite, or overlapping, anima-figures are rarely described in full, their phantom-like, sometimes even heavenly or otherworldly, presence entices and disturbs as much as it puzzles. Often the women have died, disappeared, or fled; sometimes they remain inexplicably remote. Their absence so haunts the narrator-poet that it becomes intensely present, causing the "sheer void" to stir "with the anguish / of awaiting you while I live." In this respect, the *Collected Poems 1920-1954* represent, above all, the poet's discovery, recognition, and exploration of this fundamental sense of mystery and loss, which ever shapes his perceptions of others and the world; they record sentimental and intellectual uncertainties maintained for over three decades, as he keeps himself in an amorous limbo not without metaphysical perspectives. His final three collections of poems can thus be read as an acquiescing to a certain inevitable disconsolateness, accompanied by self-sarcasm, irony, and a focusing on the quotidian. Arrestingly, the *Posthumous Diary* reverts—in a few instances—to the poet's earlier manner.

"I know nothing of you but the wordless / message that sustains me on my way," Montale writes characteristically in an important poem, "Delta," which reveals as well how womanhood and nature—as in Mother Nature—coincide in his encompassing vision, influenced by pantheism, Christianity, Symbolism, Surrealism, and numerous Italian writers. The poet is allured by Nature, as by female lovers, yet a double sense of existential estrangement or emptiness results every time from the encounter. The tension of several poems in fact increases when Montale's sudden awareness of the infinitesimal stature of man in the cosmos collides with the extreme self-absorption of his amorous yearnings. In "Mediterranean," a long sequence set near his oft-evoked childhood summer home on the Ligurian coast, the poet avows, addressing Nature as "Ancient one," that "the petty ferment of my heart [is] no more / than a moment of yours." Later he adds, bitterly: "Even an eroded pebble on my way / condemns me." Although sparked by romantic incidents, Montale's poems thus simultaneously investigate man's relationship to Nature and to Time, or his search for a meaning to existence, or his unappeased religious aspirations.

Transforming lovers into addressees both earthly and transcendent, into guardian angels and intercessors ("Pray for me now," he begs once of Arletta), into morbid enchantresses ("Your words were iridescent like the scales / of a dying mullet"), is by no means a rhetorical device invented by Montale. So the question arises: What is the function, and the justification, of his hermeticism? He claims to begin always "with the real." "What's important," he adds in an oft-quoted 1961 letter translated by Galassi along with countless other self-elucidating comments made by the author, "is that the translation from the true to the symbolic or vice versa always occurs unconsciously in me.... I'm incapable of inventing anything, but when I start to write (rapidly and with few corrections), the poetic nucleus has had a long incubation in me: long and obscure."

While perusing Galassi's exhaustively erudite edition, the reader will meditate often on this remark. The revisions made to one fascinating poem, "Two in Twilight," suggest that the Italian poet—as probably most poets—actually reworked his verse much more diligently than he lets on. Montale's revisions, notes Galassi, initially referring to this poem, "characteristically render the poem's action more impersonal." This impersonal quality involves an intense intimacy by implication; in such an ambience, often established in the opening lines of the poem by the presence of enigmatic objects or settings that are evidently highly charged with significance for the narrator (yet whose fundamental role eludes the reader), one remains tantalized by the paradoxical lack of the slightest autobiographical clarification.

One suspects that many of Montale's poems moved similarly, via revision, from the witnessed "occasion"—initially transcribed with comparative limpidity—to the allegorical or mythopoetic multi-layering typical of his final versions. It is in this respect that Montale's "nervous, astringent music" (as Galassi finely puts it) can be at once concrete, factual, abstract, and convoluted, as well as, to paraphrase the poet, "frenetically immobile." Elsewhere in his writings, the poet observes—contradicting his above remarks about rapidity and recalling the poetics of T. S. Eliot, whom he admired—that he "works his own poem like an object, instinctively accumulating meanings and metaphorical meanings, reconciling the irreconcilable within the poem so as to make it the strongest, surest, more unrepeatable correlative of his own internal experience." Not surprisingly, Montale stands at instructive antipodes from Umberto Saba, his elder by thirteen years, whose love poetry is lexically and syntactically transparent yet no less fathomless or ambiguous—on the emotional level—because of that hard-earned clarity. Epistemologically, Montale's method (and own commentary) thereby imply that poetic truth, for him, is either: 1) a quasi-automatic transcription (however triggered by some "real" detail) of certain symbolically potent configurations buried in the unconscious; or 2) a "correlative" of inner experience that the poet must strive hard to unearth, to recreate, to reflect, by reworking simple facts into elaborate metaphorical constructs.

A telling example of the latter poetics occurs in "Buffalo," an impressionistic evocation of "a sweet inferno" and a "limbo where the voices of the blood / are deafening and gleaming burns the sight / like mirror flashes." The hellish or purgatorial urban setting of this quasi-parody of Dante is actually a bicycle race, an event perhaps—though it is unlikely—suggested to some contemporaneous (1929) Italian readers familiar with France because of the title, taken from the American place-name given to a velodrome located in the suburbs of Paris. It is doubtful, however, that all readers readily grasped the genuine setting—described as an "oval / echoing with megaphones"—since only one quick perception actually alludes to cycling: "striped backs, bent and churning / on the track." The poet seeks not to render a magical, comical, exciting, or sociologically significant event of everyday life, but rather, as he himself admitted, to depict a "landscape of Acheron." The velodrome with which Montale was acquainted has been transformed into a hellscape, with all the consequent literary, philosophical, and religious connotations. Only retrospectively, once the reader has studied Galassi's annotations, is the setting fully recognizable as a velodrome.

Another telltale example of Montale's reworkings is offered by "Bagni di Lucca." Here he conceals, by rewriting, an initially more straightforward expression of his anxiety about death—another recurrent concern. An early published variant included the lines "Marble, branches, and you, / youth headlong into the ditch"; the definitive version became: "Marble, branches— / with a shake / leaves eddy, arrow down / into the ditch." The impersonalizing process, visible elsewhere as well, thus involves effacing the self, vanquishing the past's hold on the present, getting beyond the "sad amazement / that all life.../ consists in following along a wall / with broken bottle shards imbedded in the top," hoping that "one morning, walking in dry, glassy air, / I'll turn, and see the miracle occur: / nothing at my back, the void / behind me."

In contrast to these painstaking efforts to dig out and re-sculpt thoughts, memories, and feelings—the "poetic nucleus"—until the final product becomes, as it were, a truer-than-life emblem of complex inner experience, Montale sometimes uses a telegraphic rapidity to suggest brute constellations of recollected fragmentary events, as they break out of him "at the swelling point, / in the moat that surrounds the release of memory.../ before attaching / to images, or words, dark reminiscent / sense." This is his second kind of poetics, the one most akin to his later journal-like manner. In a short poem from the "Motets" section of *The Occasions,* for instance, Montale begins with untypical forthrightness ("The hope of even seeing you again / was leaving me"), then concludes abruptly, in parentheses: "(under the arcades, at Modena, / a servant in gold braid dragged / two jackals on a leash)." The image is obviously related to an experience shared with the unnamed "you" (actually Clizia, as the poet reveals in a self-mocking 1950 essay) and illustrates well how an excessively private memory must potentially provoke the reader into finding a parallel—an equally obscure, recurrently brooded-over object or event—in his own life. Only in this way can Montale's obscure symbols really move us. Yet they often do.

If Galassi's masterly edition overwhelms with its two-hundred pages of annotation, in very small print, and can greatly influence one's first impression of the poems (if one peeks at the appendix before taking on the obscurities unassisted), Arrowsmith's translation of *Satura,* albeit left in manuscript at the time of his death, is regretfully lacking in sufficient commentary—little matter that Montale himself sneers: "Poetry / rejects with horror / the glosses of commentators." Several phrases are left untranslated or unexplained in the English version (*si parva licet* in "After a Flight"; *olla podrida* in "Late at Night"; *ecumene* in "Sounds") and solecisms occur when French is, oddly, used to translate the original Italian: "à la sorbet" for *al sorbetto;* the incorrect French plural, "Guides Hachettes," for the Italian plural *le guide Hachette.* Compared to Galassi's fluent, superbly rigorous, ever-intelligent, often resourceful translations (especially noticeable when he is confronted with Montale's unusual enjambments or with Italian syntactical acrobatics difficult to mirror in smooth English), Arrowsmith's version raises many doubts. In "Two Venetian Sequences," portraying a meeting with Hemingway, Montale uses the English word "stinking" in the lines: "Parigi Londra un porcaio, / New York stinking, pestifera." Why has Arrowsmith translated "stinking" at all, let alone by the euphemistic "nauseating"? In his mature work, Montale increasingly uses nouns ("What makes the impact is the accumulation of facts," he asserts in *Satura*), as opposed to verbs, inducing bizarre catalog-like effects. Yet the poem "In Silence" employs an active verb in the line "Nella strada non passa nessuno," literally "In the street no one passes." Arrowsmith translates: "Deserted streets, no noise." The "no noise," which does not exist in the original, is amply conveyed by the next line, which moreover confirms that only one street is intended, not "streets" in general. That next line is rendered: "Only a transistor the other side of the wall." The missing preposition "on" has surely been left out by editorial neglect—and this is not the only case of misprints and oversights. These errors are unfortunate, for *Satura*—a Latin title meaning "miscellany" and recalling the pun made by Petronius's *Satyricon*—provides the key transition in Montale's oeuvre. The volume includes cynical and lapidary statements, typical of his later disabused jottings, but also disquieting evocations (as in his early poetry) of "that first refuge /...the shadows / of the eucalyptus.../ the shadows concealed / between words, unseizable, / never revealed, never written, / never wholly uttered...." It is on account of such lines that Montale will ever remain mesmerizing.

* * *

When Montale's "secret diary" appeared in Italy, in 1996, the poems sparked a blaze of rumors and recrimination. In the diary itself, the poet predicted no less:

> And now that the end is nearing I'm tossing
> my bottle which may well give rise
> to a real firestorm.

It is exciting to have this unusual poetry collection in Galassi's accurate and fluid version. Passing from studied facetiousness to a world-weary gloom, from critical feistiness to a touching sensitivity, these eighty-four short poems purportedly written "off the cuff" were composed between 1969 and 1979, a period otherwise encompassing Montale's Nobel Prize (1975) and the publication of his, in some respects similarly puzzling, last four volumes: *Satura, Diary of '71 and '72, Notebook of Four Years*, and *Other and Uncollected Poems*.
    The subject of much of this self-styled "testament halfway / between prose and poetry," and the dedicatee of the entire book, is Annalisa Cima (b.

1941), a young poet whom Montale met in 1968. Cima would visit the aged poet during his last years, becoming in the process his collaborator, inspirer, and fellow conspirator. The two were soul mates. "We had the same disease," Montale avows, "some call it *spleen*, / others melancholy." In poems celebrating her arrivals as miraculous apparitions ("You descend from the wide avenue / crowned by an azure / summer sky"), she even joins the other muse-lovers who animate his greatest collections: *Cuttlefish Bones, The Storm, Etc.*, and *The Occasions*—gathered in *Collected Poems 1920-1954*.

The opening poem of *Diaro postumo* daringly brings together Cima, "Gina" (Montale's maid, who likewise appears in late poems), and "The Fly" (the poet's long-time companion, Drusilla Tanzi, who died in 1963). "If The Fly had seen you / even once," notes Montale, "how much love she would have / granted you." But then he asks, teasingly: "What would Gina say / if I decided suddenly / to be a father"? These late erotic impulses aside, the elderly death-obsessed poet is above all grateful for the young woman's luminous, invigorating presence. "Tomorrow I'll request another meeting, / and another still," he writes, "together we make up a now / that isn't ashes, or empty." This sense of the "emptiness" of the present, a theme that is evoked repeatedly, gives a characteristic grimness and astringency not only to this diary but indeed to Montale's entire oeuvre.

As Galassi explains in his precise, thought-provoking introduction, Montale regularly presented Cima with poems that he had composed for her. In 1979, he reorganized them all, dividing most into groups of six, which he then sealed inside ten envelopes; he added another eighteen poems to a larger envelope also containing a final, eleventh, envelope of six poems. Cima was instructed not to publish the poems until five years after his death; and at that, only in a series of annual *plaquettes*. When she started bringing out the poems, six at a time, she respected the order that the poet had established: the envelopes were numbered from I to XI. A volume containing the first thirty poems was reprinted in 1991; then the entire diary was published as a standard trade edition in 1996.

As Montale's last poems eked out, one imagines the frustration and irritation of his closest friends, none of whom had been let in on the "conspiracy" or "hoax," as this testamentary game has disparagingly been called. Moreover, Montale maliciously increased the provocative impact of his "time bomb"—as other critics have termed it—by alluding, in a handful of poems, to living acquaintances. His praise for a few friends implicitly condemns others. He especially impugns critics, Angelo Marchese (1937-2000) proving to be an exception because, according to the diarist, he knows how "to explore without being cryptic / in order to make sense of emptiness." (Marchese was the author of *Visiting angel: Interpretazione semiologica della poesia di Montale*, 1977.) Although academics and book reviewers are satirized in Montale's previous work as well, he develops in *Posthumous Diary* an idea paralleling one expounded by the French writer Julien Gracq, who argues, in his lively and still all-too-pertinent diatribe, *La Littérature à l'estomac* (1950), that writing has declined because the standards are henceforth set by "magisters." "The poet gets pegged," similarly sneers Montale, "by so-called connoisseurs / who don't realize they lack / the necessary gift." Ever since verse-making has fallen under the sway of "the new censors," he claims elsewhere, poetry "has...been reduced to agony." He points to "tangle[s] of atonal sounds" and wonders whether "the music that assures / the future life of poetry" will return, thus preserving "the form / of its own being." In haughty contrast, Montale depicts himself "judging" contemporary poems written by Cima and others. His persona as a "great poet"—a supreme artist and an exacting craftsman as opposed to a posturing, power-seeking academic poetaster—is exhibited at times. However, in subtle, unexpected ways, we are also granted peeks behind the mask.

Aggravating his case is that these bold declarations are made in a volume that is hardly among his most "musical." This is not to say that he could not practice what he preached. The author of some of the most intense, densely allusive, yet undeniably mellifluous Italian poems of the twentieth century (most of which date from the early and middle periods of his career) cannot be dismissed so easily. Yet the difference between his former manner and these "prosaic" poems nonetheless perturbs. A leading scholar, Dante Isella, even went so far, in July 1997, as to claim that *Posthumous Diary* was "apocryphal." He conjectured that the poems had been concocted by Cima out of "snippets of phrases taken from oral conversations with the poet." Galassi provides the amusing details of this controversy, about which countless critics, poets, writers, and journalists have voiced opinions. Although the authenticity of the original manuscripts no longer seems in doubt (Cima exhibited them in Lugano, in October 1997), debate about the literary qualities of the book continues.

Critics should of course meditate twice on the reasons underlying an author's evolution, especially when a "second manner" ostentatiously rejects the guiding principles of a former, well-established style and intentionally taunts the reader, as *Posthumous Diary* does in several—but not all—places. There do exist "musical moments," such as when, in the significantly entitled "Time of Destruction," Montale rhymes the last word of the penultimate line with the penultimate word of the last line, thereby grimly setting off the final word, *amara* "bitter." "Et intanto il tempo si sgrana nella desolata," he writes, "realtà della vita, che è sempre stata amara" ("And still time drains away in the desolate / reality of life, which has always been bitter"). And there is the thrice-rhyming quatrain concluding "Second Testament," itself an important statement of Montale's intentions. The aphoristic effect of the quatrain is strengthened by the repetition of -*ire*:

> Non vi è mai stato un nulla in cui sparire
> già altri grazie al ricordo son risorti,
> lasciate in pace i vivi per rinvivire
> i morti: nell'aldilà mi voglio divertire.

> (There's never been a nothingness to hide in,
> already others have returned by way of memory,
> leave the living in peace to revive the dead:
> I want to enjoy myself in the beyond.)

Posthumous Diary in fact revives poetic forms developed by Roman epigrammatists and satirists during the decadent age of the Roman Empire. This is also true of Montale's last four (aforementioned) collections. Like them, this final volume remains at defiant antipodes from the rich Italian poetic heritage which, in his earlier writing, he set forth with brio, namely the conspicuously intellectual or philosophical love poem, a genre whose initial poetics were defined by Cavalcanti, Dante, and Petrarch. Like, say, the disabused, sardonic Martial, Montale can spurn and pontificate; but it is also clear—rather unlike Martial—that he is simultaneously giving advice to his young poet-friend about the traps and trappings of the practice of poetry. "Your pace will quicken," he cautions, "and now I fear for you the pains / that once were mine. In this world / devoid of hope, with unsure boundaries, / few will recognize you." Several poems of *Posthumous Diary* recall the "letters to a young poet" genre.

Moreover, Montale can write tongue-in-cheek, even to the extent of creating elaborate ironic constructs. If the poems of *Posthumous Diary* are rarely multilayered in meaning and allusion, as his earlier poems famously are, they are nevertheless often at least double-layered in emotional impact. His superficial harshness can conceal a soft lining, as it were. He can suddenly appear more vulnerable than one had suspected. Early on, he pointedly announces (in another thrice-rhyming Italian quatrain): "If you want my opinion, / illusion is the one way out, / since every day life supersedes / the limit that it sets." One of the salient aesthetic qualities of *Posthumous Diary* is its emotional ambiguity: the possibility that part of what is being stated or shown is mere illusion. Indeed, is Montale always telling the entire truth about his feelings? His disgust, for example, is rarely of one piece. His cynicism about the Italian literary milieu, about critics, or about the lasting value of our day and age can be offset by his gratefulness for Cima's solicitude or by his admiration for her own talent. Especially remarkable is his anxiety about the posterity of his own poetry, an enduring fear that makes him seem fragile, not so sure of his gifts as he otherwise pretends. Significantly, one of his most self-revealing poems justifies evasion and insincerity:

> ...irony's the only way
> not to be surprised
> with a face gone gray with sadness.
> In tristitia hilaris, I repeat.
> Man often fools himself,
> it's the perennial flight from the present:
> the one shield against pain.

This being said, Montale even more often casts down his shield in *Posthumous Diary*, painfully facing up to the present and seeking to leave behind the childhood and erotic memories which—as his earlier poetry amply demonstrates—both torture and allure him. "Truth perhaps is in.../...this spent cigarette butt," he muses, "it reappears in that bottle bottom / left on the shoreline. / The rest is nothing but a pretext / for feeling alive and less alone."

Elsewhere, he returns to this same desolate image, striving to accept ephemerality, then nothingness:

> ...If only [my cigarette smoke] could
> muffle my memories, veil them, erase
> the past and leave only a lit
> cigarette butt, symbol of what stays.

The burning cigarette butt will go out, the scant remains of paper and tobacco will rot away. Perhaps Montale came to believe that only a poetic Poor Art—an equivalent of the Italian modern art movement—could honestly express his bitter attempts to confront, then accept, the inevitability of his own annihilation. Too much artistry would be a travesty of his deep, incurable disgust. And that same disgust and desperation sometimes incite rash remarks, cruel jabs, insincerities—crimes to which he sincerely confesses in effect, by the very form of these poems.

This disturbing and challenging diary should be read on its own redoubtable terms. It is an instructive and precocious example of a literary phenomenon much more widespread in Europe than in the United States. Like several other European poets and writers, in both his and subsequent generations, Montale has produced a book that is "entre les genres," as the French put it. *Posthumous Diary* is obviously not a collection of short prose writings, though his poems are frequently "prosaic." It comprises relatively few poems genuinely stemming from the intense, intricate poetics that Montale forged, early on. Surely it is an unconventional "diary." It commemorates or anticipates a number of "occasions," notably his meetings with Cima, but there is no coherent chronology, even though some successive poems hint at a progressing narrative or sketch out variations on a common theme. And, as has been seen, the book rehabilitates the "letters to a young poet" genre; yet it includes no missives and only rarely provides explicit counsel. Despite a few cryptic remarks, no consistent amorous theme can be discerned.

Does this fundamental formal instability perhaps represent a sort of last stage in the disintegration of traditional literary forms, that is as they were wrenched every which way by twentieth-century modernism? Or does "entre les genres" writing, as practiced by some of the most profound and innovative European writers, perhaps constitute a reconstructive stage following upon a long process of disintegration, fragmentation, destruction? These are just two far-reaching historical questions raised by Montale's diary—which was certainly long meditated, if indeed, as it seems, spontaneously penned. Above all, the book starkly expresses what all aspects of a human sensibility must necessarily and multifariously converge to: a single abrupt end. And in this respect, the Italian poet's last words, as they shift from irony to brutal frankness, and back again, ultimately deeply move.

Songs of a Life
(Umberto Saba)

Equal in stature to his near-contemporaries Eugenio Montale and Giuseppe Ungaretti, the poet and prose-writer Umberto Saba (1883-1957) has been comparatively underestimated in the United States. I myself discovered Saba's writings while I was living in Paris during the 1980s. His self-searching poems and poignant stories (later available from Sheep Meadow Press as *The Stories and Recollections of Umberto Saba*) were translated into French during this period, and I was hardly alone in wishing to put the man's work into every friend's hands. Saba's *intimisme*, psychoanalytical in motivation yet not dogmatically so, suggested a new approach to autobiography; he could achieve a fascinating equilibrium between confession and understatement, stylistic clarity and lyricism, melancholy and sensual immediacy, all the while pointing to the emotions as the uncharted frontier of literature. Writing a poetry of inner suffering and acute avowal, he speaks with such paradoxically quiet sincerity that his most painful thoughts solicit complicity from his reader. Saba yearns "to be outside / of [him]self, to live the life / of everyone." Imaginatively, he accomplished this feat, for although egocentric at first glance, his poetry—more deeply—encompasses the secret joy and despair of "every / everyday man."

He wrote from the depths of a tortured sensibility. His father abandoned him before childbirth and his mother subsequently handed him over to a Slovenian wet-nurse (one of the engaging figures of his poetry) for his first four years. Because of his introverted tendencies ("The dream I live on is itself the truth," he states), one might expect from him a deeply symbolic hermeticism; and the Hermetic school, led by Montale, indeed dominated Italian poetry for a good share of Saba's lifetime. In stark contrast, Saba's poems and stories—in some cases, prototypal "personal essays"—are so limpid that their precious lasting value was recognized only gradually, even in his native language. Montale's judgment is incisive. "The language of Italian poetry," he writes, "which has almost always sought transfiguration in plasticity and relief, has rarely known an exception so singular. Saba attains the *lied* as if without realizing it."

Saba is a great modern poet of both love and his hometown, Trieste, which in his eyes had an "scontrosa / grazia," a "grace" or "charm" that is "surly," "sullen." One of his finest volumes, *Trieste and A Woman* (1910-1912), explicitly explores this dichotomy, which is also summed up in a famous line from *Autobiography* (1924): "Trieste is the city, Lina the woman /...and never to this day / have our two souls been separated." Although centered on Lina, his verse also overtly refers to extramarital liaisons, notably with shopgirls who assisted him in his famous used-book shop on the via San Nicolò; and he also, not-too-cryptically, alludes to adolescent homosexuality. However, it was only two decades after his death, when his uncompleted novel *Ernesto* (1975) appeared (he had worked on it around 1953), that the poet's homoerotic experiences were fully described. Passages from *Ernesto* elucidate lines such as these, from *Autobiography:* "To my guardian angel I left, at night, / half my pillow free; but never did / his precious form come back to me in dreams / once I had tasted the sweetness of the flesh." Referring to his wife, he confesses elsewhere: "I have known every other human love; / but for Lina I would give up yet another life; / I would gladly start anew."

The Petrarchan title *Il Canzoniere*—"The Songbook"—encompasses all of Saba's individual collections. Like Petrarch, the Triestine master focuses on his own ambiguous amorous attractions. Remarkable oxymorons tellingly appear in his lines, as well as in the titles of two well-known volumes, *Serene Desperation* (1913-15) and *The Loving Thorn* (1920). The poet is, moreover, breathtakingly honest with respect to himself and to his affection for Lina ("of the red shawl," as he designates her). He admits in one sonnet, for instance, that he "loved her for the summits of her sorrow. / For she was everything, but never false, / and could love everything, but not herself."

Also like Petrarch, Saba is a poet for whom presentiments of death often contaminate his perceptions of everyday experience. Yet in an enigmatic poem not translated in Stephen Sartarelli's Sheep Meadow Press selection, *Songbook: Selected Poems*, he paradoxically avows that "it is the thought of death that ultimately helps one to live." The remark discloses an unexpected facet of the melancholy—even the death wish—that otherwise inspires the poet's frequent intimations of mortality. The significantly entitled *Dying Heart* dates back to as early as 1925-30, not to mention *Last Things* (1935-43), penned not long thereafter. Interestingly, Saba believed that his poetry would be understood only when a new Risorgimento took place, that is when "Petrarchan values (which are related to death)...once again give way to Dantean values (which are those of life)." He expatiates on this key question of orientation—dizzying when applied to our own age, let alone to one's own life—in various passages of *History and Chronicle of the Songbook,* a self-explicating, self-justifying, and also often sharply self-critical examination, of his own lifework. Probably unique in literary history, this systematic exegesis of *Il Canzoniere* was penned by Saba in the third person. It has also been translated by Sartarelli for Sheep Meadow Press.

Exact and fluent in his renderings, Sartarelli can hardly be criticized for not approximating, most of the time, Saba's rhymes and delicate hendecasyllabics.

In the process of bringing these exquisite poems into English, he does, however—in a few places—invert the lines of the original, presumably in order to achieve greater naturalness. The inflections of Italian permit a syntactic flexibility difficult to parallel in English, yet certain stresses are thereby weakened. In the mysterious "Caffelatte," to cite one example, Saba surprises, after referring to a girl's bitterness as she arises in the morning, by placing the word "happy" at the very end of the poem: "E sente / che torna lentamente / felice." Sartarelli de-emphasizes "felice" by writing: "And slowly / [she] starts to feel happy / again." Devoid of rhetorical effects, the impact of Saba's subdued poetry almost always depends on minute nuances of word order.

This is a mere quibble, designed to praise the deceptive simplicity of Saba's craft—about which Sartarelli tells us a great deal in his richly informative, brilliantly perceptive introduction. More seriously, having taken the trouble to bring out the entire *History and Chronicle of the Songbook*, why have Sartarelli's publishers contented themselves with only a selection of *Il Canzoniere?* Missing are some superb portraits of working-class characters, a genre of poem representing an investigative, outward-turned quality in Saba. (He tellingly terms his portraits "objectifications.") A reminiscer, a tortured self-analyzer, the poet is also a wide-eyed stroller ever noting the vicissitudes of a town which, in his own words, is "more mine than anyone's / because I found her when a boy and as a man / I married to her to Italy forever with song." However welcome, this abridgement—Saba calls his *opus magnum* a "novel"—rather diminishes the importance of the city, in regard to the entire *Canzoniere,* and makes it harder to appreciate the book's (albeit occasionally repetitious) diary-like atmosphere. Saba's ambivalent relationship with his hometown was both crucial to his writing and, ironically for someone who spent most of his lifetime in one place, almost prophetically suggestive of contemporary uprootedness and existential estrangement. "Around / each thing circulates," he writes in another poem left untranslated, "an ambience both strange and tormenting: / the ambience of my origins."

Some sequences of *Il Canzoniere*—in this selection—likewise lose their narrative force or clarity because of missing passages (particularly noticeable in "New Lines for Lina"), or are themselves entirely missing. Especially unfortunate is the absence of *Girls* (1925), whose tantalizing fifth poem, structured around the haunting leitmotiv of a seamstress's eyes, could profitably have been included. In his *History and Chronicle,* Saba defines *Girls* as "a digression in the charming 'novel' of the *Canzoniere,* a parenthesis that could not be removed without harming or lessening the whole." Similarly disappointing is the absence of all the *Canzonettas* (1922-3), a series to which Saba devoted an enlightening chapter of *History and Chronicle.*

In another important missing poem, "On a Portrait of Myself as a Young Child" (from *Light and Airy Things,* 1920), Saba comes to perceive that, even though his face has changed, he is still the "same" as he was in early childhood. In his poetry, the past often suddenly becomes present in epiphanic ways, momentarily creating in his mind the initially calming, ultimately disturbing feeling that Time is somehow even immobile. However naive his pellucid verses may first appear to readers versed exclusively in twentieth-century poetics, Saba's poetry actually conceals a wealth of smoothed-out literary allusions (to Theocritus, Heine, and—quite pertinently—Herondas, as well as countless Italian classics); and he earnestly investigates the nature of Time, the function of memory, the relationship between emotion and acting. He is an inspiring, resourceful mentor. Anyone interested in subtle autobiographical narration, in the fluctuating boundaries between inner and outer worlds, or in the intricacies of desire, should seek him out forthwith.

* * *

In August 2004, in Trieste, as I stood toward the back of the Libreria Antiquaria Umberto Saba and imagined the Italian poet writing there in the 1920s and 1930s, I was gladdened by the thought that, from our English-language perspective, Saba has fared fairly well. Thanks to Carcanet (in the U. K.) and Sheep Meadow Press, we have two different selections of Saba's poetry as well as his only novel, *Ernesto*. We have many examples of his touching *Stories and Recollections*. Although not all of his poems, which he gathered under the title *Canzoniere* (or *Songbook*), are translated, we do have the poet's book-length self-commentary in the third person, *History and Chronicle of the Songbook*, which characteristically begins: "Saba made many mistakes. But ignoring Saba's poetry would be like ignoring the evidence of a natural phenomenon."

Now, from Australia, comes a voluminous and beautifully illustrated *Poetry and Prose*, which offers new (and often first) translations of numerous poems, stories, and prose pieces as well as of revelatory letters and other significant texts. This extensively annotated tome not only fills countless gaps in the English reader's knowledge of the poet, but also offers a full panorama of the man's life, from his birth in Hapsburg Trieste in 1883, through the dangerous war years (during which he hid out in Florence because he was a Jew), to his death in a nursing home in Gorizia (near Trieste), in 1957. Never has it been easier to chart properly the evolution of Saba's writing and to measure what the translator, Vincent Moleta, terms its "constant freshness and independence."

The common denominator of Saba's poems and stories is a "serenely despairing" candor. He was a gentle, tormented, proud "egoist," as the title of a 1919 poem declares. Certainly his melancholy introspection, combined with his affectionate scrutiny of Triestine life, fit his own definition of poets as "*egocentric*. For them the external world *exists*: but it circulates exclusively around their person." One of his most important collections is aptly called *Autobiography* (1924). Drawing on the scholarly Italian editions of Saba's work, Moleta now greatly highlights this incorrigible autobiographical propensity by adding missives and manuscripts that reveal much about the poet's friendships (notably with Eugenio Montale, Italo Svevo, and Carlo Levi), about his "curious antiquarian shop /...in a quiet street of Trieste," about his beloved hometown ("when I grew up / I married it to Italy for ever with my song"), and of course about his complex relationships with his two favorite "characters," his wife Lina and his daughter Linuccia.

Original in conception, *Poetry and Prose* almost seamlessly combines literary and extra-literary material. Hence, a 1937 letter describing the impoverished poet Sandro Penna is followed by a 1940 letter to Saba's friend Nello Stock (who had emigrated to New York). On the next page, we find a passage, from *History and Chronicle of the Songbook*, in which Saba comments on his poems from those years. This passage then introduces eight poems from *Last Things*. After this selection comes a 1943 letter to his publisher, Giulio Einaudi, in which he inquires about the publication of *Last Things*; and this document leads to the transcript of a clandestine radio broadcast, in 1944, about Heinrich Heine and Ugo Foscolo. Turn the page and there is a painting, by Vittore Cargnel, of the Trieste central train station in the rain. This painting faces Saba's depressed 1944 letter to his daughter, whom he has not seen for years because he is in hiding. After another section from *History and Chronicle of the Songbook*, appear two poems from the sequence *1944*.

This arrangement conjures up Saba the man, but it is important not to lose sight of Saba the poet, in Moleta's smooth, accurate, yet not always sufficiently lyrical, versions. It is probably impossible to suggest, in English, Saba's discrete haunting music, with all those metered Italian lines that end in open a's and o's.

Above all, Moleta's anthology amply illustrates the essential differences between Saba's subtle literary approach to autobiography (which aspires to universality by means of a meticulous crafting of thought, feeling, and perception) and the straightforward, spontaneous "autobiography" related by his letters and prose texts. Saba significantly did not call his collected poems "Autobiografia," as he might have done, but rather associated them with Petrarch's *Canzoniere* and Heine's *Buch der Lieder*. "I have in my heart the *song* of a life," he proclaims in "The Visit," and the italics are his. Because of his masterful versification and his deftness at selecting just those personal specifics that foster resonance in us all, Saba is a much more enchanting autobiographer in his poems, and in his best stories, than in his letters. As a poet, he often strikes a perfect balance between confession and understatement, stylistic clarity and lyrical effusion, melancholy and sensual immediacy. This is the lesson, about autobiographical writing, that be learned from perusing Moleta's anthology: it is Saba's "song" that will long be heard.

Childhood as Sacrifice and Annihilation (Alberto Savinio)

The Italian writer, composer, and artist Alberto Savinio (1891-1952)—whose real name was Andrea de Chirico—has long been overshadowed by his older brother, the metaphysical painter Giorgio de Chirico. Yet in Europe, interest in Savinio's own artistic and literary accomplishments has never completely waned, and in the United States during the late 1980s and early 1990s there was even an impressive and unexpected revival. The Marlboro Press especially defended Savinio's distinctive and provocative work by producing translations of *Capri* (written in 1926, fully published in Italian only in 1988), *Operatic Lives*, and *Dico a te, Clio* (*Speaking to Clio*, 1940). Eridanos Press chipped in with a version of an essential autobiographical novel set mostly in Greece (where Savinio was born and raised), *Infanzia di Nivasio Dolcemare* (*The Childhood of Nivasio Dolcemare*, 1941); and Atlas Press followed suit with a selection of Savinio's short stories, characteristically parodying Greco-Roman myths and entitled *The Lives of the Gods* in English. The Marlboro Press then added to its excellent series of modern Italian literature by issuing John Shepley's fine translation of *Tragedia dell'infanzia* (1937 / 1945), one of Savinio's most intriguing books. It is a penetrating look at our cruel adult world through a child's bewildered, ingenuous eyes.

Centered on several weeks of a child's illness (followed by convalescence and recovery), this likewise autobiographical novel—"essay" is perhaps more appropriate—is rich in surrealistic imagery as Savinio brings his poetic prose as closely as possible to an infant's vivid perceptions and startling metaphors. "One morning," remembers the narrator, "the sun beat directly on my bed, and in its rays thousands of homunculi came to wish me good morning. The pulp of the halved lemon shone brightly, and the bottles lined up on the bedside table glittered. The drop of syrup remaining in the bowl of the silver spoon had turned into a ruby."

Indeed, as in Savinio's (as well as his brother's) paintings, perspective is all-important. Unanticipated apparitions in the narrative lens symbolize the natural laws limiting the scope of a child's world. A child has no global view of his surroundings or of his immediate future. He has no idea what his parents or other adults hold in store for him. Savinio shows how this inability to grasp the whole temporal and spatial picture is a tragic condition enabling adults to prey upon the young, whether wittingly or unwittingly. Childhood is a "tragedy, meaning sacrifice and annihilation," he remarks. The part of the bull is played by the children."

During the darkest moments of his illness, for example, Savinio recalls journeying "endlessly down long bare corridors, across vast deserted rooms. Our immense shadows accompanied us on the wall. In the stride of whoever was carrying me in his arms, I seemed to be walking with the flabby legs of a giant. All of a sudden I was blinded by a great light, and my breath was cut short in my throat: they had plunged me into icy water that I hadn't seen coming." These significant memories, writes the author, "continue to bear witness within us with the gravity of eternal things."

Worst of all is when joy culminates in unexpected cruelty. One day, the child's feared and distrusted doctor, Saltas, pompously quotes Xenophon ("Thalatta! Thalatta!"). The child thinks that the man means his own "great playmate," also named Xenophon, "the cross-eyed kitchen boy...who pieced reeds and turned them into whistles, stole nests full of featherless little birds from the oak trees." The child's "aversion" for Dr. Saltas "vanishes in a twinkling," yet as the joyful child is about to leap into his arms, the latter turns around, sees him, "and with a mere sniff of his buttocky nose, [stops him] cold."

Tragedy of Childhood can be taken as a poignant paradigm of how many childhood stories and novels are born. "Only in artists," notes Savinio, "is adult life the *natural* continuation of childhood." He shows graphically how haunting memories build up over time into formidable obstacles that must be overcome. And how can they be overcome? The lesson is clear: by writing, by turning painful memories into art.

A Dark Degree of Suffering:
Livia Svevo's Memoir of Her Husband

The short, gentle, and unpretentious memoir of Italo Svevo (1861-1928) that was written by his widow, Livia Veneziani Svevo (1874-1957), curiously suggests much more about a writer's inner world than many biographies claiming to leave not a scandal or laundry list unexamined. And yet Livia admits that her husband, who was also a distant cousin whom she had known since childhood, never spoke to her about "his torment or his obsessions" and that she could not always understand his "dark degree of suffering." "To me he showed only his cheerful face," she writes. "He wanted me always to remain calm, simple and without inner complications, as if to draw strength from this way of being of mine."

The secret behind the moving and paradoxical effectiveness of *Vita di mio marito* (1950), as *Memoir of Italo Svevo* is modestly called in Italian, is that the woman observes her husband's outward behavior as sympathetically as the Italian writer himself observed those around him in Trieste, a "businessman's city, scarcely aware of art at all" and full of "conformist provincials." Svevo spent his entire life in the town, first working (for eighteen years) in the Correspondence Department of the Trieste branch of the Union Bank of Vienna, and later as the manager of the marine paint factory that belonged to his wife's family. Only from time to time was he able to work seriously on his novels, which he nonetheless seems to have brooded on incessantly.

Livia writes tenderly of Svevo's disdain for clothes ("he could not even undo the buttons of his shirt cuffs"), of his desire for simplicity, of his legendary absentmindedness, and of his lifelong attempt to quit smoking, a failure immortalized in his most famous novel, *The Confessions of Zeno* (1923). Like his neurotic fictional characters, Svevo, who usually wore only black clothing, "thought constantly about illness and death, listening to his body with intense attention." "Sometimes he raised his right arm with his fist clenched," Livia recalls, "as if to ward off an invisible enemy, and said, in a breathless voice: 'I can hear him coming, I can hear him coming.' And if I asked him 'What can you hear?' he would answer, 'The blow.' (This is the word ['il colpo'] used in our dialect to mean a stroke." Quoting (at times profusely) from his letters, notes, and unpublished texts, Livia reveals how Svevo was obsessed, from his earliest years, with the fleetingness of time. Indeed, at the relatively young age of thirty-seven, Svevo published a novel entitled *Senilità* (1898; *As a Man Grows Older*, as it is called in English); only eight years later he noted in his journal: "Why the devil do I speak so much about my old age?"

Yet Svevo feared artistic failure even more than death. He nicknamed "frogs" his soul-wrenching literary doubts. According to Livia, they croaked insistently. "He was pierced by two things," she remarks, "the longing for fame, and a lack of confidence in his own work, to which he could give only part of his time." Her memoir is especially sensitive and universal as she describes how difficult it was for Svevo, as for many writers, to believe in the genuineness of his artistic calling. He also suffered from one of the worst calamities that can befall an aspiring author, that of sending a first or second book to an admired, older writer who, by reacting in a certain way, paralyzes the younger writer's creativity for years. In Svevo's case, it was the German writer and Italophile Paul Heyse (1830-1914) who, replying to Svevo in 1898, paid tribute to his "art of psychological analysis" and "sharpness of observation" in *Senilità*, but regretted that these talents had been wasted "on such a repulsive subject," that of "a young man with so insignificant a life, without any moral backing." The blow was devastating because Svevo's first book, *Una Vita* (1892; *A Life*), which had gone unnoticed, had similarly been criticized (and thoroughly misunderstood) by Heyse: "You are tireless in describing the most insignificant procedures of life at the bank…. The hero…is so weak, so insignificant, that occupying oneself so persistently with him and his *milieu*, analyzing his minutest feelings, his thoughts, his soul, seem not really worth the trouble." Svevo was in fact an extraordinary precursor of the literature of dailiness and ordinariness, several classic examples of which were soon to appear elsewhere in Europe.

Luckily, nine years later after the publication of *Senilità*, Svevo's repulsive subjects, insignificant heroes, and focus on the quotidian came to fascinate a young Irish teacher from the Berlitz School whom Svevo had hired for private English lessons. This chance encounter with James Joyce, who had settled in Trieste in 1903 (and lived for a while, moreover, above the poet Umberto Saba's antiquarian bookshop), "sparked," as Livia puts it, Svevo out of his literary "half sleep." Joyce admired *A Life* and *Senilità*, praised the novels to his friends, and, as Livia recalls, "raged against the critics' blindness." Even after Joyce had moved to Paris (via Zurich) at the end of the First World War, the two men met whenever Svevo passed through the city on business.

Finally, after the publication of *The Confessions of Zeno*, Svevo received not only Joyce's renewed enthusiasm but also that of the influential French writer, critic, and translator Valery Larbaud, who was always drawing attention to the work of deserving unknown writers or poets. By 1925, Svevo became a "master" for writers in Joyce and Larbaud's circle; translations followed; his international reputation was assured. But this rightful good fortune nearly came too late. Svevo had three more years to live.

The Solitude of a Master Empathizer
(Cesare Pavese)

"Non scriverò piú." With these solemn words, which mean "I will not write anymore," the Italian novelist, short story writer, and poet Cesare Pavese (1908-1950) concluded his diary, and killed himself nine days later by taking an overdose of sleeping pills.

Of what is a writer's suicide emblematic? Of writing's inability to save a life? Ardent lovers of literature may even find it hard to believe that a talent like Pavese's could not somehow have kept on producing, plunging anew into the toils of composition as a way of resolving perfunctorily (or at least of putting off) the comparatively minor problems of unrequited love and daily living. But of course I am waxing ironic. It is arresting and, I daresay, grimly informative that Pavese's extraordinarily lucid and pessimistic diary is entitled *Il mestiere di vivere* (1952), a book translated twice into English respectively as *The Burning Brand* and *This Business of Living*, and all too significantly emphasizing the "métier" or "trade" of living—as in, say, "Mastering the Trade of Living."

If Pavese failed at this trade, he successfully—to mimic his own penchant for implacable ironies—analyzed the failure in his diary, one of the most excruciatingly honest ever composed. This is why the challenge put forward by the title must be kept in mind when reading his stories, as well as the four important novels—*The Beach* (1942), *The House on the Hill* (1949), *Among Women Only* (1949), *The Devil in the Hills* (1949)—that have welcomely been brought together as *The Selected Works of Cesare Pavese*, in a translation by R. W. Flint. As the diary amply reveals, few authors have worked so long with such a heightened awareness of the perilous gap between living and writing. Few writers have so bravely stood astride the chasm, as it were, observing how it widens inexorably, ever awaiting—while continuing to write—the fated moment when they must fall.

Yet if Pavese's fiction is personal in this essential sense, its deep-running autobiographical orientation is not immediately visible on the surface. Whereas his lifelong struggle with the prospect of self-afflicted death is exhibited straightforwardly in his diary, it is transposed imaginatively in haunting stories like "Wedding Trip" or "Suicides" (to mention just those two), or in a novel like *Among Women Only*. The unity of his oeuvre is that of a coin: two sides superficially different in the images that they put forward to the world, yet intimately connected, even perhaps ultimately identical.

Early on, Pavese alludes to this troubled relationship between living and writing by means of a subtitle, *Secretum professionale*, which covers four months during the first two years (1935-1936) that he records in his diary. Evoked as well in stories like "Land of Exile" and "Gaol Birds," this same period was marked by his arrest and ten-month imprisonment in Brancaleone (Calabri) because of his editorials in the anti-fascist magazine *La Cultura*. But surely the subtitle also recalls Petrarch's highly self-conscious *Secretum* (composed in Latin around 1347), an imaginary confessional dialogue with his intellectual mentor, Saint Augustine. Their dialogue revolves around Petrarch's poetic, spiritual, and amatory qualms.

As to Pavese, while analyzing in his diary what he calls "stylistic situations" (one of several critical concepts that he forged), he criticizes Petrarch for "confusing life and art"; he sides with Dante, Stendhal, and Baudelaire because they departed from real life by constructing self-contained "mental situations" governed by "internal laws." This distinction being made (and whatever surprise one feels upon finding Stendhal thus cited), Pavese's own conflict between life and art remains arduous to grasp. His experiences quite evidently fuel his fiction, yet he aims, stylistically, to transform them—and in no simplistic manner. (It was Stendhal, after all, who proposed that a novel, as it was borne down a road, held up a mirror to reality.)

To return to Petrarch, a pre-eminent European autobiographer, it is furthermore hard not to notice that, like the author of the *Canzoniere* and *Secretum*, Pavese is a perpetual doubter who constantly delves—in both his diary and fiction—into pre-eminently Christian questions like guilt, charity, selflessness, and necessary solitude; and secondly, that he likewise aspires to the most sensual aspects of love all the while developing an authorial vision whereby literature is the medium par excellence through which life is approached or, alternately, kept at bay. Paradoxically, for sensibilities such as Pavese's (or Petrarch's), only writing can near one to life, or to the beloved other. The life one is living daily actually remains—in one's conscience, in one's consciousness—at a strange, and estranging, remove.

Although Petrarch's ornate rhetoric in his Italian love poetry (his Latin prose is something else again) could not be more distant from Pavese's deceptively realist prose, the two writers equally idealize yet at the same time harshly scrutinize women. Bordering on misogyny (as he himself admitted), Pavese fatally linked love to morbidity. His grim final poetry collection, found on his desk after he had committed suicide, is significantly entitled *Verrà la morte e avrà i tuoi occhi* (1951), literally "Death will Come and [She will] Have Your Eyes. "Death," a feminine noun in Italian, is here associated with the American actress Constance Dowling, who had recently left him. The poems are composed in short lines and there is little emphasis on storytelling. In one tale collected in *Cesare Pavese: Stories*, the first-person narrator envisions self-destructive desires as occurring one step earlier. He coolly concedes that every time he is in love he thinks of killing himself. It seems that Pavese was driven by a perpetually adolescent romanticism with respect to women, as well as, in contrast, by an amorous philosophy so inflexibly pessimistic that any enduring partnership was excluded in advance.

Interestingly, scenes in his novels more often than not involve, not a single man and a single woman interacting, but rather a group of characters. Prolonged conversations between these characters build up tension and authenticity; the author's written words, which presumably record once-spoken words, are ontologically closer to what actually happened (was uttered) than are descriptions. As they bring to the fore the difficulties of lasting friendship, the forces of sexual attraction, the impasses of love, many passages are conspicuously theatrical in narrative structure. Plots shift decisively during parties, dances, or outings. A prime example is the *ménage à trois* artfully studied in *The Beach*, a novel otherwise portraying a small crowd of friends who have gathered at the same summer resort.

Yet this social dimension of Pavese's novel writing deftly masks a much more somber awareness of an individual's abject aloneness. A clue to this subtle double layering can be found in his diary, when Pavese advises caustically that any person convinced of a human being's utter solitude should "lose himself in countless social relationships which, in consequence, demand little." He also contended that writers "spoke" their characters; that it was essentially the same thing if a novelist employed one character or several. "My lot is to hug shadows," he confessed in a letter dated 6 July 1950, referring not only to Constance Dowling but also—I would posit—to his habit of sectioning himself off into characters. As lively and full-rounded as these characters seem to us, they were hopelessly phantom-like for Pavese.

Though resembling early twentieth-century American realism in certain ways, Pavese's stories and novels are thus more deeply structured around a series of fascinating oppositions. He once noted that he lived "with antinomies," which he began to list as "voluptuous-tragic, cowardly-heroic, sensual-ideal..." In his fiction, such antinomies add fathomless ambiguity to relatively simple plot lines; they also enable him to experiment with himself, even in novels ostensibly offering social panoramas. He imaginatively crossed distances that he could not cross in real life. He even uses a woman first-person narrator in *Among Women Only*, an engrossing novel exploring solitude and the quest for affection even as it satirizes the affluent milieus of postwar Turin, Pavese's hometown.

Some stories similarly test hypotheses about how he might have behaved in this or that amorous situation. In one of his most absorbing tales, "The Family," the fictional Corradino runs into an old girlfriend at a dance, starts going out with her again, only to learn that he is the likely father of her illegitimate son—not coincidentally named "Dino" and aged six-and-a-half. Having himself suffered from the early deaths of his father (when he was six) and mother (when he was twenty-two), Pavese seems to toy here with what founding a family—even under such circumstances—might be like. In *Among Women Only*, Momina, Morelli, and the narrator Clelia likewise debate the advantages of "accepting life" and "having children." Pavese's characters and alter egos often assay the potential happiness of lifestyles that he never possessed.

In "The Family," moreover, Corradino longs "for something...to change his life without robbing him of...his old habits." He would like "to become a different man without being conscious of it." These secret aspirations for change—effortless changes, immobile escapes—intensify Pavese's stories because the changes never come about. On the surface, his tales thereby recount "long illusions," as he himself puts it in *The House on the Hill*, a novel set during the final stages of the Second World War and charting the attempts of a Turin teacher, linked to the Italian underground movement, to hide out in the surrounding hills, the very territory of his lost childhood. During his seclusion, his recollected boyhood tellingly becomes his surrogate "companion, colleague, son." Yet beneath his acts lurks the bleak truth that no recovery of the past is possible, that no evolution in a human heart can take place. Pavese's diary (which, incidentally, comments very little on the war) discloses how relentlessly such dire axioms ate away at him. In European literature, Marcel Proust is by no means the only writer to probe the existential and philosophical consequences of the urge or necessity to remember.

Not surprisingly, Pavese elucidated, both for himself and more generally as a critic, the "static essentials" of a novel, as they are incarnated in a hero who remains the same from the beginning to the end. In "Evocation," an oddly rambling prose text departing from the classical short story form that Pavese normally practiced, the narrator accordingly despairs because "nothing happens." Sitting in an empty corner of a tavern, he tries to "fill the silence with the sound of a distant tram." Eventually a stranger sits down nearby, rests his elbow on the table and his jaw on his fist. The narrator becomes fascinated with the man's knuckles—just one of countless instances, throughout Pavese's oeuvre, where a minuscule detail is magnified obsessively, radiantly. In his poems, similarly, a nameless woman's "husky voice" recurrently crystallizes longing and resentment. Scholars have since determined that this lady with the "voce rauca" was the fiancée who broke off with Pavese shortly before his return from prison. Whatever the autobiographical inspiration underlying them, such details are "caressed," as Vladimir Nabokov counseled his disciples, and for reasons that transcend mere craftsmanship.

Of course, Pavese surely learned much from the inherent empiricism of English-language writing—a salient quality of our literature, yet one which also harbors potential philosophical limitations. As an Americanist (who wrote a thesis on Walt Whitman), he had already translated Sinclair Lewis's *Our Mr. Wrenn*, Herman Melville's *Moby Dick*, Sherwood Anderson's *Dark*

Laughter, John Dos Passos's *42nd Parallel*, as well as James Joyce's *Portrait of the Artist as a Young Man,* by the time his first poetry collection, *Lavorare stanca* (*Hard Labor* or *Work's Tiring*), devoted to village life and to his exile from it, was published in 1936. By 1943, when the second, revised and much expanded, edition of this pioneering collection came out, he had produced versions of Daniel Defoe's *Moll Flanders*, Charles Dickens's *David Copperfield*, Gertrude Stein's *Three Lives*, William Faulkner's *The Hamlet*, and Melville's *Benito Cereno*. Although he was raised and schooled in Turin, a large town, he spent childhood summers and once an entire year in his father's native village of Santo Stefano Belbo.

Yet details in Pavese reveal a still more intricate motivation. The opposition between town and countryside, as experienced during his childhood, directly relates to his conscientious use of "images." This opposition arises thematically in the plots of several stories and novels, but also and especially in probing reflections (in the diary) about how images spontaneously engage his mind while he is writing. He worries, for example, whether his "images" are perhaps nothing but "ingenious variations" on a single "fundamental image" associated with his *paese*, his homeland, the Piedmont region. Ever scrupulous about the authenticity of his inspiration (in its autobiographical aspects) and about the accuracy of his perceptions (as he scrutinized the particulars of the outside world), he sought to measure the extent to which he was naturally, that is unconsciously, a "regional writer." The earnestness and obsessiveness of his self-interrogation of course reveals how unnatural a regionalist he actually was. It is because he felt, as an adult, incurably separated from his at once beloved and tragic childhood memories, attached to village life and the death of his father, that he could use them so profoundly in his writing. This is why *The House on the Hill* (to cite just that novel) is cryptically, essentially, autobiographical.

His remarkable details, moreover, function like bridges leading away from the self, enabling the Italian writer to cross over into the pure, emotionless, objective world of matter. Such bridge-crossings perhaps brought temporary relief. The reader certainly takes pleasure whenever Pavese abruptly focuses on, say, "the toes of Cate's little shoes." But probably the pleasure (for Pavese) of these lovingly rendered close-ups, of these desperate leaps toward the "thing-in-itself," was short lived. He confessed that his "contemplation of things" was ultimately always "inquieta"—"anxious," "troubled," "uneasy."

"Inquieta" indeed. One senses that Pavese was soon gazing, no longer at the thing, but inwards. In his diary, he declares that people in a story "have a given character and that things happen in accordance with pre-determined laws." "But the *point* of our story," he insists, "must lie neither in these characters nor in those laws." For all his so-called realism, it is to his credit that such "points" are rarely easy to deduce, or define. But they certainly stir up a pervasive "unquietness" extending well beyond the narratives themselves, and one imagines Pavese—his own analysis of Dante, Stendhal, and Baudelaire notwithstanding—ultimately holding up a mirror to himself, self-splintered into a host of surrogate characters, each struggling to recover an impossible wholeness and to master that redoubtable "trade of living."

* * *

Pavese's poetry and fiction continues to be rediscovered in the United States, and this is exciting news. In 2001, New York Review Books brought out a volume entitled *Selected Works*, consisting of four important novels (*The Beach, The House on the Hill, Among Women Only, The Devil in the Hills*); this book was followed the next year by the Italian writer's most famous novel, *The Moon and the Bonfires*. Now Copper Canyon Press has published Geoffrey Brock's vivid rendering of Pavese's extremely moving poetry, *Disaffections: Complete Poems 1930-1950*. All we lack now is an available version of *Il mestiere di vivere*, one of the most intellectually fascinating and excruciatingly honest writer's diaries in modern European literature. An earlier translation, entitled *This Business of Living*, is out of print, as is the 1946 translation (by A. E. Murch) of Pavese's superb short stories that The Ecco Press re-issued in 1987.

Above all, Pavese surprised his first readers with his "American" stylistic directness and sharp eye for detail. His natural empiricism, or realism, dissociated him from contemporary "Hermetic" poets like Giuseppe Ungaretti, Eugenio Montale, or Salvatore Quasimodo, all noted for their highly personal symbolism. Pavese, moreover, had an intimate knowledge of the countryside, of its villagers and farm laborers, as well as of those who had migrated to large cities in search of work. This being said, he was never a committed writer, despite his membership in the Communist Party after the Second World War and his passing interest in Marxism. He possessed something much more precious than a political theory: a natural sensitivity to the plight and dignity of common people, be they bums, priests, grape-pickers, gas station attendants, office workers, or anonymous girls picked up on the street (though to women, the author could—as he admitted—be as misogynous as he was affectionate). Some of Pavese's most memorable poems depict peasant girls who become prostitutes in Turin. In "The Country Whore," he describes one such woman awakening, details her memory of being sexually abused during childhood, then adds:

> It often returns, in the slow rise from sleep,
> that undone aroma of far-off flowers,
> of barns and of sun. No man can know
> the subtle caress of that sour memory.

Although raised in Turin, Pavese spent childhood summers and one entire year in his father's village of Santo Stefano Belbo, located in the Langhe hills outside of Turin. Both the style and subject matter used by some American writers—surely Anderson and Lewis, not to forget Edgar Lee Masters—helped the aspiring Italian poet understand more profoundly the universal significance (and lasting enigmas) of this double childhood linked to a cosmopolitan city as well as to lower Piedmont. Certainly American writers' interest in manual labor, small towns, and the new urban working classes provided an encouraging literary paradigm for Pavese, who sought the aesthetic means to deal with what he had eyewitnessed among his family members and their acquaintances. One of his first poetic experiments, "South Seas," notably relates the life of a cousin who leaves the poverty of his village behind and, for two decades, sails the world, seeking his fortune. He finally returns and opens a gas station—which fails. For Southern Europeans, self-imposed economic exile was frequent; and not all homecomings were glorious.

In two important memoirs, "The Poet's Craft" and "On Certain Poems That Have Not Yet Been Written," as well as in the opening *Secretum professionale* section of his diary, Pavese recalls his struggle to find a poetic language that could reflect an Italy that was evolving rapidly, indeed brutally. This language would also have to express his personal pain associated with the countryside: his father had died when Pavese was only six years old. So convincing is the auto-biographical realism of his poems that it is impossible to read those (implicitly) set in Santo Stefano Belbo without thinking of their real-life models: friends and neighbors of the poet's father. Could Pavese have sensed that his father, too, was somehow temporarily revived in such poems? Masters and Whitman were especially decisive in Pavese's quest to resuscitate the archetypal figures of this doomed rural past, even if he ultimately rejected free verse along with classical Italian poetic forms. One day, as he recounts in "The Poet's Craft," he spontaneously discovered (or rather, rediscovered) the thirteen-syllable, four-foot anapestic lines that would become his hallmark: "I found myself muttering a certain jumble of words (which turned into a pair of lines from 'South Seas') in a pronounced cadence that I had used for emphasis ever since I was a child, when I would murmur over and over the phrases that obsessed me most in the novels I was reading."

This particular meter, which is rather strange for ears trained in the *ende-casillabo* and the *settenario*, is respected quite rigorously in *Work's Tiring* (as Brock prefers to call *Lavorare stanca*, as opposed to William Arrowsmith's 1976 version, *Hard Labor*). Pavese occasionally adds or deletes a metrical foot, but he otherwise creates a unified metrical impression. In the introduction to his French translation (*Travailler fatigue / La Mort viendra et elle aura tes yeux*, 1969), Gilles de Van praises the originality of this "regular rhythm, without syncopation, without abrupt surprises, without [lyrical] research, without [undue] refinement."

Brock's highly crafted translation much improves on Arrowsmith's rendering. Brock's volume also comprises poems contemporaneous to *Work's Tiring* but not included in the two editions of that book, as well as the posthumously published, dark-toned, and still very popular sequence, *Death Will Come and*

Will Have Your Eyes. In all cases, Brock finely renders Pavese's "tight-lipped rhythm," as he aptly puts it. Intensity, even sometimes despair, characterize Pavese's verse, though brief moments of hope are recorded. In "Two Cigarettes," for example, a woman asks the narrator for a match to light her cigarette, then engages in conversation with him. Pavese concludes:

> Two butts, now, on the asphalt. We look at the sky:
> that window up there, she says pointing, is ours—
> but the heater's not working. At night, lost steamers
> have little to steer by, maybe only the stars.
> We cross the street, arm in arm, playfully warming each other.

Yet such amorous optimism is rare. Pavese's ephemeral love affairs are delineated in stark lines because the poet was already tormented, at the onset of the relationship, by the inevitability of loss. An early poem, "Words for a Girlfriend" already formulates this fundamental pessimism: "I am alone, and I'll be alone always."

Though solitude is Pavese's most salient theme, his poetry also sometimes resembles the "neighborly" short story that we associate with, say, *Winesburg, Ohio*. In *Work's Tiring*, the poems are long (averaging twenty-five to thirty lines), center on a character or two, evoke action directly, or use action as a mirror of a character's thoughts. The Italian poet invented this specific literary genre, which he called a *poesia-racconto*, a "poem-story." Despite their length, however, the poems contain no excess lyricism, bathos, or extensive description. As for dialogue, a quoted remark or two suffices to conjure up an entire personality. In "Betrayal," which is typical of Pavese's simultaneous yearning for and cynicism toward women, the narrator takes a "new woman" for a rowboat ride. She responds to "the boisterous Po, its bright sun, its echoes / of quick waves and sand-diggers" with this terse comment:

> "So enchanting," she said
> without moving her body or taking her eyes off the sky.

Pavese excels at bringing out the density of such moments, in which nothing really happens. Yet also impressive are several poems in which he announces a tragedy ("Last night, there was a boy / who fell off this roof, breaking his back"), then immediately focuses on the so-called insignificant events taking place nearby:

> The wind riffles the cool leaves of the trees.
> The red clouds above are warm and move slowly.
> A stray dog appears in the alley below, sniffing
> the body on the cobblestones, and a raw wail
> rises up among chimneys: someone's unhappy.

Here and elsewhere, he develops the notion that the saddest dramas occur almost imperceptibly, a philosophy reinforcing his theme of solitude. Yet beyond this poetic exposition of an idea, it is more characteristic of Pavese to aim for a scrupulous rendering of reality—the ideas being illustrated, not explained. After all, from a strictly phenomenological viewpoint, cool leaves, slowly moving red clouds, and a stray dog indeed vie for our attention as insistently as a boy's corpse. (One can compare this poem—"Affairs"—to Auden's "Musée des Beaux Arts," in which a similar philosophy is brought to the fore, yet more explicitly.)

Few lines in Pavese's poetry are memorable, but an overall impression remains indelible in the reader's mind. Perhaps this is because many "poem-stories" are in fact "poem-portraits." In "Dina Thinking," Pavese goes so far as to adopt the voice of a prostitute who, while swimming naked in a stream, reflects on her life in the first-person personal. For a poet who evokes incurable solitude so often, Pavese was a master empathizer. With admirable subtlety, he reveals the intricacies of another person's thought patterns, even as he is describing the character from the outside, in the third person. In "Deola Thinking," for instance, he portrays a prostitute who has left a brothel for good and now "only works evenings, making slow conquests / to music, in her usual bar." Each morning she spends time in a café, drinking milk, eating brioches, and smoking serenely. "This morning she's nearly a lady," remarks Pavese, whose objective descriptions gradually merge with the woman's thoughts:

> The girls at the house are still sleeping. The air stinks,
> the madam goes out for a walk, it's crazy to stay there.
> To work the bars in the evening you have to look good;
> at that house, by thirty, you've lost what little looks you had left.

Brock's translations of these Edward Hopper-like scenes bristle with intelligent decisions. Even the hesitating quibbler (who notices a singular "street" in the English for an Italian plural, and a few other minor departures from the original) perceives how much attention Brock has paid to the way that Italians and English-language readers respectively form mental pictures with words. He often brilliantly translates at this conceptual level. And he has been very careful with the music of these poems—they are a delight to read. On the whole, this version is outstanding and deserves a wide readership. In his introduction, he alludes to American poets (like Philip Levine) who have acknowledged their debt to Pavese. Thanks to Brock, there will be others.

Appearance, Apparition, Aspiration
(Giorgio Caproni and Giuseppe Ungaretti)

For American lovers of modern Italian poetry, this is an exciting time. After recent, and sometimes brilliant, translations of Eugenio Montale, Umberto Saba, and Cesare Pavese, here come Giorgio Caproni (1912-1990) and Giuseppe Ungaretti (1888-1970). Reading their work is invigorating. Please forgive me if I am inclined to argue that, in comparison to many American poets, Caproni and Ungaretti often attain an admirable, intense equilibrium between various poetic intentions and tendencies. They can be sensual and metaphysical at the same time. They seek out vivid detail from the outside world, but also retire into secrecy, obliqueness, acute subjectivity. Their formal innovations, however striking, intelligently respect a refined literary heritage going back to Cavalcanti, Dante, and Petrarch. Like the aforementioned, their amorous passions come draped in an intricate intellectuality. They aspire to "song," to a visceral musicality, even as they seek "ever deeper and distant analogical associations" (as Filippo Marinetti put it in his Futurist Manifesto). In brief, their poetic sensibilities are rich, moving, challenging, and—I daresay—not "dissociated," as T. S. Eliot might have put it.

The opening two-liner in Andrew Frisardi's engaging *Selected Poems of Giuseppe Ungaretti* stopped me short for an entire afternoon: "Between one flower plucked and the other given / the inexpressible nothing." This is only the first of several instances where "nothingness" or "absence" takes on a haunting presence in Ungaretti's work. Whereas most poets showcase language, Ungaretti, as well as Caproni, exhibit a poetics of sparseness because they are all too aware of nothingness as the very foundation—but of course it provides no foundation—upon which our existence might well stand. They correspondingly craft language into, say, not an admirable façade, but rather an admirable door that one soon wishes to open: it leads out onto (or back onto) what cannot be crafted, even uttered, perhaps even known, except by means of rare penetrating intuitions. In "The Buried Harbor," significantly, Ungaretti calls his poetry "the merest nothing / of an inexhaustible secret." This is no false modesty, but rather a way of redirecting attention, from the poem, to what matters: the fountainhead that he has glimpsed and that is strangely akin to a weighty "silence" that precedes, underlies and nourishes all writing. "When I find / a word / in this my silence," he reports elsewhere, "it is dug into my life / like an abyss."

One does not walk away lightly from such depths. Clearly Ungaretti—otherwise celebrated for his humane embrace—harbors spiritual qualms that call into question his Christian heritage. In "The Captain," the poet remembers how, as a child, he would awake startled in the middle of the night, then be soothed by howling stray dogs more than by "the little lamp / That burned forever in that room / Near the Madonna." Other poems are more dramatic in their momentary presupposing of a God who can be confronted. In "Mercy," for instance, Ungaretti almost pleas: "Are you nothing but a dream, God? // We rashly want you to resemble this, / At least: a dream." Elsewhere, a Job-like entreaty concludes in a heartrending question: "Will it now come to pass that ashes triumph?"

Yet for all his staring at and meditation upon those ashes as the probable sole horizon of human experience, Ungaretti's passionate circumspection—no one doubt is ever declared conclusive, no one hope definitive—induces even more provocative speculations. In the sequence *Last Choruses for the Promised Land*, notably, he observes a mimosa blossoming in February, then wonders:

> As I approach the great silence,
> Will it be a sign that no thing dies
> If its appearance keeps coming back?
>
> Or will I finally know that death
> Is sovereign over nothing but appearance?

Indeed, if it is only "appearance" that death vanquishes, then what sustains and ever re-creates phenomena would be a sort of invisible vital undercurrent that destruction cannot reach: "life," in a word, though not in any banal biological understanding of this elusive concept (the pursuit of which, it increasingly strikes me, defines the deep-running, perhaps sometimes unconscious, motivation of many more contemporary writers than is commonly acknowledged). This hypothesis about appearances, so movingly stated by Ungaretti, leads me to Caproni, who is much less known in the English-speaking world.

For Caproni, too, delves into the nature of appearances. He calls them "asparizioni," a neologism combining—to return to English—"aspiration" and "apparition." In a poem entitled "Asparizione" (not included by Ned Condini in his smoothly and resourcefully translated selection, *The Earth's Wall*), the poet typically evokes a perception, or rather the memory of a perception, as little more than a vague, ghostly apparition. We "aspire" to remember, but remembering fosters only uncertainties, intellectual aporias, at best only troubling hallucinations:

In a street in Lima

Or here.
                    Little matter.

In a dream, perhaps
                    An echo.

In the already desperately dispersed
sound of a slammed door.

                    (my translation)

One remembers hearing the sound of the slammed door; one can no longer actually hear it. Conceivably, an infinite regress sets in, whereby one remembers remembering remembering...hearing the slammed door. Like Ungaretti, Caproni suspects that our daily empirical experience of the world is no more reliable; sensate "facts" are mere phantoms; each sense impression—little matter how initially strong and despite our will to preserve it—dwindles to naught. In "Controversial Verse," translated by Condini, Caproni pointedly inquires:

Live shafts of light
into eyes filled with woods
and seagulls. . .

                    Just one step

away. . .

A step from where?

Does where really exist?

Many twentieth-century European poets and writers have grappled with similar fundamental doubts, but it is to Caproni's credit that he insists on the desire and yearning (the "aspiring") intimately woven into radical (intellectual) skepticism. His insight that, as we face the world, ideas and emotions are intimately entwined is as simple as it is profound. Countless lines in his poems illustrate this marriage of thought and feeling; take this at once despairing and lucid avowal, from Condini's version of "The Barge": "I was crying and couldn't / say the root of my dying." Enveloped in the painful lament, provoked (as in several other poems) by his mother's death, is a resonant philosophical question resembling that asked by Ungaretti when he contemplated the mimosa. What is the genuine "root" (in Italian: the polysemous "il seme," which also means "seed") of this "existence" that can be said to "belong" to me if and only if I take into full account "il mio morire," "my dying? What kind of "possessions" are these?

In Caproni's opera-poem, *Il Conte de Kevenhüller*, there is actually a section called "Asparizioni," by which he implicitly asserts that poems are "asparitions" as well. So be it: that language, too, is spectral logically ensues from the kind of reasoning outlined above. In one of these "asparizioni," "Renunciation," the poet hunts for himself by hunting for his double:

I followed him.

I spotted him.

But it was not he.

It was I.

So I let him go.

Uncertain,
he took the grassy path.

In a bound he had vanished
(that is, I had, not he)

amidst the trees, into the dark.

(my translation)

Here, Caproni of course recalls Rimbaud's harrowing "je est un autre." It is not just the world which, like an "apparition," constantly withdraws from us, despite our "aspiring" for it to remain securely in our purview; we, too, are "asparitions" who withdraw from ourselves. Ungaretti puts it somewhat differently in "Resting," when he describes himself as "plummet[ing] into myself / And go[ing] dark in my nest." Yet in both cases, the final darkness implies that the poet's quest terminates in epistemological confusion and obscurity, in no redeeming self-elucidation.

With remarkable economy, Caproni's poem "La porta" crystallizes all these doubts. Various doors are mentioned. A transparent one "leads to opacity"; others are locked, blind, deceiving or useless. Finally, this series of doors—which prevent the poet from advancing or guide him nowhere—culminate in the complex image of a "porta morgana." Quite gravely, Caproni equates this "morgana door," via a mere colon, to "la Parola" (with a capital "P"), which can be rendered as "Speech," "Words," "the Word of God" (given the poet's persistent religious anguish), or perhaps—stretching things a bit—even "Poetry."

It is dizzying to imagine simultaneously all the meanings of this dense, decisive image. Since "porta morgana" puns with "fata morgana," initially "la Parola"—with its equally over-brimming signification—is linked to distortion, insubstantiality, illusoriness. The poet's very tool—language—thus constitutes a mirage, as also do human speech and all divine utterance. Interestingly, Ungaretti admonishes himself likewise: "all you need is an illusion / to give you courage // A searchlight / over there / creates an ocean / in the fog."

Yet Caproni's "morgana door" possesses still other semantic layers, even as a sturdy door might be constructed of many layers of wood. The neologistic "morgana" recalls the legendary Breton fairy "Morgane" (or "Morgan le Fay"). In a French translation of Caproni's poem, I have found a footnote mentioning Apollinaire's "La Tranchée" and its line "Morgane en son castel sans retour." The translators, Philippe Renard and Bernard Simeone (who likely consulted Caproni), leave the matter there, but their suggestion is worth pursuing. Apollinaire's "The Trench" refers to the First World War, in which he was wounded. Moreover, this poem from the *Poèmes à Madeleine* sequence is blatantly erotic. A femme fatale, Morgane—who is thus also a macabre goddess of war—is likened to an enticing prostitute and her "castle of no return" to a lethal brothel. This implies "porta morgana" in its most negative sense, and I suppose that the punctuation mark—the colon—could stand for a sort of standoff between physical sensation and the poet trying to fully experience or render it. For Caproni, as for Ungaretti, aspiring to lose oneself—even momentarily—in pure sensuality is also an illusion. One cannot merge, as it were, with sensation because one is separated from nature, from the world, not to mention from oneself; and language has even less chance of passing through the narrow gate represented by the two dots punctuating the poem. Similarly, when Ungaretti asks "to delight in just / one minute of inchoate / life," his wish, by its very formulation in the poem "Wanderer," obviously remains ungranted.

This is not all. As an enchanting fairy, Morgane also has positive connotations. Some ancient poems depict her as the savior of King Arthur. When he was wounded by Mordred, Morgane took him to the Isle of Avalon, attended to his wounds, then let him remain there until he was well enough to return to Brittany and re-unite his people. In this affirming symbolism, the adjective invented by Caproni would liken "la Parola" to that which can approach the gateway of hope and renewal. And besides these mutually contradictory symbols of death, eroticism, the sensate cosmos, hope, and renewal, one furthermore hears the echo of "morganatic" ("morganatico" in Italian), an adjective qualifying a marriage between a member of a noble family and a person of inferior rank. In this regard, "porta morgana" suggests the poet's aspirations to a higher order of reality. Yet he will be left outside, "below."

This acknowledgement of remaining apart, hopelessly remote, in fact informs Caproni's entire oeuvre. The expression "the earth's wall" used in the title of the anthology comes from Dante's *Inferno* (X, 1-3) and alludes to the poet and his mentor, Virgil, passing "onward still, following a hidden track / Between the city's ramparts and the fires." The Italian behind the translator Dorothy Sayers's "city's ramparts" is "il muro della terra," literally "the earth's wall"; but the medievalist and detective novelist has not misconstrued "terra" because, in the fourteenth century, the word also meant "fortress," "rampart," or "circle." As for Caproni, he borrows the same Dantean expression in "I, Too," in order to graphically depict his poetics of metaphysical impossibility; in Condini's tense, terse version:

> I, too, have tried.
> It has all been a war
> of fingernails. Now I know
> No one will ever manage
> to bore through the earth's wall.

Caproni's grim lesson is that, despite all our fingernail-digging and aspiration, we very probably cannot get beyond the human condition, beyond the rigorous ontological limit established by our absolute materiality, our inescapable physicality. And if "terra" is taken in its former metaphorical senses (of which Caproni was surely aware), then it moreover can be deduced that it is impossible to pass through the "morgana" door or gate shutting us off from whatever heavenly citadel might ensure salvation. Needless to say, Caproni's penetrating and oft gripping poems—like Ungaretti's—give us frequent intimations of citadels looming there above us, even as we pass below the ramparts, alongside those redoubtable earth's walls.

A Cornucopia of Italian Poetry
(Camillo Sbarbaro, Vittorio Sereni, Andrea
Zanzotto, Luciano Erba, Bàrtolo Cattafi, Lucio
Mariani, Luigi Fontanella)

Modern and contemporary Italian poetry continues to fill our bookshelves. No other foreign poetry has recently benefited as much from the efforts of translators, who have produced not just samplings, but thick "Selected Poems" and even "Complete Poems." Annotated and bilingual, several of these volumes also possess excellent introductions situating the poet with respect to Hermeticism—the most influential Italian poetic sensibility in the twentieth century—and other European literary movements and philosophies, especially those that have held sway in France. Italian poets have long engaged in dialogue with their neighbors across the Alps; and not a few have also been attentive to German-language culture, notably to the psychoanalysis of early-twentieth-century Vienna or to the aesthetic implications of Martin Heidegger's readings of Trakl, Rilke, and Hölderlin.

The abundance of Italian verse that is available in English urges us to reexamine literary history. Do our standard chronicles of modern poetry underestimate the Italians? If a reevaluation is called for, as I believe, it can now be done. A substantial portion of the poetry of seminal Italian modernists, ranging from Umberto Saba (1883-1957) and Giuseppe Ungaretti (1888-1970) to Eugenio Montale (1896-1981), Cesare Pavese (1908-1950), Mario Luzi (1914-2005), and Giorgio Caproni (1912-1990), has been rendered within the past few years; to this list can henceforth be added the prose poet Camillo Sbarbaro (1888-1967), and the poets Vittorio Sereni (1913-1983), Andrea Zanzotto (b. 1921), Luciano Erba (b. 1922), and Bartolo Cattafi (1922-1979). This is not all. Following upon earlier translations of the work of important poets who are either slightly younger than the aforementioned—like Alfredo de Palchi (b. 1926) and Antonio Porta (1935-1989)—or belong to the next generation—like Roberto Bertoldo (b. 1957) and Milo De Angelis (b. 1951)—representative verse by Lucio Mariani (b. 1936) and Luigi Fontanella (b. 1943) has likewise come out in English.

* * *

Sbarbaro's *Shavings*, which has been finely rendered by Gayle Ridinger, is a significant addition to our English-language bibliography of a genre that defies definition: short poetic prose, as opposed to the short story and even the classical European prose poem that we associate with Baudelaire and Rimbaud. Sbarbaro's melancholy pieces—christened not only *trucioli* ("shavings"), but also *bolli di sapone* ("soap bubbles"), *rimanenze* ("leftovers"), *scampoli* ("scraps"), *spiccioli* ("small change"), and *fuochi fatui* ("will-o'-the-wisps")—represent major examples of a particular kind of European brevity that retains compelling narrative qualities even as it transforms or rejects traditional characterization, description, emotional evocation, or event sequencing. Of course, American "short-shorts" are cousins to such prose, but perhaps they more often emphasize events and narrative logic, however sketchily or absurdly, whereas Sbarbaro and other Europeans tend to underscore oblique perceptions, strange recollections, troubling atmospheres, and the estranging oddness of the quotidian. Be this as it may, several Italian short-prose writers deserve renewed attention. In his incisive introduction to *Shavings*, the critic Simone Giusti mentions collections like *Goccie d'inchiostro* ("Ink Drops," 1880) by Carlo Dossi (1849-1910), *Pesce rossi* ("Goldfish," 1920), by Emilio Cecchi (1884-1966), *Frantumi* ("Splinters," 1918) by Giovanni Boine (1887-1917), and *Scorciatoie* ("Shortcuts," 1946) by the much better known Saba. Saba was also an outstanding lyrical poet who wrote rhymed, metrically strict verse. This simultaneous mastery of what usually appear to be two distinct literary orientations should remind us that, for a given author, prose and poetry can actually form a continuous spectrum in which there are no stable boundaries between genres.

Sbarbaro, who wrote many of his "shavings" while crouching in the trenches during the First World War, calls his craft "la mia poesia tanto povera" ("my so poor poetry"). This is a deeper remark than it appears. It implies the sacrifice of literary elegance in order to attain a profound genuineness. Such asceticism in fact characterizes some of the most probing and original European writing, especially since the Second World War; and Sbarbaro may be one of the first modern poets—in France, the Yves Bonnefoy of *Pierre écrite* (1965) and the Philippe Jaccottet of *Leçons* (1966-1967) come much later—to grasp the dangers of "writing well," that is to comprehend a personal aspiration to stylistic beauty as a potential obstacle to the search for truth. Rhetorical destructiveness, as in Dada, is not so much involved here as is an intentional impoverishment. (One also remembers Samuel Beckett's quip about writing in French because it was too tempting to write poetically in English.) Stressing his painful, not just social but also ontological, separation from a real world made up of material things and other people, Sbabaro's autobiographical pieces comprise startling primary sense impressions, ranging from birds "whirling through leaves like flung stones" and urinals smelling "like violent black flowers" to a "whole world" that "seemed docile and a bit comic, too, like an object inside a water bottle." No fictional inventiveness functions here, but rather a sincere

autobiographical realism intensified by the author's natural heightened awareness; his hypersensitivity can be traced in his simultaneous attraction to and
alienation from others, the Other, and things. "My only possible gesture of
love," he admits, "consists in taking my mute wonderment for a walk." He was
likewise one of first European writer-strollers who, following in Baudelaire's
footsteps, sought to penetrate the mysteries of modern life by wandering aimlessly through city streets.

Interestingly, our own Edgar Allan Poe, whom Baudelaire translated, is still
considered by many Europeans to have offered pioneering critical insights into
such unclassifiable prose, even when he was ostensibly examining the more or
less classically shaped tales of contemporaries like Nathaniel Hawthorne. Giusti
recalls Poe's notion of the reader's role in "making the poem" by "connecting the
fragments and reconstructing a poetic vision that without his or her help would
fall to pieces." Once again, a fragmentary poetic and philosophical vision—and
not so much plot, however lacunary—is at stake. Drawing subsequently on the
ever-sharp perceptions of Montale (who made acute remarks about his friend's
"poetry of failed humanity and of things that remain irremediably obscure and
out of reach"), Giusti adds: "No matter what sort of proto-*shaving* Sbarbaro
was writing, whether a short descriptive prose poem or a longer, more 'story-
like' sketch, each creation was meant to come together like the shattered but
swept-up parts of a barely fathomable, immense whole; in short, they are to be
read as the fallout of a totality that does not in reality exist, yet can be intuited
enough to bestow on those shattered pieces the dignity of a microcosm."

Sbarbaro's short prose leaves us in this uneasy limbo. Infused with the
narrator's melancholy (which is not to say the depression that eventually led
to Sbarbaro's confinement in the San Paolo Hospital in Savona), several pieces
almost desperately commemorate "blessings raining down from heaven or
undeserved delights, memories of small things." These "loose snippets" that
"seem to hang in midair," as he calls them, sometimes depict his native region of
Liguria, which he shared with Montale and Caproni. As a world-ranked lichen
specialist (some of whose specimen collections are now housed in American
museums), Sbarbaro would also walk in the countryside. He was looking for
lichens more than for poetic inspiration, but he would later enjoy spontaneous
Proust-like reminiscence of, for example, a craggy apple tree located in the hills
in which he had hiked above Spotorno. In such memories, Sbarbaro's happiness
is depicted as momentary, literally. A moment, like a suddenly tangible then
suddenly vanishing dust mote of an eternity ever out of reach, is all he can hope
for. But lichens last, comparatively. While writing about his vocation, Sbarbaro
reveals his yearning to get a grip on a reality that ever disappears:

> My herbarium of lichens clutters the room and saturates the air with a smell of
> underbrush. A Sample Kit of the World—or nearly so—is what it contains, in the
> form of wood splinters and rock fragments. Because collecting plants means collect-
> ing places. Noting retains more about a site than the plant that sprang to life there.

Intrinsic to it as only a living portrait can be, and affected by every circumstance, it embodies a vivid, concrete sense of place. Evoking the voice of a waterfall or the breath of the sea, preserving a whiff of the air in the city or up in the hills, a plant captures for the person who picked it a precise hours and seasons. Dried out and brittle, it still holds out the knowledge of how the sun caressed it.

The ultimate image in his pieces is often one of aridity or infertility. "These memories resurface for no reason, so sweet as to seem unreal," he concludes in his text about Spotorno, "for my parched life, grass that keeps growing in city cement." Similarly, in a fine portrait of his carefree friend, Natta, who "floats on top of appearances and lives off nuances," Sbarbaro initially circumvents the sadness formulated in so many of his diary-like jottings, and notes: "Being with him puts me in a similar state of grace. A cane chair and the crystal of a glass suffice to make me feel unutterable happiness." But the conclusion is once again pessimistic: "Only I'm not able to keep it up."

* * *

I first came across Vittorio Sereni in a simple but ultimately haunting line that de Palchi quotes in the ninth poem of his long sequence, *Sessions with My Analyst*: "non lo amo il mio tempo, non lo amo" ("I don't like my times, I don't like them"). In one or two other poems by this same Italian poet who has long lived in the United States and whose *Collected Poems* have recently been published in Italy as *Paradigma* (Mimesis/Hebenon, 2006), allusions to other aphoristic lines by Sereni are similarly made. The author of *The Human Implements* (1965) and *Variable Star* (1979 / 1981)—Sereni's best-known collections—is eminently quotable. I find myself still pondering, after reading the extensive *Selected Poetry and Prose* that has been excellently introduced by Peter Robinson and carefully rendered by Robinson and Marcus Perryman, lines such as "This timorous living among the dead," which is found in the poet's first book, *Frontier* (1941); and especially this distich in a short piece dated "Christmas 1944," from his second collection, *Algerian Diary* (1947): "And let the God made flesh today / be distance for us in the darkest hour."

Sereni's more characteristic manner is to elaborate complex, less immediate imagery in which abstractions and physical phenomena are brought together into heady combinations. "It's choked in the heat, / life's concert that quavers / in outermost swirlings of water" is a typical example showing how he also favors synaesthesia, which here involves intersecting sensations of sound, sight, and temperature. His images are long and sinuous, as it were, unwinding in continually surprising ways. In the following four lines, note how nearly every word adds something quite different to, and sometimes even shifts the perspectives of, the emerging extended image: "Disheartened delights, no better than the thread / of breeze that in the morning / of wisteria / infiltrates on the bombarded coastline." (The English syntax mirrors the Italian, with the exception, of course, of the inverted "costa bombardata.") Sereni often proceeds accordingly, convoking several levels of cognitive experience to his contemplation of a deceptively simple event, here a coastline over which blows a slight breeze.

Perryman and Robinson's annotations suggest how the poet attained these effects of compression and kaleidoscopic semantic density. While rewriting, he would strip off certain realistic details from his first drafts. The eight-line "Pin-up Girl," which is based on a thirty-four-line version that was published in the first edition of *Algerian Diary*, is a revealing extreme example. The definitive poem reads:

> Look at the sorry cutting grown limp
> in the dazzling air:
> the July afternoon
> has hints of bad weather,
> stray voices of alarm.
>
> And for a while the thirst
> is quenched on your lips
> still moistened in the wind.

In the longer draft, the poet addresses the pin-up girl with a recurrent "you" that puts her in the forefront as a character. If Sereni's much more oblique final version had not retained the same title, readers might have imagined that the poet was even somehow addressing himself with the "you" while gazing at the "ritaglio." (Perryman and Robinson are British, and here and there American readers may be slightly confused by their vocabulary: "cutting [from a magazine]" as opposed to "clipping.")

Sereni's verse often exhibits a scrutiny of reality, followed by a reorientation toward the self. In a quatrain called "A Return," he begins: "On the lake the sails made a white and compact poem." But the next three lines find him looking in a mirror: "but my breath was no longer equal to it / and it was no longer a lake but an astonished / mirror of me a lacuna of the heart." In a well-known poem entitled "Italian in Greece" and set in Piraeus in August 1942, Sereni similarly moves from a relatively objective evocation of the setting ("First Athens evening, drawn-out goodbye / of the convoys") to this characteristic introspective remark: "Europe, Europe who watch me / descending unarmed and absorbed / in my slender myth within the ranks of brutes, / I'm one of your sons in flight who knows / no enemy if not his own sorrow." In his most memorable war poems (and many are memorable), his observations, however self-focused, universalize the individual's (or an entire generation's) plight in the course of history. In "The Unjust Pity," he describes

> the disaster's unbuttoned battle dress, a helmet
> rolling between craters, on torn embankments
> face after face down a canal behind a wall

a platoon collapsing, stripping, not giving a damn
about surrender with dignity, but on everyone
that wrecked look, of youth in ruins,
with its flush of resentment, of failure,
of expulsion from the future.

One of the dichotomies that can be studied in Sereni's poetry is the relation-ship between factual circumstances and the poet's immediate, or delayed, writ-ten response. Some lines, such as those I have just quoted, seem to have been written nearly on the spot; they at least give that lively impression. A perception like "those semblances on bridges / in the headlamps' glare" seem jotted down in diary-like fashion by this soldier-poet who found himself on the outskirts of Athens in 1940. Tellingly, however, in a poem that appeared for the first time only in 1971, Sereni admits to being "still benumbed with war, with that war." As his later poems sometimes indicate, tragic events that he eye-witnessed continued to haunt him. He is an extraordinary evoker of both on-the-spot experience and the enduring presence of the past in memory. His stature as a major European war poet should grow rapidly with this volume.

Perryman and Robinson's annotations also reveal that there is much more intertextuality than one might expect in Sereni's intensely intricate verse. Along-side several admired fellow poets and writers (including, interestingly, William Carlos Williams), René Char, whom Sereni calls his "salutary antagonist," is the salient figure. Sereni translated Char's *Feuillets d'Hypnos*, the wartime journal chronicling in aphorisms and short prose his participation in the French underground movement, and later rendered additional poems by the Frenchman for his volume *Ritorno sopramonte e altre poesie* (1974)—which corresponds to Char's *Retour amont*. In "Translating Char," Sereni addresses his friend and explains his method: "In my way, René Char, / with my only means / on your materials." In his author's note to *Variable Star*, he specifies that his own poems are "moments of life, or better, recoveries (not exercises, not 'studies') related to the time I was occupied with that work." The Char-influenced verse shows how Sereni uses quotations from others' poems as impetuses to write. Indeed, in his prose text "Self-Portrait," he confesses: "To sit down at a desk, or, rather, to make experiments, I need a mediator.... The mediation may come from a foreign text I'm tempted to, or, perhaps, have been asked to translate."

Perryman and Robinson translate closely and accurately, and this monumen-tal bilingual edition will be invaluable to students of Sereni. Once in a while, however, their syntax too stiffly mirrors the original. In a touching poem about the suicide of Antonia Pozzi, a poet who was a friend of Sereni's and who left a note for him—"Addio...mio caro fratello" on her body, Perryman and Robin-son write, for instance, "that still for us / you die a little every year" as a strict equivalent of lines that are not as unnatural in Italian, a language that permits more syntactic flexibility than English: "che ancora per noi / tu muoia un poco ogni anno." Sometimes the increasingly generalized tendency, among English writers, to suppress the completive conjunction "that" for colloquial rapidity leads to phrases that cannot be fluidly construed. "On the Zenna Road Again," for example, opens with the question: "Why do these troubled branches touch me?" Yet the reader may have to read the answer twice because two potential meanings of the verb "repeat" coexist when "that" is deleted: "Maybe because they repeat [that] the green renews..." (for "Forse perché ridicono che il verde si rinnova"). And the use of "me," whose grammatical counterpart is necessary in the Italian, is unidiomatic in Perryman and Robinson's version of "Birthday," which in addition comprises the stilted inversion "who to glances is serene": "you renew me the time, / return me the memory / of a woman who to glances is serene, / bitter summer." (The Italian is "mi rinnovi il tempo / d'una donna agli sguardi serena / mi ritorni memoria, / amara estate.") Similarly, in "Journey There and Back," the translators write "There remains to me a city close to sleep / in earliest springtime" for "Mi resta una città prossima al sonno / di prima primavera." A few other minor examples could be cited. These are quibbles about Perryman and Robinson's otherwise laudable and Herculean effort to bring Sereni into English. I point them out with respect to this generally excellent translation only because I have increasingly noticed, among otherwise commendable scholarly editions like this one, a propensity to translate rather too literally, at the expense of stylistic naturalness in English.

* * *

Another major figure whose work has welcomely come into our language is Andrea Zanzotto. Patrick Barron and five other translators have produced an authoritative, meticulously introduced, and extensive *Selected Poetry and Prose*, which indeed also includes essays about poetics, personal essays, and sundry texts. (See the exalted descriptive prose of "Rebirth of the Hills," which, like Sbarbaro's brief pieces, can be studied alongside other unclassifiable examples of European short prose.) Complex like Sereni, yet more austere and even abstruse in his intellectuality, the author of *Behind the Landscape* (1951), *Glances, Facts and Senhals* (1969), *What was the point?* (1970), and *Superimpressions* (2001) is playful, not just with ideas and words within poems, but also directly with his reader. Sometimes the implicit dialogue between poet and reader becomes bizarrely explicit. In the long-poem "The Perfection of the Snow," for example, after puzzling lines like

> and all—all—and all-eros, all-lib. Liberty in the snare
> it's there in my embrace: it goes along,
> it goes along with the invitation, the program, the whole affair.
> A smile, right? And the (li)fe (id-vid)
> about which you can do nothing, cannot hypthesize,
> it gets (caressed?) on the threshold,

Zanzotto suddenly evokes a telephone call: "Hello? Who's speaking? Hang up." At the end of the poem, he simply tells his reader that he may leave: "That's all, you may go."

Zanzotto is an erudite gamester. To the countless semantic and phonetic puns that come naturally to him, he adds Latin words, terms from the various Italian dialects, funny neologisms, and quotations ranging from children's jingles to

> Hölderlin: "we are a sign without interpretation":
> but where do the two series come into contact?
> But is it true? And what will happen to us?
> And you why, why you?. . .

The reader is constantly challenged to determine where the whimsy ends and the serious insights begin. What is profound, even poignant, often crops up unexpectedly among distracting observations, leaps between details and abstractions, and makes abrupt juxtapositions. Yet even in the wackiest passages, Zanzotto is engaged with "this / sacred and fierce brevity of things / senses and signs," an incisive observation that summarizes the motivation behind his verse and, more generally, bespeaks an intense awareness of facing up to—that is, of also being separate from—life. "By Now" suggests the existential wounds that are hidden beneath the unsettling surface of this poetry:

> By now the primrose and the warmth
> at your feet and the green insight of the world
>
> The uncovered carpets
> the loggias shaken by wind and sun
> tranquil worm of the thorny woods;
> my distant pain, distinct thirst
> like another life in the breast
>
> > Here all that's left is to wrap the landscape around the self
> > and turn your back.

The translations of Zanzotto's sometimes exceedingly difficult lines almost always reflect the Italian exactly, but—as with Perryman and Robinson's versions of Sereni—this strategy now and then induces syntactic unnaturalness. Moreover, whereas the poet often employs little punctuation in the original (an asceticism that works easier in an inflected language like Italian), suppressing commas, semi-colons, and periods in English sometimes introduces unnecessary ambiguities.

* * *

The still-too-little-known older poet who emerges strongly from this group is Luciano Erba, who was Sereni's high-school student in 1939. Well-known in his native Italy, where *L'Ippopotamo* (1989) won the Librex-Guggenheim "Eugenio Montale" Prize, Erba writes subtle poems that much less provoke the reader than leave him in a meditative state, caught up between doubt and wonder, between acceptance and anxiety. Made up of the odds and ends not only of everyday experience but also of reverie and philosophical whimsy, his work is striking in neither its forms nor its subdued lyricism. Yet for all the poet's gazing at the surface of the world, he probes deep—almost without telling us so. His poems question more than they assert, speculate more than they conclude—and this is a virtue. Ann Snodgrass has carefully translated the deceptively simple poems of *The Hippototamus* (Guernica), which actually comprise many discrete literary allusions and are often based on artfully ambiguous feelings. She is to be thanked heartily for rendering a collection so finely balancing thought, emotion, and delicately crafted verbal beauty.

Erba's poems often point to that all-too-human predicament recreated daily as we awake to a world made up of a myriad of appearances. As our eye flitters from object to object, from glimmer to glimmer, from atom to atom, we cannot help but wonder whether any ultimate meaning surpasses or underlies them. Such is the dilemma formulated by the title poem, which begins with a hippopotamus rather comically opening a path through a jungle to a river. Yet Erba characteristically (and often humorously) eschews smooth logical transitions, preferring instead to chart the genuinely oblique veerings of thought, as opposed to straightening them out narratively, *a posteriori,* with clever rhetorical artifice. So he soon leaves the hippopotamus to his "sultry slaughter of orchids" and moves on to the designs made by flower beds in a small town (the "infiorata di Genzano"), before finally alluding to the "canals" of Mars. "Maybe," he muses at the end, all these patterns are nothing "but shadowless events that reflect / just a sign signifying itself."

The poet desires to strip off the mirages of metaphor (the "canals" are decidedly not canals), to return to things as they are, and only at this stage begin to ponder them; that is, to measure the transcendent shadows, if any, that they cast. Although our dream of a "thread" tying us to the "eternal *invisibilia*" of Christian metaphysics is now "broken" (as Erba puts it in another poem), the mere "things" or "signs" with which we are left define a sort of uncharted vista—a not entirely pessimistic perspective, after all, in poems that tend to discourage facile credences. "Did this life not by chance just happen?" the poet similarly reflects in "The Metaphysical Streetcar Conductor," "Are we just talking to ourselves, / using make-shift questions and answers?" It is up to us to begin anew, he seems to suggest, to seek out more justifiable paths toward whatever significance might nonetheless await us—a significance perhaps consisting solely in our stubborn willingness to pursue the lures of significance. The poem just mentioned notably trails off in a series of further questions.

In this respect, Erba's poetics partly link him to other European poets of the "back to things" movement, which was given its aesthetic impetus by Rilke and its epistemological foundation by Husserl. Interestingly, Erba—a fine connoisseur of French literature—has translated Francis Ponge (1899-1988), the "poet of things" par excellence, while other aspects of his work—the occasional imaginative flight beyond the self's confines—recall that very different sensibility, Henri Michaux (1899-1984), whom he has rendered into Italian as well. In most cases, Erba commemorates "intermediate spaces" as the locus of suddenly arresting perceptions. In "Travelers," he notices from a train window "a field just outside the city / between things abandoned and not, / between houses without balconies / and the railway's gravel shoulder." Among the "many sheets...drying" on a line in this unexceptional field in fact hang "other feminine signs." The poet of course focuses on them as well. One suspects—though this is unstated—that for Erba this ordinary moment becomes richer in pure living (if perhaps no more forthcoming in ultimate metaphysical verities) because of the erotic thoughts aroused. (In which case, certain signs would have signified more than themselves...) It is Life itself that the poet perceives in the suspended (under-)clothes, Life itself that he feels flowing in his own veins.

The philosophically minded Erba indeed half-hides a touching (and sometimes touchingly funny) love poet. Some poems memorably describe the tormenting presence of a permanent amorous absence, though even sad pieces are not without tongue-in-cheek humor. "In the Woods" notably begins:

> And you had thought it would be enough
> to lean cross-legged like an eastern sage
> at the protruding roots of a beech tree
> to distance the thought of her
> and become the blue between the branches
> or maybe an ant, bark, blade of grass. . .

This poem depicts "loving without," as Erba succinctly defines it, and the imagery builds upon Petrarch's famous long lament, "De pensier in pensier," which includes these verses: "I often saw her living.../ in the clear water, in the green grass, / in the trunk of a beech tree, in a white cloud..." Yet Erba, inclined to view solitude as a metaphysical absolute (not just the consequence of lost love), inverts Petrarch's argument. Whereas the latter discovers his beloved Laura objectified in (and thus somehow surviving as) natural elements, Erba seeks to forget his lover by projecting himself—in vain—into a strictly material, unanthropomorphized, outside world. This poem, too, ends with an introspective enigma: "Three tufts of clouds have passed / and you're still you— // you love, but you love without.../ the best way?"

Robinson's broader selection of Erba's verse, *The Greener Meadow* (Princeton University Press), includes twenty-six poems from the same book, plus work from *Il nastro de Moebius* (The Moebius Strip, 1980), *Il male minore* (The Lesser Evil, 1960), *Il prato più verde* (The Greener Meadow, 1977), *L'ipotesi circense* (The Circus Hypothesis, 1995), *Nella terra di mezzo* (In the Middle Ground, 2000), *Poesie 1951-2001* (2002), and *L'altra metà* (The Other Half, 2004).

With these two translations, Erba's reputation should grow rapidly in English-speaking countries, as it already has in France. Like Zanzotto, the Milanese poet can be funny, though not at all in the same idiosyncratic manner as his contemporary. Erba is a master of the tongue-in-cheek. A contemplator of daily happenstance who also relishes metaphysical conjecture, he subtly enhances his verse with an occasional odd detail or foreign term. In "Mailand," for instance, he employs two Italian loan-words from German, which mean something like "doughnuts and pastries." "I'd tell her goodbye," he recalls, "from her bargain fur coat / an odor of just treated pelt remained // truth was going home myself I'd be wearing / a heavy odor of *krapfen* and *kipfeln*." In "Only Signs?" he puns with the etymology of "cancel," all the while making, with characteristic false naïveté, some quite serious philosophical remarks about language and perception. His touch is always light; note the gentle jibe at T. S. Eliot's "Ash-Wednesday" at the end:

> Before there descended upon my eyes
> one of the heaviest dreams I recall
> (. . .)
> What remains
> is animated hatching, slightly electric
> with delicate colors, luminous
> as if someone wanted to cancel
> (from *cancellum*, "barrier" or better "fence")
> what it was I saw and have forgotten.
>
> If what exists is preverbal
> lights lines colors without name
> nothing else but lights, lines and colors
> how do I explain John 1 verse 1
> In the beginning was the Word
> (or the Cantabridgian proud of his word-world)?

Many literary and philosophical allusions sneak into Erba's poems, almost without our noticing. More ostentatious are those livening "With Doctor K," a hilarious anthology piece about psychoanalysis, and those filling out a spoof, entitled "Dasein," on the philosopher of *Being and Time*. The latter poem pokes fun at Heidegger's concept by placing it among everyday appurtenances. "The preemptory being (*Dasein*?)," commences Erba, "of the carpet or a fillet of parquet / after a while makes me think of nothingness."

Like Sereni, Erba has been linked to the Linea Lombarda, a group of six poets, based in or around Milan, who were featured in Luciano Anceschi's influential homonymous anthology (1952). Included in that book are Sereni (who wrote one of the first articles about Erba), Erba, Nelo Risi (b. 1920), Giorgio Orelli (b. 1921), Roberto Rebora (1910-1992), and Renzo Modesti (b. 1920). As

Robinson explains, Anceschi defines these poets "as sharing a poetry of objects, of understatement, irony, and self-criticism, which included social commentary and cultural commitment—but only if meditated through a skeptical grid of humanistic intelligence and aesthetic detachment." Erba later distanced himself from this unofficial group; in his poem "Linea Lombarda," he jokes about the appellation "Lombard Line" as if it were a train line running between the Milan train stops Lambrate and Garibaldi. The respective oeuvres of Sereni and Erba, to mention only those two poets, are indeed nearly antipodal in ambience and tone, not to mention disparity of imagery.

This being said, Anceschi's attentiveness to the role of objects in the work of such poets is worth pursuing. Erba's highly personal angle on everyday (and sometimes slightly eccentric) things enhances his originality. He is not the first European poet to tackle the problematics of things, but his approach differs from those who seek to evoke the thing-in-itself in order to reconcile themselves with the daily world or to reduce what they experience as an ontological gap between themselves and Nature. Irony and self-irony distinguish Erba, as well as his simultaneous attraction to, and humility about, metaphysics. For him, objects above all provoke unanswerable questions. "These things without prestige," he points out, "objects with no *design* / the necktie for my birthday / the eastern block's *Trabant*. / They trouble, but whatever does it mean? / Maybe better than others / they express a tension of their own / an aura, as we used to say / towards what's surrounding us here." Sharply but also affectionately observed details like these, along with the gentle paradoxes that always animate Erba's verse, often end in an admission of ignorance. In "Seven and a Half," he confesses:

> Probably between seven and eight
> of an evening in July or August
> kids between seven and eight
> can understand something / of this world...
> (. . .)
> If it happened to me? in any case
> I wouldn't have known I could understand
> and now? I've understood that I can't know.

In his self-elucidating essay "On Tradition and Discovery," which is included in Robinson's edition, Erba reveals, moreover, how gazing at objects induces the geometrical patterns that he also introduces into many of his poems. This poet of ordinary objects is also a geometrician with a love for abstractions, logic, and pure shapes. "In the appearances of the everyday," he observes, "there are things that stick out. I grasp them whatever they are: eternal dimensions, forms at their highest level of abstraction, simply geometrical-like lines, half-lines, diagonals, curves, triangles, squares, circles, or their shadows on the ground, or their imprints in the sky." In "Iron Wire," which is eventually revealed to be about the poet's persistent memory of a certain woman, the poem itself turns into an abstract painting made up of the wire and "a wall entirely white." In another poem sketching a geometrical figure and raising a still deeper question, Erba quips: "It's difficult to get one's bearings / on nothingness's outskirts." With this remarkable paradox, he declares that the outskirts that we inhabit are not necessarily also nothing: on the "outskirts," there may well be something other than nothing, and it is our duty to think about the consequences. Often this Cartesian full of childlike wonder raises, poetically, this question that has engaged philosophers ever since antiquity.

Associating ideas is one well-honed tool of his trade. He often pens verse that pleasantly and enigmatically meanders down the page, from associated image to associated image, all the while building to a powerful unexpected emotion or, at times, to a final unsolvable riddle. "Quartiere Solari" begins with a statement about Milanese "golden red" sunsets, shifts to a derelict housing complex, which leads to the smells of a nearby coffee factory and distant foundries, which in turn causes the poet to daydream about being "in Piedmont in France who knows where / it seemed to me I was in Europe," which suddenly causes him to recall his mother with moving precision: "my mother knew only too well / that I wouldn't be a long time near her / she was smiling nonetheless / on a background of dahlias and clustered violets." Such sequences artfully replicate how our thinking really does wander; they also arrive at essential speculations, queries, or memories—the kinds of cognitive termini to which we ourselves do not always arrive when we are musing randomly, without the Muses' assistance. In Erba, there is often a sense of great liberty (his ever-moving intellection, shifting from mundane routines to metaphysical riddles, from intentional vagueness to extremely fine points), but this is hardly to suggest that he exerts no control. For all their seeming naturalness, syntactic clarity and straightforward phraseology (however slyly studded with an amusing or unsettling detail or two), Erba's poems show the highest craft. Some poems are structured around a few rhymes toward the end, which constitute a subdued lyrical conclusion to his ruminations. Like Saba, Erba has a distinct music.

Robinson and Snodgrass are careful translators, so it would be churlish to detail the sometimes very fine differences between their respective versions of all the pieces that they have both translated. In "The Metaphysical Tramdriver," a telltale poem about the ambivalence of belief, Robinson translates the final lines as:

> I believe, don't believe, when believing I'd like
> to take to the beyond with me a bit of the here
> even the scar that marks my leg
> and keeps me company.
> Sure, and so? Another voice *in excelsis*
> appears to say.
> Another?

Snodgrass, an American, calls the piece "The Metaphysical Streetcar Conductor" and writes:

> I believe. I don't believe. When I believe
> I'd like to bring with me to the hereafter
> a little of this side, also the scar
> marking my leg that keeps me company.
> Right, and so? Another voice
> Seems to say *in excelsis*. . .
> And another?

I interpret the final "altra" in the very last line ("Già, ma allora? sembra dica *in excelsis* / un'altra voce. / Altra?") as referring to the preceding "other" voice. So Snodgrass's solution for the last line would be somewhat misleading, even if her version of the preceding lines is somewhat more engaging.

In "The I and Not-I," Erba characteristically empathizes with a squirrel ("over the abyss of violet air / the bushy-tail goes from bough to bough / and I'm with him towards pink rocks") and admits that he is "mentally / skipping to myself beside one point and another." Snodgrass interprets "rupi rosate" differently: "and I cross the pinkish cliffs / with him mentally, / leaping myself from one subject to another." "Cliffs" is more arresting symbolically but does not seem quite right when a squirrel is involved, even if, as in other lines elsewhere, Snodgrass is smoother and more idiomatically inclined than Robinson. It's a tossup whether she is more vivid than Robinson in "The Hippopotamus," a key sonnet in which Erba raises the question—like Hölderlin once again, and then Zanzotto, not to forget Ferdinand de Saussure—of whether signs signify themselves alone. (A sensitivity to semiotics is indeed common to all these poets.) Snodgrass's "sultry slaughter of orchids" is more striking than Robinson's "damp trampling of orchids" for "un umido scempio di orchidee," but he justifiably paraphrases "l'umile 'infiorata' di Genzano" as "Genzano's humble 'flower show,'" whereas Snodgrass retains the Italian expression and explains it in her notes. Here is Robinson's version of the last three lines:

> . . . or a canal on Mars, are none other
> than events without shadow or reflection
> just a sign signaling itself alone.

* * *

Bartolo Cattafi, a generous selection of whose prolific output has been smoothly translated by Rina Ferrarelli as *Winter Fragments*, is also sometimes associated associated with the Linea Lombarda, even though he was not included in Anceschi's anthology and was born about as far away from northern Italy as possible: in Sicily. (He did work in Milan in journalism and advertising.) If parallels with Linea Lombarda poets must be drawn, they are likely to be found in Sereni's war poems, for Cattafi likewise inherited a postwar anguish that fuels his verse. He is more candid about his personal life than Erba, who even in his love poems prefers indirect allusions or vicarious egos (like squirrels). Moreover, whereas Erba's poems remain at a stoic, bemused remove from moroseness and death, the author of *The Bone, the Soul* (1964) often writes confessional verse full of disillusionment, even discouragement. "Your monotonous game continues / with the loaded dice, the cards, / the many means at the heart's disposal," he avows in one poem, "And time passes, / the years and your efforts up in smoke, / your work come to nothing." By the way, heart imagery is so ubiquitous in Cattafi's oeuvre that it cumulatively indicates an unstated search for a center, a wholeness, in an overall poetics otherwise stressing lucidity and harsh existential facts.

Obsessed by "the shadows that pursue us" and ever conscious of "the voracious / colonies of germs engraved / inserted like a living / epitaph in the heart of things," Cattafi is a grave poet who conceives of his poems as "fragments wandering / in the void in the dark." But he significantly qualifies the preceding image as "struck for an instant by light." This dark-light duality suggests the deeper psychological opposition informing his oeuvre: utter pessimism struggling against a resolution to muster his will and defy the inexorable. Related to this fundamental dichotomy are his several erotic poems, which stand out in this selection. Vaporous romantic yearnings are out of the question for this poet who cannot help but spot death wherever he looks; but he nonetheless insists on celebrating the transitory pleasures of the flesh. Defiantly, moments of pleasure and sexual union are held up to inevitable extinction:

> I'm not speaking of the moon in the well.
> I'm speaking of a chocolate shade
> barely tinged with pink
> but I'm not speaking of roses and chocolate.
> I'm speaking of tender animal
> tissue, of the entrance
> to the mystery the sweet darkness,
> beautiful moist linings,
> triple, tremulous opening,
> venus of dark
> skin, of very black fleece.

Such poems, with their staging of a struggle between death and pleasure, might be defined as neo-baroque. I suggest this epithet because Christian allusions and symbols are mostly absent in this selection, except perhaps in the intriguing metaphorical geometry of the final poem, presumably written when the poet was dying from cancer at the age of fifty-seven: "In you in you I trust / I have stolen everything from the world / you are the Cube the Sphere the Center / my mind is at ease / everything was stacked inside of you." It is moving that Cattafi's quest for a center, signaled elsewhere by so many conspicuous hearts, seems to have attained its goal.

In her well-researched introduction, Ferrarelli points out that the critic Giovanna Wedel De Stasio calls Cattafi's poetry "a significant testimony of a baroque style in twentieth-century Italian literature." "Like the English Metaphysicals," Wedel De Stasio continues, "Cattafi tried to grasp the fragments of an unseizable reality by exploring verbal logic to the verge of absurdity. He bestows a metaphysical significance upon common physical objects; existential interrogations mold the ethical and aesthetic import of his poems." Personally, "verbal logic to the verge of absurdity" strikes me as describing Zanzotto more than Cattafli (whose style is, moreover, semantically less complex than the Metaphysicals, though Ferrarelli also has some pertinent comments to make about the challenges of the poet's Italian style). But it is arresting that Cattafi's vision of objects is, once again, considered to determine his originality. Decidedly, objects, signs, and perhaps also geometry (as an alternative cosmological and metaphysical model to one that would posit the chaotic haphazardness of Being) provide keys to understanding twentieth-century Italian poetry. One of Cattafi's collections is in fact called *Signs* (1986). Despite all the differences between his verse and that of the other poets under review here, certain telltale themes recur. Even Hölderlin and his signs without interpretation seem to reappear in "Plaza de Toros," when Cattafi gazes at the bulls, bullfighters, and flags in the arena and states: "We are images inscribed without pause / in this circle, / manikins, men and emblems."

* * *

Lucio Mariani is also attentive to signs from the very onset of *Echoes of Memory*, a selection fluently translated by Anthony Molino. "Now / through what sign / will you respond to the silence?" the poet asks in "Savings," adding that one must not "forget that this is the silence / that follows a chess move / the only sensible saving / amid the sounds / the sounds / the combinations." One finds this same anti-rhetorical skepticism about words and the same scrutiny of signs in a French poet whom Mariani has translated into Italian: Yves Bonnefoy. The point is reiterated often. One of Mariani's titles, borrowed from Ecclesiastes, is no less than "Tempus tacendi tempus loquendi" ("a time to hush, a time to speak").

Several of his poems not only distinguish between times to hush and speak, but also explore Time itself. The author of *Qualche notizie del tempo* (2001) and the cyclical poem *Del tempo* (1998) explores history, "echoes of memory" (as the apt title of this selection puts it), timelessness, and especially synchronicity. In "Timaeus 1983," for example, the poet first makes a whimsical calculation ("Plato's seed is removed from mine only / eighty-six mothers of mothers and a bit of luck"), goes on to mention "TV / slurp[ing] up the last drops of transcendence," then finishes with a much longer temporal and cosmological perspective: the soul's remains "will be specks of dust / that waves of sun / stir in the malignant void." Amid the garish and, perhaps here and there, too facilely evoked contemporary detail, conclusions like the latter are meant to impress. And Mariani sometimes revives ancient poetic forms to depict foibles of the present day. "Daughter, don't be like me," he notes wittily in a quatrain that an Epicurean epigrammatist would have appreciated, "who / to smoke more doesn't brush his teeth. / Mishaps lesser than death / can be avoided." Superposing disparate historical periods especially enables Mariani to lament our own age. In "Crèche," which describes a nativity scene, he regrets that there is "no one beyond the hedges of wonder, / beyond the ironic form of the shell. / No one [who] comes anymore with word / of the oracles." Such lines provoke thoughts in a heterogeneous volume that also exhibits flippancy. "Players of superfluousness" is what Mariani calls poets: "they know by heart / the rules of the void."

* * *

Like de Palchi, Luigi Fontanella has long lived in the United States. Though translations of his poetry have already been published on our shores, *Land of Time* is his first major selection. This volume, to which five translators have contributed, includes work from most of Fontanella's Italian books, beginning with *Tentative Evidence* (1972).

This latter title already indicates the uncertainty and sense of fleetingness that continue to inform his oeuvre. A telling poem entitled "The Transparent Life" aligns images that each suggest the immateriality, emptiness, or constant mobility of what we see:

> bicycles go by riderless,
> a woman's face in the window
> appears then vanishes,
> shop windows offer fetishes
> for every season,
> lives turning,
> a slender agile couple dances
> in the deserted piazza...

Such is "the intimate life," as Fontanella puts it elsewhere, "that slips away," a perception that is reinforced by his corollary declaration that we persistently imagine, not ultimately real events, but only mirages. "I'm / continually distracted," avows Fontanella, "by what doesn't happen"—a remark that essentially reformulates Rimbaud's (self-)warning that genuine life is "elsewhere." Rather like Mariani, Fontanella initially defines this separation from various aspects of reality as depending on our inescapable insertion in human Time, whereby "everything instantly becomes the Past" and our anticipations remain illusory, unfounded. Many pieces grimly probe into "the calm terror of discovering that perhaps life is / nothing but this."

Yet some of Fontanella's poems attempt to get beyond these imprisoning strictures of the human condition. In this respect, *Land of Time* charts a thinking poet's progress. In an untitled poem beginning "Down there / a piercing glittering brightness / shattered image / of some rippling pool," Fontanella describes dizzying impressions of a "presence swiftly restitched / between the apparition and the absence." Finally, however, he realizes that the shimmer is due to an unambiguous natural event. "But / look," he exclaims to himself as much as to his reader, "it's raining, it's merely raining." This poem and others provide a still different vantage point from which to consider the European poetic problem of dealing with objects and, here specifically, phenomena. Raining (as opposed to a raindrop) is less an object than a process, and it is not surprising that Fontanella, ever sensitive to movement and ungraspable ephemerality, is startled by it. But here the raining especially functions as a corrective to both the natural flights of the poet's imagination and his fascination with immateriality. As in other poets under review here, reality—be it defined as nature, war, or the quotidian—jars the poet into sharp suspicions about language, mental images, and the self.

The sense of one's own self, perhaps temporarily (deceivingly) effaced during the eye's fascination with shimmering impressions, cannot lastingly disappear from our daily experience. Nor can one's personal history be forgotten, even at a substantial remove from childhood. Fontanella's expatriation to the United States also comes up in *Land of Time*, a title that can be interpreted as an exile from a specific homeland to that eminently transitory country, Time, as well as to a new land in which the poet becomes more painfully aware of Time. In a particularly moving sequence, Fontanella pays homage to his father, then asks: "Can it be that I understand you better today / after spending almost twenty years some / distance away, a bit lonely, a bit selfish?"

Such verse can be read alongside the eight-part "Stanzas for Emma," in which the poet himself has become a father. The first poem depicts his baby daughter grasping for water, a graphic picture of the fleetingness that ever engages Fontanella and that here contaminates, for the first time as it were, the girl's pristine innocence about existence. "You can't hold onto / that translucent, liquid shaft," writes Fontanella, "just for a moment you pensively reflect, / perhaps reflect / upon the impossibility of ever grasping it." Other poems in the same sequence express the impossibility of explaining "the desperate joy that comes from / this pure vision of your curls in the wind / of your tiny little nape," or turn to the baby's unawareness "of the cry, the laceration / hurled behind [her father] inside [him]." These poems are more than touching; they deeply engage with another human being, through love. Here and elsewhere, Fontanella develops the idea of a divided self which cannot know happiness, yet which maintains the hope that his lover or his offspring will. I know of another example in contemporary European poetry that focuses, with similar sincerity, on this dilemma. In "Ken Avo," the great opening long-poem of *Poèmes bleus* (1962), Georges Perros addresses his lover, Tania, and repeats the line "toi au moins" ("you at least") three times in his desire that, because of his "attentiveness" and his "silence," she at least will be able to say to herself that "the horrible ennui is vanquished." As the journey chronicled in *Land of Time* shows, Fontanella fully knows what this means.

Between the Horizon and the Leap
(Alfredo de Palchi)

It is tempting to declare that Alfredo de Palchi (b. 1926) is the François Villon of contemporary Italian poetry. The poet himself solicits the comparison. Not only does he borrow lines from the fifteenth-century French poet in order to introduce each of his own six collections (now gathered and sometimes rearranged, enlarged, or revised in an authoritative *Paradigma: tutte le poesie: 1947-2005*), but many of his poems—their subject matter drawing on poverty and imprisonment, their razor-sharp images, their tense concision, their syntactic boldness, their forthright eroticism, their bitter yet somehow plucky existential outlook—recall the candor and chiseled craftsmanship that we admire in the author of *The Testament* and the "Ballad of the Hanged Men." Even a recent poem, beginning "In rue de l'Arbre Sec," dated 29 June 2003, and included in the sixth collection, *Ultime*, stages an imaginary encounter between the admired French poet and his "gradito compagno di sventure," that is his pleasant and likeable sidekick, fellow traveler, comrade-in-arms. The dried-up tree evoked in the name of this thirteenth-century street, which is located in the once-teeming first *arrondissement* of Paris and famous for the gallows—the dead tree?—at its northern end, conjures up the legend, indeed the possibility, that Villon was hanged, perhaps right there, for the diverse crimes of which he was accused. Interestingly, there is a restaurant called the "Caveau François Villon" near that northern end, and de Palchi claims to have composed his poem while he was lunching there. Villon has obviously been a cherished mentor for and comfort to de Palchi in dark times.

De Palchi's dark times lasted so long and were so oppressive that his jagged-edged, emotive, yet also intellectually intricate verse at first beckons to be read as personal testimony, if not exactly as a "last will and testament" in the Villonesque sense. His poetry deeply and genuinely tells his life's story, but it also goes beyond this strict autobiographical circumscription in that it represents an "example," an *exemplum*, as the title of his fifth collection, and now his *Collected Poems* in general, makes clear. *Paradigma* is exemplary, and his short poems are especially emblematic in this sense, though one should equally remark that his verse absolutely never proffers moral judgments; instead, it unearths, discloses, points to, without the slightest superfluous commentary. Its lessons must be inferred, though they are rarely obscure. Let it suffice to say that *Paradigma* reveals the deep structure, the "pattern"—another meaning of "paradigm"—of intensely lived moments, hours, days, and years. Taking off from still another, this time linguistic, sense of the word, one could venture the analogy that the book displays a life in all its "inflected forms."

These exemplary aspects are, of course, all the more compelling and instructive in that the poet experienced harsh setbacks and humiliations during his youth and early manhood. Repudiated by his father at birth (in the town of Legnago, near Verona) and thereafter raised by his maternal grandfather (who was a noted anticlerical anarchist), de Palchi suffered through an impoverished childhood in the countryside. There, as he states in the "Bag of Flies" sequence (dated 1961, written in New York, and included—with this psychologically revealing English title—in his second collection, *Sessioni con l'analista*), his childhood was lonely and deprived; he was "shut off / even from playmates—patched, shoeless, / or in winter, / clogs, warmed by the living hide / chewing cud in their stalls." Amidst these hardships, de Palchi admired his grandfather, whose presence is beautifully rendered in "Cancer," as the poem was called when it was published in the American bilingual edition of *Sessioni con l'analista* (*Sessions with my Analyst*, 1970). This piece, now untitled (as are several other previously titled pieces in the definitive *Collected Poems*), has been moved to the "L'Assenza" ("Absence") sequence and is comprised in the collection *Paradigma*, which opens with an apt Villonesque epigraph: "Vivre aux humains est incertain." One of de Palchi's most moving pieces, the long poem pays homage to a man who

> . . . doesn't write down his poems like debts
> in a notebook
> the Psalter of the poor
>   with anarchic invention
> he recites his earthy ones, unadorned,
> raw so they stink of garden manure,
> his cigar stump, corrosion...

> (trans. I. L. Solomon)

The child's eyes were opened to the world in at once attentive and trenchant ways by this man who, in reply to his grandson's disgust at a nauseating first-communion bowl of chocolate, sneered sardonically that priests boil meat in water. Instead of attending church on a sultry Sunday, a "domenica con l'afa," de Palchi's grandfather would call out a city—like Rome or Paris—then place the boy on his bicycle handlebars and pedal off, in his imagination, to these and other remote capitals. Actually, the capitals were no more than the grain store or the tavern, but surely these whimsical inversions stimulated the boy's mind. In *La buia danza di scorpione*, a collection appearing for the first time in a bilingual Xenos Books edition as *The Scorpion's Last Dance* only in 1993, although it was actually composed in prison between 1947 and 1951, de Palchi recalls that "at the elbow of the Adige [he] grew up / on guesses, rumors of other cities." In de Palchi's early poetry especially, the Adige River remains the last refuge of purity, even though it, too, is eventually defiled by smokestacks, fertilizer works, sugar refineries, barges, and drowned cats:

> Smokestacks fertilizer-
> works and sugar refineries
> barges loaded with gravel and a few cats
> flung from the bridge
> pervert this slab of river
> this Adige.

(trans. Sonia Raiziss)

An even worse perversion occurs when, as recounted in "Bag of Flies," Tony the hunchback throws the poet's dog into the Adige, its paws tied and a rag in its mouth. "Is this love?" de Palchi can only ask. It is a question implicitly raised throughout his oeuvre, and almost always answered with a resounding negative, at least in poems written before his recent erotic poetry. The poet lets such flies out of the bag, a fitting symbol here of the torments of his past as they stubbornly return to pester his present mind.

Interestingly, in de Palchi's later poetry, the Adige recovers more positive connotations. In an untitled poem translated by Barbara Carle for the Spring 2001 issue of the review *Gradiva* and now comprised in the "Essenza carnale" ("Carnal Essence") section of the *Paradigma* collection, the river becomes his lover's body: "the Adige / is your body sinuously spare, powerful / vortex that welcomes my thirsty mouth." The beginning of the poem ("The clarity of waters regenerates me / pure in the river, which from the top of your head, / surges in springs whirlpools quick streams") exemplifies numerous other instances in which liquid or aquatic images are associated with a lover's body or, more precisely, in which a lover's orgasmic or menstrual fluids are boldly praised. This being said, de Palchi's erotic vision nearly always goes beyond the corporal per se. Present in his erotic poems is a cosmic dimension, an experience of amorous union and the epiphanies of pleasure surely, but also a yearning for the primeval, the primordial, the ab-original. Another untitled poem from the same sequence conspicuously mentions spiritual symbiosis and equates his lover with—and enables the poet to experience—the "originary water" of creation: "An arcade of carnal prosodies / expands proposing flood streams / of spiritual symbiosis / solid with salt and spores / you are the originary water." The poem ends with a telling declaration:

> As a serpent I absorb you whole
> and you terraqueous mother
> call my return to birth in the dawn
> of the womb, the abode
> of ascending devotion for a spirit in fragments.

(trans. Barbara Carle)

This important philosophical dimension of de Palchi's work will be discussed below.

After arriving not in the Café des Deux Magots but rather in the disheveled rural tavern, the boy would study old men "suck[ing] their cheeks stuffed / with tobacco, spit[ing], drink[ing,] / at their card game and mumbl[ing] curses." At the end of these card-playing sessions, and after tipsily avoiding the perilous ditches bordering the road on the way home, de Palchi's grandfather would, as the poet remembers, "sing over my neck hoarsely: the stink / of wine and the Barber / of Seville." In these and other acid-etched remembrances, fondness is expressed through crude, down-to-earth detail; social realities surge forth with a solidity normally attained only through novelistic description. Carlo de Palchi died in 1941. His final moments are memorialized by his grandson with lucidity:

> And in the same bed, inventing
> verses nobody writes down
> or tells me, he shields me
> under his armpit that smells of hair and cigar; cancer eats him
> alive in my thin arms
> dirty with his shit, and in pain, disgusting,
> his breath whooshes into the sharpened smile
> of a cat
> that is dead.

(I have rearranged I. L. Solomon's translation of the last two lines so as to reflect the surprise ending created by the postposed adjective "morto" in "d'un gatto / morto".)

Concluding tragically with the Second World War and his grandfather's death, this early period of de Palchi's life nonetheless comprised his "anni verdi" or "green years," as he phrases it in the "Carnival of Exiles" section of *La buia danza di scorpione*. In childhood, as de Palchi recalls (in the same poem), "the roads were dust-white / I wandered along ways flooded with gardens / fluid with sun and my slingshot / would hiss against the telegraph poles." Along with Villon, Arthur Rimbaud watches benevolently over such lines, which celebrate a sensuality and willful anti-societal individualism that are also pure de Palchi. Conspicuously, however, the quatrain is set in parentheses. It is preceded by lines expressing despair and self-incomprehension ("each season / a stone in the sea and I don't know / who I am—trying myself with wild / strokes, a bad swimmer") and followed by this dark ending describing the environment in which he must struggle to find himself: "I succumb to the rough rages of hate / flesh mind word."

There is not a gram of false pathos here: joys like shooting slingshots were short-lived. Toward the end of the Second World War and three years after his grandfather's death, de Palchi was rounded up and tortured by Italian Fascists and German soldiers. Then, just after the war, he found himself accused of involvement in a political homicide. He was sentenced to prison on a trumped-up charge. Once again he was tortured, as he explains in the biographical note appended to the American edition of *La buia danza di scorpione*, this time "by Communists and mythomaniacs of the ludicrous Italian resistance." Between the spring of 1945 and the spring of 1951, the poet remained incarcerated, successively in Venice, Rome, Naples, Procida, and Civitavecchia. During his imprisonment, to cite his own words, he "defied and insulted the government, the army, the church, and decried Italy as a country inhabited by vileness." But his outrageous bad fortune and the ruthless injustice that had been applied to him also induced his first stabs at writing. "Stabs" is to be taken literally here. In 1946, he scratched his first poem onto a cell wall in Naples, an event commemorated in these firm lines from *La buia danza di scorpione*: "coming of age I gnaw at myself / and scrape on stone for a different life." During the next year, he started to write more seriously, encouraged by Ennio Contini, an older poet and critic who was also incarcerated. (A touching note of gratitude about Contini is included in the *Collected Poems*.) De Palchi was coming of age both as a man and a poet.

However, as he was yearning for a different life and writing the terse, pungent verse that would eventually go into *La buia danza di scorpione*, the poet's mental and physical suffering was surpassing the limits of the bearable. A "heel of stale bread feeds me," he notes on the spot, "a gasoline taste / I chew it with lemon / rinds scrounged from the dump." Elsewhere, he describes himself as "a stranger roving with both fists / clenched," adding that the prison "bullies have the last word." "I ask for water," he declares in inverted Christic and Psalmic phraseology, "—they inflict thirst / I want light / — they enforce darkness." Although he vituperates against institutionalized Christianity in several poems, and directs scathing irony at an "impostor Christ" from whom he demands compassion in vain, a few early pieces nonetheless exhibit his close reading of the Bible and his subtle psychological understanding of Christian symbolism:

> but here I am
> believing myself
> what others observe I am not—
> how can this be
> if there on the cankered cross of us all
> I gasp with empty cheeks
> and crowded around me there's no one to
> slake my thirst
> only to curse me.

>   (trans. Sonia Raiziss)

Although inhabited by rage and disgust, de Palchi is nonetheless symbolically accompanied by a Christ-like model (a paradigm?) whose suffering parallels his own and whose persistence encourages his urge to write (and thus save himself). At the heart of his predicament lies the paradoxical, likewise Christic, "believing myself / what others observe I am not," as in the lines above. As the years go by, de Palchi will increasingly associate Christian symbolism with eroticism. This is especially true of the fourteen erotic poems written in 1999-2000, put to music by the composer Carlo Galante, and recorded by the group Sonata Islands in 2003. In the poem (from the CD) that gives the title "Carnal Essence" to the entire sequence, de Palchi notably writes:

> The cell window is shut, the exit blocked,
> the whitewashed walls absorb your silent screams
> and you nun-like divaticate your scalded flesh
> and with saturnine mouth full of meandering luciferian tongue
> you envelop my inflamed Calvary in the concept,
> conquered with the religion of your carnal essence—
> take me as you will, in all your mouths swollen with rose,
> turgid with Passion,
> fill yourself with your Saviour.

(trans. Barbara Carle)

A second poem, "Mi / immedesimo in te, Cristo" ("I immerse myself in you, Christ"), from the same sequence, transfers the symbolism of communion to an erotic union:

> I break myself like the dinner bread
> and bleed, like the offering of wine—symbol of precious
> blood; I'm the carnivore
> the tonguing cannibal devouring her body
> drinking the blood of the wound
> to be remembered:
> and you nail my love on the same cross
> for her majestic flesh.

(trans. Barbara Carle)

(The poems originally used in the CD have now been incorporated into the longer "Essenza carnale" sequence of twenty-three poems that is included in the *Collected Poems*.)

As the poet Luigi Fontanella specifies in his article "Vita e poesia di Alfredo de Palchi" (included in the invaluable *Scritti sulla poesia di Alfredo de Palchi*, a special supplement to issue No. 6 of the Italian review *Hebenon*, October 2000), it was only in 1955 that the Court of Assizes, in Venice, acquitted de Palchi of all charges and proclaimed his total innocence. Villon of course experienced similar despair, rejection, banishment, hunger, cruelty, solitude, and injustice. It prompted him to sum up the world as relentless "abusion." This acerbic acknowledgment—"ce monde n'est qu'abusion"—is used as the epigraph of *La buia danza di scorpione*. As it were, de Palchi had already given a personal translation, into Italian, of the biting apothegm. "Concluso fra pareti vilipendio / e menzogne," he writes in the same volume, "mi sfinisco per quello che succede / mai." His longtime American translator, Sonia Raiziss, gives this equivalent: "Between walls, abuse and / men's lies I'm finished / I waste myself for something that never / happens" (*The Scorpion's Dark Dance*).

Yet miraculously, de Palchi still had life ahead of him. Against all odds, he was not vanquished by torture and unjust imprisonment. He long performed "the scorpion's dark dance," as he harrowingly phrases it, but did not give himself the ultimate sting. And after his release from incarceration, his life remained arduous but changed directions radically. The "vita dissimile" or "different life" to which he had aspired, while engraving verse into the cold stone wall of his prison cell, took shape. De Palchi left Italy for good in the autumn of 1951. He moved to Paris and, using the French capital as his base, traveled throughout Europe, sojourning in Barcelona for a while as well. In 1956, he took a second decisive step by departing for the United States. He sailed into New York City on Columbus Day, an auspicious coincidence, and initiated an exile that continues to this day. In the first poem of the sequence "L'Arrivo" ("The Arrival"), originally included in the American edition of *Sessions with my Analyst* and now part of the *Paradigma* collection, de Palchi describes his first sight of the Hudson; he expresses the resolute independence that is characteristic of all his autobiographical poetry. "I belong to my breath," he writes tersely, that is to his own physical life and his uncompromising poetic inspiration; he rejects all other allegiances.

In the United States, the individualism, revolt, existential unease, and acute sensibility underlying his inspiration by no means vanish. In his first volume of poems composed mostly in America, *Costellazione anonima* (*Anonymous Constellation* was published bilingually by Xenos Books in 1997 and now represents the third collection in the *Collected Poems*), he finds himself "among an incongruous jumble of / objects directionless people." These lines are presumably set in New York City, where he still lives. Settling in the United States enabled de Palchi to put his Italian past behind him, at least in his daily comings and goings, though of course not in his musings and nightmares. The sequence "Reportage" (dated 1957 and a part of *Sessioni con l'analista*), which describes New York City, notably begins with excruciating memories, "a tearing at my guts by sudden / remembering." Even in the imposing, alluring, constantly surprising present of the New World metropolis par excellence, the poet's European past haunts him still. And the long title poem "Sessioni con l'analista," which stages fictive encounters with a psychoanalyst (whose unique reaction to his patient's confessions is "perché?", "why?"), builds to a suicide poem as well:

        unpredictable suicide

                        I have an archaic reason
                        hidden in lasting
                        sleep

"don't do it" . . a voice
says

      —it's easy to say
      don't do it . . —

I won't commit the coup
de grâce on me, but
      I don't love our time, I don't.

In a note appended to the *Collected Poems*, de Palchi specifies that he had sessions with a psychoanalyst only after the publication of the book.

Sessioni con l'analista is still marked by de Palchi's familial past and disastrous Second World War experiences as well as by his scrupulous honesty about a persistent existential malaise. In one particularly despairing moment, the poet wants to put his head "inside the terracotta jar and scream / [his] failure at [his] divided self." (In the *Collected Poems*, this poem—originally entitled "Topo ossessionato" or "A Rat Obsessed" when it was published in the American edition of *Sessioni con l'analista*—has lost its title and been switched to the sequence "Movimenti" in *Le viziose avversioni* [*Addictive Aversions*], the fourth collection.) Such lines, which touch on solipsism, individuation, and the sudden pangs of conscience that derive from the presence of the past, illustrate how de Palchi's more or less realistically detailed autobiographical poems almost always include more abstract psychological or philosophical ramifications. Reading his poems merely as personal narratives is insufficient. Moreover, now that all the individual poems are untitled (only sequences—and they are numerous—have titles in the *Collected Poems*), the reader is even more encouraged to seek out the philosophical or cosmological horizon implied or glimpsed by de Palchi. Like untitled modern paintings, the poems invite interpretations, but they rarely direct the reader to a single one. For all their tension and terseness, there is ever a sense of spontaneity, openness, and freedom in de Palchi's work, mirroring the essential biographical fact that his writing of poetry was linked, from the onset, to an aspiration to liberty. Furthermore, the regroupings and revisions undertaken by the poet for the *Collected Poems* suggest that his lifework—as it must be called—should be read more thematically than chronologically, that is as a multifaceted yet coherent social, psychological, erotic, poetic, and philosophical autobiography wherein several personal evolutions, on several different levels, are charted (though hardly as strict linear progressions). Except for the collection *Ultime*, whose poems were composed between 2000 and 2005, the five other collections all include verse going back to the late 1940s and early 1950s. More importantly still, in distinct pieces of the collection *Sessioni con l'analista* and in passages of the long title sequence (whose formal originality as a long sequence of dialogues has been overlooked by most critics), not to mention his other collections, de Palchi reveals a remarkable sensitivity to the broader implications of his own present and past experiences. When, with a characteristic appeal to geological and biological symbolism, he declares to the psychoanalyst that

> I don't know where in my geologic
> age
> to begin: to extract the magma;
> impossible
> to communicate the inconclusive
> twisted
> jargon, a thicket alive with snakes,

he represents all human beings—all his "frères humains," as Villon puts it in his epitaph. De Palchi reveals that it is an integral part of the human condition to be unable to make sense of, even sometimes to formulate, unhealable sorrows and unfathomable treachery. The pessimistic conclusion of the sequence "Sessions with my Analyst" is that he is—we are—"alone, out of touch, / incommunicable."

For a poet such as de Palchi, it is poetry's responsibility to take on this paradoxical predicament head on. In this regard, de Palchi is also an exemplary writer. He extracts the self's magma by the very act of writing; yet what he extracts verges on the incommunicable, not only because of its familial, social, historical, or political gruesomeness, but also and especially because of the ontological depths to which he digs. His constant awareness of the limits of language, which necessarily remains his only tool, suggests why his succinct, spare, forthright yet fragmentary verse sometimes resembles, in its intellectual and lyric intensity, that written by the Italian Hermetics, namely Salvatore Quasimodo (1901-1968), Giuseppe Ungaretti (1888-1970), and especially Eugenio Montale (1896-1981), whose poetry de Palchi helped to introduce in the United States. Leonardo Sinisgalli (1908-1981), Giorgio Caproni (1912-1990), and Vittorio Sereni (1913-1983) can also be mentioned. A few lines by Sereni are, in fact, quoted in "Bag of Flies" and "Sessioni con l'analista," notably the desperate "non lo amo il mio tempo, non lo amo" that has already been mentioned. And a nod is seemingly made to Montale when the title "Movimenti" (a section in Montale's *Ossi di sepia*) is used in *Le viziose avversioni*, though de Palchi obviously has the arresting progression "Momenti"—"Movimenti"—"Mutazioni" above all in mind as he organizes this collection into these three successive sections. In any event, like the aforementioned Italian poets (as well as the French symbolists who preceded and, in some cases, nourished them), de Palchi favors the collision of vivid images and symbols as he digs into, excavates, and expresses his innermost experience. He generally eschews narrative expatiation, with the possible exception of the sequence "Sessions with my Analyst," which is uncharacteristically open-ended in form; and it nevertheless consists more of searing avowals and flashes of self-analysis than of storytelling. De Palchi's poetry evidently emanates from—why not complete the metaphor?—a volcano in which subterranean heat builds up over a long period of time, causing occasional eruptions. He is not a prolific poet, but he writes from a dire inner necessity.

This eruptive necessity, of course, brings back to mind the inner turmoil, inwoven with combativeness, that must have incited Villon to record, and revolt against, his fate. Yet whereas the French poet remains a lively autobiographer and a compelling sympathizer with his fellow rogues and down-and-outers, he is perhaps not as philosophically and scientifically alert as de Palchi. Already in *La buia danza di scorpione*, the Italian poet generalizes on the biological act necessarily preceding not only his, but any existence. "The first cause / engrafts the nebulous aorta / and quickens consciousness," he writes almost clinically, "with the abject drop that splits / the egg / starting the womb / fit for affliction."

The very words with which he opens this poem, indeed the entire collection, is "il principio," here rendered by Sonia Raiziss as "the first cause." Like its Latin antecedents and the Greek *arkhé*, the concept is charged with philosophical resonance. "Il principio" is also "the origin," "the beginning," indeed the overriding or fundamental "principle," and the Greco-Roman idea of a *necessitas* or an *ananké* is related to it. De Palchi returns several times to this notion of a first cause, emphasizing its austere physical materialism: for him, arguably, "life" is *bios*, by no means the transcendent *zoé* of the Gospel of John, and thus mere copulation, followed by a single spermatozoon splitting an ovum. But such a conception harbors its own mysteries. As the contemporary French writer Pascal Quignard has also pointed out in several texts, we have no access to this first cause from which we have emerged. We cannot go back to the instant when we were conceived, even as we cannot go back to the instant in which "life," as we understand it, began in the cosmos. Our coming into the world is perpetually held out to us as an empirical certainty, but at the same time it remains intangible, elusive, remote. It is thus essentially a speculative, more than an empirical, certainty. We are ever separate from "il principio." And the abiding, sometimes shocking, pessimism of de Palchi's work partly stems from his cynical view of this onset. The words "egg" and "ovum" are used, not as positive symbols associated with the perpetuation of one's genes in particular and of the human race in general, but rather negatively, disparagingly. A somewhat more neutral instance occurs in the five numbered erotic notes in the twelfth poem of the sequence "Sessions with my Analyst." The poet recalls his lovemaking with a long-limbed girl and quips in the fourth note: "I exist and / in your ovum / I hear myself." The idea of hearing himself in the woman's ovum is funny, but it also points to the puzzling phenomenology of self-awareness. Can one in fact sense oneself existing only through the mediation of another person?

Acquiring some kind of tangible proof of, or at least a momentary feeling for, one's own existence is a theme of several poems. In "Reportage," de Palchi concedes with autobiographical precision that "at bottom it is I / a son rejected / broken by trades / who knows not in what faith to waste / the belief in my presence." Incidentally, a grammatical inexactitude mars I. L. Solomon's version here. The Italian ("il convincimento della mia presenza") is more clearly construed as "the certitude of my presence," "my belief in my presence" or, to expand the avowal into a paraphrase, "my conviction that I exist (based on the empirical evidence at hand)." In any event, this certitude, conviction, or belief harbors an implicit doubt: the very real possibility of absence, not presence. The doubts go back at least to 1954 in Paris, where de Palchi was writing the poems about loss that would eventually constitute the sequence "L'Assenza" ("Absence"), now part of the collection *Paradigma*. In *Costellazione anonima*, the poet in fact less ambivalently contemplates a permanent absence: "the heart's pear... split by the worm digging / methodically at what remains forever absent." Both the autobiographical and the more symbolic poetic approaches to this persistent absence, which is as ontological and even metaphysical as it is historical (familial) and psychological, posit that the center of the self consists of an emptiness that somehow yearns for an impossible fullness. Both poems suggest that, even if one feels oneself yearning, such an emotion relies on false beliefs, and that the desire for plenitude is wishful thinking. The life we feel ourselves living, in moments of heightened awareness, is physiological—nothing more.

Other poems, notably in *Costellazione anonima*, even show de Palchi seeking detachment from the self. It is a quest not uncommon in contemporary European poetry, especially among the French, where the corollary problematics of the Cartesian *cogito ergo sum* continue to challenge writers concerned with the foundation of the self, the phenomenology of consciousness, and one's apperceptive sense of being in the world. Yet whereas some European poets dismiss their own petty needs, decide to avoid the ineffable, remain silent about that which apparently cannot be uttered, and focus on the vagaries and vicissitudes of the outside world, de Palchi and others (from Thomas Bernhard and Dinos Christianopoulos to Louis Calaferte and Charles Juliet) plunge so deeply into themselves that they approach their goal only after an excruciating process of self-dissection and self-destruction. Even when the Italian poet declares that the "resolve to meet myself is squarely / behind me, useless, I'll never have the guts / to confront my identity," he actually does nothing else than meet himself in his poems. In light of his tragic past, this process of self-deconstruction is particularly gripping when he considers himself to be his "own rash / inquisitor, no walls / no laws, everything wide open, / doors windows the bed, / where no other scum on two legs shall / judge me." The sessions with the (fictive) analyst—with himself as his own rash inquisitor—continue. It should be clear by now that de Palchi's is no facile autobiographical poetry concerned merely with the self's everyday events and ephemeral emotions.

His poetic tour de force is that his literally egocentric poetry casts a revealing light on the dubious existential foundations of all mankind. Much more than a single self attached to a given historical time and place, the poet convincingly becomes "the blaze where the species swarms." Especially in his more recent work, de Palchi time and again turns himself into a sort of anti-idealistic, anti-sentimental Everyman-poet whose imagery increasingly draws on science, especially geology and biology. "There's no way out," he observes in *Costellazione anonima*, "I'm a chain of insidious origins / orders mechanisms fantasies / already charged with extinction." Ever since the 1960s, which were crowned by the publication of *Sessioni con l'analista* in Italy (by Mondadori in 1967) and then by the 1970 unexpurgated, somewhat augmented, American edition (see I. L. Solomon's "Introduction" for a few details about the editorial censorship, in Italy, applied to five poems in the original manuscript), it seems that the Italian poet's American exile has enabled him to achieve a greater compression and symbolization in his poetry: despite painful memories, perhaps specific details from his Italian past have lost some of their pull on his poetic conscience. A general thematic movement can be traced from the familial and the social to the erotic and the cosmic. And yet, as the above quotation makes clear, "there is no way out" for him, that is for the Everyman-poet, for any human being.

The tense, epigrammatic, sometimes darkly droll poems of *Costellazione anonima* are indeed most impressive when de Palchi becomes obliquely auto-biographical and provides a cosmic setting. He uses science incisively. To wit, envisioning himself as the food chain ("watery grease insectivorous oil /...the ocean fat / with corpuscles, plankton / functioning with zeal for crustaceans"), he ends up as a not yet extinct coelacanth. The bitter postulate underscored here is that we, at best, are configurations of matter inscribed with persistent (genetic) memories of our fish-eat-fish heritage. "Under each fallen leaf a war / of insects," he likewise observes, "everywhere the rage / of survival." Elsewhere, he quips savagely that "today mimics yesterday / and limits tomorrow—what does it matter / there's always carnage / or another cleanup." Whatever our historical, social, national, religious, and familial backgrounds, we necessarily participate in this permanent agon or polemos. The war may be out in the open, or concealed, clandestine; in all cases, it is war. We can escape neither the debasement of our origins, nor the embattled present, nor our ultimate destination. "Everywhere dust on all things on all of us dust," concludes the poet, who sees himself as locked into his "future cadaver / already buried under the cumulus of dust." Yet in their relentless desperation, such poems also cumulate into a redoubtable wisdom: accepting one's identity as no more permanent than an "anonymous constellation" of dust. De Palchi often leaves us with this perspective to contemplate.

This same materialistic, biological, physiological world view governs his erotic poems, many of which are comprised in the aforementioned *Le viziose avversioni*, a book first published in a bilingual edition as *Addictive Aversions* (Xenos Books, 1999). It comprises work written between 1951 and 1996. In such an individualistic poet, the erotic poems are especially telling because they stage confrontations with a potentially positive protagonist, an "other" unlike the deceitful personages targeted in the several justifiably misanthropic poems of *La buia danza di scorpione* and *Sessioni con l'analista*. The first section of *Le viziose avversioni*, a sequence of thirteen short poems called "Momenti" ("Moments"), expresses little, if any, romantic sentiment, but instead much corporal delight, even humor:

> fulminations beneath the house and trees
> fertile with rain, watched over by a medley
> of birds as splendid
> as my own bird—.
>
> *
>
> and as in the Bible I betroth
> with my left hand
> the left breast
> with my right the caressing compactness;
> in my mouth I engulf the right breast
> and you say the sperm nourishes you,
> perfectly,
> "like meat and eggs"—.

(trans. Sonia Raiziss)

Elsewhere, de Palchi views erotic encounters as contests, struggles, additional illustrations of the fundamental agon in which we find ourselves engaged, whether we like it or not. Lovers act at once like plant lice and atomic particles. "We are phylloxera, / compulsion, temper, / fission," the poet remarks bluntly, though the reader (especially the American reader) should not deduce too quickly that the Italian poet is using such imagery only with negative connotations. In de Palchi's work, amorous attractions are irrepressible, free of guilt and moral restraints. The "Carnal Essence" sequence—with its suggestive epigraph from Villon about "spying on well-sculpted thighs being washed," as one might adventurously render "voyant laver cuisses bien faites"—comprises lines such as "the centrality of my gaze is drugged / on your figure's magnetic cleft / the only unpredictable stability / of an unknown world," "you want me to enter you / and reach the depth of your throat / you want your sex to be excavated / when you say 'burst me open, complete me,'" and "I know how to turn on your blood to the pure / trickling of monthly wounds in my mouth / how to violate you / ready for the mystery of wanting violation." But taking off from explicit sexual imagery as such, de Palchi often points not only to the psychological intricacy, ambiguity, or enigma of one's sexual penchant for another person, but also to something stranger, hidden, more profound. De Palchi's erotic poetry rarely lacks an ultimate, if sometimes oblique or implied, search for the "origin," the "first cause" ("il principio"), or essential "roots":

Expose your hands, touch
and concentrate me in the centrality of your body
at times bellicose or fluvial
beneath the intensity of our evolving light
justifying our roots.

(trans. Barbara Carle)

Yet de Palchi's erotic poetry is not without its paradoxes. In the aforementioned poem "A Rat Obsessed," for instance, the poet goes so far as to confess
that "each animate or inanimate object is a woman, / a sewer where my sex, a
rat obsessed / lurks" (American edition of *Sessions with my Analyst*, p. 68). It
is difficult to conceive of a metaphor—the sewer equated to the feminine, the
male to a rat-phallus—further removed from any kind of amorous transcendence, though it is important to take into account a change made in this poem
when it was republished (see page 46) in *Addictive Aversions* in 1999, then in
the *Collected Poems*: the sewer indeed becomes "luminosa" (p. 250). When
reading de Palchi, one is constantly faced with the negative-positive tension of
such imagery. The oxymoronic title of this same collection sums up this erotic
momentum toward that which is antipodal, opposite, even negative, licentious,
dissolute. The English title is even more frank: one becomes addicted to what
is adverse.

In *Le viziose avversioni,* the thirteen-poem sequence "Mutazioni" —the
sequences "Un ricordo del 1945" and "Momenti" also consist of thirteen
poems—ends with an appeal to the "incorruptible / Justine" of de Sade's
like-named novel. The poet awaits her "coming" ("arrivo"), perhaps ernestly,
perhaps ironically in that her arrival seems to parody the coming of a Messiah.
Does this mean that some kind of hope or salvation can be envisioned? It is
unlikely, unless salvation is understood as ephemeral physical pleasure, the last
resort and revolt of the *homme revolté* against a godless world that also often
represses carnal pleasure. "I'm nothing but empty / gusto," exclaims de Palchi,
"or rather a cry in the void, / existing in a smother of mutations / no defenses
no exits." A more ambiguous and intriguing image is almost, but not quite,
solipsistic: "we stare at each other with sexual looks / but in the grand scheme
of senseless things / I doubt that you exist." And does the ideal Justine exist
more convincingly in consciousness than any real "you"? In "Carnal Essence,"
de Palchi similarly writes of a "soliloquy" as plunging him between the telluric
thighs of his beloved. The subsequent description is graphic in its exaltation of
sexual exploration, yet it is also not without abstractions indicating the constant
simultaneity of sensation and self-consciousness, indeed a self-consciousness
charged, once again, with Christian symbolism:

I split my lips following each curve each line
of your slight form that moulds itself in the dimension

of one unified spirit
religion of your fluctuations,
sustenance of your consecrated host that shines on my face
which has become yourself.

(trans. Barbara Carle)

Such are the puzzles of living. Already in the 1950 piece originally called "Le Sacre du printemps" and now introducing the collection *Paradigma*, de Palchi perceives life—indeed the whole history of biological life on the earth—as "pointless genesis pointless evolution / only matter—the nemesis." "Nemesis" has at least two meanings. The first would imply that matter would inflict retribution and destroy human bodies (as the like-named goddess mercilessly would); and to be sure, bodies waste away, rot, disintegrate. The terrible lesson precociously learned at his grandfather's bedside was never forgotten. Yet matter, as "the nemesis," would also signify the formidable opponent, or obstacle, facing individuals who, like de Palchi, incessantly scrutinize the origin, the first cause—"il principio"—of biological life. Even when we break living matter down into its vital systems and infinitesimal components, it still turns its shiny, impenetrable surfaces to us; they loom, obstacle-like questions, over our own life. They also loom like mirrors. This standoff belongs to the human condition. One poem in *Le viziose avversioni* especially captures the momentous existential consequences of these face-to-face encounters with the goddess. "Let's turn over the stone pocked with scribbles, / worms, blanched spermatozoa, molecules," remarks de Palchi in lines that also seemingly hark back to his green years, "such is the incessant beginning, the glimmer / that locks us between the linear horizon and the leap." We are ever locked between the horizon and the leap.

A Quest for Continuity and Communion
(Mario Luzi)

In English-speaking countries, the poetry of Mario Luzi (1914-2005) has been present in a few translations but still remains insufficiently known. More than thirty years ago, the translator I. L. Solomon pioneered by bringing out *In the Dark Body of Metamorphosis and Other Poems* (1975), a selection that was later complemented in Ireland by Catherine O'Brien's *After So Many Years: Selected Poems* (1990). Luigi Bonaffini then rendered *Per il battesimo dei nostri frammenti* (1985) and *Frasi e incisi di un canto salutare* (1990), two major books that were published in English by Guernica in 1992 and 1999. This was a promising start, but in comparison, in France where I am writing this, fifteen books by Luzi have appeared; that is, most of his poetry, several of his luminous essays, his play *Libro di Ipazia* (1993), which stages the violent transformation of paganism and Neo-Platonic thought into Christianity, and a version of *Trame* (1982), his collection of elegant, gently moving evocations, diary-like jottings, brief reminiscences, and travel narratives. This volume offers excellent examples of "short prose," that fertile, multifaceted genre—as opposed to the comparatively circumscribed "short story"—in which contemporary European poets and writers also often express themselves.

It is important to read as much of Luzi's seminal work as possible, though this is not essentially because he was a prolific poet, not to forget a penetrating critic who brought to the fore crucial philosophical and spiritual issues that have engaged major European authors. (His analyzes of Leopardi are incisive, and he deeply explored the Dante vs. Petrarch dichotomy. His grappling with the poetics and pessimism of Mallarmé, as expressed in *Studio su Mallarmé* [1952], is no less significant.) Above all, during a career that spanned seven decades—his first collection, *La Barca*, appeared in 1935—his studied innovations and self-transformations were remarkable. What must be grasped is the admirable personal and poetic outlook that provoked this long development. An excruciating "honesty" is not a trite word in this regard.

This is why it is not really helpful to classify Luzi, as critics sometimes do, as a major representative of the second generation of Italian Hermetic poets, even if this grouping rightly points to a certain intellectualization, specifically an intertextualization, of his work during his middle creative period, beginning with

Avvento notturno (1940). The poet later moved toward a more straightforward (if no less psychologically and philosophically rich) mode of expression and toward a humanistic vantage point emphasizing the Other as much as the Self. His mother's death in 1959 is often cited as the turning point, followed by the poetry dedicated to her in *Nel magma* (1963). All the while, Luzi continued to question his formal poetic techniques and his Christian metaphysics. In fact, from the beginning to the end of his career, much of his verse focused on doubt and the difficulties of maintaining any certitudes whatsoever, let alone a Christian faith. So persistent was his circumspection that he was still defining himself as an "absolute beginner" when his collection *Dottrina dell'estremo principiante* (2004) came out. The nonagenarian was not being falsely modest. Like the French poet Philippe Jaccottet, who has also translated some of Luzi's poems and whose own book of verse and short prose, *Après beaucoup d'années* (1994), echoes that of his friend, the Italian writes a poetry of genuine groping. In both cases, the notions of poetry as a quest, as a relentless examination of possible truths, as an epistemological tool, and as a touchstone for measuring how one should live, take on an impressive seriousness. Significantly, as the years went by for Luzi, individual occasional poems mattered less, and even less so heterogeneous "collections" of them; he came to favor sequences of interrelated poems and coherently structured book-length poems. This formal propensity likewise reflects an unceasing search.

Let me now announce the good news. Bonaffini has produced for Green Integer a fine translation of *Viaggio terrestre e celeste di Simone Martini* (1994), a mysterious, polyphonic, book-length poem that crowns Luzi's oeuvre and also meditates on its ever-evolving themes. The book forms a loose trilogy with *For the Baptism of our Fragments* and *Phrases and Passages of a Salutary Song*, so a still clearer idea of Luzi's development can now be obtained. Moreover, Green Integer is also announcing the same translator's version of *Sotto specie umana* (1999), to be published as *Under Human Species*.

Earthly and Heavenly Journey of Simone Martini takes off from the last years of the life of the Sienese artist (1282-1344), who reputedly died in Avignon. Luzi imagines, however, that Simone Martini in fact left the French town (and Papal capital) at the end of his life, for one last "return? / or a retreat..." to his hometown. The artist must bid farewell rather too quickly, it seems, to his dear friend Petrarch, who would watch him paint, inspecting "the laborious shaping / of the faces, the drapery," awaiting "anxiously / the almond of the eyes." As an artistic companion for Simone Martini and a tutelary figure for Luzi, Petrarch of course represents par excellence the persistent tension between Christianity and Humanism, between learning and spontaneity, between the Self and the Other (and, subsequently, between autobiography and biography), as well as between erotic desire and the desire for what he called "religious rest" (in his Latin treatise *De otio religioso*, penned three years after Simone Martini's death).

This fictive journey otherwise involves the artist's wife Giovanna, his brother Donato (a painter), and the latter's "beautiful and strange wife, also called Giovanna" (as the poet specifies). Their daughters and a few servants accompany them, as well as a student ("one assumes of theology," notes Luzi ironically) who is "a witness, interpreter, and chronicler as well as integral part of the adventure." To this description of a quasi-theatrical cast, Luzi slyly adds that "the scribe is each of them a little and none in particular." The definition reveals from the onset that the narrative structure is complex. The poet ("the scribe") is thus "a little of" the student-chronicler and the entire poem is thereby narrated by a narrator capable of adopting other narrators' voices, of quoting their words, or of remaining strictly himself, as it were. The occasional independence of Luzi's voice is evident whenever he mentions contemporary objects, notably a "vocafono" in the lines:

> Careful. Don't open.
>   Whoever is ringing
> and saying her name on the vocaphone
> is not really her,
> she is not the one you think
> and await
> with ancient tenderness...

By the time "ancient tenderness" appears, both Luzi and Simone Martini are already back in the fourteenth century, trekking along near, say, Genoa, and once again caught up in the many trials and occasional pleasures of the journey.

Constantly moving in his mind between present and past, that is between his own present (pen in hand, on a given day in 1993, as he is writing a page) and this fourteenth-century story that he is telling (imagining) in the present, Luzi recounts Simone Martini's trip but also hints, in fragmentary fashion, at his own chronicle of creation: the story of the writing of this book that is also about poetic creativity and a poet—Luzi—at the end of his life. "For whose love / does he, / wandering cleric," asks Luzi (who also asks himself), "write and live with / these papers / of exile, of travel? / of homecoming, of estrangement..." The student-chronicler here recalls Luzi, who of course recalls Simone Martini. Or later, in another cryptic autobiographical allusion underscoring the poet's concern with artistic honesty and authentic self-metamorphosis: "Where are you taking me, my art? / into what remote / deserted territory / are you suddenly thrusting me?" And still later, this even deeper question about the truth-revealing capabilities of art and poetry: "Art, what does your gaze illuminate for me? / life or memory / of life? its flashes, its continuity? / the bed and flow of the eternal river?" These latter questions show how Luzi is himself riveted by a human being's frequent sense of being ontologically separated from Life (in both biological and Christian meanings of the term); and they indicate the poet's intense wrestling with the enigmas of Time, another central theme of the narrative poem.

When reading, it is thus also impossible not to think of Petrarch's cherished mentor, Saint Augustine, who developed the concept of a "presence of things past," a "presence of things future," and a "presence of things present." Luzi's verse employs and embodies these and other concepts about time and consciousness, which is why *Earthly and Heavenly Journey of Simone Martini* may often seem abstract to readers who rarely venture beyond the typical empiricism of Anglo-American poetry. In any event, the philosopher of *The Confessions* is perhaps an invisible companion for Simone Martini's group, and surely a fellow traveler for Luzi, who indeed meditates on Time from the very first lines onward:

> Nature,
> always uttered, named
> from the origins...
> > As it was,
> as it stayed in the mind
> and sense of men—
> > in that prison, in that wind,
> very alive, very cautious.
> Time neither gave nor took anything from it.
> It itself was time, it was eternally.
> Human history being born in its womb
> and consuming itself in it
> without leaving a trace...
> > Without?

Moreover, throughout *Earthly and Heavenly Journey of Simone Martini*, Luzi's literary term *trama*, whose meanings shift from "weft" and "woof" to "plot," "intrigue," and, here perhaps, the "framework" of a narrative, is perfectly fitting. The various sub-genres—diary-like notes, travelogue fragments, sudden reminiscence—of short prose that the poet used in *Trame* are poetically metamorphosed in the narrative poem. Dreams, daydreams, hallucinations, and expressions of despair also crop up. At one point, Donato's wife Giovanna is suddenly "beside herself / frozen with terror." "She tortures / images and memories (. . .)," writes Luzi, "discovers / snares and monsters / in the common / monotonous occurrences." The omniscient "scribe" reports: "Why, life, / this injury / done to you, they ask you / in dismay."

Take a second look at the preceding quotation. The English syntax, which mirrors that of the Italian original (as very often elsewhere in Bonaffini's close and accurate version), already shows how Luzi blends one voice, or the illusion thereof, into another. The first eight words ("Perché, vita / questo sfregio / che ti è fatto"), which are not set off by quotation marks, initially seem pronounced by the narrator (the scribe, Luzi), as if they were an outburst, an interjection; but the ninth and tenth words ("ti chiedono") disclose that he is actually reporting what the voyagers have exclaimed. Sometimes philosophical reflections are similarly attached *a posteriori* to a concrete human speaker. Note the sudden appearance of "he thinks" after the dash in:

> The instant has no meaning. Time does
> so does its mysterious
> continuity—he thinks.

Although the book sometimes evokes the concrete details and events of Simone Martini's journey, including sensual exaltation ("your unique aroma / so very sweet and raging") and especially startling manifestations of nature ("astonishment of ultra-morning light"), the narrative typically moves from act or fact to metaphysical reflection. This is one sense of *Earthly and Heavenly Journey of Simone Martini* as a narrative poem—the itinerary is as much philosophical and spiritual as geographical—and, specifically, of each narrative event as a "bewitched" (as Luzi phrases it once) sensibility acutely perceives reality, ponders it, lets himself be infused by it, sometimes transforms it into art, and ever seeks a comprehension of both its and his ultimate ends. "In the sky / beyond the hills, / it dawns, it grows blue," Luzi relates at one point, for example, before inducing that this perception implies an opening "to its sybilline future, / year suddenly sprung today / from its own nothingness." Inversely elsewhere, Simone Martini (and thus Luzi) is "dazzled / by the visible / invisible everywhere present / revelry of reflections, of transparencies." This sparkling immanence of transcendent mysteries seems so evidently and spontaneously within reach that mere "pigeons / cut clean across it / in their taut flight."

This is not the only instance where the Christian cross is symbolically generalized into a philosophically more polysemous intersection of the horizontal and the vertical. There is nothing facile about this symbolism in Luzi, as can be observed when he associates the horizontal, not only with realistic perishable pigeons cutting straight across the sky, but rather with conjectured horizontal geometries such as the eternal, river-like continuity of Time. From Joyce's "epiphany" and Proust's unexpected sensation or perception enabling a recovery of "lost time," to those discreet magical moments that are celebrated by any number of poets and writers, contemporary European authors have perhaps now mostly turned away from the search for continuity. They prefer to focus on more tangible discontinuities. Not so Luzi, who certainly seeks transcendence in illuminative instants (which might be termed "vertical discontinuities"), but who also hopes to contemplate something lasting, ever-flowing, that is a horizontal yet no less transcendental continuity.

As the journey progresses, this search for a communion with transcendent mysteries, in the here and now, intensifies. Once again, the poet brings forth his fundamental dichotomy of ontological union and separation. In a prayer, which offers still another example of Luzi's varied poetic approach, the artist beckons the Virgin for "a moment / of universal co-presence [*compresenza*], /

of total evidence— / things go into / the thought that thinks them, they go into / the name that names them, / the miraculous coincidence blazes."

Such pleas increase a mystical suspense that has been slowly but surely building all along. It seems that the poet, though his various personae and especially that of Simone Martini, will at last attain serenity; that his struggle with opposites is heading for a divine conclusion; that his wish for "the advent of the light / that unites us and absolves us" is going to be granted. The soothing opening lines of the final poem, with their vision of totality, reinforce this impression of union and continuity:

> Being is. It is.
> Whole,
> unconsumed,
> equal to itself...

Luzi then sees a flame, realizes that "everything blazes without shadow." He defines this mystical manifestation as "essence, advent, appearance, / all utterly transparent substance." Does this not announce a Christian apotheosis? But in an unexpected turnabout, the poet then calls into question this ultimate, all-encompassing certitude. "Is this paradise / perhaps?" he wonders, or instead a "luminous trap, / a smile of ours never conquered, / dark ab origine?" Ultimately, Mario Luzi's quest must continue, and this was not his last book.

The Nexus of Contradictory Verities
(Roberto Bertoldo)

"Poetry is not for beginners," warns Roberto Bertoldo ironically in a poem included in *The Calvary of the Cranes*, a collection whose complex meanings emerge perhaps only after the reader, as Rimbaud put it, has himself undertaken a "long, boundless and systematic (*raisonné*) disordering of all the senses."

I exaggerate these preparatory efforts only slightly. Arguably informed by Surrealism, by Italian Hermetic poetry, and by contemporary philosophical debates about "writing and silence," or about the instability of the writerly "I" and the readerly "you," Bertoldo is assuredly no facile or spontaneous lyric poet. Though his poems are short and sometimes about love, they show the labor of much meticulous word ordering—which is not to say that they are unemotional. Bertoldo confronts us with bold oxymorons ("You flay the water in Your windmill, / burn it, fill it with holes"), with brow-knitting illogicalities ("stories in the hole / of the rain"), with troubling metamorphoses ("the broken air flowered thorns / on your paleness, the rose scratches / were cicadas on the dunes"), and with intriguing private symbols ranging from significant "commas" and "holes" to polysemous "magpies," "cicadas," "cranes," and "cockroaches."

As the title indicates, Biblical imagery likewise haunts this book in strange and original ways. There is a paradoxical allusion to Noah's ark. Elsewhere, Bertoldo calls out to the cicada—a symbol of singing and thus lyric poetry—while evoking the crucifixion of Christ: "for you queen on the cross.../ For you I commit my wood and nail you down." In "Letters to the Magpie," second-person pronouns are capitalized, suggesting a divine interlocutor, though "magpie" is otherwise equated in an epigraph with "false poet." The third "Letter to the Magpie" exhibits further imaginable senses of "You":

> I know why You,
> settled on the rocking chair,
> have defeated the ball of wool.
> Because You have an exit for each entry.

Whereas "you" unambiguously becomes "death" in the "Letters to the Pallet":

> What are you, death, that counter-currently
> carve hearts and arrows into the bark of trees?
> And you lay down into life:
> to make it brief, of memory?

These examples of thematic multi-layering illustrate the difficulties but also the emotional, intellectual, and spiritual scope of this poetry. Moreover, a certain initial opacity of both stylistic surface and semantic depth is to be expected, because Bertoldo's poems are also "about" his struggle with speaking genuinely, with seeking "words with core." (In the final poem, he laments that he is now left with only "words without core.") This search for what can be uttered, and for a listener to whom *povere parole*, "poor words," can be addressed (whence the shifting or composite "you's"), is a concern informing much essential European writing since the Second World War. Bertoldo's poetry stems from, or at least recalls, this over-half-century-long existential, linguistic, and historical malaise, which is sometimes linked to the Shoah and the impossibility of writing poetry afterwards. In any event, Bertoldo eerily insists on empty spaces, or scrutinizes the edges of redoubtable gaps, and if this recurrent geometric symbolism ultimately has little to do with the Holocaust (the poet was born in 1957), then surely it reflects the conviction that sense, significance, and (not least) feeling dwell, if at all, only on the margins of what was once considered essential and now is grievously missing. Noting in one poem that "caverns have lips," and in another that "the bead of a story" is being born on "your bloodless lips," Bertoldo indeed gropes for meaning along austere borders, remote limits, rims:

> You speak to me of a silence
> I've had to swallow
> between the fragments of words
> like a hole and its cornices.

Elsewhere he notes that "distance is: / a hole I smell, a — gramma," where "gramma" means both the metric "gram" and the suffix "-gram" (derived from the Greek *gramma*, "letter," and *graphein*, "to write"). Hence, distance is a burden, but also a gap, a lack, an emptiness that can be conveyed. It is an absence or a nothingness that is a communicable presence (where the epithet "communicable" would possess all its positive and negative connotations). Interestingly, many of these poems are explicitly epistolary.

With respect to these dialectics of impossibility and endeavor, of annihilation and reaffirmation, of aphasia and entreaty, poems ending on a slightly positive note are particularly arresting. "Nihilism," for instance, concludes with an uplifting "surprise of a song that moves the waters / with hands of paddles." Similarly, "Mill Pond" locates potential epiphanies in rubbish and rubble:

And in the rubbish the man searches the grass
that may skim that cuts that engraves miracles.
This is the reason for the riddle of flowers;
the rubble and the gift. This evening.

Bertoldo's poetry, too, is full of riddles and, as it were, is wrought (with great care) from rubble, from the odds and ends of nature and civilization. He shows time and again that new composite wholes can be made out of striking diversity. The poet himself calls his poetry "intersemica" and "tonosimbolica," which the translator, Emanuel di Pasquale (who provides an accurate equivalent of this challenging verse), renders in an endnote as "intermeaning" and "tone-symbolic." Would *intersemica* perhaps be more clearly understood as the more literal "inter-semic," where "semic" would refer to "semes" and the compound adjective thus to the intrepidly heterogeneous, authentically surrealist units of elementary meaning that build together into such perplexing, yet compelling, global meanings in Bertoldo's poems?

One is long haunted by these intense, tightly crafted, at once introspective and resonant poems, which often surpass common logic in their imagery and which remain so multifariously interpretable. Think of a nexus of contradictory or competitive verities, rather like those falling autumn leaves evoked by Bertoldo which resemble a splendorous "carnival" or "confetti," yet which "celebrate" no less than a human being's "hell."

Unresolved Betweenness
(Milo De Angelis)

Milo De Angelis's dense, complex poems should each be read at least three times. As the title, *Between the Blast Furnaces and the Dizziness*, of the second American selection of his poetry indicates, a first exposure can be dizzying. (An initial selection, *Finite Intuition*, was made in 1995 by Lawrence Venuti for Sun and Moon Press.) One doubts that coherent meanings can be construed from the Italian poet's daring juxtapositions of images, symbols, and obscure personal allusions. His cognitive leaps are many in the volumes from which Emanuel di Pasquale has chosen fifty-four poems: *Somiglianze* (Resemblances, 1976), *Millimetri* (Millimeters, 1983), *Terra del viso* (Land of the Face, 1985), *Distante un padre* (A Father's Distance, 1989), and *Biografia sommaria* (A Summary Biography, 1999).

A second reading, however, assuages the reader's vertigo. As it turns out, De Angelis (born in 1951) is closer to concrete facts than one had noticed. He evokes trucks, brine, poplars, sporting events, a "bar that fills up / in the early hours," an "8mm film shown at the gymnasium," "long and black gloves of young ladies, telescopes, military / maps," and other such empirical details, suggesting that his own efforts to grasp the unified sense of a teeming moment of consciousness has run up against, or must take into account, these all-too-real particulars. This is the "blast furnace" side to his writing.

Is there a link between the two poetics, between dizzily arranged abstractions and stolid blast furnaces, between a banal phone call from a pollster and the "brightness inside the ruin" that the boy's voice suggests?

An epigraph gives a clue: "You will feel each beat of your heart / like a small obligation." This perhaps implies an obligation—self-deceiving or not—to move up and outwards from one's body, from one's corporeity, and obtain an independent perspective (as it were). At any rate, De Angelis often depicts himself caught up in a similar "betweenness," suspended between ideation (or the transcendent urge) and the utter materiality of the world (and human flesh). Sometimes the poet glimpses a greater unity, or dual harmony, as when "the trains from Certosa...parked there" seem "spiritual." But more haunting, in this generous selection of his work, is when the betweenness is left unresolved, and lasts—a source of immitigable yearning.

How We Would Live
(Giovanna Sicari)

Giovanna Sicari's poetry asks "how we would live," as she puts it in *Rome during the Vigil* (1999), one of the six collections from which poems have been selected for *Naked Humanity: Poems 1981-2003*, and translated by Emanuel di Pasquale. Like many postwar Europeans, the Italian poet (1954-2003) aims her verse at this at once existential and metaphysical question. Many poems, not to mention the aforementioned title, then simultaneously evoke her "keeping watch" while she is pondering the matter; in other words, waiting, suspending all action, indeed watching, as if she could not decide how to live. While remaining attentive to what might happen, is happening or—alternatively—while becoming aware of all that can never be fulfilled or recovered (as regards the absences and losses that haunt her), she finds herself enveloped in an "anxious darkness that trembles / that does not breathe." However, the suffocating vigil kept by this single individual is not the only strange, and estranging, wakefulness depicted. A state of vigil can also define the human condition; it can be maintained by all of "naked humanity."

To be sure, Sicari—or at least one of her vigorous narrative voices—declares that she will "leave [behind] maps of [her] peculiar prisons." She thereby underscores the personal impetus of her verse, all the while associating it with enclosure and separation, as well as with a plea for retrospective comprehension. Yet beyond her own self's specific torments and hesitations, her vigil has a universal quality. Sicari's allusions can be so acutely personal that they border on obscurity, yet not so much that they no longer represent other individuals' groping for coherence in a world that has little, or none. Sicari peers into the self (toward her "inner ex-voto," as she phrases it memorably), but she also continues to seek for meaning "outside." Her double quest necessarily runs up against our unmerciful age. Conveying well the heady, throbbing rhythms of modern secular life, she at one point equates her poetry with "a manuscript of this age without nightingales: / over the baroque muttering, / the endless arpeggio of the civil world." Other poems or passages describe violence, especially against women. It is perhaps important to know that she taught in a penitentiary for twelve years, and there is even a temptation to read some poems, not only as I have suggested above, but also as if they were spoken or confessed, through the poet's sympathy, by prisoners or prostitutes.

Given such a world, it is arresting that several poems persist in appealing to Christian symbolism, notably Easter. Sicari emphasizes the preliminary suffering in the paschal death-rebirth dichotomy, such as when (in *Decisions*, 1986) she describes "the mystic red of / a March lashing," beckoning at the same time for Jesus to "take" her "in the blot of this / obtuse century." Here, "take" is arguably polysemous—as are many other phrases in Sicari's work. Similarly, in the important sequence "The Mother" (from *Seal*, 1989), an otherwise unelucidated allusion to "your childhood sickness" especially compels when the poet avows that she has "prayed" that the sickness "be given as food to one who had blood— / the sacrifice God asks for / is the execution of an April Sunday." Incidentally, the semantic leaps, disorienting juxtapositions, and perceptual bizarreness of this poetry—which create its stark intellectuality—are often given strong emotional underpinnings through repetition, assonance, consonance, or insistent injunction. Like other Italian poets through the ages, Sicari skillfully creates a lyric intellectuality.

Related to the preceding are litany-like effects, as in a long untitled poem included in *Naked and Wretched, May the Human Triumph* (1998). It again refers to the key event, the "sick infancy," and bewails an unfeeling God:

> O alleys of the newborn, O God who does not comfort
> violated infancy, O autumn always
> for the saints alone, for all the saints who've prayed to
> God until they lost their voice.

As in the solitary plight of the Biblical Job, God is deaf to the narrator's pleading. Also like Job, the individual poet can be left "naked with no return [possible]," as she remarks in "Open Morning"; and so are we all, as the title of the entire book reminds us once again.

As is already clear, maternity is a complex recurrent theme. It can be negatively or poignantly portrayed, as well as with fleeting affirmative images that deserve reflection. This especially obtains in "The Mother," whose seventh poem concludes with still another image of death and birth:

> I disinterred the bones in a small, desecrated church,
> the crying of the newborn did not vex
> the necessity of all births.

In such dire situations (the sequence begins with a napalm bomb falling), the specific original question—"how would we live?"—must face up to the even more general miracle of regeneration. Acknowledging the ongoing processes of life as necessity—in the full philosophical force of the term—engenders compassion. Sicari follows this train of thought at times, and her poetry evolves accordingly. She learns to isolate "calm instant[s]" in which "you see compassion." In the same collection, revealingly entitled *Naked and Wretched, May the Human Triumph*, she looks well beyond the self when she perceives Time itself as coming "with the broken voice of innocent and hurt children, / of the bodies petrified in the ditch, of all / the world's bodies that lack access to the day." And the title poem declares "may the human triumph," before formulating the wish that

> for one not loved, a wonder,
> recompense and wonder for one that is gentle, for one
> that feels humans
> and with voice and look offers the word like a prayer.

In other words, in some late poems the vigil has perhaps come to an end or at least has acquired renewed purpose. In Sicari's last book, *Immobile Epoch* (2003), she notes that "in this emptiness there is compassion, in this outlaw / zone, one can save [one]self." This, she implicitly concludes, is how we would or should live.

Slovenia

A Generous and Courageous Lucidity
(Edvard Kocbek)

I first read the moving and mysterious verse of the Slovene poet Edvard Kocbek (1904-1981) at one remove: in a Croatian fishing village. After leaving France, then northern Italy, we had driven past the southeastern Alps of Austria, crossed the Slovene foothills where Kocbek was born, then headed south down the winding cliff-hanging highway of the Dalmatian coast. Even well south of Split, in Igrane, Kocbek's Slovenia was not far away. As generals, kings, diplomats, dictators, "ethnic purifiers," and—alas—peaceful civilians have known for some twenty centuries, the Balkans represent a mountainous, geopolitically turbulent, yet relatively small European region. And if I still felt close to Kocbek, even as I was otherwise immersing myself in Croatian life and manners, it was also because Slovene—as a southern Slavic language—is akin to the Croatian with whose rudiments I was wrestling by means of a conversation manual and the only dictionary at my disposal: a French-Serbian bilingual lexicon that I kept hidden. (This French-Serbian dictionary was obviously a reworked re-edition of a Serbo-Croatian lexicon; today, no one speaks of "Serbo-Croatian," but for historical, linguistic, and literary reasons the recent divorce of the adjectives that has become *de rigueur* because of the ethnic bloodshed is actually quite a complicated affair.)

Back to Kocbek. As I perused Michael Scammell and Veno Taufer's splendidly fluid translation of Kocbek's *Nothing is Lost: Selected Poems*, I could thus peek to the left at the Slovene original and try to make out cognates and determine grammatical parallels with Serbian and Croatian. One poem, "Kaj je z goro," "What Happens to the Mountain," even offers a conjugation lesson, as it begins (in English): "The mountain has not yet been a mountain. / The mountain is not yet a mountain. / The mountain will soon be a mountain...." As will be seen, Kocbek often ponders what, if anything—a mountain? a tree?—might prove to be an enduring, ever-renewable presence surpassing human fickleness, cruelty, and ephemerality. Grasping what, at its core, that deceptively simple term—"life" might consist of and imply thus also constitutes one of his primary motivations. Can words reach "life," even as they merge with "tree" in one remarkable poem? Whenever Kocbek is puzzled by his own "words," as he avows elsewhere, he "yearn[s] for one only, / one only that is unutterable." A sensitive self-searcher, he is hence equally a self-minimizing seeker of the One. At once optimistic and doubting, he remains gravely cognizant of human shortcomings, all the while keeping his eyes open for glimmers on the spiritual horizon.

Whenever possible, I try to read *in situ* such poets, hoping to grasp the here and now as they once did. I hoped that the fishing village could somehow replace hilly Slovenia. For Kocbek, the "sun...wreathed in cobwebs" or the "lazy hum of the late bees / over the buckwheat" are sensate launching pads from which an enigmatic "something" lying beyond the senses can perhaps be intuited. Yet from the patio where we ate our evening meals, I spotted no cobwebs. I could only sense the sun—concealed behind a thicket of silver-green olive trees—setting into the tepid Adriatic. There was no buckwheat: the steep karstic mountain slopes behind us, terraced with abandoned olive groves, were otherwise spotted with bold white boulders, with an undergrowth of thyme and savory, and with gigantic towering agaves. Surely the steady stream of traffic on the highway above the coastal village recalled no "pair of strong young oxen" that go "slowly / along the road as if unaware they are hauling a load," whose saliva drips from their muzzles and leaves behind "a thin / wet trail of circular blobs," and whose "russet hides smell warm /...as they enter the wood with their dreamy / driver."

Little matter. These lines from *Earth* (1934)—the pastoral first collection that established Kocbek's reputation—create a sense- and mind-stimulating world of their own that competes, at least for a while in the reader's mind, with the so-called real one. In the collections that followed (*Dread*, 1963; *Report*, 1969; *Pentagram*, *Embers*, and *Bride in Black*—the latter three published only in the *Collected Poems* of 1977), Kocbek broadens his philosophical scope and sometimes increases his use of symbolism as he incorporates into his rural focus a deep concern with Slovene history (see his celebrated long poem "Lippizaners"), with Christian and pantheistic metaphysics, and with the conflicts of an individual fully aware, as he phrases it, of the "mysterious...link / in this world between history and nature." Taken as a whole, his poetry portrays a pensive Slovene Everyman caught up in moments replete with ethical or spiritual complexities, as well as contradictions. In his fine foreword, Charles Simic rightly remarks that "the first person pronoun we encounter is more likely to represent a sensibility, a moral consciousness, and a view of the world rather than a person detailing the events of his life. Kocbek is a connoisseur of philosophical paradoxes and impossible moral predicaments."

For these reasons, it is just as appropriate to read Kocbek, not in Slovenia proper, but rather elsewhere in ex-Yugoslavia. I would argue that it has never been more important to read Kocbek in ex-Yugoslavia, war-torn just yesterday and still suffering today from the gashes. (As for Slovenia, which managed to stay out of the Balkan war, the country became, in 2004, the first Balkan state to belong to the European Union.) After all, the former seminary student—who after traveling in Germany and France was influenced as much by surrealism as by the Catholic humanism of Emmanuel Mounier—had lived through the years of the Kingdom of the Serbs, Croats, and Slovenes (1918-1931); he had eyewitnessed the three-in-one country becoming (in 1929) a monarchist dictatorship that was later (in 1931) renamed "Yugoslavia"; and although Kocbek was not a Communist, he had fought so bravely alongside Communist Partisans resisting Nazism that he found himself made into a general by the end of the Second World War. In Tito's Marxist Yugoslavia, Kocbek (still a non-Communist) even briefly became an important political figure, an experience that arguably underlies his famous poem "Hands." "I have lived between my two hands," he confesses, "as between two brigands, / neither knew / what the other did. The left hand was foolish because of its heart, / the right hand was clever because of its skill." Characteristically, even an initially—if this is truly the case—political poem like "Hands" soon develops other spiritual dimensions. It ultimately discloses a Job-like torment:

> Today as I ran from death
> and fell and rose and fell
> and crawled among thorns and rocks
> both were bloody.
> I spread [my hands] like the cruciform branches
> of the great temple candlestick,
> bearing witness with equal ardor.
> Faith and unfaith burned with a single flame,
> ascending hotly on high.

Kocbek's political responsibilities diminished in 1949, with the publication of his war diary, *Comradeship*; and they were curtailed abruptly by the government in 1951, after the publication of his war stories, *Fear and Courage*. The two books unsparingly related the harshness of some Partisan acts, and the writer did not shirk from examining his own deeds. In his excellent introduction to *Nothing is Lost*, Scammell notes how Kocbek expressed "his ethical qualms with an objectivity and realism that had not been seen in Slovene (or Yugoslav) literature before." Scammell then chronicles Kocbek's fall from political grace, explaining how the poet thereafter lived as a "nonperson"—his apartment watched, his telephone tapped—and survived only by translating, under a pseudonym, from French and German. Throughout his life, Kocbek thus lived at the heart of a Balkan region struggling to endure as "Yugoslavia" yet destined to fall apart. Moreover, his political banishment led to a "Pontic exile" within his own fatherland, as he admits in his subtle and poignant homage to Ovid.

And now Yugoslavia has fallen apart, violently, leaving underneath the surface of everyday life—a decade later—a myriad of potential tensions even in places—such as the Croatian fishing village—that knew no manslaughter. A past when "the world ran amok," as Kocbek puts it in another context, "and lusted for horrors," is still discretely omnipresent. Let me give a banal example. In Igrane, my twelve-year-old son started playing every morning with a boy on the beach. They shared no common language but, side by side, they would peer through diving masks and use long-poled nets to hunt for and compare sea urchins. One morning, my wife approached the boy's mother—always sitting at least two dozen feet away from us—and asked in broken Croatian what the boy's name was. "Ivo? Petar?...," Françoise suggested, pronouncing sample Christian names. After hesitating, the wary mother uttered only two words in explanation: "Sarajevo. Ahmed." She said nothing else, but it was clear now that the family were Muslims who had ventured over to the coast from one of the towns that had suffered most during the Balkan War. Because of the specific conflict between Christians and Muslims in Bosnia (exemplified in Mostar, where the two religious groups first allied against the Serbs, then turned against each other), it was important for this Muslim family to keep a low profile in Christian Croatia.

Allusive phrases and conspicuous silences—there were others—kept bringing me back to compassionate, meditative Kocbek. He would have empathized with the Sarajevo woman, I think, even as in his time the high-pitched songs of peasant women "coming from work and / climb[ing] the sloped fields" made him imagine stuffing his mouth "with bitter soil / in sorrow over their sound." It must be added that Kocbek was sensitive to the relativity of social positions and prestige. Like Mark Twain, he knew all too well how a prince could be turned into a pauper; the pauper, into a prince. By extension, the Muslim boy, of Slavic origin, whose babyhood was wracked with bombs and ethnic hate, might have been born elsewhere—and vice versa. In his striking long poem "The Game," depicting a Partisan camp, Kocbek sharply observes how each Partisan similarly turns into another person, as if "someone has changed and defined us, / as though shuffling a pack of cards." He remembers:

> He who burrowed now walks upon air,
> the declaimer of speeches now stammers in his dreams,
> he who slept upon straw now commands a brigade
> and the quiet woodcutter is full of questions;
> he who quoted Homer is building bunkers
> and he who dined in Paris is shaping a spoon...

Moreover, in this poem, the narrator "reel[s] under the weight of dreams" that seem to be inside him "as in a young mother." The burden of comprehending the cares of his comrades thus becomes a creative chore, procreative of poems and also—I suspect—fostering the kind of understanding that induces peace. Elsewhere, as Kocbek scrutinizes evil, he practices the circumspection of the wise. In "Dialectics," for example, which is set during the most rigorous Communist era, he mentions "a loaded rifle at the neighbor's, / a microphone under the bed," and he adds that "the daughter is an informer." But then he elucidates and ultimately forgives such conduct by generalizing on the behavior of individuals, not just in the former Iron Curtain countries, but everywhere: "Everyone clings to a ram's belly / when sneaking from the Cyclops' cave."

Christian ethics, especially the notion of forgiveness, inform such verse. A few poems employ Christian symbolism, notably pertaining to the crucifixion. Yet one senses that Kocbek's Christian beliefs ever blossom outward, enabling him to embrace other philosophical viewpoints. When he appeals to Christian eschatology and writes that "I am more / than oblivion, /...immeasurably more / than nothing" or that "all that exists / is eternal, / birth is stronger / than death," and that "never / shall I cease to be," the poem is significantly entitled "Prayer." Throughout his work, such declarations are philosophical hypotheses formulated in a spirit of hope and entreaty. I daresay we need such a poetics today, and not just in ex-Yugoslavia. Kocbek's poems artfully blend lucidity, insight, and generosity. Not least, all the while the man kept his faith—despite what he was living through—in poetry as "the condensed power of all human / abilities."

A Much Delayed Letter from Ljubljana
(Veno Taufer, Aleš Debeljak, and others)

On page 144 of the tattered Bantam Classics edition of *Walden* that has traveled with me ever since my high school days in the late 1960s, Henry David Thoreau remarks: "We are eager to tunnel under the Atlantic and bring the old world some weeks nearer to the new; but perchance the first news that will leak through into the broad, flapping American ear will be that the Princess Adelaide has the whooping cough."

I hope that Thoreau's quip sufficiently excuses my tardiness in writing to you about my trip to Ljubljana. I was there in late April 2006; it is now mid-March 2007. Yet rather like concern for the Princess Adelaide's health, had I described my stay on the spot, I might have emphasized only ephemeral news of this European capital of 276,000 inhabitants. One needs the benefits of hindsight, such as can be earned by perusing old magazines in the waiting rooms of doctor's offices and meditating on the course of human events. Now I am rereading my notes and thinking of a much-touted contemporary art exhibit, "Interrupted Histories," that was taking place at the Museum of Modern Art, the Moderna Galerija, which otherwise presents Slovene modernists (like the engaging portraitist and self-portraitist Gabrijel Stupica, 1913-1990). Several provocative installations had been set up in the central hall, most of them involving television sets. I can report that only one installation has left a trace in me: Tanja Lažetić and Dejan Habicht's photos and video taken from The Trail of Remembrance and Comradeship.

The Trail is a twenty-two-mile-long walking and bicycling path that encircles Ljubljana. It commemorates the sinister barbwire enclosure that the Italian Army set up and guarded for more than three years during the Second World War in order to quell the Slovene underground movement. In 2005, Habicht photographed the town center from a hundred spots along the Trail; these snapshots were then arranged, for the installation, into a large rectangle on a whitewashed wall and accompanied—by means of a nearby television set—by Lažetić's video, which shows a man (probably Habicht) and a child riding their bicycles along the Trail. According to a poster, Lažetić and Habicht had tried to organize a regular bicycle outing with friends; it was to take place the first Sunday of every month; some of their friends had initially agreed, "but for a variety of reasons," as the artists explain, "no one ever joined us." The entire installation was thus entitled "No Remembrance, No Comradeship." Lažetić and Habicht likewise protest against the use, even on official maps, of the name "The Green Ring" instead of "The Trail of Remembrance and Comradeship."

Most of us hear this disgruntlement with sympathy. Affluent societies certainly tend to efface remembrance so that activities like bicycling or jogging along tree-shaded paths can take place without our thinking too much about what might have occurred in such places. Yet these effacements always (and often rightfully) provoke tense reactions in Europe, where history has been bloody and tragic for millennia and no pristine places exist. "Words are stitched together, but thoughts / break in as they will," as Meta Kušar (b. 1952) puts it in a poem from her sequence *Ljubljana* (2004), published in *The Voice in the Body: Three Slovenian Women Poets* (2005); and she adds: "Along dry, grey tendrils of wisteria / history climbs out onto a long balcony. / In the morning it tumbles over." Let me add a personal touch to this image of history-as-wisteria. Because I frequently have to prune back an energetic wisteria that grows alongside the front of my house in France, I know well that wisteria roots and branches grip like boa constrictors, even strangle, whatever support they entwine: wrought-iron balcony railings are favorite victims. Both individuals and entire nations must inevitably do some pruning now and then, that is establish a delicate balance (so as to move profitably into the future, nevertheless) between the duty to remember and the inclination or desire to forget, the latter tendency increasingly fueled by inevitable forgetting as each year's lot of babies is born ever further in time from the events that one must remember.

This balance is crucial to Slovenes, who have experienced upheavals in recent times. The nation has been jolted into a future that must be built. Following upon Tito's long Communist rule (which actually began among underground partisan ranks as early as 1943 and lasted until his death in 1980) of federated Yugoslavia, and as the Balkan War was about to rage in the republics of Croatia, Bosnia, and Serbia, the population courageously voted by referendum on 23 December 1990 to secede from the country; then the Slovenes officially proclaimed their independence on 25 June 1991. Having mostly stayed out of the Balkan War (which was waged until the Dayton Agreement of 21 November 1995), Slovenia became a member of the European Union on 1 May 2004. The country is the first and still the only ex-Yugoslavian republic to have been accepted.

The proverbially hardworking and ingenious citizens of this forested and mountainous nation are proud to have become at last an independent country. Until 1991, Slovenia had always been absorbed into empires, countries, protectorates, or pan-ethnic entities of various kinds, including the Roman Empire (when Ljubljana was called Emona), the territory controlled by Attila's Huns, the Austro-Hungarian Empire, the Realm of Serbs, Croats, and Slovenes, and finally Tito's federated Yugoslavia. Moreover, in April 2006, at a time when the French and the Dutch were about to vote, also by referendum, against a projected European Constitution, all the Slovenes whom I met were enthusiastic Europeans. Their mastery of several languages, and notably English (among the young people), was invigorating. (Umberto Eco has joked that the language of Europe is "translation." Wedged in among Italy, Austria, Hungary, and Croatia, Slovenia is an apt country in which to witness the frustrating and amusing truths of the statement.) In brief, the Slovenes, who in the meantime have also adopted the euro, are eager to move into the future and thus "forget," partly or wholly, rightly or wrongly, certain periods of their past. To return to the polemical aspects of Lažetić and Habicht's installation, the urge to replace "The Trail of Remembrance and Comradeship" with "The Green Ring" or the like is comprehensible. "Comrade" and "comradeship" are Communist-connoted terms in any language. At the same time, their title, "No Remembrance, No Comradeship," sums up the dangers sensed by other Europeans from the former Eastern Bloc countries (little matter in this regard that Yugoslavia was a non-aligned nation): namely, that Europe's plunge into the future signals the disappearance of vital historical knowledge and the end of social bonds. Apropos, why did I keep coming across books on yoga and meditation in bookshop windows?

* * *

Now I must explain why the one thing that I initially wanted to see in Ljubljana—the apartment building where the Slovene poet Edvard Kocbek (1904-1981) had lived—I did not manage to see and why this failure was ultimately unimportant. The year before I traveled to Ljubljana, I had written in *The Antioch Review* about the Princeton University Press edition, *Nothing is Lost*, of Kocbek's selected poems. I had been deeply moved by Kocbek's engaged humanism and spiritual quest as they came through vividly in English renderings made conjointly by Michael Scammell and the Slovene poet Veno Taufer (about whom more below). From Scammell's introduction, I knew that Kocbek's apartment had been watched, his telephone tapped, and that he had long been "kept in enforced quarantine." For various reasons (including a bedridden bout with lumbago, which almost made me cancel my trip), I had not researched, before leaving for Ljubljana, where exactly Kocbek's apartment was located; but I assumed that a tourist brochure or probably even the manager of the Pension Pri Mraku, the small hotel at which I would stay, would direct me to the last dwelling place of a famous poet, Second World War resistance hero, and dissident. I was wrong about this.

On the second day of my stay, while I was still perambulating the town very cautiously, my right hand pressing against the capricious muscles located in a triangle formed by my right hip, the small of my back, and my coccyx, I found myself at the National Museum, the Narodni Muzej Slovenije. There I was captivated by a curiosity, a Roman stele commemorating FULG(UR)

C(ONDITUM) or "Buried Lightning." A spot where lightning had struck had been entombed, as it were, so that the lightning—rather like lumbago—could not bolt back out of the ground and strike again. Upon leaving the museum, I turned to the left, shuffled under some towering trees, and then arrived in Tomšičeva Street. My intention was to proceed to Tivoli Park, where I wanted to see the Jakopičevo Sprehajališče, the Jakopič Promenade designed by Jože Plečnik (1872-1957).

Plečnik is rightly considered a brilliant precursor of postmodern architects. He was above all a humanist who was as sensitive to formal beauty as to the constraints and pleasures of daily life. He clearly loved his hometown. As an innovator with an unmistakable personal signature (often involving Doric columns with light bulbs), he superbly improvised on the Greco-Roman architectural heritage, making Ljubljana the showcase of his inspiration. Plečnik's buildings, colonnades, and even lampposts are omnipresent. I think that he also designed some of the comfortable public benches that I sat on near the Lubljanica River, which flows rather vigorously through the town. Moreover, he was responsible for redesigning some of the street layout as it branches off from the medieval Old Town with its looming castle atop a very steep promontory. The results are consistently attractive and offer a variety of enhanced perspectives, sometimes of oblique angles formed by his own graceful colonnades (along the Marketplace on Pogačarjev Square, for example); at other times of snowy Alpine peaks in the distance, beyond the ends of certain streets. He paid attention to overall impressions and minute details. The high walls of the National and University Library, the Narodna in Univerzitetna Knjižnica, for instance, display an audacious use of hewn and unhewn stone (and thus connect the building aesthetically to some adjacent vestiges of a Roman wall); he also ensured that the Ljubljanica had stable banks so that local citizens could relax and have picnics on them.

His bridges over the Ljubljanica are no less than stunning. They are short, solid, and yet—despite their massiveness—elegant because of Plečnik's at once classical and original deployment of straight lines, curves, three-dimensional harmonies, and pragmatic decoration (his unmistakable Doric-column lampposts, once again), not to mention his sensitive use of the most common building materials, notably concrete. His masterpiece is the Tromostovje, a single bridge that is also (as the name indicates) three bridges: two for pedestrians and the central one for cars. It is located at the very heart of the town. By the way, much of the inner city is pleasantly more adapted to pedestrians and bicycle riders than to automobile drivers; local citizens take advantage of this. Other Plečnik bridges, such as the Zmajski Most (the "Dragons' Bridge") and the Čevljarski Most (the "Shoemakers' Bridge"), are equally pleasing to the eye. The latter bridge is an obvious meeting place for the many young strollers who arrive in the evening for a drink at one of the cafés lining the Ljubljanica. While I was reading the indispensable anthology *Fragments from Slovene*

Literature (2005), I was not surprised to come across a rather sprawling poem, "The Scent of Tea," by Primož Čučnik (b. 1971). The poet mentions a Buddhist friend—another sign of the Eastern religions and their by-products that I kept noticing in Ljubljana?—who will perhaps "read the Tibetan secret / tantras and then we can all have a laugh together on Shoemakers' Bridge." A guided tour of Plečnik's house-museum in the Trnovo suburbs—a mere ten-minute walk along the river from the bridge—is moving because one then learns how modestly he lived and how dedicated a professor he was. Nearly everything in the house, from chairs and tables to vases and verandahs, he designed and made with his own hands.

* * *

Actually, I was methodically studying Plečnik's architectural marvels a few days later. Before I digressed about them, you will remember that I was advancing, wary of back pain, down Tomšičeva Street with its lofty trees. I glanced to my right and noticed a plaque at No. 12, indicating that there stood the headquarters of the Slovene Writers' Association. This organization is famous because of the role that it played during the democratization of pre-1991 Slovenia. It dawned on me that someone inside could at last indicate where Edvard Kocbek had lived.

Soon I was conversing with Barbara Subert, the hospitable and resourceful director of the Association and the general coordinator of Litterae Slovenicae, a stimulating forward-looking series of books and literary anthologies that are brought out in English, French, Spanish, or German translations. I have already mentioned *The Voice in the Body* and *Fragments from Slovene Literature*, published in the same series. There are also anthologies of contemporary Slovene short stories, poems, plays, and essays, as well as volumes gathering work by the poet Kajetan Kovič (b. 1930), the novelist Lojze Kovačič(1928-2004), and others. Subert of course knew where Kocbek had lived; it was not far from where we were just then, she remarked; but first she generously put me in touch with Veno Taufer. She gave him a call. Our mutual admiration for Kocbek befriended us immediately; other literary affinities were already at work as well, but I would perceive them only after I had read his own poetry.

Taufer (b. 1933) is a remarkable man. We could not meet because he was about to leave for the PEN World Congress in Berlin, where he intended to retire after two three-year mandates at Chairman of the Writers for Peace Committee. As the Slovene translator of Ezra Pound, T. S. Eliot, Gerard Manley Hopkins, Wallace Stevens, and Ted Hughes, as well as numerous modernists writing in Macedonian or Serbo-Croatian (these days, one must say "Serbian" or "Croatian" or "Bosnian"), not to forget as a striking poet and dramatist in his own right, Taufer is greatly responsible for having encouraged an internationalist, innovative outlook among his fellow Slovene writers. Beginning in the mid-

1950s, he was intimately involved in key literary reviews (*Beseda, Revija 57, Perspektive*), all of which were eventually banned. He also played a leading role in democratic protest groups during Tito's reign, serving a prison term in 1959 because of his dissident activities in support of cultural and political freedoms and otherwise suffering several times over the years from long hours of police interrogation. His participation in the Slovene independence movement was decisive. He served as the secretary as well as the chairman of the Committee for Freedom of Speech and Writing of the Slovene Writers' Association, which was the first "unofficial" public organization devoted to human rights; he was a co-founder (in 1989) of the first democratic political party in Slovenia and the co-author of the May Declaration of 1989, the fundamental document initiating the Slovenes' declaration of independence.

A thematically coherent sampling of his poetry can be found in the North-western University Press volume, *Waterlings*, which was originally published in Slovene in 1986 as *Vodenjaki*. The poems are based on an archaeological discovery in Lepenski Vir (located along the Danube River), where Neolithic stone sculptures in the form of half-human, half-fish creatures were found. When examining the sculptures at an exhibit in Ljubljana, Taufer was moved, as a brief editor's note explains, "by the statues' gaping mouths, their wide, staring eyes, and their expressions of helplessness and horror. He...tried to imagine what cataclysm had caused such fear and pain." Taufer adds: "Seeing these creatures, I wanted to give their mute cry a voice. What could I do but give them my own experience, that of a modern man?" Two lines sum up a volume unlike any American poetry collection that I have ever read: "in the dead dark of space / the water people's world is heard."

Taufer creates six sequences of short poems, which are translated by the poet and Milne Holton (and for the initial sequence, by the poet and his Kocbek collaborator, Michael Scammell). Evoking the "tongues," prayers, games, cries, incantations, songs, dances, myths, legends, and monuments of the Waterlings, the sequences sketch the eerie resonant vestiges of this "water people's world." There is sometimes an atmosphere of Delphic oracles; the cryptic utterances, underscored by the poet's very short lines and intricately rhymed formal struc-tures, invoke a civilization whose specific details we can only infer. The highly inflected Slovene language, which does not use definite and indefinite articles, is brilliantly suited to concision. Taufer makes the most of these grammatical and syntactic qualities. He forges a stark lyricism that sometimes draws on ancient folksongs, all the while remaining abstract and indirectly suggestive. A typical line in Slovene will have two or three fewer words than the, albeit tersely rendered, English.

Upon a first reading, some poems seem to conjure up the beginning of human language and simultaneously point to how language induces an ontological shift whereby humans are cut off from the immediacy of nature: "short word / stone without root / long word / fern without flower / angry word / breeze without tree." And yet such images also represent a world in ruins, a wasteland, where flowers and trees no longer grow. This apocalyptic world is also our own, as the phrase "black hole" in the following line makes clear: "i / break / an egg / i give / the night / a black hole / i bore / a stone / i pray." The Waterlings have also arrived at the end of language, at a desperate impotence of speech; their prayers grope back to lost meanings now hopelessly beyond formulation.

Images of entrapment also recur, and they grasp the reader by the throat. "Rising / coming / gaping / or singing," exclaims Taufer, "no voice no voice / but all around us / breathing / breathing us in / catching us overtaking us." There is a sense of helplessness, of being hunted down, of awaiting imminent destruction or, conversely, of having barely survived a cataclysm. The claustrophobic atmosphere is increased when Taufer emphasizes darkness. In one piece, he asks when he will see the sun again; the implicit answer is "never." Again, despite the archaic or prehistoric setting, it is impossible not to envision contemporary ecological disasters or warfare. "Flametimes these / wavetimes these," Taufer pointedly states at one point, characteristically creating neologisms ("plamenkrat," "valovkrat") in the process. Yearnings are confronted with impossibilities and paradoxes: "when the stone looks out of my head / when the stone floats / when the fish drowns." Sometimes, Taufer conjures up an unspecified "it" that threatens to annihilate the Waterlings: "nearby, silently, / far away, it waits."

One of the most haunting poems, consisting of seven three-line stanzas, takes off from the Slovene folk song "Riba Faronika nosi svet." In the song, Faronika the Fish bears the world on his back; but the lyrics also reveal that the fish will eventually turn on himself, destroying the world. Reinforcing this foreboding theme is a relentless formal structure that is impossible to reproduce fully in English, however crafted and gripping the translations of all these poems otherwise are. The first line recurs as the first line of each stanza; end-rhymes in Slovene follow the pattern a-b-b, a-c-c, a-d-d, etc.; and the words "ki" ("which [is]") and "tak" ("such [as / it is]"), which respectively introduce second and third lines of each stanza, are used with stunning effectiveness as internal rhymes, especially when their order is reversed in the sixth stanza and then reestablished at the end. Taufer tellingly reiterates the question "does it stand firm," where "it" is the world on Faronika the Fish. (Interestingly, question marks are not used.) At the end, he asks again:

> does it stand firm
>   as firm as this
>   this firm

"This" is, presumably, the tightly knit poem itself—a human construction which, like a folksong, is also exceedingly fragile. In other words, Taufer asks grimly, harrowingly, how much time is left for the Waterlings and thus for us as well. Moreover, according to the translator Jana Unuk, with whom I corresponded about this poem, the lines "does it stand firm / as firm as this / this firm" can have an additional connotation in Slovene. They recall an old children's game, called "Is it firm, the bridge?" Rather like our own game of "London Bridge is Falling Down," two children hold their arms in the air, forming a bridge. A line of other children moves under their arms and asks: "Ali je kaj trden most?" ("Is it firm, the bridge?"). The two children forming the bridge then answer: "Kakor kamen-kost" ("As stone, as bone").

Taufer is a master of these poetic formalisms, and with a force of conviction that I rarely encounter in American poets. He does not "apply" a traditional form to subject matter; instead, the forms derive from a profound necessity and are indissociable from both feeling and contents. In my correspondence with him since my stay in Ljubljana, I have received copies of many other poems that have been published in English, French or German in magazines or anthologies. These include a variation on the villanelle, written in November 1993 after the Serb-controlled Yugoslavian Army fire-bombed the Sarajevo University Library; the dark, deeply engaged lines begin:

> two thousand years in the library books maps
> in flames the wind carries leaves away from memory
> blood sticks letters and pages in stiff fingers
>
> pens tremble as the sound of the spheres reaches the listening
> who have only commentaries to resist death
> the age pursuing the shot to the heart struck by the echo in sarajevo...

(translated by the poet and Michael Scammell)

Although I am a mere (though inveterate) dabbler in Southern Slavic languages, I am convinced that Taufer's formal structures, because of their deep roots in Slovene folksong (rather like Béla Bartók's music drew deeply on Central European folk music), fully participate in the stern and solemn feelings that are created in the originals and re-created so intensely in the translations. Let me give a final example. A similarly intricate structure, including a meaning-bearing inversion, occurs in a poem ("the wind sways the fern") that consists of five three-line stanzas, the first three of which (in Slovene; the translator makes an interesting reversal here) are based on the incantatory refrain "reši nam telesa" ("save our bodies"). Here, the opening end-rhyme scheme is a-b-b, c (half-rhymed with b)-b-b, d (half-rhymed with b and c)-b-b, e (half-rhymed with b, c and d)-b-b; and the final stanza reverts the rhymes by beginning with b; and there are other, internal, rhymes in the original as well. The poem in English reads:

> the wind sways the fern
> it spreads its seed
>   save our bodies

the wind caresses the darkness
it climbs up the trees
    save our bodies

the wind wades in the water
it brightens the eyes of the fish
    save our bodies

the wind moans sadly
and clings to the leaves
    save our bodies

it stirs our bodies
it shakes our souls down upon us
    through out ravening eyes
    it enters us

All these highly crafted forms, which nonetheless look so natural on the page (there is a sort of mathematical elegance to them), reinforce the sense of suffocation and confinement. It is clear that Taufer's permutational structures, here and elsewhere, have nothing to do with verbal game-playing, rhetorical ostentation, or even a "return to traditional forms": elaborate formal schemes enable a resolute contemporary vision to draw on all the emotional force of archaic laments.

* * *

Taking off from a rich Slovene folkloric and literary heritage, as well as from the cultures of the country's several neighbors, contemporary Slovene writing can indeed be sophisticated and provocative. As Andrej Inkret reminds us in his "Two Melancholic Essays on Slovene Literature" (included in *Fragments from Slovene Literature*), the national literature maintains a particularly intense, even unique, relationship to language and identity. "For long centuries," explains Inkret, "the Slovene identity was almost exclusively a matter of language. Thus it is logical that poetry, in which language achieves its ultimate and most complex realization, became established as the most direct, reliable and authentic expression of the Slovene nationality principle." One of his striking observations is that "Slovene verbal art was never an unambiguous and pragmatic manifestation of a monolithic common conscience or national ideology." He adds:

> The "Sloveneness" to which poetry with its own language belonged in an essential way and in which it played a mythical "Orphean" role, was almost always marked with an essential skepticism and tragic irony and not infrequently with resistance and a catastrophic sarcasm. It is precisely because *both* were present in its lines that it can also be spoken of as true and authentic poetry.... Accordingly, poetry was never solely a foundation for the Slovene national conscience and social action but was in some manner always their problematization.

This spirit can be found in some of the many poets and writers anthologized in *Fragments from Slovene Literature*, which has been edited by Vanesa Matajc. Florjan Lipuš (b. 1937) even spoofs at the very idea of identity for a Slovene author by drafting a pseudo-biographical résumé of a writer whose "greatest works can only yield comparable effects in German translations"; Lipuš then lists, not the Slovene originals, but only the German titles. The aphorisms about communism and its discourse that are composed by Žarko Petan (b. 1929) sum up another integral element of the Slovene past. "All socialist fairy tales begin with the same words: 'Once upon a time, there will be...'" and "Those who sow words must import wheat" offer two examples. Petan slyly concludes: "I take back everything I have ever written between the lines." Other impressive pieces, though in a different key, are a long poetic prose text by Drago Jančar (b. 1948), entitled "The Look of an Angel," and a subtle love poem ("Eyes") by Gustav Januš (b. 1939). The anthology gathers texts from the onset of Slovene literature as well. Interestingly, two essential early texts are "Reflections on Language" written by the Protestant theologians and translators, Primož Tubar (1508-1586) and Adam Bohorič (1520-1598). The earliest text included is an ancient folk song retold by the highly influential and admired Romantic poet France Prešeren (1800-1849), one of whose poems—"Zdravljica" / "The Toast"—has become the national anthem and whose ubiquitous presence in Ljubljana is reinforced by countless memorial plaques, place names, postcards, souvenirs, and, most enchantingly, the bust of his idealized lover, Julija Primić, who gazes from an upper storey on Wolfova Street at his statue on nearby Prešernov Square. Significantly or not, I came across quite a lot of love poetry in Slovene. The aforementioned *The Voice in the Body* includes intriguingly succinct poems by Erika Vouk (b. 1941). Her sequence *Undulation* (2003) obliquely chronicles a love story (or perhaps stories); an absent lover often becomes increasingly present, as symbols are channeled into the precise sensate detail of an "icy sip of tequila":

> The night of corals and snow tide,
> a tower of solitude, cicadas,
> a gentle luster in the wolf's eye
> and tracks of bloody paws;
> a blunted wave, a shudder of remembrance
> across flowers and blue silk—
> icy sip of tequila.
> A word's scream is silence.

(translated by Ana Jelnikar and Kelly Lenox-Allan)

Maja Vidmar (b. 1961) also includes some of her arresting love lyrics in the same volume; they too end with a troubling taste in the mouth:

> A raised sword
> is the heart-sky—

without a breath
it touches the lips,
is the tongue-sky—
without pulling back
it savours the heart.

Never again
to pierce so precisely,
never again
to depart.
The taste of smooth metal
throbs in the mouth.

(translated by Ana Jelnikar and Kelly Lenox-Allan)

Before leaving Ljubljana (and with my lumbago successfully kept in check, indeed entombed like the lightning bolt), I spent much time examining the three full bookcases of "Slovene Literature in Translation," a section located on the second floor of the big crowded bookstore on Slovenska Avenue. Among various finds (including German versions of the short stories of Ivan Cankar, 1876-1918, who is the preeminent Slovene prose master), I came across a White Pine Press edition of Aleš Debeljak's *The City and the Child* (1999), smoothly translated by Christopher Merrill. Debeljak (b. 1961), who received his Ph.D. from Syracuse University and whose *Anxious Moments* (1994) and *Dictionary of Silence* (1999) have also appeared in the United States, writes densely imaged, intellectually elaborate sonnets that sometimes bring to mind the sensual "hermetic" poems of Eugenio Montale and other Italians. These particular sonnets are set during the Balkan War as well as during the first years of the life of the poet's first child, a girl. It is an at once touching and grim juxtaposition. One piece, entitled "Bosnian Elegy," is dedicated to the incisive Bosnian short-story writer Miljenko Jergović (the author of *Sarajevo Marlboro*, 1994) and encourages his friend not to "give up now, / when the gunners' fevered sights are trained on the stained façades / of museums and palaces." The penultimate piece focuses on "Edvard Kocbek, wherever you are."

This brings me back to the beginning of this letter. I must confess that I simply forgot to ask Veno Taufer or Barbara Shubert to give me the exact address of Kocbek's apartment building. When I remembered, it was April 27, Insurrection Day, a rain-drenched national holiday that turned into a rain-drenched long weekend during which all shops as well as the Slovene Writers' Association were closed; and on Monday morning I had to fly back over the Alps to France.

I later learned that Kocbek's apartment was located on the fourth floor of a complex that stands behind the Cankarjev Dom, the Cultural Center on Prešernova Avenue. (That's the name of the Romantic poet, once again.) I had walked by the complex several times, without realizing it. It matters little that

I was unable to pay homage *in situ* to Kocbek during my trip, for I am resolved to return to Ljubljana. As you see, I have discovered much else in the meantime. Debeljak's sonnet invokes Kocbek as a poetic and moral force during a period in which Yugoslavia had been torn apart. Even though Slovenia is now thankfully beyond the threat of interethnic war (which is still viable in several areas of former Yugoslavia), the final seven lines indicate how Slovene literature continues to seek a compelling genuineness:

You sing calmly. Landslides and floods and the death masks

of poets proclaim their secrets through you. In the hourglass, the thread
of sand has stopped. A dove has returned from a great distance,
and the ark slowly glides into the unknown. The pale sun expands

in the hearts of the masses when they hear you. For you sing to them.
A compass needle trembles: a migraine's endless wave. Pregnant women and
old men sing with you, their throats growing moist. No one can stop them.

Bosnia and Herzegovina

A Letter from Sarajevo
(Miljenko Jergović, Vidosav Stevanović, Aleksandar Hemon, Velibor Čolić, and Svetislav Basara)

If you struggle with the moral questions raised by the disastrous political commitments of certain otherwise stimulating or even essential writers, then ponder this anecdote. It goes back to the years 1992-1995, when Sarajevo was besieged by Serbian paramilitaries and the Serbian-controlled Yugoslavian Army, and when civilians—dashing through the streets for water or food—were being killed daily by snipers hiding in the surrounding high hills. The Russian novelist Edward Limonov (who is the author of the best-selling *It's Me, Eddie*, among other books, and who had become pro-Serbian with respect to the Balkan War and ultra-nationalist with respect to his homeland) arrived at an army outpost on the Trebević mountain flanking the town, then was filmed as he shot machine-gun rounds down at scurrying Sarajevo inhabitants.

This may be old news to you: the event was featured in Pawel Pawlikowski's 1992 BBC documentary "Serbian Epics," and the footage was later used as prosecution evidence at the trial, in The Hague, of the Serbian ethnic cleanser Radovan Karadžić, whom Limonov had befriended. *Mea culpa*: like most European and American writers—Juan Goytisolo and Susan Sontag are conspicuous exceptions—to whom the Balkan War, however close geographically, was at best a very distant concern, I was unaware of much of this until I arrived in Sarajevo for ten days in the spring of 2005.

A decade had passed since the Dayton Agreement (21 November 1995) brought a still fragile end to the Balkan War, yet memories of this gruesome anecdote involving Limonov had not faded. It was spontaneously recounted to me on three different occasions by Sarajevans, none of them writers, who were trying to convey what the treacherous siege was like. The specter of a novelist aiming at men and women lugging jerricans epitomizes, for such survivors, the widespread calculated cruelty and murdering that marked the war and changed probably forever a town famous for its centuries-long, more or less peaceful, cohabitation of Muslims, Roman Catholics, Orthodox Christians, and Jews. Indeed, the square (Trg Oslobodenja) where I drafted parts of this letter, while

I was sitting on a bench near the bust of the too-little-known novelist Meša Selimović (the author of the deep-probing, Sarajevo-set, psychological novels *Death and the Dervish* [1966] and *The Fortress* [1970]), is flanked by the large Serbian Orthodox Church; if you pass by the many outdoor chess players and cross the square, then turn right, the Catholic cathedral stands just a little off Ferhadija, the pedestrian shopping street; continue on your way, down Ferhadija, and you soon arrive at the great Gazi-Husrev-Begova mosque; and a few yards more, to the left up a narrow passageway, is the old synagogue, now a museum devoted to the history of the local Jewish population, most of whom were exterminated by the Nazis during the Second World War. Within a few minutes' walking distance from there is the bridge near which the Archduke Ferdinand was assassinated by the Serbian nationalist Gavrilo Princip on 28 June 1914—the event that sparked the First World War. Under that bridge flows the muddy, reddish Miljacka River, an incessant symbol of earth mixed with copious blood.

One of my interlocutors, named Igor, insisted on driving me up a winding road to the spot from which Limonov had fired his rounds. It is an overlook not far from the former bobsled run of the 1984 Winter Olympics, and the slope descending from there down to the town is still specked with thousands of anti-personal mines. Signs warn hikers to stop. "No walking anymore in these lovely mountains, let alone skiing and sledding," Igor pointed out, adding that his own adolescence had been nipped in the bud and that he himself had taken up arms to defend his hometown. The offspring of a mixed Croatian-Serbian marriage, he was not alone among non-Muslims in deciding to remain and side with his fellow Sarajevans, the majority of whom are of Muslim origin. "It was only during the war," he related, "that we learned to listen to first names ethnically—sometimes with disastrous consequences. Up to then, I never paid any attention. We are all Slavs and speak the same language." Now, after the war, Igor sometimes finds himself painfully stigmatized—depending on whom he is talking to—for being neither "purely" Serbian nor Croatian nor Muslim. In one of the moving short stories of *Sarajevo Marlboro* (1994), Miljenko Jergović (b. 1966), recalling the war, similarly notes that

> as time went by the Muslims and the Croats began to listen to the firebrands among their leaders. They began to look askance at each other and then to set fire to one another's houses. Each community went its own way—some escaping to Zenica, others from Zenica to neighboring towns. They dug trenches for several weeks and then the chaos began. Wherever you went there was blood and shooting.... We battled over each field, over plots of land to which none had given a second thought until then.

From Trebević mountain, Igor and I had "an excellent view of the hills around Sarajevo, which are dotted with white Turkish tombstones," as Jergović also states with bitter irony. Resembling so many small Arlington cemeteries (each similarly impressive in its stark row-by-row accounting of manslaughter), well over a dozen Muslim graveyards sprouted up every hillside during the war. Some ancient graveyards adjoining modest neighborhood mosques likewise became overcrowded with white, turban-crowned, pillar-like stones. And this sight continued to bring back all the horror and hubris of the Limonov incident. It was, moreover, all the more tangible for me in that I had run into and chatted with the Russian novelist a few times during the 1980s, when we were both living in Paris. We had writer-friends in common. His act has kept me thinking about writers' oft-troubled relationship to reality, and I thus do not mean reality as it is aimed at merely through the sights of crafted language. A cynical French novelist once speculated that "perhaps in the final reckoning...the goal of this coup d'état, with all its consequences, was simply to offer attractive scenes enticing talented men of letters to write about them."

Gustave Flaubert knew well how human conflict and suffering can allure writers (independently of any sympathy for the victims), sometimes politically deluding them in the process. His remark is quoted by the dissident Serbian novelist Vidosav Stevanović (b. 1942) in his memoir *Voleurs de leur propre liberté*, which became available in French in 2003. Living in political exile in Paris since 1992, Stevanović takes the Frenchman's comment literally in order to raise the question of how aesthetics relate to ethics. "Ethics nonetheless still concerns [writers]," cautions Stevanović, "who use aesthetics as an excuse for hiding their head in the sand and refusing to participate, to accept responsibility."

This is a classic call for political concern and direct writerly commitment. A democrat and a long-standing adversary of Balkan nationalisms, the novelist had returned to his homeland during the crucial period mid-December 1996—mid-July 1997, in order to take part in the growing opposition movement against Slobodan Milošević. It then seemed that Serbia could become more democratic. Stevanović's memoir recounts the failure of this movement, and castigates the intellectuals who eventually exchanged their ideals for political privileges. His chronologically intricate novel, *Abel et Lise*, which was also translated into French in 2003, similarly evokes the personal destruction waged by the rise of nationalist sentiment, in this case as it tragically affects the now separate lives of two former lovers, an Albanian man and a Serbian woman.

In Stevanović, the political dichotomies are clear-cut (however literarily engaging), but let me return to Flaubert's more psychological observation about the motivations of some writers attracted to war and suffering. Several of Jergović's stories in *Sarajevo Marlboro* scrutinize authorial or journalistic inspiration per se, raising the additional question of how events are consequently construed from various vantage points. The lesson formulated both by him and another compelling Bosnian writer, Aleksandar Hemon (b. 1964), much of whose formally sophisticated collection *The Question of Bruno* (2000), written directly in English, concerns the dilemma of a young Sarajevan writer who finds himself in Chicago on a scholarship when the war breaks out in his hometown, is that even well-meaning outside observers are inevitably trapped into viewing events according to their wishes about how such events should be viewed. Both Hemon and Jergović are interested in the phenomenology of violence, hatred, and survival, as well as in how such phenomena are perceived, especially by writer-eyewitnesses, writers-newly-arrived-on-the-scene, and writers-in-exile. More generally, they overturn the too simplistic Western understanding of the Balkan War as an *irrational* ethnic and nationalistic confrontation.

The two short-story writers are not alone in espousing this viewpoint. As quoted by Ammiel Alcalay in his preface to *Sarajevo Marlboro*, the Slovene theorist Slavoj Žižek, for example, posits that

> in former Yugoslavia, we are lost not because of our primitive dreams and myths preventing us from speaking the enlightened language of Europe, but because we pay in flesh the price of being the stuff the Other's dreams are made of.... Far from being the Other of Europe, former Yugoslavia was rather Europe itself in its Other-ness, the screen onto which Europe projected its own repressed reverse.... Against today's journalistic commonplace about the Balkans as the madhouse of thriving nationalisms where rational rules of behavior are suspended, one must point out again and again that the moves of every political agent in former Yugoslavia, reprehensible as they may be, are totally rational within the goals they want to attain—the only exception, the only truly irrational factor in it, is the gaze of the West, babbling about archaic ethnic passions.

I'm sure that Flaubert would have understood Žižek's point about passionate or violent behavior actually concealing a devastating, rigorous, Machiavellian logic—applied by outside, sometimes initially opaque and undesignated sources—that one must pinpoint and define if one is to make some sense of the reality transpiring before one's eyes. Such is the gist of Jergović's story "The Letter," in which the narrator finds a missive that has been sent to a man in Sarajevo who, before receiving it, was killed by a sniper while he was standing in his doorway smoking a cigarette. It turns out that the letter has been written by an African who had originally come from a non-aligned country and had settled in Sarajevo during the years (between 1948 and 1980) when Yugoslavia, ruled by Marshal Tito, was itself a non-aligned Communist nation. In his letter to his Bosnian friend, the African explains why he has fled the city and details how hard it is for the foreigners, where he is now living in exile, to understand the war. Significantly and tragically, the letter cannot be answered; it is in the writer's hands, in all senses of the expression.

"The Gravedigger" likewise stages an encounter between the writer-narrator and an American journalist. "I understand that he is researching the subject for his article," pointedly explains the writer (who has become a gravedigger), "except he can't write the piece because he already knows what it's going to say." This, too, is a caveat for any well-intentioned writer desiring to probe behind the epiphenomena of reality. Even more incisively, a story about one

Slobodan, who is an idiot, describes how one of the first CNN bulletins from Sarajevo contained footage of the retarded man wandering aimlessly through the city as dozens of shells exploded on all sides." "The camera followed him for about seventy yards," adds Jergović,

> no doubt because the journalists were expecting to capture the moment when the Serb onslaught destroyed an innocent life in Sarajevo. Slobodan very casually sauntered over to the cameraman and gave him a warm smile.... He didn't stop. He just went on his way as the shells continued to fall. That night the reporter, with some disappointment, informed viewers that there were insanely brave people living in Sarajevo.

While I was exploring the streets and back streets, I thus often thought of the different ways in which writers have responded to, or spurned, objective reality. I thought of how reality has been variously defined by writers and philosophers alike. In Sarajevo, it is certainly hard not to be overwhelmed by the brute (and brutal) factuality of nearly everything in sight. War scars are omnipresent: bomb-devastated edifices that have not yet been razed and replaced; weeds and even trees that have sprouted up through shattered concrete; the half-destroyed helicopter, tank, and sundry artillery vehicles that are rusting behind the Historical Museum and next to the National Museum with its stunning Bogomil gravestones and excellent wild animal, bird, and insect collections; countless shell-dented walls and bullet-pelted balconies (sometimes with blooming flowers in a pot or two); numerous smoke-blackened windowless apartments in buildings also containing attractively curtained flats that have been repaired. In the small shops of the Bascarsi Muslim quarter in the old town, not far from the phosphorus-bombed National Library (everything was lost), you can buy obuses of all shapes and sizes that have been transformed into vases, pen holders, and ashtrays. Dire contrasts such as these pop up at every corner.

As for the human realities of the Balkan War, two remarkable collections of short prose by the Bosnian Velibor Čolić (b. 1964) focus—like Hemon and Jergović's stories—on the kinds of telltale detail which, if you prefer keeping your emotions intact, you had better avoid. Written on the spot during the fighting and available in French, *Les Bosniaques* (1993) and *Chronique des oubliés* (1994) recall both the short-prose interludes of Hemingway's *In Our Time* and Daniel Zimmermann's terse eyewitness accounts of Algerian War scenes (*Nouvelles de la zone interdite*). One also thinks of Marcel Cohen's volumes of short-prose reports on all sorts of disturbing contemporary phenomena. Like Cohen, Čolić's concise texts record extremely grim facts, without proffering the slightest moral judgment. For this reason, the images are all the more harrowing:

> The guards of the Doboj concentration camp dragged Jozo the prisoner *by the balls* to the toilet of the former Federal Army barracks, now transformed into a prison. When he was finally able to prop himself back up, he saw the Serbian emblem (the four C's) drawn on a mirror with human shit. The guards forced him to lick it off.

No direct transition can link this despicable scene and *Chinese Letter*, a novel by the Serbian writer Svetislav Basara (b. 1953), yet the book provided an unexpected coda to my Sarajevan sojourn. Published in Serbian in 1984, the novel is unrelated to the Balkan War. But from the very first sentence, with its evocation of jarred identities ("My name is Fritz. Yesterday I had a different name.") and with the author's tense first allusions to a 100-page statement that he has been ordered to write by two unnamed, threatening men, a grim political tragedy seemingly looms on the horizon. *Chinese Letter* is informed by the communist ethos of Eastern Europe and, more specifically, by the increasing tensions, following upon the death of Tito in 1980, among politically manipulated ethnic populations in a Yugoslavia already falling apart. Yet this historical and political background does not sufficiently describe the unsettling ambience of the book. There are echoes of Kafka and Beckett, but also of Stephen King and Agatha Christie. Major philosophical concerns are what it means when "something happens," and the question, too, of what the writer should do with whatever he thinks an "event" or "incident" means.

These questions alone were sufficiently pertinent to what I had seen and learned in Sarajevo. Indeed, Basara ominously (and sometimes jocularly) tells various stories and conjures up quite a lot of disturbing trivia, all the while reflecting on the logic underlying everyday life. It is impossible to sum up his at once capricious and hyper-logical narration, which constantly moves from the routines and common facts of the quotidian to something opaque and undefined and threatening. As I was reworking my notes for this Letter, long after I had returned home to France, two sentences from *Chinese Letter* kept haunting me. Let me quote both as tentative summaries of my Sarajevan experiences. The first points to the problem of determining the rational connections among what one sees, how one lives, and what one writes. "On paper everything has its direction, its logic," claims Basara, "but in reality everything that happens except for this logic is unclear." The second quotation concerns a girl without an arm: "What is this girl going to do, asks the author, "in [a] world in which even two hands aren't enough to cover your face with?"

Serbia

Pleasure and the Deeper Ambivalence
(Radmila Lazić)

Radmila Lazić (b. 1949) is a Serbian feminist and was the founder of the Civil Resistance Movement during the Milošević years. Yet it would be a mistake to confine the thirty-six poems of *A Wake for the Living*, which have been vividly translated by Charles Simic, to the specific realms of political poetry or woman's literature.

Above all, Lazić writes about sensing and accepting one's body as perishable matter nonetheless capable of giving and receiving exalted sexual pleasure; and thus about boldly asserting one's individuality — in the face of inevitable death — through such pleasure. In her forthright evocations, she often rejects all concomitant aspirations for lasting relationships. "Many times I fell in love forever," she admits in "Sorry, My Lord," "My heart was a hot stove. / Now the jug is broken. / Let there be sex unsustained by love / Is my slogan now."

Such lines build on the lucid eroticism of any number of European folksongs, not to mention the lyrics of our own (uncensored) Blues. In her "Dorothy Parker Blues," notably, Lazić avows: "I'm putting on my black panties, / Covering my still-hairy crotch. / I paint my lips, fluff my hair, / Climb on a pair of heels. / I'm ready for you." Yet after several like assertions, this telltale confession suddenly appears in italics: "*I'm writing my life hour by hour.*"

By means of such phrases, Lazić adds unexpected perspectives to her funny, ribald lyricism. "The history of solitude is long," she more quietly notes elsewhere, "It's made up of a string of individuals / That resemble one another like blades of grass.../ Each speaks one of the dead languages / The way a lake speaks with its silence." A vigorous antidote to prudery and moral correctness ("goodness is boring," she quips), *A Wake for the Living* simultaneously explores existential loneliness and hopelessness. The title perfectly sums up this deeper ambivalence.

Greece

Intricacies of Exile
(Georgios Vizyenos)

Translations of works such as the six stories by Georgios Vizyenos (1849-1896) that are included in *My Mother's Sin and Other Stories* remind us that the history of modern prose should not be viewed as it is often taught: as a linear progression of forms invented by a select group of writers. Vizyenos, like his contemporary Alexandros Papadiamantis, is an innovative author who deserves a chapter in any history of European fiction. As Roderick Beaton remarks in his foreword, Vizyenos's stories have been "dramatically" re-evaluated in recent years. (He is writing in 1988.) Indeed, adds Beaton, "compromise over the language question has encouraged a new look at the *katharevousa* [purist Greek] writers of the last century, and twentieth-century modernism and radical critical approaches to literature have placed a new emphasis on the complexity and intellectual subtlety that distinguish [Vizyenos's] work." The language question has also made a writer such as Vizyenos of particular interest to contemporary poets.

Beaton situates Vizyenos's fiction within contexts of European realism and its Greek counterpart in the 1880s and 1890s, *ithographia*. Mentioning the author's sympathetic portrayal of the Turkish character Moscov-Selim and his implicit rejection of militarism and Greek nationalism, Beaton goes on to demonstrate how, "by setting his characters so they straddle the most sacred boundaries that determine identity for each of us and define, in consequence, our perception of reality, Vizyenos…brings into question the nature of identity and of reality as constructed by reason and the senses."

Will Vizyenos be quarry for psychoanalysts? Mothers are domineering in his stories; some male characters are raised as girls. The story "Who Was My Brother's Killer?" begins with a description of the "coquette," a French male servant who, according to the narrator's mother, "had a feminine, that is to say, smooth-shaven face and was unable to stand on his feet without bowing his head and shaking his tail." The suffering of the unaccepted, unloved, or maladjusted is an underlying theme of every one of these tales. Vizyenos's penetrating examination of the ambiguous relationships at the heart of family life is equaled in contemporary Greek literature perhaps only in Kostas Taktsis's fiction, especially his novel *The Third Wedding Wreath* (1963).

Vizyenos's psychological insight is reflected in the structures of his complex narrative art. Often the primary narrator, sometimes named Yoryis (note the resemblance to the author's first name, a fact masked by transliteration), has little to say and turns over the burden of telling the lengthy story to another character: his mother, his grandfather, his brother, his friend, or his fellow passenger. The hapless soldier Moscov-Selim indeed talks for pages on end. But do the "frightful dramas" which these characters relate and in which the narrator sometimes becomes an actor constitute the essential tales? As mother or brother expatiates on their woes, the estrangement of the well-meaning son or sibling is gradually revealed. He has been "far, far away"; he has "got ahead in the world and taken a name from learned circles"—even as Vizyenos, baptized simply "George the son of Michael," took his surname from his village in Eastern Thrace, Vizo or Vizy, prompting his own mother to remark later: "Nowadays, when they write about him in the newspapers, even I don't know if it's really my own child they're talking about, or some European!" This estrangement becomes all the more poignant when Yoryis returns to his role as the primary narrator and, as if he had been an eyewitness, describes scenes that occurred during his absence: "Once they told [my mother] I had run into money problems in Constantinople and had turned Turk.... Once they told her I had shipwrecked on the shores of Cyprus and was dressed in rags and begging in the streets." Vizyenos's stories give to the common Greek theme of exile an unsurpassed intricacy.

Only a stylistic quibble or two can be made about William F. Wyatt's skillful and accurate translation of these difficult texts. Vizyenos occasionally employs words of Turkish origin. In most cases, Wyatt, having defined the terms in the introduction to each story, leaves them as such in the English. However, in stories such as "Who Was My Brother's Killer?", "The Only Journey of His Life," or "Moscov-Selim," the translation is somewhat overburdened with italicized foreign words. Nearly all such terms are (and as the translator remarks, were) understood by the Greek reader, found in Greek dictionaries, and thus should be regarded as assimilated foreign terms in modern Greek. However interesting from the folkloric or lexicological viewpoint the terms may be, should not some of them (like *duniá* "the world, this life" or *dértia* "griefs, troubles") have been translated into English? Similarly, terms such as *harémi*, *kalpáki*, *konáki*, *kaïki*, or *fermáni*, italicized and accented as such in Wyatt's version, are in fact the Hellenized forms of Turkish or Arabic words that are found in English-language dictionaries ("harem," "calpac," "konak," "caïque," "firman"). "Giaour," also found in the dictionary, is italicized and given an accent (*giaoúr*); "kiosk" is given an accent and a Greek ending (*kióski*); "bazaar" becomes *pazári*. Wyatt rightly seeks to retain "a bit of the color of the original," but by adopting the Hellenized forms of such words and not those by which they are known in English he overshoots his target.

Invoking Saint Alexandros Papadiamantis

With exception of Nikos Kazantzakis (1885-1957), Greek fiction writers, classic and contemporary, are rarely and never extensively translated into English. This neglect, which contrasts with the worldwide popularity of several outstanding Greek poets, is reason enough to applaud a translation of twelve short stories by Alexandros Papadiamantis (1851-1911). Elizabeth Constantinides's translation, entitled *Tales from a Greek Island*, has been impatiently awaited: only a few of Papadiamantis's 170 stories have previously appeared in English, though three different versions of his powerful novella about a poverty-stricken child-killing mother, *The Murderess* (1903), have existed in the past.

In Greece, the interest of Papadiamantis's prose is considered to lie well beyond his mere chronological place in literary history, his career coinciding with the beginnings of modern Greek fiction. Ever since the lifetime of this "saint of modern Greek letters" or "father of modern Greek prose"—as he is often called by his literary disciples—a critical battle has been fought over the so-called technical shortcomings of his novels, novellas, and short stories. Professors of literature have tended to square off against the numerous poets and writers who have championed him from the very beginning. In his classic *A History of Modern Greek Literature* (1972), for instance, Professor C. Th. Dimaras declares in effect that Papadiamantis's work can be read with pleasure only by people who are not connoisseurs of serious literature.

However, if until recently—I am writing in 1987—a large number of professors of literature have seconded this judgment, a classic poet like Kostis Palamas (1859-1943) was already among Papadiamantis's early defenders. For C. P. Cavafy (1863-1933), Papadiamantis was the "pinnacle of pinnacles." Odysseus Elytis (1911-1996), who devoted a book to him, wrote in Psalm XI of *The Axion Esti*:

> Wherever evil finds you, brothers,
> wherever your mind clouds over,
> invoke Dionysios Solomos
> and invoke Alexandros Papadiamantis.
> Their speech that knows no lie
> will bring rest to a martyr's face
> with a little glaucous dye on the lips.

(trans. Jeffrey Carson and Nikos Sarris)

To these praises can be added the articles, studies, literary memoirs, sundry homages, and creative works written by dozens of other Greek writers, such as the materials collected in *Alexandros Papadiamantis* (1979), *Phota olophota* (1981), and a special double issue of the review *Diavazo* (No. 165, March 1987). With the simultaneous publication of an exemplary critical edition by N. D. Triantafyllopoulos, it can be said that even academic interest in Papadiamantis is growing. A consensus of approval seems at last to have formed. In Greece, Papadiamantis is now rightly considered to be a writer of no less importance than Cavafy, Elytis, or George Seferis (1900-1971), the latter also being one of his early admirers.

Above all, it is Papadiamantis's mastery of the Greek language that the Greek poets have praised. His richly textured musical prose is typically composed of the purist idiom (*katharevousa*) in the narrative parts and of the dialect of his native island, Skiathos, in the dialogues—rather in the manner of Mark Twain, an author whom he had translated into Greek. Moreover, as Constantinides points out, Papadiamantis's style is further enriched by his use of straightforward demotic forms, Byzantine ecclesiastical Greek, and even ancient Greek. Excepting his near-contemporaries Emmanuel Roidis (1836-1904) and Georgios Vizyenos (1849-1896), who also used *katharevousa* in combination with other levels of diction, no Greek writer is more difficult to translate.

Constantinides's selection offers several of the best and most famous stories. Through them, all of Papadiamantis's characteristic themes are expressed with graphic realism and unequalled passion: the superstitions of village life, the corruption of the Orthodox faith, the plight of women abandoned by their husbands or sons, the oppressive obligation of dowering girls, the necessity of economic emigration, the pernicious influx of foreign mores into Greek life, the extreme poverty afflicting much of the population, and the ravages of tuberculosis and alcoholism.

Other stories, more personal in tone, have a quality of reverie, the author recollecting his childhood in Skiathos while eking out his living in Athens as so many islanders and provincials of his generation were forced to do. Also present in Papadiamantis's writing is an undeniable mythical or Biblical dimension. In her introduction, Constantinides observes that long before James Joyce, the Greek author "had used myth as an organizing principle" for the plots of stories such as "The American," "Love the Harvester," and "The Haunted Bridge," and "had made, to quote Eliot on Joyce, a 'continuous parallel between contemporaneity and antiquity.'" Constantinides compares Papadiamantis to Thomas Hardy, Alphonse Daudet, Theodor Storm, and Giovanni Verga. The latter parallel is particularly apt. Let me add that, although their respective styles differ to the extent that Papadiamantis was a realist who must have found more direct affinities with the French, English, or American realists whose stories he translated (Mark Twain, Bret Harte, Rudyard Kipling, Émile Zola, Guy de Maupassant), some of his tales distinctly recall the Puritan world of

Nathaniel Hawthorne: both authors were perspicacious explorers of evil, of the shadowy realms of the soul, and of the role of religion in a tightly knit village community. "The Matchmaker" notably depicts a shy narrator who is tortured by religious guilt and longs in vain for an inaccessible sweetheart. No Greek author, as Constantinides remarks, has created such an abundance of characters, plots, and settings.

With greater explicitness, however, than in Hawthorne's ever-allusive *Twice-Told Tales* or *The Scarlet Letter*, several of Papadiamantis's stories are marked by a delicate, voyeuristic eroticism. In "Love the Harvester," for example, the narrator notes: "As soon as they left the little town, the girl had said she was hot and removed her bodice. Then, with only a long-sleeved chemise over her white cotton camisole, her slender waist, graceful stance, and smooth breasts showed to greater advantage. The swelling flesh beneath the thin camisole hinted that here was a store of pale lilies, dewy and freshly cut, with veins the color of a white rose." The most memorable erotic scene occurs in "A Dream among the Waters," as the narrator, hiding behind a boulder, observes Moschoula bathing in the nude. In "The Homesick Wife," there is a more modest, yet no less evocative, image of an accidental joining of hands. Papadiamantis often evokes the tension of amorous longing; he is a master of the difficult art of suggestiveness, ever keeping it in stylistic balance with his meticulous descriptions of local customs or landscapes.

Constantinides's translation follows the original faithfully and for this reason reads more felicitously in the narrative descriptions than in the dialogues. Although when searching for an equivalent of the Skiathos dialect she rightly eschews English dialectical forms that for the reader would "bring associations and connotations that do not belong in stories about a small Greek island at the turn of the century," the mere use of a slang term or a contraction does not suffice to render a dialect; a syntax mirroring that of colloquial speech must also be employed. Sometimes, in the dialogues, Constantinides follows the Greek too closely; sometimes the speeches, with a slang term or a contraction inserted, are corseted in the same syntax used in the more elegant English of the descriptions. And of course it is important when translating dialogue to determine whether a character is shouting, whispering, or speaking in a normal tone. If shouting in English, wouldn't Mr. Monahakis shout "hey!" instead of the sibilant "say!" ascribed to him (the Greek is "e!")?

A fault more grievous than the occasionally inadequate English equivalent—once again, the obstacles involved in rendering Papadiamantis into English are overwhelming—is that the paragraph breaks in the Triantafyllopoulos edition are not respected. In a translation, paragraphs cannot always be started and ended as in the original, but here they are rarely so and Papadiamantis is a writer for whom a paragraph is often a matter of only two or three sentences. In addition, in the Greek text direct discourse is indented, that is only rarely embedded in a paragraph or attached to an introductory sentence. The author's prolix descriptions and digressions read much more easily when the paragraphs are arranged as in the original, than when they appear in unjustifiably cumbersome lengths. Several of Papadiamantis's notorious repetitions, so often criticized by the professors, can likewise (in the short paragraphs of the original) be seen as the natural detours or recapitulations of the engaging storyteller. They have a curious narrative logic all their own.

There are a few other problems. The translator might have respected the italics sometimes used by the author for emphasis (the "yet," for example, in "So you haven't yet decided to remarry," p. 55). Here and there, a phrase is suppressed without explanation (e.g., the phrase "ego o satyriskos tou vounou" is missing, p. 90). In Papadiamantis's most famous story, "A Dream among the Waters," "Ksarmeno" is introduced as a local variant of the place-name "Xanemo." Papadiamantis then typically explains its etymology; there is no reason to replace the former term by the latter in the translation (p. 85). One of the most telling characteristics of a story by Papadiamantis is topographic and toponymic precision, a quality that in turn reinforces the credibility of the narrator as an "insider." Movingly manifest in the care with which the author designates and describes places is also his love, indeed his nostalgia, for his native island. More generally, this ethnographic concern of Greek (and other European) writers, faced with the destruction of landscapes and lifestyles that they loved as children, is never superfluous. This is one of the aspects of modern European writing that are not always readily understood by American readers.

Similar is Papadiamantis's genealogical precision. He ever specifies who exactly is the mother or father of whom, a stylistic trait perfectly suited to the village community that he describes and to the language that therein was spoken. Such genealogical alignments sometimes lead the translator into unnatural avoidances of the Saxon genitive, unless of course a level of diction reminiscent of the King James Version of the Bible is intended (cf. "Zogara, Zakhos's mother," p. 97, and "Kratira, the daughter of Andreola," p. 48). And why in "Fortune from America" is the name "Yiannis" translated as "John," a former practice of translators, whereas elsewhere the Greek names are transliterated? Why is *laghouto* sometimes translated as "lute" and sometimes simply transliterated? Why is *viola* (or a derivative term) sometimes translated as "violin" and sometimes, more correctly, as "fiddle"? Repeated in the introduction is the common bibliographic error that Papadiamantis, who published his stories in magazines, never saw a selection published in book form in his lifetime. In fact, a French translation of two stories appeared in book form in 1908.

As Greek writers and poets have long insisted, it is to Papadiamantis's style that one must look to comprehend the force and originality of his narrative art. He is far from being—perhaps because of his extensive early experience as a translator—the country bumpkin author that he was accused of being by academics; behind his apparent naïveté lies a sure sense of literary technique. Criticized for the seemingly haphazard construction of his stories, Papadiamantis consciously followed the impulses of an authentic, profound inspiration. What once seemed to be a regional art, more of folkloristic than of literary interest, moves us still, nearly a century later. It can only be hoped that these twelve stories will one day encourage the translation of all the others, so that Papadiamantis can at last take his rightful place, outside of Greece, as a major author.

A Bayeux Tapestry à la grecque
(Stratis Myrivilis)

A classic well-known in Eastern Europe, Italy, and France, Stratis Myrivilis's *Life in the Tomb* (1924) is, as the translator Peter Bien remarked (in 1987), "the single most successful and most widely read serious novel in Greece in the period since the Great War, having sold 80,000 copies—an astonishing figure for that small country." His excellent translation (a first edition appeared in 1977) could not be more welcome. Only two other books by Myrivilis (1892-1969) have been available in English, *The Schoolmistress with the Golden Eyes* (1933) and *The Mermaid Madonna* (1949). Along with *Life in the Tomb*, these two novels form a trilogy about human behavior in war. The original Greek title is drawn from a lamentation sung in the Greek Orthodox church on Good Friday: "Thou O Christ, the Life, in the tomb was laid, and armies of angels were amazed, and they glorified Thy humiliation."

The novel consists of fifty-seven short chapters, every one except the first purportedly a letter written by one Sergeant Anthony Kostoulas, during the trench warfare on the Macedonian front in 1917-1918. Kostoulas is described as "a university student, tall and olive-complexioned," and he sends these letters to his beloved. Yet the narrative structure of *Life in the Tomb* is more intricate than a mere epistolary novel. In the first chapter (or "prologue"), Myrivilis employs the literary artifice of claiming that he himself had fought with Kostoulos during the war—the author in fact spent the decade 1912-1922 fighting in the Balkan Wars, the First World War, and the Asia Minor campaign—and that while he was rummaging through an old chest he had come across a bundle of copybooks, the Sergeant's manuscripts. (Kostoulas, we learn, was accidentally incinerated by a flame-thrower while he was in battle with the Bulgarians.) The author resolves to publish the manuscripts, remarking that if the "girl is real, not imaginary, and if she is still alive, I must ask her to forgive my audacity."

This rather sophisticated narrative structure—the author finds not a bundle of letters, but rather a bundle of copybooks containing the manuscript of an epistolary novel—has other subtle qualities. Many of the letters can be read independently, as if they were short stories, to the extent that one might first sense that the book, as a novel, exemplarily lacked "the immense force derivable from totality"—to recall Edgar Allan Poe's criticism of novels in general.

Yet it is precisely this heterogeneous aspect of the anecdotes, vignettes, and transcribed thoughts that verily mirror the Sergeant's life as a volunteer in the Greek Army. He notably experiences those "monotonous, sluggish, wearying days" when soldiers must seek out distractions while awaiting battle, "the irremovable shadow of death which weighs relentlessly upon [them]." Instead of appealing to a more concise, unified plot, or taking advantage of the narrative cohesion that battlefield suspense would provide, Myrivilis grips his reader on a more profound level; beneath the many digressions flows a single, not always visible undercurrent: the inexorable progression of a human being towards the front, towards combat, towards death. Only by revealing the everyday life of a soldier through haphazard anecdotes, or by means of ethnographic details, can Myrivilis ask this question toward the end of the book: "How could the 'human being' inside me have disappeared so completely, leaving only the patrol-leader and warrior behind?" *Life in the Tomb* is thus also the diary of a volunteer who loses his illusions and grows capable of the most penetrating self-observation. Through the Sergeant's voice, Myrivilis makes this declaration toward the end; it also implicitly justifies his original combination of fiction and exact reportage:

> These blasted papers have begun to take up too much room in my pack. Maybe I shall even roll them up and stuff them inside the casing of a .15 shell, inscribing on the bronze with a nail, in great big striking letters: "The true story of a soldier." Because sometime, surely sometime, this evil crisis which the conscience of humanity is experiencing will dwindle away—this crisis which leads those who have seen war to produce counterfeit versions of it in various genres of printed matter, out of fear, fanaticism or vainglorious conceit. When the end does come, perhaps at that time—sometime—the voice of a plain soldier will emerge into the light of day, a voice which will possess the courage to tell the whole truth without fear of court-martial or defamation, because it will be the voice of a corpse…. You must possess close, first-hand experience of this improbable life so full of despicable baseness and pseudo-chivalry if you want to see what role this dumb-show plays in a multitude of fine upstanding men—grown-up, settled characters with a whole armful of mustache beneath their noses.

Focused well beyond ideological and nationalistic concerns, Myrivilis above all scrutinizes human behavior. The battlefield might have been any battlefield from Homer's Troy to the Skra di Legen here depicted; the war, any war of brutal carnage fought "in darkness…so thick [that] probably even God himself was unable to witness it." Soldiers, officers, friends, enemies, prisoners, mothers, children, and loved ones are portrayed with realism and humanity. They are stitched one by one into this Bayeux Tapestry *à la grecque*, of memorably epic proportions.

The Innate Passion and the Apotheosis (Odysseus Elytis)

Despite his 1979 Nobel Prize, Odysseus Elytis (1911-1996) remains less known in English-speaking countries than C. P. Cavafy (1863-1933). No two poets could be more antithetical. The work of the latter is realistic, pessimistic, agnostic, ironic, emotionally sober, and limpid in style (though certain idiosyncratic spellings and syntactic originalities are masked by translations), while the poetry of Elytis is lyrical, optimistic, exuberantly erotic, surrealist in metaphor, cosmic in scope, often oracular and sometimes quite obscure. Moreover, whereas Cavafy revives minor historical figures, focuses on societal margins, and half-discloses his own experiences as a hesitant homosexual in turn-of-the-century Alexandria, Elytis's jubilant "I" sings the "glittering sensations[s]" of the Aegean islands, exalts "korai beautiful and naked and smooth as a beach pebble," and possesses that Whitmanesque quality of standing for all Greeks in all ages. When Elytis asks—with an exclamation point—in his masterpiece, *The Axion Esti* (1959), "where can I find my soul * the four-leaf teardrop!," the narrator characteristically speaks as an Adamic figure: "he who I truly was He many aeons ago / He still green in the fire He uncut from the sky." Even a pellucid phrase such as "secret syllables through which I strove to articulate my identity" refers only secondarily to the poet's struggles with self and language (with the "huge crimson rose...tangled in my tongue," as he puts it elsewhere) and more generally designates the toils of a Greek Everyman-Poet who recurs in, and unifies, a multifaceted lifework.

Given the continuity of Greek literature (a theme stressed in the Nobel lecture), perhaps it could be said that two poetic lineages are brilliantly set forth by Cavafy and Elytis: on the one hand, a humanistic vision reaching back to Archilochus's confessional utterances, to the realistic passages of Sappho, to the epigrams of *The Greek Anthology,* and to the "mimes" of everyday life as were written by Herondas and other Alexandrians; on the other, a pantheistic, indeed cosmogonic lyricism comprising Pindar's odes, the pronouncements of the pre-Socratic philosophers, Platonic idealism, and especially neo-Platonic mysticism. These traditions of course occasionally coalesce, and Elytis (who admitted both boldly and modestly: "I was given the Greek language; / a poor house on Homer's beaches. / My only care my language on Homer's beaches") would have pointed out that opposing literary sensibilities sometimes unite miraculously, notably in Homer (Elytis's Everyman also incarnates Ulysses), as well as in modern Greek mentors such as the poet Dionysios Solomos (1798-1857) and the short story writer Alexandros Papadiamantis (1851-1911). Redoubtable for the translator (Jeffrey Carson and Nikos Sarris are to be thanked for their careful, close, annotated versions in the *Collected Poems* that Johns Hopkins University Press published in 1997), Elytis's diction ambitiously gathers in all levels and historical stages of Greek. The result differs appreciably from Eliot's or Pound's insertions of allusions or quotations into their long poems; here the Greek language, *ta ellenika* (the Greeks rightfully refer to their language in the plural), is molded by the poet into a fascinating continuum, rather like those smooth marble Cycladic idols and alluring *korai* that Elytis invokes often.

With these unifying linguistic aspirations, Elytis naturally embraces all aspects of Greekness: from paganism to the Greek Orthodox liturgy; from the Heraclitean vision of Nature as ever-changing to the Plotinian conception of Oneness and Timelessness ("Each moment a sail changing color," reads one early poem, "And no one / Stays the same / In changeless space"); from a Thucydidean concern with men caught up in war (as in the solemn prose sections of *The Axion Esti*, recalling the poet's own Second World War experiences and numerous past conflicts in which Greeks were tragically engaged) to joyful celebrations of nakedness and stark landscape; from elegy and threnody to exuberance, incantation, and enchantment. Even discreet erotic images reminiscent of Cavafy appear in Elytis's all-assimilating poetics, such as when—in his first book, *Orientations* (1939)—he evokes those "Light fingers to caress a brow" or recalls "desires' early whispering" in which "you felt for the first time the painful happiness of living!" That final exclamation point, however, sharply defines the extreme temperamental differences separating the two poets.

Elytis's exhortations to make an effort—"Guess, toil, feel"—and to exalt are most memorably expressed in *The Axion Esti*, his famous book-length poem. It is in this volume that the surrealist metaphors are consistently the clearest and the most striking. Quoted from a liturgical hymn, the expression *axion esti* means "worthy it is." The literal translation of the title would hence be *The Worthy It Is* (as one might say, referring to the Lord's Prayer, *The Our Father Who Art in Heaven*). The final "Gloria" section provides a stirring litany of countless praiseworthy deeds and things. Beginning "AXION ESTI the light and the first / wish of man incised in stone," the long sequence includes some magnificent erotic imagery:

> The hatching of whispers in the conchs
> a girl lost like a dream: Arignota
> a distant light that says: sleep
> perplexed kisses like a crowd of trees

> The bit of blouse the wind wears out
> the grassy down along the shin
>   and the deep violet salt of the vulva
>   and the cold water of the Full Moon.

Similarly, Eros pervades those magical moments in which a multitude of contradictory sentiments, images, and ideas are brought together; in brief, when chaos is given form anew. In these moments "the world recommences," as Elytis phrases it in an eruditely metered poem from *Stepchildren* (1974). (His lifework is a vast catalog of poetic forms, including a moving pseudo-fragment, published in *The Little Seafarer* in 1985, that pays homage to the mutilated verses of ancient poets.) Elytis celebrates, time and again, bewitching instants of full being in which merge "the innate passion and the apotheosis." Echoing Sappho, he exclaims for example in *Sun the First* (1943) that "What I love is born incessantly / What I love is at its beginning always." Although his optimism is often expressed gravely, this ongoing search for signs of rebirth and renewal reveals him to be a positive-thinking poet, one ready to fight "the Not and the Impossible of this world." Tellingly, the refrain from the "Genesis" section of *The Axion Esti*, "THIS / the world the small the great!," is echoed throughout his work. In the innovative sequence *Maria Nephele* (1978), in which a young woman and an "antiphonist" dialogue by means of alternating poems, the "world" is similarly referred to as an "Announcement." Elytis's poetry is bent on capturing and celebrating these "announcements"—the ever-re-emerging newness of the present.

How, though, can these life-enheartening annunciatory signals be perceived, recognized? Like the French surrealists (who influenced his thinking), Elytis situates essence on "the third heights," a superior state of the spirit where opposites are reconciled and the limitations of rationality surpassed; only on this level "thrives the Invisible." It is advisable to view Elytis's oft-hermetic poetry as having been written—as it surely was—from this elevated, quasi-mystical vantage point. Synesthesia abounds ("we fluttered the eyelids of all our emotions in the pandemonium of buzz and color"), as do recurrent symbols (the sun, the winds, the islands) and color-adjectives (namely "cyan" and "glaucous"). The personal mythology thus composed is never fully decipherable, yet it is undeniably Greek.

More, however, is at stake than a literary or even an epistemological insight enabling one to perceive reality in deeper ways. Elytis maintains that arriving at this elevated vantage point—sometimes compared to employing a "sixth-sense"—implies a crucial ethical end. In a prose poem from *The Little Seafarer*, for instance, he writes: "Doubtless for each one of us there is a separate, irreplaceable sense which if one does not find it and isolate it on time and cohabit with it later, so as to fill it with visible acts, one is lost." Elsewhere he adds: "When we discover the secret connections of concepts and we follow them in depth we shall come to another kind of clearing which is Poetry. And Poetry is always one as the sky is one."

A life-changing message thus runs through this intricately interconnected lifework. One must elevate oneself to these spiritual heights in order to live fully, to find oneself, to finally return home, a well-wandered Ulysses. The soul-seeking evoked from the very beginning in Elytis's poetry ("Where is a man to go / Who is nothing but a man," he asks in the aptly entitled *Orientations)* should be interpreted in this light. Not surprisingly, in *Three Poems under a Flag of Convenience* (1982), the poet warns:

> a million signs
> omega zeta eta
> and if these don't form a word for you
> tomorrow
> will be yesterday forever.

The Greek word hidden by the anagram is of course "zeta-omega-eta"—*zoe,* "life"—the vibrant living which Elytis is ever holding up to us and to whose glories and mysteries he devoted his extraordinary gifts.

From Sorrow to Celebration
(Andonis Decavalles)

Andonis Decavalles (b. 1920) belongs to that generation of Greek poets—
some have called it the "Generation of Anguish"—which, as the poet observes
in an interview included in *Ransoms to Time* (a major selection in English of
his poems), saw its "youth taken away," its "dreams destroyed," and its "ideologies betrayed" by the Second World War and by the Civil War (1946-1949) that
followed. The literary responses to that anguish, however, have been diverse.
Manolis Anagnostakis (1925-2005) wrote a poetry of political commitment,
Nanos Valaoritis (b. 1921) an erotic poetry influenced by Surrealism, and
Takis Sinopoulos (1917-1981) a poetry whose principal theme is death. As
for Decavalles, who also often meditates on death, he attempts "to create his
own world of values in the heart of evil," as the translator Kimon Friar notes
in his thorough, perspicacious introduction to these sixty-five poems chosen
from *Nimule-Gondokoro* (1949), *Akis* (1950), *Oceanids* (1970), and *Joints,
Ships, Ransoms* (1976). (Two new poems are also included.) As in the poetry
of Odysseus Elytis, continues Friar, for Decavalles "irrevocable tragedies and
sorrows of life must be transcended into the higher realm of man's assimilat-
ing imagination and there given their proper place in the ultimate glorification
of the universe."

Indeed, in "Dark Rose," Decavalles makes the surprising affirmation: "Yet I
don't mean death with the deaths I speak of." Elsewhere, while he is sitting in
the grass and closely observing insects, he concludes with a sense of Plotinean
oneness. And in "For the Tree to Remember," he establishes the criteria for
commemoration; it demands waiting, modesty, and awe:

> even the smallest moment is excessive.
>
> But it needs a little aeon for the word to become clay
> in your fingers,
> to measure the size and to fit
> the weight of things,
> and it takes the flame a little aeon to chisel
> the ineffable.

In *Ransoms to Time*, the poet celebrates the Aegean Sea, his ancestral island of Siphnos, the coastal landscape of New England (he has lived in the United States since 1954), and—in his most transparent, moving poems—his wife, his three daughters, a few old mentors, several relatives and ancestors, his childhood nurse, and especially his father, his "other self," whose bones, in accordance with the Greek ritual, he disinters and washes with wine, then asks:

> If only I knew what I am washing here, what is
> being cleansed—if it is your bones
> or my own self that so much in vain
> sought you and never found you...

Some poems have an old fashioned air to them, but Decavales's attempt to write "festive elegies," to use his own term for them, is stimulating and situates them alongside so many other European poetic struggles with affirming and negating. Often with subtlety, Decavalles explores the "dark recesses" of affection, the "deep turnings" of love, and the "unexpected crevice called death."

A Chromatic, Obsessional Poetics
(Miltos Sachtouris)

Twenty years ago in the *Times Literary Supplement*, I briefly reviewed John Stathatos's British versions of thirty-six poems by Miltos Sachtouris (1919-2005). The other day, when I reopened *Strange Sunday* (Bran's Head Books) in order to compare it to Karen Emmerich's new, and much more extensive, rendering of the Greek poet's work (*Poems 1945-1971*, Archipelago Books), I discovered that I had penned a red asterisk in the margin whenever the word "black" occured, an orange asterisk for "blood" or "bloody," and a green asterisk for "dead" or "death." Most pages of my copy are thus color-coded by at least one and sometimes two such reminders, while two short, skeletal poems are marked by as many as four asterisks; one fourteen-liner repeats "black" five times. Such is Sachtouris's chromatic, obsessional poetics. The author of *Colorwounds* (1980) similarly employs only a very few recurrent symbols and motifs, some of them implicitly hued as well: fire (or burning), birds, dogs, the sky, the sun, the moon, and rain. Back then I wrote: "A metaphysics [of salvation] is rejected as an illusion in the terse, dark, occasionally nightmarish poems of Sachtouris. His is a minimalist poetry which evokes the innate tragedy of the human condition; twinges of sarcastic humor accompany the pervasive mood of hopeless impotence and imprisonment."

This "innate tragedy" includes the traumas experienced by Sachtouris and other Greek writers during the Second World War, then the Civil War (1946-1949). In her subtle and informative afterword, Emmerich quotes another of Sachtouris's translators, Kimon Friar, who pointed out that this generation saw "the whitewashed walls of Greece suddenly splattered red" and that Sachtouris's poetry was "colored by this terror." Full of violent imagery involving knives, revolvers, lost eyesight, and severed limbs (the lines "now our arms and legs are hanging / from the trees" exemplify a frequent theme of humiliation and helplessness), Sachtouris's verse indeed at times seems to respond realistically to wartime murdering, torture, and cruelty. The prose poem "The Nightmare" refers to "five Germans," and lines such as

> You stretched always stretched out your hands
> to help the sick men on the balconies
> climb down

with their big eyes their skinny legs
        and their flowers
while all around from the dark windows
everyone fired their guns

obviously describe a battle. A "Moment" such as "The painter has a painting / in his heart / and a knife in his head / he wants to pull out the painting / he wants to pull out the knife / to slash the painting" likewise suggests the extreme tension of artistic and literary creativity in or after a time of treachery. Several poems evoke "unforgivable forgetting," which in light of the atrocities committed remains a major problem for the Greek national conscience.

Yet linking Sachtouris's haunted and haunting verse exclusively to these dark years is insufficient, as Emmerich herself observes, even as its heightened strangeness cannot be explained away by situating it alongside the equally vivid though otherwise differently lyricized oeuvres of other surrealist-influenced Greek poets, notably his friends Nikos Engonopoulos (1907-1985) and Odysseus Elytis (1911-1996). Surely the reader puzzling over Sachtouris's disarming mixture of apparent eyewitness account and apparent hallucination should take the poet seriously when, in "The Dream," he quotes Céline, who graphically depicted First World War manslaughter yet claimed that his "voyage was fully imaginary—whence its force."

Moreover, Sachtouris's verse draws on other kinds of symbols: some Christian (see "Three Tears of God"), some ironically anti-mythical ("Ilias from the vegetable market" is decidedly "not Oedipus"), while still others conspicuously involve a polysemous "forgotten woman," as the title of his 1945 volume and its key poem-sequence state it. One early piece, "Christmas 1943," increases the interpretative complexity by referring to the "forgotten woman," Christ, and remote, perhaps illusory, hopes:

children hurl crumbs into the sky
the holidays have smooth faces
a tiny Christ in each of the forgotten woman's tears
a little lamb a drop in her frozen palms
a bird a starry pin in her hair.

Sachtouris's focus always shifts abruptly, sometimes in mid-line, giving a dream-like impression or, as Emmerich defines it while recalling how "each volume builds upon previous ones," "a kind of cumulative madness, a paralogical perspective that keeps coming at the world—or fleeing from it—at an angle." In one uncommonly direct confessional poem, Sachtouris admits: "A few dangerous pieces / of chaos / is my soul / which God cut / with his teeth." Still another facet of his sensibility is revealed by love poems, though these, too, bring disparate themes into uncomfortable configurations. In "The Savior," Sachtouris invokes a lover in a context of menace and mutilation: "I count on the fingers of my severed hands / the hours I've wandered through these rooms of wind / I have no other hands my love and the doors / don't want to close and the dogs are unrelenting."

Perhaps a clue to his unique and disturbing poetry lies in the mere fact that he dedicates "Sunset" to the Greek painter Alekos Fassianos. Although Fassianos's paintings are much more optimistic and luminous than Sachtouris's poems, they analogously employ primary colors and stage symbolically resonant, at once timeless and time-specific, scenes consisting mainly of human figures whose pure forms recall or slightly parody the aesthetic canons of ancient Greece. (Realistic details crop up as well, such as flies, scarves, bicycles or watermelon rinds.) Of course, Fassianos's art, which often depicts dark-hued "shades" (in the ancient Greek sense) posing statuesquely or naked couples whose erotic play is temporarily postponed, exhibits a harmonious wholeness that starkly contrasts to the festering wounds, discontinuous thoughts, and torn-off limbs brought to the fore by Sachtouris as emblems of man's crippled ontological state, his bitter brooding, and his all-too-real destructiveness, which is to say that the poet, too, envisions lost wholenesses. With remarkable economy of means, both men create multiple potential meanings that at once compel and elude. Emmerich is to be thanked for bringing so many of Sachtouris's poems into fluent English. She is occasionally a less concrete translator than Stathatos, who once or twice also shows a surer grip on syntax, but her work is fine and meticulous in many other ways. This is an essential collection.

Erotic Knowledge, Self-Knowledge
(Dinos Christianopoulos)

It would be an error to restrict Dinos Christianopoulos (b. 1931) to the ranks of "Greek homosexual poets." He is a major contemporary poet *tout court*. Although selections of his sensitive and transparent poems have appeared in several European languages, strangely enough I have found relatively few traces of his prose and poetry in English, and none whatsoever in readily accessible editions.

From Kimon Friar's excellent introduction to his poetry, a selection of which was published in the *Journal of the Hellenic Diaspora* (Vol. VI, No. 1, Spring 1979), we learn that the poet was the son of Yannis and Persephone Dimitriou, and that two months later was baptized Constandinos. When he was one and a half years old, however, he was adopted by Anastasios and Fani Dimitriadis, who chose this particular infant because of the similarity of surnames. In 1945, the poet began using the pseudonym "Christianopoulos" ("Son of Christ"), which reflects as well the Christian themes that would soon appear in his oeuvre. After earning a degree in literature at the University of Thessaloniki in 1954, he founded the important literary periodical *Diagonios* (Diagonal) in 1958; later he began publishing books under the logo Diagonal Publications. (Diagonios is also the name of an important intersection in Thessaloniki.) Nearly all his own books have been self-published at his own press in sober, exquisite editions. Intimately associated with his hometown, Christianopoulos has spent his entire life in Thessaloniki, visiting few places in mainland Greece or the islands, making only the most necessary trips to Athens, primarily to give readings of his poetry.

Early on, Christianopoulos's poetry took off from that of C. P. Cavafy (1863-1933). When in the poem "The Centurion Cornelius," which was rendered by Friar for the anthology *Modern European Poetry* (1966), Christianopoulos writes

> ...for these reasons, Lord, and for many others,
> make Andonios well, slave of your slave.
> If need be, I can even turn Christian.
> Only make him well, all I ask of you, nothing else.
> Anything else I might dare ask of you would be immoral[,]

Cavafy's delicate touch of irony and implicit eroticism is immediately recognizable. In his first collection, *Season of the Lean Cows* (1950), Christianopoulos includes several such poems, which manifestly draw their inspiration from Cavafy's "Historical Poems." One of the best is "Antigone: In Defense of Oedipus," which Friar translated in *The Charioteer* (No. 10, 1968):

> Men of Athens, why do you look at us so curiously?
> This is my father, Oedipus
> who at one time was a powerful king and now
> wanders in your market place, wounded
> by fate, ragged and blind,
> playing with his small broken-down barrel-organ.
>
> Men of Athens, every obol you give us
> adds a crack to your hearts;
> the secrets of our Royal House grow heavy
> with all that your imaginations have heaped on them.
> Let us alone—until when will you continue to drag us
> here and there, like a gypsy with his bear....
>
> (. . .)
>
> ...is not enough for you that my
> father was once a poet,
> the first to introduce symbolism,
> who with his epigram "Reply to the Sphinx"
> saved the lives of many of you—not to mention
> the aesthetic pleasure derived—why
> do you poke into his private life
> and search for Oedipus complexes,
> illicit loves,
> and pleasures which the current morality forbids?
>
> The "Reply to the Sphinx" should have been enough for you.
> You should have left the rest in semi-darkness.
> After all, he did it in complete ignorance,
> whereas you do it with complete consciousness.

The "barrel-organ," the "gypsy with his bear," and the image of Oedipus as the first Symbolist poet reveal Christianopoulos's attempt to establish a certain distance between his and Cavafy's more veridical poetic historiography, whereby the latter usually respects the unity of time and place even when he uses the present tense. The influence at work here is that of T. S. Eliot, as Friar has noted: "[Eliot] introduced [Christianopoulos] to the expression of Christian agony in contemporary times, to the modern structure of verse, and to the juxtaposition of historically anachronistic situations." Similar juxtapositions appear in the work of another important twentieth-century Greek poet, George Seferis (1900-1971), upon whom the impact of Eliot was profound and lasting.

Christianopoulos, however, is no mere epigone of either Cavafy or Eliot, and it would be unjust to appraise his work exclusively in their terms. With his subsequent collections, *Knees of Strangers* (1954), *Defenseless Craving* (1960), *Suburbs* (1969), and *The Cross-Eyed Man* (written between 1949 and 1970, and published, like the other volumes, in *Poems 1949-1970*), the poet discards historical settings and composes, to use the Greek term, *erotika poiimata*: "erotic poems" or "love poems." Although similar to Cavafy's "Erotic Poems" in their directness and simplicity, and likewise void of metaphor, they move beyond the mentor's in their greater boldness, explicitness, and contemporaneity. The poems commemorate emotions, corporal sensations, rendezvous, chance encounters, nights spent searching for love in city parks, and evenings spent in a lover's embrace far beyond the city limits. Here is "Interval of Joy," as rendered by Friar in the *Modern European Poetry* anthology:

> just as I was saying I would stop writing about love and lust
> and write something instead about the unhappiness of my neighbor
> I met you and fell into complete confusion
> and all my resolutions went up in air
>
> now see where I sit and write songs again
> burning for your saliva
> recollecting our one love-walk in the country
> when the mosquitoes bit us in confused bewilderment
> at this incomparable devotion of ours
> and the thorns pierced into our bodies
> astonished at the extent of our indifference
>
> it was an interval of joy
> may the unhappy forgive me for it
> I have not yet suffered enough
> for the pain of my neighbor to touch me.

As Friar has noted, "Interval of Joy" (from *Defenseless Craving*) announces a theme that recurs in Christianopoulos's subsequent work: the guilty conscience of a poet who discovers that, because of his pursuit of pleasure, he has been indifferent to the suffering of his fellow man. The most explicit expression of this theme occurs in "The Splinter," which evokes the assassination of Grigoris Lambrakis, a leftist political leader and member of the Greek Parliament. On the night of 22 May 1963, Lambrakis, while leaving a political rally in Thessaloniki, was run over by a *trikyklo*, a small three-wheeled delivery truck, and clubbed to death by hired henchmen. The event became known abroad through Vassilis Vassilikos's novel *Z* (1966) and through Costa-Gavras's film version (1969) of the same. Christianopoulos's own memory of the event involves an "imperceptible splinter" that continues to torment him; in the *Journal of the Hellenic Diaspora* selection, Friar translates:

The night they killed Lambrakis
I was returning from a date.
"What's happened?" someone on the bus asked.
No one knew. We saw policemen
but could make out nothing more.

Three years went by. Once more I fell
into the same indifference about political matters.
But that particular night disturbed me
like an imperceptible splinter that won't come out:
some clubbed down for their ideals,
others roaring about on their tricycles,
and I mindlessly running off to make love in the meadows.

In a poem from *The Body and Remorse*, a collection written between 1960 and 1977 and entirely republished in *Mikra poiimata* (Short Poems, 1975/1982), Christianopoulos similarly remarks, in Friar's version:

my country, i stand ashamed before you
you drain away bit by bit
while i play my own fiddle

but by keeping company with your lads
i got to know you better
and feel your pain.

Many of Christianopoulos's poems are intimately attached to Thessaloniki. Place names often crop up, such as when, in "Western Quarters," he begins by naming three specific suburban districts: "Stavroupolis, Ilioupolis, Polihnis, / neighborhoods of my secret love life, / how stirred I am every time I find you / improving in youth and beauty" (from *Suburbs*, my translation). In this respect, his work joins that of the mentor of many younger Thessalonican writers, Nikos Gabriel Pentzikis (1908-1993), about whom Christianopoulos himself wrote in *Diagonios* (Vol. 4, No. 2, 1961). In the work of both writers, one senses a great respect for the town that Pentzikis calls "Mother Thessaloniki," and a sometimes bitter nostalgia for its vanished former street life and folk architecture. There is a sense of irreparable change, loss, and impossibility, as in "Walk in the Meadow" (from *Defenseless Craving*, my translation):

This is no place to lie down in.
The thorns prick and the burrs stick and betray.
The muddy stream, mosquitoes everywhere,
Hardly like the sparkling pure rivulets running near your village.

This is no place to come back to.
Another house has been built, I see a light in the window.
The dirt road passes too close to us.
Couples are riding back on their mopeds.

This is no place to be quiet in.
That rebetic song has ruined my good mood.
My insides are rimmed with tears as I hug you.
It makes me sick to hear about emigrants.

This is no place for us.
Even the countryside has its way of wounding us.

Such melancholy is prevalent in the work of other Greek writers of Christianopoulos's generation, namely Kostas Taktsis (1927-1988), Yiorgos Ioannou (1927-1984), Elias Petropoulos (1928-2003), and Elias Papadimitrakopoulos (b. 1930). In such poems, Christianopoulos maps out a "topography of love" of the city and its surrounding countryside. The word "topography" recalls Pentzikis's own well-known poem "Topography," translated by George Thaniel in *Homage to Byzantium: The Life and Work of Nikos Gabriel Pentzikis* (1983): "Higher than the houses hidden by mist / at the upper part of the square with the many churches / (...) there on the marble piece rolled down from its base, / my love is sitting." In Christianopoulos, an erotic memory is similarly linked to a particular street, quarter, or suburb; in the *Journal of the Hellenic Diaspora* selection, one finds:

This place was once called "Almond Trees."
I was in time to see them. The place was filled with fragrance.
Periwinkles teemed, and a small river
carried down dry chaff from the threshing floors.

We used to come here at night for a body.

One by one the almond trees were all cut down. One by one
small houses sprouted in their place.
We were the first to inaugurate them. Our love
was given shape amid the scaffolding and the cement.

Not even one almond tree has remained.
The place has filled up with shops and apartment buildings.
They gobbled down one more place for love in the country.

"Afternoon" similarly specifies the location of props and people, for the final emotion depends on a sort of stage scenery:

That afternoon was beautiful, with our endless talk out on the sidewalk.
The birds were chirping, the people passing, the cars driving by.
In the window opposite, the radio was playing rebetic songs
and the girl next door was singing out her yearning.
The acacia smelled so sweetly, the jasmine was so fragrant,
and near the ramparts children were playing hide-and-go-seek; girls were skipping rope —
they were playing near the ramparts and didn't know about death,
they were playing near the ramparts and didn't know about remorse,

and I loved people so much that afternoon,
I don't know why, but I loved them so much, like a condemned man.

(from *The Cross-Eyed Man*, my translation)

* * *

Beginning in 1960 and continuing to the present day, Christianopoulos has also been writing extremely short poems, today collected under the aforementioned title *Short Poems*. (Friar calls them "Small Poems.") These poems are available as a separate volume, and they have also been logically included in the 1985 edition of the collected poems. Along with *The Body and Remorse*, *Short Poems* contains the collections *The Body and Longing* (written between 1969 and 1972), *The Buffet* (1969-1981), and *Freshwater Tales* (1976-1981). The latter title, *Istories tou glykou nerou*, has pejorative connotations; in Greek, "freshwater" implies that something or someone that is of inferior quality. Accordingly to the poet and folklorist Elias Petropoulos, the expression probably derives from the fact that, in Greece, fish from inland waters are considered inferior to those caught in the sea. In this regard, the implications of the title are telling. Friar rightly notes that Christianopoulos's short poems are "brief notations that have a personality uniquely their own, unlike either the Japanese *haiku* and *tanka*, or the ancient Greek epigram."

It seems to me that the differences stem from Christianopoulos's being, not first and foremost a poet of images, but rather of emotion and irony, especially self-irony. He writes concretely, but not of things-in-themselves; rather, he invokes his own emotions or the emotions he perceives in others. When he describes the body, for instance, his primary aim is not to create images of physical beauty (or decrepitude): poetically self-sufficient images, so to speak; instead, he strives to evoke—*via* the body—desire, loneliness, passion, or cruelty. "Night" is explicit in this respect:

Night aggravates loneliness,
cultivates our secret ruins.

Night works beauty into perfection,
reduces our supplications to rags.

Night unbuttons our veins,
finds our hidden dreams and eats them.

Night hacks tenderness to pieces,
renews our wounds—

and when we provide ourselves with a body
immediately unleashes its moons.

(from *The Cross-Eyed Man*, my translation)

These are inevitably self-centered, confessional, not really aphoristic, poems, which aim to convey a message of universal truth. Moreover, an erotic short poem such as

> I go to kiss you
> but you turn away
> you won't trust your lips
> to a cesspool
>
> only beneath your navel
> are you for sale[,]

rendered by Friar in the *Journal of the Hellenic Diaspora* selection, may superficially recall verse by Martial (e.g., I, 84; II, 10; II, 50), but the differences between Christianopoulous and the Roman decadent poet are fundamental. All too absent in the epigrams of a poet like Martial is that search for self-knowledge and for the knowledge of the nature of love which has been the hallmark of Christianopoulos's poetry since the very beginning.

One must also keep in mind the difference between homosexuality stemming from Middle Eastern traditions—the "active" and "passive" roles adopted in regard to sodomy—and the "Gay Movement," against which Christianopoulos has sometimes taken a stand, especially in its emphasis on fellatio. In his prose poem "The Names," he trenchantly writes (in my translation): "In 1950 it was called *mineto*. The word evoked European-like debaucheries…. In 1960 it was called *tsibouki*—a deceiving return to Ottoman lasciviousness. Queers started to delight in the act as if it were a delicious delicacy, and hustlers felt more virile when someone knelt down in front of them…. In 1970 it was called *pipa*…. Sodomites vanished; in their places, a thousand little weenies grew. Wretched effeminates started licking each other off. Who knows what we will hear next, what new words will drape inability?" In another prose poem, Christianopoulos observes: "For better or worse, we were unable to get used to the new situation. We eternally remained miserable queers, the last worms of a quagmire that was drying up, the survivors of a social group annihilated by prosperity and the easy life." And yet it is only in such solitude and distress that the poet senses himself fully living. Solitude, distress, humiliation, and cruelty thus become positive values in his poetry as well.

I mentioned topography above; I'll extend the image. When reading Christianopoulos's poems, I often think of those *cartes de tendre* (such as the map game conceived by the novelist Madeleine de Scudéry), which were popular in seventeenth-century Paris salons. It was a game devoted to "love's progress" and involved a "country" or "realm" of Tendre (the old French word for "tenderness"). The "new friendship" commences; the road to the "unknown lands" of love (on the other side of the "dangerous sea") first winds its way between "complaisance" (an accommodating attitude), "inégalité" (inequality), "orgueil" (pride), "médisance" (malicious gossip), "méchancété" (meanness), and "oubli" (forgetfulness). The relationship progresses much like that of the pilgrim in *The Pilgrim's Progress*. In some respects, Christianopoulos's poems unfold a "map of tenderness." They constitute the diary of a poet slowly making his way, with many false turnings, towards those "unknown lands." We linger long at "solitude," "soumission" (submissiveness), "perfidie" (perfidy). But Christianopoulos's poetry expresses another journey, taken at the same time, over the same vast and dangerous territory: the journey of self-knowledge:

> Now that at last I have found an embrace,
> better even than what I had hoped for,
> now that everything I wanted has come my way,
> and I begin to feel comfy in my secret joy,
> I feel that something inside me is rotting.

(from *The Cross-Eyed Man*, my translation)

The *Short Poems* are particularly intense in that they are seemingly written at the intersection of the two paths, or perhaps at that point where the paths divide, tearing away from each other, or indeed at that point where, unexpectedly, the paths come together again. Be they only two lines long, Christianopoulos's poems express the complexity and ambiguity of human feeling which are implied by such proximity:

> i took you to repair me
> and you took me apart

*

> every time I think I have you in hand
> I see that love is not handwork

*

> call it masochism
> call it whatever you wish
> I feel inadequate for so much tenderness.

(trans. Friar, *Journal of the Hellenic Diaspora*)

* * *

Alhough Christianopoulos is best known as a poet, he has also written short stories, prose poems, and what in Anglo-American literary jargon have come to be called "short shorts." Examples of the latter are the fourteen pieces in *Oi rebetes tou dounia* (1986). The title is untranslatable: the word *rebetis* (plural: *rebetes*) refers to an archetypal figure from the old Greek underworld, a rebellious rogue or troublemaker who lived outside the accepted standards of traditional Greek society and who showed contempt for the establishment in all its forms. As Elias Petropoulos notes in *Rebetika: Songs from the Old Greek Underworld* (1992), the *rebetis* "didn't marry…and wouldn't walk arm-in-arm with his girlfriend; he didn't wear a collar and tie and refused to carry an umbrella; he scorned work, helped the underdog, smoked hashish, bitterly hated the police, and considered going to jail a mark of honor." Associated with his character is intense feeling and virile passion, such as becomes manifest when—as in "Hippokleides," the first text of Christianopoulos's collection—the *rebetis* dances alone in the taverna, at times solemnly and defiantly lifting several chairs or even a table off the ground by using his mouth and teeth alone. Christianopoulos's title is surely borrowed directly from a famous underworld "rebetic song" that was composed and first recorded in 1938 by the great singer Markos Vamvakaris: "Oli oi rebetis tou dounia," literary "All the Rebetes of the World." Christianopoulos has written a study entitled *Historical and Aesthetic Development of the Rebetic Song* (1961).

In the collection of short prose texts, only "Hippokleides" and "Roza Eskenazi," which sketches in moving details the life story of one of the early popular singers of rebetic songs, allude to this underworld; but the title of this atypically heterogeneous gathering, if taken metaphorically—where *rebetis* would signify an "outlaw" or "outcast"—encompasses several other texts, especially when the term is given the additional nuance, specific to Christianopoulos's writing, of outlaws or outcasts of love. As in Christianopoulos's poetry and other prose writings, the main character (usually a first-person narrator) is an outlaw or outcast because of the very intensity of his or her sexual desire. In most cases, this desire is that of a solitary homosexual who, when young, is attracted to other young men ("Sweets") or who, as an adult, cruises the streets of Thessaloniki in search of amorous relationships ("Christmas Eve," "Maundy Thursday"). With stylistic clarity and succinctness, Christianopoulos evokes the passionate "drunkenness" that causes the narrator to unknowingly leave behind in a field the pullover generously knit for him by a friend; he tells of a picked-up lover who suddenly remembers that it is Maundy Thursday and for this reason decides not to make love. In these stories, Christianopoulos reveals his talent for concentrating, in one telltale erotic detail, all the emotion linked to a painful memory or, less often, to a pleasurable one. In this and other respects, he is the worthy descendent of Cavafy. Certainly "The Votive Lamp," from an earlier collection *Nekri piatsa* (1983) of short poetry and prose, provides discreet echoes of the Alexandrian:

> An old abandoned mansion with a garden out back, and at the end of the garden a little chapel. A crazy old woman, who lived inside all by herself, used to light the votive lamp every evening. I would see it through a crack in the door, glimmering through the leaves, and my soul would be at peace. I always felt ravaged when I returned home in the evening from my room of love. Without understanding why,

that votive lamp had become my most secret consolation. And I understood why in this world thousands of people still continue to light their votive lamps.

One evening it was extinguished. It seemed that something had happened to the crazy old woman. A little later I too lost my room of love; I walked down that street no more. Ever since, no votive lamp has given consolation to my life.

(my translation)

Written between 1982 and 1985, *Oi rebetes tou dounia* marks a broadening of Christianopoulos's scope with respect to characters and themes. In "Arethas, Bishop of Caesarea," which like "Demosthenes" and some of Christianopoulos's earliest poetry is a first-person narrative of a scene from the distant past that is set in the present, Arethas recounts the ennui of provincial life and conveys his disgust at hearing barbarians, "with their sloppy errors in syntax and with their wretched rhythms," sing Greek odes. In "Stefan Zweig," the narrator (Zweig himself) tells of his disappointing first impressions of Franz Kafka, whom Max Brod enables him to meet in Prague. Similar texts concern the Greek writers Yiannis Vlahoyiannis (1868-1945) and Adamantios Koraïs (*alias* Coray; 1748-1833). Such narratives explore themes outside of the autobiographical, oft-sexual, sphere from which Christianopoulos typically finds his inspiration.

"Roza Eskenazi" and "On the Island of Skyros," however, bring forth in unexpectedly positive formulations a theme present in Christianopoulos's work from the onset. In the former, a truck driver from Corinth "moves Heaven and Earth" to locate the impoverished and mentally deranged Roza. In more fortunate days before the Second World War, the singer had helped him out in some way or perhaps had even loved him. Now he takes care of her until she dies. "All by himself he served and nursed her," writes Christianopoulos, "he washed her, combed her hair, took her out for walks, and whenever he had to leave on long trips he entrusted her to the women in the neighborhood." "When you hear such stories," concludes the narrator, "you gain faith in man." In "On the Island of Skyros," a foreign girl (a tourist) chooses to walk all night back to town with her Greek boyfriend—they had apparently made love in the countryside, then on the way back their motorcycle had been damaged—rather than to accept a ride with the narrator and his friend. Because of the late hour, the narrator and his friend have not been able to make their "pilgrimage" to the grave of the English poet Rupert Brooke, but now they are struck with equal admiration for the girl's love. In Christianopoulos's work, such faithfulness, whether to others or to oneself, is rarely depicted as leading to anything but a "catastrophe."

Rather than as turning points, however, these two cautiously optimistic stories should doubtless be viewed as adding additional facets to the complex image of human love that Christianopoulos has been fashioning in his work, poem by poem, story by story, during the past fifty years. What the short narratives in *Oi rebetes tou dounia* confirm, after the longer stories in *I kato volta* (1963/1980) and the prose poems in *Nekri piatsa* (1981/1983), is that Christianopoulos is a master, not only of poetry, but also of prose; and that his oeuvre is rigorously of one piece. One is moved by the same stylistic simplicity, sometimes charming, sometimes brutal; by the same acute emotions; by the same forthright expression of the protagonist's desire. Whether he is Hippokleides or the poet himself, Christianopoulos's protagonists hope to "be" when they cannot "become." This is why Christianopoulos's poetry recalls the writings of Jean Genet. "I wanted to be myself," declares Genet in *Le Miracle de la rose*, "and I was myself when I turned out to be a burglar." Christianopoulos likewise makes this confession: "I want neither to die nor to be healed / I want simply to adjust to my catastrophe" (translated by Friar in *Café* [No. 1, Summer 1969]).

Poetry, Anti-Poetry, and Disgust
(Elias Petropoulos)

Elias Petropoulos (1928-2003) was notoriously well known in Greece as an urban folklorist, but I am not alone among his friends in suspecting that he attached an equally great—perhaps even greater—importance to his poetry. Wasn't Nikos Gabriel Pentzikis's faithful (if turbulent) pupil a poet at heart, even in his folkloristic work? Wasn't one of Elias Petropoulos's main goals as a folklorist that of recovering and preserving what can properly be called, from our fin-de-siècle perspective (I am writing in 1993), the "poetic" vestiges of a now nearly vanished popular culture? Wasn't his very methodology as literary as it was "scientific" or "empirical"? For although many prose writers (and even scientists) have versified on the side, Petropoulos's case was different. Writing poetry for him was no pastime, but rather participated fully in the vision underlying his entire oeuvre.

This unity between the folkloristic writings and the poems can best be discerned in the arresting melancholy informing them both. For even in his prose writings, he never hypocritically conceals his personality, or his subjectivity, behind the multitude of "objective" facts that he catalogues or describes. He wasn't Pentzikis's pupil for nothing! Petropoulos was too interested in language and perception to be deceived by naive notions of so-called "scientific" rigor and objectivity. And yet there is unquestionably an attempt on his part to objectively express the world—in his poetry as well— by means of an exposition of brute facts. This is no contradiction. Petropoulos knew all too well that observing entails selecting, the subjective act par excellence. Not only the poet, but also the urban folklorist must live "harmoniously," as he puts it in a poem in *Pote kai tipota* (Never and Nothing, 1993) with his "innate melancholy."

Never and Nothing marked a new step in the continuing evolution of Petropoulos's poetry, notably from *Soma* (Body, 1969) and *Avtoktonia* (Suicide, 1973), and even more strikingly from the lyricism of his earlier book, *Elytis Moralis Tsarouhis* (1966), the latter volume ostensibly a critical work about the poet and two well-known Greek artists. Rereading these works gives one the impression of a metamorphosing unity. "Deep inside me a battle wages," writes Petropoulos in *Body*, and his poetry, from his earliest efforts to *Never and Nothing*, chronicles that ongoing war. In this latest stage, which dated from

Mirror for You (1983) and *In Berlin* (1987), the war was reported on in a much more direct fashion than ever before. One is tempted to say, in the aftermath of the first war in Iraq, that well-penned letters from the front have been replaced by the willfully fleeting images of CNN cable television.

War indeed. For the inner strife that Petropoulos evoked with increasing forthrightness in his poetry likewise originates in his memories of "all those friends who were shot by firing squads" (*Pente erotica poiimata*, Five Erotic Poems, 1975) and, still more painfully, in the murder of his father in 1944 (evoked in *In Berlin*). The latter event—surely a key to the writer's personality and oevure—was never elucidated: like Petropoulos himself, his father was in the Resistance Movement; the corpse was never found. Much has already been written about the impact of the Second World War and the Civil War on the Greek writers of Petropoulos's generation (he was seventeen years old in 1945), and his poetry, as well as his entire folkloristic approach, can profitably be viewed in this light. Behind even his most brutal remarks nearly always lies moving remembrance. Petropoulos is brutal because of remembrance. As he avows in *Never and Nothing*, in a self-revealing notation, "But the women, the friends, whom I loved / are not phantoms. / And they know that I'm constantly thinking of them."

Before and after these meditative moments in *Never and Nothing*, Petropoulos characteristically rages against the Establishment, against Academe, against bourgeois values, sometimes even against countries or groups of nationals (especially the French, often the Greeks; in fact, nearly everyone). A genuine *poète révolté*, Petropoulos also relishes leveling his guns at pretentious, academic—one thinks of the term "cacademic" forged by his friend, *Maledicta* publisher Reinhold Aman—uses of language. Already in *Body*, *Suicide*, and *Five Erotic Poems*, a few lines end abruptly, with a period, in mid-sentence, creating the effect of an interrupted scream. Such stylistic provocations take on renewed vigor when the writer, starting with *Mirror for You* and *In Berlin*, begins incorporating "kitsch" into his poems. After experimenting (in those works) with intentionally ridiculous uses of traditional meter and rhyme, Petropoulos came to make blatant voluntary grammatical errors, as in his poem, included in *Never and Nothing*, beginning: "Ston leoforo to avtokinito." The poet concludes: "I fuck your grammar." "Obscenity" is indeed his "pride," as he declares in *Body*.

Yet the opening poem of *Never and Nothing* surprisingly claims that the poet is "harsh...out of tenderness." Given the violence of some of these verses, it is difficult to take him at his word. Or is it? For as is obvious in the folkloristic writings, an innate tenderness—a sympathy for the underdog—obliges Petropoulos to look closely, meticulously, at life; and often, in consequence, to speak out strongly. Petropoulos likewise knows how fragile artistic creativity is; unforgettable is his warning, in *Five Erotic Poems*, to a younger poet, Manolis Xexakis: "patience Manolis patience my soul / because the shabby bastards will crush you without shame." Moreover, concealed behind the writer's proverbial aggressiveness are ceaseless ruminations on mortality. Explicitly rendered in *The Graves of Greece* (1979), death is present in all of

Petropoulos's writings, especially his poetry. And even more especially in the last period of his poetry.

For this very reason, Petropoulos's late poems unambiguously express what he already announces in *Mirror for You*: "I don't believe in so-called Great Poetry." "I'll have to write a Manifesto of Ugly Poetry," he likewise proclaims in *In Berlin*," adding: "Throw away the Poetry of Ideas and of Symbols and of Colors. / Prefer Everyday Images / and insignificant Snapshots, one after the other; / that is, Poor Poetry." Yet this ongoing "manifesto," set forth in *Never and Nothing* with still greater resolution, is based as securely on the author's unequivocal theories—a "non-poetry" or an "anti-poetry" representing an aesthetic position, after all—as on the irrepressible, haunting fact that he (and those whom he loves) are aging—yes, dying. Perhaps it is best to read his voluntarily un-poetic poems as expressions of what happens when grim observations of time's and death's ravages are allowed to overwhelm all the nuances, refinements, and restraint of classical poetics. "The closer you get to the coffin, / the more you abandon *fioriture*, / the beautiful hollow words," he writes in *Never and Nothing*.

Petropoulos is not the first poet for whom, with age, idealism veers to melancholy; and melancholy to disgust. Yet he is one of the very rare poets who, affected by extreme feelings, is willing to relinquish all ties to formal literary elegance. And although he has always taken great risks with his readers, never were the risks as great as in his late poems. For he shows that the very form of a poetry inspired by melancholy and disgust must necessarily be melancholic, even disgusting. The reading of *Never and Nothing* is disquieting, to say the least.

The Mentor of Pyrgos
(Elias Papadimitrakopoulos)

Though hardly a prolific author or one whose name is constantly on the lips of the average Greek reader, Elias Papadimitrakopoulos (b. 1930) enjoys the greater merit of being esteemed by his peers, by his fellow Greek writers and critics, as a stylistic virtuoso, a sensitive, perspicacious craftsman of the emotions who has given voice to a community neglected by modern Greek letters, the small provincial town, in the present case the town of Pyrgos in the Peloponnesian province of Eleia. In a national literature crowded with mountain villages, island villages, Thessaloniki, and of course Athens, Papadimitrakopoulos reveals the human richness hidden in this seemingly nondescript burg, dominated commercially by Patras and touristically by the nearby site of Olympia.

His first two collections of short stories, *Toothpaste with Chlorophyll* (1973) and *Maritime Hot Baths* (1980), established Papadimitrakopoulos as one of the leading Greek writers, one whose work recalls such painters of the *triste* and ephemeral as Peter Altenberg, Sait Faik, and Dezsö Kosztolányi, with here and there a maudlin, funny-sad brushstroke of James Thurber. Born in Pyrgos in 1930, a military doctor by profession (he retired from the Greek army in 1983), Papadimitrakopoulos otherwise writes film and literary criticism for several Greek magazines and newspapers. His later books include collections of incisive book reviews, film reviews, articles, and essays; studies devoted to the novelist Nikos Kachtitsis (1926-1970), whom Papadimitrakopoulos was partly responsible for discovering, and several other writers; and a few other collections of stories, notably *O Genikos Arkhiothetis* (The General Archivist, 1989), *Rozamoundi* (Rosamund, 1995), *O Ovolos kai alla diiyimata* (The Obol and Other Stories, 2004).

Like Kachtitsis and Nikos Gabriel Pentzikis (1908-1993), another innovative writer whose work has interested him as a critic, Papadimitrakopoulos has forged as his mode of expression a language immediately recognizable as his own. Ever concise, melodious, with much attention given to the overall rhythm of the story—the very music of the prose in "Eleonora" imitates the huffing and puffing of sexual intercourse, thus paralleling plot on the prosodic level, creating what the author himself has described as a "metaphysical calembour"—the language in *Toothpaste with Chlorophyll* and *Maritime Hot Baths* reveals a delicate juxtaposition of "purist" (*katharevousa*) and demotic Greek. Not least among Papadimitrakopoulos's gifts is that of parody. In "The Spanish Guitar" and "The Money Order," for example, the author parodies the infelicitous *katharevousa* of the local newspaper and of the well-meaning provincial townsman, a stylistic tour de force that attains unprecedented heights in "The General Archivist," the title story of his third collection. In that tale of twenty-four printed pages, the longest story that he has written, Papadimitrakopoulos lampoons small-town journalism by providing hilarious examples of the showy foreign phrases and the grammatically dubious *katharevousa* that are employed by half-literate reporters vainly seeking clever effects. Similarly, in the dialogue "Did It Agree with You?", included in *Maritime Hot Baths*, Papadimitrakopoulos mimics the Greek of nouveaux riches. The dialogue, set in a train compartment, could be transformed into a lively one-act play. Papadimitrakopoulos's humor is usually to be savored, not devoured, and can sometimes be missed; one of the characters in the same dialogue indeed remarks that she suffers from "something like interior varicose veins on [her] left leg."

Papadimitrakopoulos's writing is also distinctive in ways that become clear when his polished prose texts are placed within the context of the contemporary Greek short story. Excellent practitioners such as Kostas Taktsis (the stories of *I yiayia mou i Athina* [My Grandmother Athens, 1979] and *Ta resta* [Small Change, 1982], not his famous novel *The Third Wedding Wreath* [1963]), Yiorgos Ioannou, or Menis Koumandareas (b. 1931) derive their first-person confessional modes from the classic European or American models. For his generally much shorter texts, Papadimitrakopoulos's literary paradigm seems closer to the prose poem, a genre perhaps brought into Greek literature by the Surrealist Andreas Embirikos (1901-1975). This affiliation becomes even more visible in his very short prose texts that suggest dreamlike atmospheres, especially those collected in *The General Archivist*. At the same time, Papadimitrakopoulos's shortest texts also resemble *billets d'humeur*, those brief, funny, or sarcastic pieces once common in newspapers.

A further influence is surely the great (and internationally still underestimated) short-story writer Alexandros Papadiamantis (1851-1911), who wrote so poignantly and perceptively about Athens and his native island of Skiathos. Papadimitrakopoulos, long a studious reader of Papadiamantis, has devoted articles to his work, notably to his humor, a quality not widely recognized in that author's tales. (The articles have been collected in *Epi ptilon avras nykterinis* [Upon the Down of a Nocturnal Breeze, 1992].) In both writers, one senses an extraordinary intimacy with the folkways, the various levels of language, as well as the most minute sociological and topographical details of their hometowns and of the cities in which they came to live. In "A Love Story," for example, we are taken through the back streets of Athens, where Papadimitrakopoulos resides when not at his summer home on the island of Paros. Very little of the setting is described, other than that the streets are "full of watery potholes";

the narrator and his lonely girlfriend talk, while walking to the train station; yet we feel immersed in that typical ambience at dusk in Athens, when only a few lights have come on, that unexpected peace and quiet once "the crowds and traffic of the busy avenue[s]" have been left behind.

Papadimitrakopoulos usually achieves his astonishing stylistic economy by evoking key details from an insider's or a participant's viewpoint, an ancient rhetorical technique that not only renders prolonged description superfluous but also transforms the reader into an insider or a participant as well. "Once, she consented to meet me early one Sunday evening behind the soccer field," he writes in "Dancing Lessons," for example. Nothing else about the soccer field needs to be said; only a native of the town would use the definite article "the"; in consequence, not for an instant do we doubt that we, too, are intimates of Pyrgos.

More generally, when appraising the carefully conceived narrative structure of Papadimitrakopoulos's stories, one must keep in mind the extremely long history of short narrative forms in world literature—and not just the modern short story. Papadimitrakopoulos's great talent is that of compression, "abbreviation" (as Greek, Roman, and medieval rhetoricians termed it); one suspects that he has learned much from reading, if not from writing, poetry. Had Papadimitrakopoulos been born in ancient Alexandria, would he not perhaps have penned epitaphs and amorous epigrams or, even more likely, rivaled Sophron, Xenarchus, and Herondas in those concise comedies of everyday life called "mimes"?

Moreover, his minimalism differs significantly in tone from the North American variety. His stories celebrate life in its transitoriness, and even when he derides ridiculous human acts we are invited to look on compassionately. In "The Courtyard," a story from *The General Archivist*, the author recalls tongue-in-cheek the folklore of inner courtyards (beneath which typically lie cesspools), before drawing a moving portrait of his blind grandmother who, while sitting in the courtyard, can miraculously surmise the colors of the clothing worn by her children and grandchildren. "Ah Yiannis! What a joy to look at you are! I see you're wearing your white socks!" The folklore of the courtyard (including the cesspool) is also vividly evoked in "Greek Summer," in which the narrator's wife reminisces about eating fried eggplant and zucchini in her neighbor's courtyard, during her childhood.

However, in *Toothpaste with Chlorophyll* and *Maritime Hot Baths*, we are given relatively few long looks at the author's adult world. (This is less true of *The General Archivist*.) At the same time, we are deftly made aware of—or are made to feel, implicitly—the expanse of years separating the narrator from the events that he is narrating. It takes little to create this effect: an opening line such as "On New Year's Day this year I suddenly started thinking about Vassilis ("The Red Flag") suffices; or an ending such as "A few days ago, while leafing through the local newspaper that has been sent to me for years…" ("The Spanish Guitar").

As in Saint Augustine's formulation: "When we describe the past correctly, it is not past facts which are drawn out of our memories but only words based on our memory-pictures of those facts, because when they happened they left an impression on our minds, by means of our sense-perception. My own childhood, which no longer exists, is in past time, which also no longer exists. But when I remember those days and describe them, it is in the present that I picture them to myself, because their picture is still present in my memory." Further on in his *Confessions*, Saint Augustine speaks of "a present of past things, a present of present things, and a present of future things." And therein lies the key to that especial melancholy (and occasional sarcasm) associated with Papadimitrakopoulos's writings: the unbridgeable gap between the presence of the past (in that instant when the narrator recalls a past event and we become absorbed in the telling) and the sentiment of irreparable loss, once he realizes (and we realize) that the event has, except in our voluntary acts of memory, vanished forever—vanished like the narrator's "sole heroic deed" in "The Obus."

The past, moreover, returns to his mind, not in a continuum (the illusion often perpetuated by novels), but rather in compelling fragments. Epistemologically, the short story is perfectly suited to this fragmentary quality of reminiscence, in particular that type of story in which much of what actually happened is omitted or merely hinted at because it is no longer known or remembered in its entirety. And Papadimitrakopoulos (seemingly) eschews fiction as a means of filling the gaps, the lacunae, the blanks. In "The Nightingale," the plot in fact pivots around a lack of knowledge: about what actually happened when the editor-in-chief invited the cantatrice to dinner.

It is the literature of the American Midwestern small town to which Papadimitrakopoulos's stories set in Pyrgos might be contrasted, with the evident difference that his parody contains none of the scorn of a Sinclair Lewis or the relentless, sometimes artless, drive of a Sherwood Anderson to lay bare the sexual facts. Papadimitrakopoulos's touch is gentle; he prefers to suggest rather than to describe; it is around the modest upturns and mishaps of everyday life that his stories revolve. The leitmotiv, however, is death: of the narrator's father in "In Memoriam"; of several classmates in "The Last Survivor"; of the ever hapless, yet happy-go-lucky Mihalis in "The Red Flag"; of the lovelorn bathing beauty in "Toothpaste with Chlorophyll"; of the old church cantor in the rest home in "The Money Order"; of the thievish Yiannis in "The Spanish Guitar"; of the young Russian show-off in "Maritime Hot Baths"; of the courageous ne'er-do-well Nikos in "Nikos the Seretis"; of the Civil War combatant in "The Execution."

Even in "Cushions," by form more a succinct personal essay than a story (and, in this piece, Papadimitrakopoulos also improvises on the nineteenth-century newspaper sketch), the narrator recalls "the day when Yiannis the Sailor slit the throats—according to some with two knives, according to others with just one—of twelve in a row right in the middle of the sheepfold." The setting is of course the Greek Civil War (1946-1949) and those whose throats are slit are not sheep, but men. Papadimitrakopoulos's prose texts differ from many stories and novels written by his (Greek) contemporaries in that the tragedy is ever human, not ideological. The author suspends his political and moral judgment. Exemplary in this regard is "The Execution," in which the horror of the Civil War is observed, from both sides, by villagers not actively participating in the conflict. Like Chekhov, Papadimitrakopoulos seeks not to provide solutions but rather to describe situations so truthfully that we can no longer evade them. He is a master at evoking the effect that the experience of witnessing another's death has on the minds of the living. The reader is brought into a meditative, though not dark, state of mind, and life is felt fully in all its fragility and mystery.

It is to the emotions that the critic of Papadimitrakopoulos's work must look for meaning—not to ideas, ideologies, or radical narrative experimentation. And it is the emotions conjured up by images in his stories which ring so true: the septuagenarian editor-in-chief's hand poised on the pack of white paper after his relationship with "the nightingale" has ended; Nikos, in "The Last Survivor," hurriedly calling back to the narrator as they are separating in the airport: "I didn't have time to tell you about my illness. My liver has been giving me fits." An anecdote recounted by Papadimitrakopoulos is usually only slightly extraordinary. His stories rarely (or only partly) respect Goethe's dictum that a *Novelle*—albeit, a novella more than a short story—should recount a "sich ereignete unerhörte Begebenheit," an "unheard-of event or incident that has happened." Papadimitrakopoulos usually prefers the less immediately alarming changes in the normal course of events; he seeks to show us what is profound and moving in mere ordinariness.

It is the narrator—perhaps not quite the same person as the author, after all—who emerges as the principal character of the twenty-three stories of *Toothpaste with Chlorophyll* and *Maritime Hot Baths*, all but one of which are written in the first person. ("A Summer Afternoon" is the exception, but, not surprisingly, the manifestly ironic use of the third-person only more conspicuously indicates the author as the true subject of interest.) Through the wry descriptions given of the traditional objects, customs, and everyday occurrences of the Greece of the author's childhood—Papadimitrakopoulos's generation is the one par excellence that not only suffered through the German Occupation and the Civil War, but that also saw the last vestiges of the Old Greece bulldozed away during the 1950s and 1960s—the narrator reveals himself to be melancholic, nostalgic, even embittered. But the genuine source of the narrator's melancholy is less the remembrance of an age that has passed than the recognition that he himself has aged; his nostalgia for the objects and events of his childhood reposes upon the intermittently occurring awareness that time is passing. Often apart, severed, excluded, ever an observer even when also a participant, the narrator of *Toothpaste with Chlorophyll* and *Maritime Hot Baths* has frequent intimations of mortality; and what upon first reading seem to be so many objectively or humorously described acts and gestures reveal themselves in time—such is the subtle effect of the stories—to be subjectively colored at heart with the painful connotation of transience.

*   *   *

One day two small books arrived in the mail, my name and address penned, in sky-blue letters, on the far left side of the envelope. I would come to know well the author's liking for eccentrically addressed envelopes, let alone for unusual stationery products, but—as I had now opened the envelope—for the time being I was concentrating on the deceptively simple first sentence of "Ripe Figs," the first story of a collection entitled both banally and oddly: *Toothpaste with Chlorophyll.* "As I was coming back home from school that noon, it suddenly started showering and I got sopping wet." I realized by the end of the paragraph (as Eleni walks toward the narrator, "her hair crowned by the sunbeams, her perfectly round breasts jutting out from under her school uniform") that the prose of Elias Papadimitrakopoulos—who was completely unknown to me—was already helping me find what I was seeking. It was the poet and folklorist Elias Petropoulos, whose books I was translating at the time, who had told his friend to send his books to me.

After living in Europe for several years, I was seeking to reconcile myself with my Midwestern upbringing and to come to peace with certain deeply felt experiences of my childhood and adolescence, not to mention with my mother's death in 1981. Papadimitrakopoulos's writing, set in Pyrgos, opened up a new perspective on my own past, enabling me to perceive my former emotional surroundings so acutely that I immediately understood how much I needed to re-create them in my own work—however different the middle-class suburb of the much larger American town, Des Moines, in which I grew up during the 1950s and 1960s, was from the quarters evoked in "Nikos the Seretis" or "The Nightingale." Yet differences in sociology, history, architecture, or folklore, not to forget those existing between two languages, matter little when an aspiring author encounters a like sensibility in an older, accomplished writer; the specificity, sometimes untranslatable, of certain details, indeed instructs and encourages. The typical Greek *taverna* evoked in "The Red Flag," for example, suggested how intimately a typical American tavern, located close to my grade school and called "The Bon Ton," was linked to several of my most troubling recollections.

More important, however, than a few transposable insights and far-fetched analogies (the expression "toothpaste with chlorophyll" reminded me of a girlfriend's "raspberry lipstick"), the sincerity of the emotions that Papadimitrakopoulos had fashioned came as a liberation. His way of making the literary and personal spheres one urged me to elaborate certain past experiences and feelings that had lingered, in my mind (and body), well into adulthood. Such experiences and feelings were like vestiges whose significance I had not yet recognized or like obstacles around which I had not yet passed. Papadimitrakopoulos's accomplishment gave me confidence in the literary validity of those experiences and feelings. A voice kept whispering: "Write down those memories you can't avoid, however fragmentary they have become, and try to specify the feelings they provoke in you as an adult." Masterly prose, I was learning, does not have to be "fiction."

By like sensibility I also mean that Papadimitrakopoulos's themes (the fleetingness of time; the deaths of contemporaries and of a beloved parent; the exile from the security of a hometown; the evanescence of the tightly knit neighborhood; the remembrance of adolescent love; the premonitions of one's own mortality) are precisely those that welled up inside me whenever I conjured up my own hometown memories. In comparison to several American classics that I was then rereading (particularly novels and stories set in Midwestern towns and expressing similar themes), I was struck by the stylistic economy of Papadimitrakopoulos's evocations. I had rarely come across such highly concentrated, crystal-clear, evocative prose. The extreme concision, the constant suggestiveness, the emotional authenticity were ever, in my mind, pointing Prose back toward Poetry—as if some original poetic source, absent in the more descriptive prose of other writers to whose subject matter I was nonetheless attracted, had been rediscovered, re-tapped, by this discreet craftsman from Pyrgos. I, too, was aiming for a kind of *intimiste* prose poetry, not mere storytelling. A young writer's problem is to become aware of—and develop confidence in—his unique way or perceiving the world. I learned from Papadimitrakopoulos to set aside the aesthetic dogmas of the classical short story and to persevere, to explore my intuitions. *Toothpaste with Chlorophyll* and *Maritime Hot Baths* taught me what most writers claim to learn from Flaubert: style reflects both the man and his philosophical standpoint.

Papadimitrakopoulos's philosophical standpoint is hued with melancholy. The especial brevity of his stories counterbalances and nuances this universal feeling. Nostalgic in no facile sense of the term (one cannot pine away in rigorous syntax subtly mixing elements of purist *katharevousa* and demotic Greek), he artfully uses melancholy to gradually shift our attention from the spectacle of the everyday world (which he sketches so vividly) to finalities. After reading a few pages, my thoughts inevitably grow meditative. Why we are here once again seems a riddle. A strange quietude, both tense and unsettling, envelops me (or arises within me—it is difficult to tell which), rather like the ambience described at the end of "The Nightingale," when the editor-in-chief, his eyes half-shut, touches the pack of white paper. I imagine what awaits us all and find the world at once sad, fragile, disturbing and very beautiful.

Eros and Other Spiritual Adventures (Veroniki Dalakoura)

A precocious poet who published her first book, *Poiisi '67-'72* (Poetry 1967-1972), at the age of twenty, then a second volume, *I parakmi tou erota* (The Decline of Eros), at twenty-four, Veroniki Dalakoura has also been a literary critic and an important translator of French literature into Greek: she has rendered work by Arthur Rimbaud, Gustave Flaubert, Stendhal, Charles Baudelaire, Henri de Montherlant, Robert Desnos, as well as, pertinently, the *Journal* of the Polish-Russian ballet dancer Vaslav Nijinsky (1890-1950). Let us remember that Nijinsky, after his marriage to a Hungarian ballerina and his subsequent breakup with his homosexual lover and impresario, Sergei Diaghilev, gradually lost his mind.

Dalakoura's haunting, richly allusive prose often similarly evokes intense amorous, artistic, or spiritual emotions, not to mention their disastrous consequences—those "catastrophes" to which she alludes at times, sometimes ambivalently, as in a recent verse-mixed-with-prose text that begins: "So don't leave me alone don't leave me // In dear Hell // This earth has low clouds the notes are flying above my umbrella" (translated by Yannis Goumas). Although she has written a few short stories (notably in *O pinakas tou Hodler* [*Hodler's Painting*, 2001], which also includes a one-act play based on the work of Christopher Marlowe), she habitually introduces dreams, visions, unsettling scenes, and intentionally sketchy plots into her narratives in such ways that the boundaries between poetry and prose (and not just prose poems) are blurred. Her audacious suppression of transitions or endings in places where the reader expects them only increases the ambiguity between lyricism and storytelling—and thus augments the allurement of her writing. Her collection of interconnected, sometimes untitled, prose texts and narratives, *O hypnos* (Sleep, 1982), illustrates her originality.

Much of *Sleep* is set in France, specifically in or near Montpellier, where the writer, who also has a law degree from the University of Athens, studied human geography. The texts weave together the powerful erotic sentiments, disturbing nightmares, and occasional real-life memories—which ultimately seem equally dreamlike—of a more or less anonymous woman narrator whose identity is, nonetheless, teasingly associated with that of the author. Literary references abound, such as to Mallarmé's "Hérodiade" (surely a promising allusion for a researcher to explore), to poets "who died in the 1930s" and who fill the narrator's "soul with an emaciated melancholy," and even to a collective "poetic wombs" in her bold reply to a letter from one Haris, a key figure who reappears as the main character of the title story of *Hodler's Painting*. (This first name echoes the noun *haris*, which means "charm," "enticement," and "grace.") "I also exist, Haris," declares the narrator, "through the knowledge of the senses. What meaning do sounds have today, how shall we recognize the few things that are left, that repose in our poetic wombs?" Related to this epistemological remark giving precedence to sense impressions is the at once physiological, philosophical and mystical aphorism "oculus meus memoria est" that is cited at the end of another text, "The Transubstantiation of Spring," and that may well derive from Saint Augustine's *Confessions*. In any event, thinking of *Sleep* with respect to Saint Augustine's ideas is not unfruitful, especially as regards Time and the ways in which memories are experienced by the mind, the past often invading the present consciousness of Dalakoura's narrators and present time thus becoming a "present of things past," before evolving smoothly or brutally back into a "present of things present (or future)"—and so forth. Despite her talent for rendering heightened sense impressions, Dalakoura is thus no strict empiricist, let alone a realist: she is constantly engaged with the interplay of mental pictures, even as the forceful facts of desire accompany, even spawn, transcendent aspirations. This combination of graphic eroticism and spirituality, typified in French literature by Pierre Jean Jouve, Georges Bataille, Pierre Klossowski, and others, is nearly absent among American poets and writers, by the way. The Greek poet and prose writer Andreas Embiricos, who introduced surrealism into modern Greek literature, also represents this sensibility. As for Dalakoura, the elaborate philosophical underpinnings of her somber, sometimes puzzling, yet also somehow seductive and spellbinding oeuvre, must be kept in mind by any reader pondering the complex representations of autobiography in her writing. She is hardly an autobiographer in any ordinary sense of the term.

This being said, she is very playful in this regard. One text of *Sleep* is entitled "The Second Death of Ang. D.," which suggests both the author's family name and a first name ("Angeliki") rather resembling her own, whereas the prose poem "What Verefon Said to Pegasus" more directly puns Veroniki with Bellerophon. "A young woman I am no longer, Horse," begins this erotic piece that characteristically merges myth and avowal, "which is why, when you fly so high, my heels keep their silence while touching your ribs: what do my feet have to say once your body enthralls my thighs?" Christian symbolism also amply crops up in *Sleep*, notably in this confession at the end of the untitled text that responds to the letter from Haris:

Deep is my gratefulness for lies, adulteries, debaucheries. I thank the brandished chastisements of the angels whom I distressed by following the dictates of my rot-ten will, without the slightest intention to repent. I am grateful—what else can I say?—for the whole Passion Story, for its wise development over the centuries, for that particular end of a silent and just path.

You were silent, Christ, as you watched the gale flooding the streets with the water of a fruitful communion.

But the gifts of that nightmarish truth were destined to remain in my conscience and only there—seeds, simply, of my long enduring guilt.

Amidst such soul-searching, the Other and perhaps the Christ figure as well are essential to Dalakoura's vision. Some texts briefly chronicle the obscure quests of spontaneous *amants*, "(formerly carnal) companions"—as she incisively phrases it in a recent prose poem called "Aversion"— or estranged yet unforgettable ex-lovers, such as an artist named Patrick who now washes dishes in an out-of-the-way restaurant. Other texts, in their depiction of the mind-and-body's dwelling on passions past and present (or future), mysteriously portray down-and-outs or vagabonds like Thierry, whom the narrator chances upon while she is "trying to think of something that would give a special significance to [her] nightly rambling" and who himself hears "a strange music." "The Other One" similarly depicts an encounter outside standard societal norms. Here the narrator comes across a drunken man in the street. This random meeting soon takes on unexpected dimensions, and realistic detail accordingly waxes surrealistic. From the small shopping arcade where the two have taken shelter from the rain, they eventually go up to the narrator's room. There, the man discovers on her face "the paradoxical features of his ancestors":

> On my mouth was his girl cousin. On my right thigh rested his dead child, who before its birth, dazed by the glittering reflections of the maternal womb, exploded. But he whom he loved most, his sister's husband, the one who sailed the seas, hung from my earlobe, sometimes rocking rhythmically back and forth, sometimes changing positions, crossing one knee over the other and snuffling.

Finally, an even more fantastical event ensues, when an icy-eyed blonde woman with "nearly azure clothes" suddenly passes through the wall and remains for a few moments in the room. Much less angelic than deathly, the woman is acknowledged by the man with a mere "It's her," followed by speechlessness. Such hallucinatory emblems of yearning, remorse, or loss surge forth often.

Lost or sought love, and persistent solitude or unfulfilled desire, thus thematically unite *Sleep*, whose Greek title of course also includes the root from which our "hypnosis" is drawn as well as suggests the voluntarily unconscious, truth-liberating, states of mind that fascinated the surrealists. The evolution of each, indeed mesmerizing, story line is never predictable. Sometimes the plot veers from a sequence of fragmentary or lacunary events—set in the present or the past—into lyrical affirmations or more abstract reflections. In "The Second Death of Ang. D.," the narrator, after being violently pushed to the ground by one of two traveling companions (who is now drunk at a student party), is spontaneously asked if she would be able to bear "the revelation of utter solitude." Now occurs one of those transitionless narrative shifts that make Dalakoura's writing so strange and compelling. The violence that the narrator has just suffered suddenly seems totally forgotten. She rationally replies: "I don't know. That would depend on the number of senses I had. In truth, how many senses do we have?" The drunken man, who up to then has mostly been portrayed in all his sordid everyday banality, takes on a powerful, almost magical, prophetic presence. He tells her that one of her wishes will come true, adding, however, that his own "power is human." "I am simply drunk on a heavenly wine," he continues. "And since the heavens do not have, by their very nature, the ability to distinguish good from evil, my power is a product of your own mind, which took me in. So what do you wish?" The narrator beckons him to use his power in such a way that, "bewitched," she will never be allowed to love again.

Bewitchment is essential. In their quest for self-truth, erotic union, mystical communion, or the kind of "amour absolu" that the French surrealists espoused, Dalakoura's narrators delight in intensity per se, little matter if their heightened states of mind and body are linked, as above, with impossibility or resolution. At times, narrators almost relish what seem to be predicaments—as long as the excitement of the (usually amorous) quandaries surpasses the drabness of solitude and the quotidian. Pain can also be pleasurable, as Dalakoura's prose text "Excessive Aestheticism" (*The Decline of Eros*) puts it. In her reply to Haris's letter, the narrator in *Sleep* similarly remembers a night when she "heard the grass growing with a sound [that she] qualified as 'splendid' from the very beginning. It had exactly that sound of a love we are trying to forget." Several other such sustained contradictions, from the emotional viewpoint, crop up. "Amor Omnia" goes on to depict a woman "desperately seeking love," but not knowing where to turn. The story opens in the public park of "No-Ville," a town name suggesting at once nullity, anonymity, amorous rejection, and the dialectics of negativity and affirmation (and of absence and presence) that run through Dalakoura's book. In the story, the narrator has nearly fallen asleep while lying on the grass; she then describes the "erotic splendor" of an abandoned dog's long, wet tongue licking her neck, mouth, and hair; a memory of her (ended) relationship with Patrick follows, before the reminiscence shifts abruptly to "the main port of the country," where she is waiting for "the one and only boat." Tellingly, the prose poet concludes, not with a genuine ending, but with a transition introducing the next text in the book: "Only when the boat had taken to the open sea for good did all my thoughts turn, entirely on their own, to Mary the Egyptian." (Ascetic, spiritually driven figures such as Mary the Egyptian enter into, or are mentioned, in other writings.) Such stories aim less at creating suspense (though several nevertheless carry off this feat), than at accurately tracing how a woman narrator's memories and thoughts "turn," and continue to "turn," moving back and forth between present and past (or the anticipated future), between objective perception and introspection (or hallucination), between exact sense impressions and multifaceted feeling. Saint Augustine joins company with surrealists often.

After *Sleep*, Dalakoura produced a similarly ambitious prose work. Literally entitled *The Game of the End* (*To paihnidi tou telous*, 1988), which can thus also be construed as a Beckettian "Endgame" (though the respective books have nothing in common), the book consists of three long, likewise intriguingly interrelated, stories that are accompanied by an enigmatic introductory text, "The Meeting." At the beginning, the woman narrator comes across a character named V., with whom she discusses the relative merits of poetry and prose, as well as the limits of perception and literary description. Once again, the initial is suggestive.

As in the shorter prose texts of *Sleep*, the tales of *The Game of the End* are told by narrators who (when they discover, for example, that the curtains are not closed but open) entangle themselves in mysteries. The mysteries lead them on nocturnal investigations, adventures, "voyages out," "voyages of the soul." Between the world of dreams and the world of reality, between consciousness and unconsciousness, curiosity and fascination turn into fear—fear even of the kind that Edgar Allan Poe knew how to arouse in his reader. And like the Poe whom Baudelaire and, later, the French surrealists admired, Dalakoura celebrates what normally repels or perturbs: chaos, random chance, bizarreness, lust, disquiet, and insecurity.

A concern with the means and ends of literature is never absent from these prose texts. Various rhetorical devices are brought out and toyed with; other characters besides V. bear as names mere initials; their genders change in mid-fiction; settings are only vaguely described; why and wherefores are obsessively pursued, but only rarely elucidated. As in dreams or hallucinations, sometimes objects, emotions, and events take on exaggerated magnitudes and intensities. This is writing that has been informed, less by the fundamentally realistic tradition of most modern Greek prose, which was founded by Georgios Vizyenos and Alexandros Papadiamantis in the late nineteenth and early twentieth centuries—Greek poetry is another matter—than by romanticism, surrealism, and modernist narrative techniques developed in the literatures of other European countries.

* * *

Dalakoura's more recent poetry and short poetic prose, all revolving around love, lust, "mal de vivre" (as one of her prose poems is entitled), "difficulté d'être" (as she puts it elsewhere), and spiritual yearnings, have been collected in *Meres idonis* (Days of Pleasure [or Lust], 1990), *Agria angeliki photia* (Wild Seraphic Fire, 1997) and *26 Poiimata* (26 Poems, 2004). Once again, dreams, nightmares, visions, prayers, paradoxes, synaesthetic perceptions ("beneath this stone / strange syllables can be heard"), numerous literary references, and enigmatic narratives are found in all these poems and prose pieces. And again, the symbol-driven language, formulated in the first person, is accompanied by such credible emotions, ranging from despair or melancholy to longing and exaltation (and also comprising self-controlled audacious confession), that an illusion of autobiographical writing obtains even in extreme fictive cases invoking madness or dereliction. The poem "Garden" of *Days of Pleasure* is one such case, with its initial evocation of what seems to be a specific childhood memory and then, as punctuation breaks down, its concluding cry of madness and vengeance. The poem also comprises Dalakoura's characteristic juxtaposition of gardens and forests:

> No one had ever accompanied me
> into the dark garden.
> So I hid behind the first bush,
> listening to the flowing water and screaming
> amid the silence of a day
> that should never happen again.
> Time thus flowed through the branches.
> The slightest instant of time was pulverized.
> Each night promised a future darkness,
> while day announced mere fleeting light
> and nothing, nothing, resembled what
> had occurred.
> Damned be those
> who led me into a garden
> that was not a forest!
> Yes, I curse Nature
> mountains
> the nauseating soil
> my hovel is a ditch
> I eat nothing but mud
> nothing else
> is left.

Subjectivity, identity, and identification with others are thus key issues in this writing. Such themes can materialize in hostile environments other than the social worlds where love is found, played out, and lost. Dalakoura centers some of her poems on a woman narrator's sense of threat and imprisonment within natural surroundings that, at the same time, are ontologically remote, in fact separate, from her. In the above poem, the narrator cannot get any closer to Nature than crouching behind a bush, as it were. She listens, intuits—with what seems to a sixth sense—and arguably screams because there is no possibility of communion (or communication). Only when a kind of illuminating insanity invades her does the stark separation cease: her house becomes a ditch and she eats mud, this brutal union with pure matter enabling her to escape from, at least temporarily (and in the final reckoning, illusorily), the mental torments caused by her introspective observations of the silent day, each instant of time, the "future darkness."

The tense "My Last Love will be with You" similarly begins: "Lies! / Summer is a poison / The sunshine icier / than the imprisoned / spring." Seasons or natural elements thereby become correlatives of exacerbated negative emotions and existential wretchedness. In the short but exceedingly complex "No," entrapment and impossibility are implicit, as a mystical vision ends with a prayer-like entreaty. As in the un-thirst-quenching water of "Garden" (above), the woman narrator is first confronted with another, seemingly unattainable, flowing liquid: rain. Rain is also habitually associated with nourishment. Yet then, even if the snow is melting in what has suddenly become a more tangible setting (transformations of visionary vistas into more realistic land- or cityscapes, and vice versa, is hardly uncommon in Dalakoura), no beneficial or curative water emanates from it. Infertility, represented by the ash-covered boulders and floating dust motes, persists:

> Rain, incessant rain, and humankind's fear
> enters the realm of light.
> All that begins with marvel ends in fright.
> How many memories are hidden in this fertile garden!
> The snow is melting, but no water flows
> over the gray surface of the ash-covered boulders:
> just a myriad of dust motes dangling in a festive mist.
> I keep getting ever further away, God, from the
>   clarity of Night.

Giving voice and form to this "clarity of Night," a phrase resonating from Saint John of the Cross to Novalis, sums up well one of Dalakoura's deepest aims.

* * *

The title *Wild Seraphic Fire* is drawn from Robert Burns's long poem, "The Cotter's Saturday Night," in particular this passage:

> The priest-like father reads the sacred page,
> How Abram was the friend of the God on high;
> Or, Moses bade eternal warfare wage
> With Amalek's ungracious progeny:
> Or how the royal bard did groaning lie
> Beneath the stroke of Heaven's avenging ire
> Or Job's pathetic plaint, and wailing cry;
> Or rapt Isaiah's wild seraphic fire;
> Or other holy seers that tune the sacred lyre.

Dalakoura often appeals to "angelic" symbols and, as has been seen, has used the first name "Angeliki" for characters or narrators. In *Sleep*, a short poem inserted early in the book announces: "You all welcome / the Vita Nuova / that a creature / —angelic like me— / promises you." Her work in fact increasingly shows a spiritual quest within a broad Christian framework, though without diminishing in the slightest the electric erotic charge that has characterized her oeuvre from the very beginning. Some of Dalakoura's symbols are recognizably biblical, such as a cherub repeating "steadfast love, resplendent body" who pops up in a prose text entitled "Phili" ("Woman Friend"). But as happens often elsewhere, this Christian symbol is not to be taken literally. It is actually a voice heard in a dream or daydream, the state in which the poet has access to, literally, "sur-real" realms; the words soon turn out to be spoken by one Sonia, a no less phantomlike figure who makes a sudden appearance here and about whom nothing else is revealed. "As I approached," simply reports the narrator, "she appeared ever further away, but the tracks that I noticed in the snow, in the forest clearing, were hers." Other oneiric, troubled, desirous, and perhaps delirious states of mind and body are sketched in this book, each associated with unresolved crises. A prime example is "Adana," the title of which (designating the Turkish town) remains a private symbol that nonetheless speaks to our own secretly magnetic place-names. The text also cryptically alludes to the story of Joseph, Jacob, and the Ismaelites (Genesis 37: 12-36); moreover, it obliquely evokes aging and erotic desire:

> My battered face cannot ensure a sequel to any fling. This does not mean that I have forgotten: your own face never actually existed, even if fate made us neighbors—friendship is excluded. Later I gave in. Unborn yet already my brother's guardian, I keep returning to a town that I did not acknowledge when I incited the guffaws of its dark-haired men.

> Dark like circumspection:
> the image on the lake's edge.
> An exodus toward the sea?
> A disorderly march to Nothingness.
> This is insane.

26 Poems continues to explore the subject matter that has long haunted the poet. Verse poems and prose poems invoke such revealing archetypes as Demeter, a "Heavenly Father who acquires feeling when / crystalline awe vibrates," a "Christo caído," as well as a seemingly disturbed man sitting on a bench in an unlighted basement and the "old woman of indeterminable age" who is confined with him. The latter couple recalls the dereliction and abandonment invoked in *Sleep* and other books. A telltale piece ("Machines") combining prose and verse makes this severe statement: "Dead are all those who stay at Love's hotel." (The Greek word here is "agápi," not "éros.") But Dalakoura then enjoins us to "struggle naked on the jagged stones."

Two poems of this collection especially bring the personal and the mythical to an even more intense merging, or standoff, than in her previous work. "Solitude" is surely addressed to her mother. "I owe you everything," writes

Dalakoura. "Potter's clay the precarious / structure of divine guilt / the shadow of whomever shaped / the pyramid / with a sense of goodwill. // Before I could say 'save me' I was born / of you. Inside your soft belly / throbbed the odd substance / creating, O god of superfluity, / fear / of the future existence / I owed." Dalakoura's entire oeuvre can be studied with these lines in mind. That is, if one also remembers these, from "Ghosts": "This writing is not theater, just as I have nothing to do with the drama."

Bulgaria

My Life as Someone Else's
(Kapka Kassabova)

Kapka Kassabova (b. 1973) is a Bulgarian who, after living in her homeland, England, France, and Germany, settled in New Zealand and began writing in English. Already at an early age for an author who chose as her literary language one that she had learned only in young adulthood, and not at school, she wrote two novels and two books of poetry, *All Roads Lead to the Sea* (1997) and *Dismemberment* (1998). The well-received *Someone Else's Life* (2003) then included revised poems from these first two collections, as well as twenty-one new pieces. And in 2007, she published *Geography for the Lost*, gathering forty-eight new poems and comprising "Skipping over Invisible Borders," a prose account of her childhood in communist Bulgaria, her multilingualism, and her family's expatriations, first to England, then to New Zealand. She tells the story of how she, like Joseph Conrad, might more logically have decided to write in the French that she had mastered at her Sofia-based French *lycée*. Kassabova is one of several writers from the Eastern European Communist Bloc countries who, in the postwar decades leading up to the fall of the Berlin Wall in 1989, and sometimes even thereafter, chose or were obliged—in one way or another—to exchange a mother tongue for a different, literary one, usually French or English. The full story of this diaspora remains to be told.

Understandably, Kassabova often evokes home-leavings. "All my life," she declares in "Angel's Lament" (*Someone Else's Life*), "I have wanted this: / to be inside the story / to have a street with a name and a corner shop / to have a window with curtains."

Accompanying these yearnings for domestic stability, however, are deeper philosophical problems that this promising poet expresses with melancholy clarity. Being "inside the story" first entails being inside one's life—which is rarely possible. As the title *Someone Else's Life* suggests, a sense of unreality arises whenever Kassabova glances in the mirror. Who is it, she asks in "Mirages," who wakes up every morning "in the same skin"? We need "more and more evidence," she observes, of who we are and even (one might add) that we are. "I listened carefully to doubts and revisions / of someone else's life," she notes similarly, "safe in my room of tomorrow, / a passing witness to sorrow and wonder. // Then night came and I was quickly / drifting inside that life. I was leaving mine."

The reasons for this troubling impression of living "someone else's life" extend beyond the consequences of geographical mobility, which Kassabova actually emphasizes less than one might expect. In some poems her symbolism is conventional, but, overall, her haunting and sensitive poems memorably express a paradox that is all too tangible for the body and the mind: the self apperceiving itself and finding, at best, only an estranged ghostlike substance.

Geography for the Lost again focuses on this theme. As before, it is not really displacement that gives the poet a sense of being a stranger to herself. "I imagine my life as a city," she observes more generally, "and I want to be a tourist / in the city of my life." Other individuals, even loved ones, produce the same effect on her. The ironic, intentionally prosaic "Travel Guide to the Country of Your Birth" concludes with "dark, empty apartments" in which "the people you love live inside mirrors." Although Kassabova is no poetic experimenter, the form of this poem is unusual in that the first line has one word ("which"), the second four ("has over 300 natural lakes"), the third eight ("is one of the oldest countries in Europe"), while subsequent lines become longer; already prosaic at the onset, the poetry increasingly becomes prose, an anti-lyrical progression and a distancing effect that reinforce the narrator's numbed bewilderment, even restrained bitterness.

Along with two pieces devoted to a former lover left behind in Europe and a poem narrating her grandfather's suicide ("how easy after all / to never see the mountains, the kids, / to never say goodbye again. Seven storeys down..."), the most memorable poem is dedicated to her parents. It seemingly depicts them watching a sunset.

Being myself a longtime expatriate, I can mention that observing natural phenomena—a sunset is emblematic—in an adopted foreign country is often accompanied by superposed mental images of those same phenomena occurring in the distant homeland, perhaps during childhood. The juxtaposition can be moving, even disturbing, as Marcel Proust famously showed with his analogous example of uneven courtyard paving stones, at the Hôtel des Guermantes, conjuring up those at Saint Mark's in Venice. The past becomes overwhelmingly present to the mind, as also sometimes does the uncertain future.

Something similar happens to the sunset gazers. As they watch "the miracle shrink behind the hills," they are invaded by panic, a sentiment of doom, impossibility. "We started sliding," continues Kassabova, lending her voice to the couple,

> from our best lives, here at the slippery
> centre, and we ran
>
> behind the moving sky
> in stupor of transience,
> in a slow motion of terror.

God, we felt like yelling,
how much remains to us,
how do we measure it?

Then, this poet who usually stresses irresolvable existential instability and mirror-like reflections of emptiness, tenders a sort of wisdom, or at least a compromise: acceptance. She implicitly reestablishes the "centre" as where one is, be it Sofia, Essex, or Mission Bay. The running away has merely gone on in the couple's mind. "We just held hands," reports the plural narrator, "Then it was gone behind the hill. // Dusk fell and we walked on." Yet this is not all. The final distich answers the questions that cannot really be asked of God by these "inhibited...sceptic[s]." "This is the only world," understands the couple, "this is the only measure." It seems that this postulate, as applied to both life and literature, is the precisely one that will continue to challenge Kassabova.

Hungary

Milk Teeth Biting Granite
(Attila József)

Rather like Béla Bartók weaving the melodies and rhythms of Central-European folk music into his own intense, exacting compositions, Attila József (1905-1937) uses the sophisticated rhymes and meters of traditional Hungarian poetry to express themes that vary from the painfully personal to the humanistic concerns of many avant-garde writers of his day. József's own experience of squalor and trauma (he was placed in a cruel foster home by his destitute mother, and he barely knew his father, who abandoned the family) made him sensitive to the acute suffering and poverty of other Hungarians. "With milk teeth," he typically asks both himself and his *semblable* in one of the last poems written before his violent suicide, "why did you bite granite?" At the same time, the death-obsessed poet, who penned his epitaph at twenty-three and who elsewhere imagines a "blackening corpse coffined within [his] heart," knows how to move beyond the strictly intimate, or the facilely political, and open up philosophical vistas looking out on the "last retreat of being" or on a "nothingness" that "flits and dances / as if it a something were." The title of a generous Bloodaxe selection, *The Iron-Blue Vault*, derives from his odd perception, characteristically mixing cosmology, theology, social irony, and modern physics, that "in heaven's iron-blue vault revolves / a cool and lacquered dynamo."

One may quibble with Zsuzsanna Ozsváth and Frederick Turner's systematic desire to reflect the complex poetics of the original; their versions at times exhibit irritating half-rhymes or syntactic unnaturalness, even if the translators thus provide an impression of the prosodic richness and intricacy of the Hungarian poems. This latent musicality must, of course, always be kept in mind when reading József. The ample and excellently introduced Bloodaxe selection is thus an important translation that can be complemented by the more natural, yet also sometimes rhymed, renderings of Peter Hargitai in *Perched on Nothing's Branch* (White Pine) and of Gábor G. Gyukics and Michael Castro in *A Transparent Lion* (Green Integer). The latter includes a few very short poems, one of which—a single line—obliquely but also quite subtly depicts the sense of pending doom that the poet must often have felt during his brief life: "The ice on the lake is covered with slushy snow." A distich more directly states: "I don't belong to anyone, my word is a flying mold / I'm light and heavy like the cold."

In French translation, all of József's poems and much of his prose have appeared as *Aimez-moi: l'oeuvre poétique* (Phébus). This title is rather maudlin, but it is nonetheless right on target. The man's poignant, profound verse courageously chronicles the despair of a failed lover, an abandoned son, and a desolate if consummate artist, "one"—as his last poem heartrendingly puts it—"who hopes for hearth and home and family / only for others, when all's done."

The No-Man's Land of the Nameless
(Ágnes Nemes Nagy)

In an essay appended to *The Night of Akhenaton*, a selection of the poetry of
Ágnes Nemes Nagy (1922-1991), the Hungarian poet argues that her work is
situated in "a no-man's land of the nameless." It is a striking phrase which, moreover, points to analogous aspirations of other key twentieth-century European writers. Recalling Rilke's remark about poets standing arrested at borders and grabbing
at "nameless things," this image of an unclaimed or uninhabited land—ambiguous
or indefinite in character and perhaps extending between opposing armies—provides
a graphic way of thinking about how certain poets have lingered solitarily in zones
ignored or avoided by others. Some of those zones are perilous.

Nemes Nagy conceives "no-man's land" and "nameless" in no mystical
way. She is speaking about ordinary Budapest streets and certain "nameless
emotions" that can be garnered in them. Later she contemplates mere forests,
lakes, or falling snow:

> This downpouring of silence, I
> don't even know if I'm hearing it,
> this hardly-there snow-pallor, I
> don't even know if I'm seeing it
>
> Only the pine tree, only the roof,
> outlines on which it falls
> as it hesitates at peripheries
> brightens and appalls.

What she means by emotion thus comprises questioning, self-questioning,
and learning, all cognitive phenomena that are usually associated with rationality
alone. It is this poetic angle and critical viewpoint that provoke thought; only
a few stubborn observers, from philosophers David Hume and Maine de Biran
to the contemporary neurologist Antonio Damasio, have likewise considered
emotions to be essential for understanding the human condition. Some poets
may be "specialists of the emotions," as Nemes Nagy contends, but certainly
the overall role of the emotions in literature has never been satisfactorily elucidated. For her, poetry wages an "epistemological campaign...in the domain
of our own unnamed emotions in order to enlarge our awareness."

Be assured that she does not equate poetry with epistemology. She is extremely attentive to the music of the Hungarian language, especially its rhymes—of which her most recent translator, the poet George Szirtes, provides pleasing parallels. Her critical remarks are in fact prefaced by a technical description of how "agglutination" in Hungarian is one of the reasons

> why twentieth-century Hungarian poetry—taking advantage of the language's assonantal riches—is much more rhymed than is usual in most other literatures. As for rhythm, the sharp juncture of the syllables has made it possible for three rhythmic systems to live side by side in Hungarian poetry : one stressed, one quantitative, and one a combination of the two. This unusual feature…proves without doubt its thorough prosodic sophistication, its rich poetic possibilities.

The reputation of this incisive poet was launched just after the Second World War. She and her husband, the critic Balázs Lengyel, co-founded the best Hungarian literary magazine of the day, *Ujhold* ("New Moon"). Yet after a brilliant start, during which T. S. Eliot, Eugenio Montale, George Seferis, Eugène Ionesco, and Samuel Beckett were associated with the review, it was banned in 1949 by the Communist government. Lengyel and other contributors were sent to prison, while Nemes Nagy was silenced for a while. She subsequently wrote children's books and translated foreign poetry, all the while writing poems (though never prolifically). An initial *Selected Poems*, translated by Bruce Berlind, appeared in 1980, followed eight years later by Hugh Maxton's *Between: Selected Poems of Ágnes Nemes Nagy*. During those last years of her life, her work was rediscovered by younger Hungarians. As Szirtes explains in his sensitive, witty, and penetrating introduction to this new selection, Nemes Nagy "was always too distant, too unbending, too disdainful of popularity to be a popular writer, but was at the same time acknowledged to be of the first importance. (. . .) She has exerted a lasting influence on poets coming after her: on Zsuzsa Rakaovszky, on Gyözö Ferencz, and on Mónika Mesterházy. To some degree it is a moral influence as much as a matter or range or technique, something to do with integrity."

Despite her suffering at the hands of Stalinist hard-liners, Nemes Nagy was never an *engagé* writer. Yet she sometimes alludes to recent Hungarian history, most notably in the Akhenaton sequence (which gives an overall title to Szirtes's selection). It is a series of long and short poems, portraying the revolutionary and spiritual-minded Egyptian pharaoh, who keeps a notebook and desires to invent a new kind of god:

> In carving myself a god, I kept in mind
> to choose the hardest stone that I could find.
> Harder than flesh and not given to wincing:
> its consolation should appear convincing.

Yet this renewal of faith in affirming acts and sentiments (in the last poem, "love" as embodied in Nefertiti becomes the new deity) must first come to terms with the bloody 1956 uprising of the Hungarians against their tank-driving Soviet overlords. Employing the modernist technique of juxtaposing disparate historical periods, Nemes Nagy passes these tragic events through Akhenaton's mind:

> *I only wish that you, my love*
> *were as small as the god on the wafer.*

And the tanks were already coming.
> The street ran along
> its stone bed before mountainous waves of metal,
> and soft bodies ran between stone and metal
> still trailing a few balloons behind them ...

I dwell on this underlying political element because Nemes Nagy masterfully evokes intricate emotions that seem, upon subsequent readings, to comprise even more aspects than one had noticed. Szirtes pinpoints the "crystalline" quality of her verse, "something both highly clear and highly structured in the experience of reading her poems," and he adds that "this does not mean that the clarity is itself the poem: as with a crystal there is an awareness of refracted light, of light held and turned about various facets." Some facets are political and especially historical, for she is sensitive to how the past coincides with the present. Her poems are tightly crafted and often succinct, with formal metrical and rhyme schemes at work, yet they express more polysemy, provide more interpretative possibilities, than most concise poems composed by other hands. An allusion to imprisonment is perhaps even hidden in this late poem, a terse quatrain presumably dealing with ennui, weariness, forebodings about death and nothingness, or the unsurpassable border of sheer physical materialism:

> The empty sky. The empty sky.
> I can't tell what might satisfy.
> No more perhaps than a few bars
> across the window to stop my eye.

In other words, Nemes Nagy highlights a single perception, but not a single emotion; she brings forth nexuses of coexistent feelings, some of them mutually contradictory. Moreover, the repetition of the opening words indicates a movement from perception to apperception, from awareness to self-awareness. This, too, is typical. Staring at the sky culminates in self-conscious staring, musing, then wishing. By the way, if her wish about the window bars is fulfilled, will it result in inner peace or a sentiment of entrapment?

Probably both. Emotional ambivalence is all too human, and it functions as an equivalent of poetic truth for Nemes Nagy. She is lucid about human contradictions and paradoxes. A poem squarely narrated in the first person, yet on a "strange afternoon," becomes no less than "evidence" of the narrator's "not-me sense." The me and the not-me? The self and the other; that is, the self as other? It is here that the concept of no-man's land once again proves useful.

For Nemes Nagy (like all of us) is caught between irresolvable antinomies: subjectivity and objectivity, ideas and things, physics and metaphysics, faith and disbelief, heritage and rupture. Her list would include art and science, as well as thinking and feeling. She lingers in such no-man's lands not because she prefers states of limbo, but rather because she is acutely aware of the truth they represent; how, in human experience, oppositions at once struggle against each other and interrelate.

The latter dichotomy of thinking and feeling is crucial. It is not ideas about existence, but rather unsettling, uncanny, not immediately definable feelings that open up access to our most genuine relationship with aliveness. By focusing on feeling (while naming no specific ones), Nemes Nagy seeks to restore the immediacy of this deep relationship, which—she avers—can be sensed at any moment: on the corner of Kékgolyó Street, for instance, when sunlight falls at a certain angle on the Castle.

What she calls emotion is thus neither sentimentality, as she explains in her essay, nor modernist surrogates for traditional poetic emotions. Pointing to the "recurring waves of avant-garde revivals, [and] the various fads and schools" of twentieth-century poetry, this Hungarian avant-gardist cautions: "Not that emotion does not sneak back into the poem under various excuses and guises: instead of private emotion collective emotion, instead of manifest emotions suppressed emotion, instead of 'beautiful' emotion 'ugly' and 'true' emotion, instead of a complex of related emotions fragments, allusions, visions; instead of pathos irony, and so forth."

In her quest for rarer, life-revealing, "post-illusion pockets of emotion" (as she defines it), she expands her purview to include "crucial things in our lives [that] happen in domains beyond the senses, among atoms and solar eruptions, nucleic acids, and ozone shields." Modern science by no means intimidates her. On the contrary, in her long-poem "Between," she combines facts and perspectives from ornithology, meteorology, geography, geology, and astronomy, in order to announce "decimations and incisions, / droughts and visions, / inarticulate resurrections, / the unbearable vertical tensions / between up-above and down-below." This apocalyptic or primeval natural pageant may at first seem beyond humanness and thus beyond emotion, though the spectacle itself necessarily engenders an emotion. And in the following, and final, stanza, Nemes Nagy leaves the reader with an even stranger sentiment. Rather like Mozart, who claimed that music lies between the notes, the Hungarian poet outlines an almost palpable "betweenness." But is this betweenness, including the cryptic "between sky and sky," the locus of a metaphysics? These "betweennesses" are all no-man's lands, in any event:

Various climates and conditions.
Between. The stone. The tracks of tanks.

A line of black reed on savannah border,
written on pond and sky in lines, in double order,
two dark stones with cryptographs
stars' diacritics, acutes and graves—

Between sky and sky.

In comparison to the "explosions in deep mountain bores" of "Between" and other poems drawing on geology (a favorite subject), the "cumulations of concrete anxieties" unearthed by archaeologists in the prose poem "A Terraced Landscape" seem pathetically funny. Among other appurtenances of existence, these "anxieties" are often hats: turbans, a velvet beret, a swineherd's fur-toque, a coolie hat, a sailor's cap. "Objects carry 'news,'" proclaims Nemes Nagy, then continues: "If we try to enclose in a poem the being of an object that has somehow touched us *as it is*, then—perhaps—we may capture a corner of a *Ding-an-sich* world sufficient unto itself. And where is the poet to find objects for this purpose? In Kékgolyó Street."

This ideal *Ding-an-sich* world is of course that of her mentor Rilke and the philosopher Edmund Husserl, whose respective examples encouraged questioning, among Nemes Nagy's contemporaries and immediate precursors, of the poet-observer's overly anthropomorphic vision of the material world. The idea spread that objects should be depicted as they really were. Poets experimented with this paradox of recovering, through words, not "me and the mimosa tree," as the French poet Francis Ponge famously put it, but rather the "mimosa tree without me." In a late poem entitled "In the Garden," Nemes Nagy offers a more complex variant by imagining wiping "the as-if from the as-if-now, / the as-if-it-existed."

As in the Akhenaton sequence, superposing the past on the here and now enables this self-styled "objective lyric poet" to discover still another no-man's land. "In the Garden" adds a temporal dimension to the object-in-itself world. "A person might in fact believe," she writes, "the past would fade away. But no, / it vanishes, then reappears, / (...) just like the seasons which sometimes / condense into seed and sometimes extend / down the unmarked highways of space-time." Some objects, like seeds, grow into objects that produce more seeds; perceiving reproducible living things must thereby take time into account. Nemes Nagy's allusion to Einstein is hardly gratuitous.

Hence, those who have previously visited the garden return to "walk round in circles, during the whole monotonous / journey turning their backs on us, / though sometimes they might turn round to face us." Even an inert coil of cable left behind on a boulder once again seems charged with electricity and to resemble the luminous faces of the revenants, "now blazing, now fading / away on the spiral cables / of time." The prisms of consciousness, in the present, are indeed multifaceted. The unresolved dialectics of another poem, "This I have seen...," similarly evoke this feeling of not so much *déjà vu* as *déjà vécu*:

This I have seen (This I have never seen)
Here I have been (Here I have never been)
(...)
Perhaps in some other life
(Some other dying, possibly)
Wearing veils, I came this way.

Such lines show Nemes Nagy at her most enigmatic, though it is important to remember that, long before her, Saint Augustine similarly analyzed the presence of things past (and things future, not to mention "things present") in the present time of consciousness. Sensing the presence of the past causes the Hungarian poet to suspend belief in superficial appearances and objects-in-themselves—an act that itself creates a particular emotion. This especial ambivalence about the real world is probably best summarized in a poem more likely set in primordial Central Europe than in California. The poet imagines herself wandering through a stand of gigantic sequoias. At first, they represent a "Platonic idea of pine forest. / Pine forest but ten times greater." Dendrological details then become precise and sensual:

...a fibre-knotted husk
whose pocks suggest a breasted creature,
a breasted deity, whose touch
might be the salvation of your palms
could you but reach above her swollen root.

At the end, Nemes Nagy turns her imagination—the verbs remain in the conditional tense—to sunlight peeking between trees. She concludes that "its glance would mark a shining path that lit / here and nowhere else and answered no known question." For some readers, such (imagined) perceptions surely open out onto the spiritual, or at least the mysterious. Yet here as elsewhere, Nemes Nagy cogently restricts herself to what can be known, which is very little. She scrutinizes the shining path of photons; it gives an answer, surely; but the question, she knows, lies in another, still unexplored, no-man's land.

Holding Hungary's Broken Peony
(Sándor Csoóri)

Are robust poems still written in America? This question will perhaps occur to other readers of Sándor Csoóri's vigorous collection *Before and After the Fall,* vividly translated by Len Roberts. Born in 1930, Csoóri is a prolific Hungarian poet, essayist, and novelist who has distinguished himself by criticizing Hungarian society and politics both before and after the 1989 collapse of Communism (whence the title, which in some poems also seemingly alludes to a symbolic Eden).

Csoóri experienced firsthand the ravages of the Second World War (see the graphic "Returning Home from Flight after the War") and began writing during a perilous, deceitful period of Hungarian history. His first collection, *The Bird Takes Wing,* was published two years before the 1956 Soviet invasion; his second collection, *Devil-Butterfly,* one year afterwards; his third volume, *Escape from Loneliness,* in 1962. He still evokes those years in *Before and After the Fall,* most memorably as he alludes to torture in "Wandering in a Former Party Office Building" or to street fighting in "Remembering November, 1956." "I was weaponless," he recalls in the latter poem, "no flag, / no knife, /...but the names and faces / of revolutionaries executed / outside Márie Therése Barracks / were hidden beneath my skin."

His forcible poetic discourse notwithstanding, Csoóri's reactions to dire events are indeed not shallow, immediate, or skin-deep. Despite sometimes directly suffering from political iniquity, Csoóri has by no means produced unsubtle engagé poems whose dubious prosody it would be better to pass over in silence. On the contrary, his metrically forthright verse solicits (and bears) rereading. Ultimately complex in sense and sentiment, the poems can be both studied quietly and, conceivably, heard as dramatic monologues recited in a spacious theater.

Walt Whitman comes to mind. Like the American, Csoóri might sum up his poetics with a bold: "I am the man, I suffer'd, I was there" ("Song of Myself"). Evidently an acute sensibility, he never hedges when expressing his emotions; all the while he remains a precious eyewitness undaunted (if infuriated) by what he sees or remembers. His narrative "I" belongs to an endangered species: the impassioned, compassionate Individual. This Individual has a few variants, of course. Csoóri is capable of empathy ("I, too, might have been a drunken / dirty frontline soldier"); he also gives brief, somehow more specific (and self-ironic) glimpses of himself, as when he converses with his mirror rather unsuccess-fully, before concluding: "Just stare at... / ...the middle of the whitewash, / the whitewash. What's left of your endlessness / still whirls in it, as the morning light / whirls in a pupil strung tight." In another poem, he adds that he is at once "Nobody" and "the memory of an unstoppable, demonstrating crowd / marching like a voiceless procession from street to street, / the concrete behind it tapping, / time tapping." The last two lines give an idea of the intricate meanings that Csoóri often ties, like afterthoughts, to more facile images.

In the Book of Revelations, an angel tells John: "Write down what you see." Csoóri acknowledges similar interlocutors (Christian allusions mark several poems) while conjuring up time and again an apocalyptic atmosphere that is looming, not in the future, but now. In the prayer-like "The Time Has Come," he speaks Jeremiah-like to God: "I... / can see continents loaded with garbage gliding into each other daily, / and indifferent empires spitting into the sea. / Smoke, smoke, poisoned dust and the gang of poisoned words roam among our quiet hours."

These "poisoned words" reveal Csoóri's sensitivity to the ways in which languages—not just German—were first perverted by Nazi and other Fascist speech, second by Communist doublespeak, and finally by the debilitating abstractions, mollifying euphemisms, distracting trivia, and downright lying of those holding linguistic sway today. In this poem and others, there is equally a notion of a lost (or perturbed) Paradise from which the poet, inclined to con-templation, has "fallen" and now must speak. As Csoóri sits among bucolic ferns in Finland, for instance, he initially enjoys "plenty of time / ...fate doesn't hiss at me from the underworld grass." But destiny does call. Harbinger-like sea gulls drop in on him, leaving the sky above him white with "scribbling." His thoughts turn to how "in the city, / gold watches throb nervously / and fifty million half-mad wheels revolve in the street, / revolve in the ground, above the ground, / in the bowels of machines." Now that his sylvan introspection is interrupted, Csoóri wonders more generally whether a poet can remain aloof, whether he can ignore the violence that is done to contemporary man, can "drift / in an idyllic way... / along the path of poisoned needles / and fire-branded missiles, / accompanied by imperial ear-ringing music." Yet his answer gives pause because it is artfully postponed; it is in fact left unstated. He decides to linger a little longer among the ferns and hearken to the "old, very old" forest talking to itself. For all his spotting of evildoing and injustice, Csoóri's verse typically ends with an arresting image, not a definite conclusion, revealing a search for a wisdom greater than ready-made replies can provide. Interestingly, his energetic poetic rhythms often engender a meditative silence.

Csoóri typically notes the precise locations of these tense moments of self-rediscovering withdrawal and outward-gazing decision-making. Gellert Hill,

Szentendré, Basalt Hill, Bakony, Sashegy's slope, Fehérvár, Zámoly (the village where he was born), the Matras Peaks, the Esztergom Hills, the Danube—such place names nail a poem to a specific here and now and provoke the reader into defining similar personal loci of heightened awareness. One leaves such verse—occasional in the noblest sense of the term—with the conviction that Csoóri, unlike the mentors ("madmen, poets, / alcoholic saints") whose absence he laments in "My Masters," is fully and provocatively among us, "holding Hungary's broken peony in [his] hands."

Good-Bye Mother
(Péter Esterházy)

What can a writer say—write—when his mother dies? Can writing help him come to terms with her excruciating pain? With her final days in an anonymous hospital? Can writing overcome grief? And what about the ethical dilemma of writing about a loved one's death? Is it "deplorable," as the narrator of *Helping Verbs of the Heart* (1985) wonders, when writing "grows out" of another's death?

These questions are raised by the Hungarian essayist, playwright, and novelist Péter Esterházy (b. 1950) in his stylistically unsettling, obliquely moving novel, which was the first of his many books to appear in English (in a consistently smooth version by Michael Henry Heim). Esterházy's response to these questions is equally unsettling because he conceals his emotions—almost to the end—within a provocative page layout and an exuberantly baroque narrative structure. Presumably autobiographical, *Helping Verbs of the Heart* lines up a series of comic episodes, each of which concludes with an unattributed, sometimes ironically mangled, quotation printed in capital letters at the bottom of the page. Each page is, moreover, enclosed in a black rectangle, as in a funeral announcement.

Where does Esterházy leave off and another writer take over? Reviving T. S. Eliot's and Ezra Pound's technique of stealing from past masters, Esterházy overtly (and admittedly) pilfers passages from Donald Barthelme, Georges Bataille, Thomas Bernhard, Jorge Luis Borges, Albert Camus, Anton Chekhov, Stéphane Mallarmé, Robert Musil, Blaise Pascal, Jean-Paul Sartre, Leo Tolstoy, Ludwig Wittgenstein, and at least as many Hungarian writers.

Fleeced more than anyone else is Peter Handke, whose memoir *Wunschloses Unglück* (1972) about his mother's suicide—it has appeared as *A Sorrow Beyond Dreams* in English—contributes its last sentence ("Später werde ich über das alles Genaureres schreiben") to the entirely capitalized last sentence ("SOME DAY I'LL WRITE ABOUT ALL THIS IN MORE DETAIL") of Esterházy's book; and passages from Handke's book fill out at least half of a deceptively personal "Foreword" dated "the 16th of June" (which is James Joyce's "Bloomsday"). Readers can compare pages 7-10 of the Suhrkamp paperback edition of *Wunschloses Unglück* to pages v-vii of Esterházy's "Foreword."

Yet it is wise not to dismiss Esterházy's modernist or post-modernist antics too quickly. Strangely, they are effective. The surprisingly coherent mixture of his own prose with that of his living or deceased *confrères* is a convoluted, yet sincere, way of expressing the painful distance between the cerebral writer and his redoubtably real "object." "I don't speak, but I'm not silent," remarks Esterházy (or another writer?), "which isn't the same. I'm cautious: this is about my mother." Borrowing the words of others in order to speak about a loved one's death implies and points to the fundamental alienation of language—a personal idiom—as it confronts and nonetheless must express both the inner and outer worlds of an individual. Even disorienting shifts in narrative perspective suit the narrator's secret mourning, especially in the second part, when the mother narrates, mourning the death of her son. She reviews her own life for him, and poignancy grows as insignificant details take on commemorative significance. All such vestiges are noble, after all.

Of course, the original narrator, the son, has all along been imagining his own demise and his mother's comforting words for him. But this imaginary death, concealing a touching confession of the son's egocentrism, represents a roundabout, but no less desperate, attempt to keep her alive. At the end, we find the son with his mother in the hospital. In an unforgettable scene (written by Esterházy or borrowed?), he helps her out of bed, then down the corridor to the toilet. She is helpless, but not without humor, as her son accompanies her through every movement of an all too human act. After a few funny-sad moments, the story closes with a complex emotion that lingers long after this book has been set down. Despite the ludicrousness of many scenes, a moving certitude has been established: the dying mother has retained all her dignity, and the memory of her dignity will long remain with the son.

German-Speaking Countries

Dark Struggles for a Utopia of Language (Ingeborg Bachmann)

Now and then someone reminds us that the Austrian poet, playwright, short story writer, and novelist Ingeborg Bachmann (1926-1973) is too little known in English-speaking countries. May I myself take on this role? For once, the problem does not really derive from a lack of translations. In the late 1980s, Mark Anderson rendered an important selection of poems (*In the Storm of Roses*), while Mary Fran Gilbert and Michael Bullock respectively translated Bachmann's two short story collections, *Three Paths to the Lake* (1972) and *The Thirtieth Year* (1961). These books were crowned in 1990 by Philip Boehm's version of *Malina* (1971), one of the most absorbing and complex European modernist novels.

Yet whereas the first translation mentioned is out of print and the three others sleep on a backlist, I can stroll up the rue du Pressoir, hop on Bus No. 3, drop by my provincial French bookstore, and find on the shelves a cheap paperback copy of Philippe Jaccottet's French version of *Malina*, which dates to 1973. Jaccottet's own reputation may somewhat keep the novel in the public eye in France, though I notice that his name is not on the front cover. Alas, *Malina* has never received in English-speaking countries the critical esteem that it enjoys in Europe. I daresay that few novels are farther removed in style, narrative structure, and philosophical scope from mainstream American fiction.

Reading *Malina* is like wandering deeper and deeper into a dark, pathless forest. With every step, the temptation is to turn back, yet something invisible and magnetic draws one relentlessly forward, at the risk of getting hopelessly lost. And this is the point. As Bachmann explores the origins, manifestations, and consequences of the artistic urge and amorous attraction (in *Malina*, they are sometimes antagonistic, sometimes intertwined), she depicts a labyrinthine sensibility at once exalted and depressed, desperate and resolved. Yet all along, the nameless "I" (as the narrator soberly designates herself) intends to emerge re-unified from what can be likened to a mapless journey through an Inferno, both inner and outer.

As in Dante, the reader must abandon all certitudes at the onset. No genuine first sentence opens this elaborate novelistic collage (which German critics have compared to an opera), but instead an intriguing list of characters ("The

Cast"), each of whom is briefly and tangentially described. The narrator, in great part autobiographical, is a female writer working on a book entitled none other than *Todesarten* (Death Styles)—the title that Bachmann had in fact given to an ambitious novelistic series, of which only *Malina* had been published when the author died tragically, at the age of forty-seven, from burns caused by a bedroom fire in her Roman apartment. In the novel, the narrator lives with one Malina, a man whom we come to know only late in the novel; and she loves Ivan, an equally shadowy Hungarian who lives on the same side street (tellingly termed Ungargasse, or "Hungary Lane") in Vienna. The time, we are told, is "today."

After these unsettling stage directions, the reader is immediately immersed, not in the midst of action, but rather in the author's penetrating yet self-paralyzing doubts about the nature of "today." "But I had to think long and hard about the Time," commences Bachmann, "since 'today' is an impossible word for me.... This Today sends me flying into an anxious haste, so that I can only write about it, or at best report whatever's going on. Actually, anything written about Today should be destroyed immediately, just like all real letters are crumpled up or torn up, unfinished and unmailed, all because they were written, but cannot arrive, Today. Whoever has composed an intensely fervent letter only to tear it to shreds and throw it away knows exactly what is meant by 'today.'"

After this nearly self-destructive incipit, *Malina* unveils the narrator's burning infatuation for Ivan, a character who may partly be modeled on the German-writing Jewish poet Paul Celan, with whom Bachmann had an impassioned unhappy love affair and who also seems to be the "stranger" of her fairy tale, *The Mysteries of the Princess of Kagran*. The writer-narrator is also working on this fairy tale, cited in italics in *Malina* as are other short passages reflecting texts-in-progress that she produces and revises in troubling ways. In the tale, the princess meets up with a stranger who "kept his face hidden in the night." "She knew that it was he who had lamented her plight and had sung for her so full of hope," adds the narrator, "in a voice never heard before, and now he had come to set her free.... She had fallen in love...she obeyed him, because she had to obey him.... Then he turned and disappeared into the night." Elsewhere, the narrator superimposes her and Ivan's "identical, high-pitched first initials," an alphabetic coincidence which could of course not involve Paul (Celan), but which is true of "*ich*" ("I"), Ingeborg, and Ivan.

This symbolic triad of characters—I, Malina, Ivan—is central, not only to the barely perceptible progress of the plot (which resembles more a excavation of "I's" conscious and unconscious turmoil), but also and especially to Bachmann's meticulous investigation of what it means to be a person. The author explores the ever-shifting boundaries between a human being's inner and outer worlds, but even more so those which separate and distinguish two human beings who are intimately linked. As the narrator remarks in one of several cryptic passages, "Ivan and I: the world converging. Malina and I, since we are one: the world diverging."

What is this strange "oneness"? In fact, Malina is not always distinct from the narrator, who is a famous writer in the story—as Bachmann herself was; her early poems, essays, and radio plays had rocketed her to fame. Yet by now, years, even a decade or so, have passed. One of Bachmann's tours de force is to describe what goes on in a mature writer's mind when he or she is not writing. In this sense, *Malina* is a meta-novel describing how another novel—ostensibly belonging to the *Death Styles* project—is being written or, rather more frequently, not getting written because the narrator is so obsessed with her elusive, busy lover. Perhaps that other novel is a more realistic, chronologically ordered version of *Malina*, a sort of *Ur-Text* of the book we have in hand; or perhaps it is *Der Fall Franza* (The Book of Franza) or *Requiem für Fanny Goldmann* (Requiem for Fanny Goldmann), two unfinished novels that belonged to the same ambitious project and that were published posthumously in 1979. Still, the distractions of love—chiefly, as they torment the mind—do not always keep the narrator from her oeuvre. She even exclaims that Ivan "has come to make consonants constant once again and comprehensible, to unlock vowels to their full resounding, to let words come over my lips once more."

Be this as it may, the most intriguing quandary for the reader remains Malina's ontological independence with respect to the narrator. In his well-informed and insightful afterword to the American translation, Mark Anderson reports critics' speculations "that [Malina] forms an anagram for 'animal,' and a partial anagram for '*anima*'...while the narrator appropriately remains an unnamed *persona*, a mask and simple pronoun."

Malina surely often seems to represent, not a full-rounded character, but rather the rational side of the narrator's mind—what Jung termed, for better or worse, the "male" side of a woman's personality. "He never forgets anything, I never have to ask," declares the narrator in one telltale scene, when she is looking for money to pay her housekeeper yet ultimately finds the envelope "very conspicuously stuck in the Grosser Duden Dictionary, secretly marked by Malina." Yet who really has put the envelope there, Malina or the narrator? "I am double," she confesses at one point, "I am also Malina's creation." Paradoxically, the narrator also declares that she created Malina. "You came after me," she reminds him in one of the many dialogues, "you can't have preceded me, you're completely inconceivable before me."

These mutually contradictory remarks—reminiscent of the mystical relationship between God and Christ as it is expounded by John in his Gospel—represent just one of several Biblical allusions woven into *Malina*. For example, as the narrator tries to increase her "patience" as she awaits a message from the oft-silent Ivan, she observes: "It has happened to my body against all reason, my body which now only moves in one continuous, soft, painful crucifixion on him." The three at once independent and mutually inter-blending characters evidently form a sort of Trinity. In early passages, the exalted amorous atmosphere of *Malina* recalls *Solomon's Song*. This is particularly telling in that the beloved Shulamith (which in Hebrew suggests "plenitude," "peace," "pacification") of *Solomon's Song* appears starkly in Celan's most famous poem, "Deathfugue" (1945), with its intersecting images of literary creation, the Shoah, and "writing," as Theodor Adorno phrased it, "after Auschwitz":

> Black milk of daybreak we drink you at night
> we drink you at morning and midday we drink you at
>   evening
> we drink and we drink
> A man lives in the house he plays with vipers he writes
> he writes when it grows dark to Deutschland your gold hair
>   Margareta
> Your ashen hair Shulamith we shovel a grave in the air
>   where you won't lie too cramped.

(trans. John Felstiner)

This interplay between Christianity and Judaism grips the reader whenever Bachmann alludes to the Shoah ("before I can scream, I'm already inhaling the gas, more and more gas"), especially in the second, "dream-journal" part of the novel. All the while, the narrator contemplates the possibilities both of "redemption" and of composing, not a work called *Death Styles*, but rather a "beautiful book," in accordance with Ivan's wishes. This affirming, healing work is to be given the title of Mozart's motet for soprano, *Exsultate, Jubilate*. But this wish, like her love, will remain unfulfilled. The dialectics of negativity and affirmation, so typical of modern European literature and certainly one of its outstanding achievements, foster no easy, comfortable solutions.

Despite the extremely precise details brought forth, which range from minutely dissected feelings to acute perceptions of the outside world and its "trivia," we never obtain clear pictures of the three main characters. We observe each particle of an atom, as it were, without being able to deduce what the atom looks like. This is a literary and philosophical position—one which Bachmann takes great narrative risks to maintain. The characters are not ultimately definable in any psychoanalytical shorthand, although Bachmann alludes often, if at times ironically, to Freud and other Viennese psychoanalysts. Even the appealing Jungian anima-paradigm cannot consistently obtain; Malina seems more individualized, that is ontologically separate from the narrator, in the third part (which is entitled "Last Things," in probable homage to the Viennese philosopher Otto Weininger). We gradually observe Malina acting more often in the world, in ways that seem describable as distinct events, not just symbolic projections of the narrator's rational or social capabilities.

Nor are Malina and the narrator stable sexually. "Am I a woman or something dimorphic," the narrator asks herself toward the end of the novel, "what am I, anyway?" Almost the same degree of sexual ambivalence defines Malina, whose name can, moreover, be a family name or a first name. *Requiem for Fanny Goldmann* in fact brings forth another Malina, who is a woman; in Slavic countries, Malina or its cognates is a common female first name. As to Ivan, equally elusive and ever on the brink of departure, he is nonetheless a more solid human entity than either Malina or the narrator. "Are Ivan and I a dark story?" she wonders at one point. "No, he isn't, I alone am a dark story." Ivan is an object of ardent love, and is more or less imaginable in this respect, but he represents above all the painful presence of absence. He rarely has time for the narrator. They talk on the telephone much more often than they meet. His mysterious, mesmerizing aloofness suggests that all that we yearn for, all that really counts for us in the end, is hopelessly out of reach.

In this decidedly dark story, the side street, Hungary Lane, is the narrator's "only country"—"which I must keep secure, which I defend, for which I tremble, for which I fight"—and provides an oblique vantage point from which post-World War II war Vienna can be evoked. Like other Austrian writers (notably Peter Handke and Thomas Bernhard), Bachmann must struggle not only with Austria's collaborationist, anti-Semitic past, but also and especially with the corruption of the German language by Nazism. Spatially, temporally, and linguistically, Bachmann is estranged; and in *Malina*, she delves headlong into this estrangement.

Her answer to remnant Nazi linguistic perversions—a dilemma that likewise engaged Celan—is above all her powerful, idiosyncratic style, partly based on stream-of-consciousness techniques; but her ultimate response can more simply be extolled as an obstinate labor with language. The narrator's rambling, exhausting, frenetic monologues ("a shower of words starts in my head") are by no means gratuitous; they represent much more than literary experiments. Language is used not only to tell a story; the language used is that story.

Malina illustrates more elaborately and graphically than the short stories of *The Thirtieth Year* (1961) and even those of *Three Paths to the Lake* (published in German as *Simultan* in 1972) Bachmann's concept of a "utopia of language." She developed this notion in five important lectures given at the University of Frankfurt in 1959-60. In her fifth lecture, she notably observes that literature "cannot itself say what it is." Then, appealing implicitly to Heidegger's analysis of the anonymous "one" (the German word *man*), she adds that literature "presents itself as a thousand-fold, many-thousand-year-old affront to 'bad language' (*schlechte Sprache*)," by which she means badly made, mediocre, ordinary, daily language. In her view, "life possesses only this *schlechte Sprache*," against which writers must oppose a "utopia of language," even when the language that they forge ultimately depends closely on the present and its mediocre speech. Even though the failure to achieve this ideal is inevitable, literature should "be praised for its desperate march toward this Language...[which] offers humanity a reason to hope."

Having written her doctoral dissertation on Heidegger's existential philosophy, Bachmann was also fully cognizant of his idea of a genuine writer's or poet's getting *"unterwegs zur Sprache"* ("on the way to Language"). And it is as a description of how a writer "heads toward language" that *Malina*, as a meta-novel, must also be read.

Yet herein lies another paradox. This most significant activity of the narrator's life cannot be observed; the novel can only attempt to help us see what cannot be seen. In her acceptance speech for the Anton-Wildgans-Preis, received in 1972, Bachmann pointedly commented: "I exist only when I am writing. I am nothing when I am not writing. I am a fully a stranger to myself, when I am not writing. Yet when I am writing, you cannot see me. No one can see me. You can watch a director directing, a singer singing, an actor acting, but no one can see what writing is." In this sense, the narrator and perhaps also Malina are "nothing," "no one," in the novel. At best, they are apparitions or strangers. They exist authentically only in what is unstated, in what cannot be told. Bachmann leaves us with the redoubtable task of grasping their essence "behind the novel," as vital sources that can be intuited yet not named.

Heading toward language thereby implies pushing words to their limits, nearing them to the ineffable; analogously, of driving the self to its frontiers, and perhaps beyond. And in this regard, the ominous pronouncements ("the boundaries of my language mean the boundaries of my world"; "of that which one cannot speak, one must remain silent") of another salient Viennese personality likewise underlie the very conception and narrative processes of *Malina*. In her essay on Wittgenstein, Bachmann notably praises the philosopher's "despairing pains with the inexpressible (*das Unaussprechliche*), [pains] which charge the *Tractatus* with tension." This same tantalizing tension characterizes *Malina* from beginning to end.

Bachmann's deep struggle with the German language was, appropriately enough, waged while she was in voluntary exile from her native Austria. Her poem "Exile" bears witness to both her status as a "woman without a country" (even as the narrator's passport, in *Malina*, has the addresses crossed out three times) and to her taking shelter, though a polyglot, in her unique possession: "I with the German language / this cloud around me / which I keep as a house / press through all languages" (trans. Peter Filkins). Much of her career was spent in Rome, a city in which she had to live in order to write about Vienna and its Hungary Lane. She once flatly quipped: "I feel better in Vienna because I live in Rome."

This Roman retreat enabled Bachmann to compose the pre-eminent modern Viennese novel. The city is obliquely present even in the almost unbearably long second chapter—otherwise set "Everywhere and Nowhere"—because it is entitled "The Third Man," in homage to Carol Reed's 1949 film. In *Malina*, distant parallels with the film are drawn often. In *The Third Man*, an American writer seeks to track down his friend Harry Lime (whom Orson Welles memorably plays) in postwar Vienna. He eventually learns that his friend has become a black market dealer in penicillin. Rather similarly, Ivan's profession is never clear. "He pursues his neatly ordered affairs in a building on the Kärtnerring," writes Bachmann, "an Institute for Extremely Urgent Affairs, since it deals with money." The film is, moreover, accompanied by Anton Karas's haunting zither melody, even as music plays an essential role throughout *Malina* (and especially in the third section, where the author adds Italian musical terms to illustrate how the dialogues should be read). Like the death at the end of *The Third Man*, *Malina* abruptly concludes in a murder. Yet is this murder a real or a psychological one?

In contrast to the timeless "today" and the explicit Viennese setting of the first and third sections, in the second part of *Malina* "Time no longer exists at all." "It could have been yesterday," the narrator explains, "it could have been long ago, it could be again, it could continually be, some things will have never been. There is no measure for this Time, which interlocks other times, and there is no measure for the non-times in which things play that were never in Time." This non-Time is that of dreaming, when "the basic elements of the world are still there, but more gruesomely assembled than anyone has ever seen." The narrator recounts chilling nightmares involving her father, Nazism, death camps, electroshock therapy, and much more. At one point, she shouts: "A book about Hell!" This dire avowal surely designates, alas not the intensely desired *Exult, Be Jubilant*, but rather the book that "I" must ultimately come to terms with, and write. The dark book, which cannot promise facile redemption but which tries to align "true sentences." In other words, *Malina*—which Ingeborg Bachmann did write.

* * *

Shouldn't we be lending our ears to a poet capable of writing such perpetually thought-provoking aphorisms as "What separates you, is you," as Peter Filkins renders "Was dich trennt, bist du" in an important new American edition of Bachmann's collected poems? Or to a poet who meditates relentlessly on "the one / and only world," all the while admitting: "to know / just whose world is forbidden to me"?

Bachmann indeed explores the fundamental, though—for her—not always unbridgeable opposition of the "I" and the World (or the Other). Her poetry, like all her writing, is tensely, if obliquely, autobiographical, all the while drawing on German romanticism, Biblical symbolism, folklore, fairytales, Viennese psychoanalysis, and the philosophy of language. She engages with multifaceted aspects of personal identity, yet never neglects the responsibilities of literature after the Shoah, the treacheries of her homeland, the destruction of nature, the battle of the sexes, the ambiguities of gender, as well as exiles and imprisonments of all kinds. "One must rush...," she writes, "from one land / into another, beneath the rainbow, / the compass points stuck in the heart / and night the radius." Time and again in her verse, as in *Malina*, she evokes estrangement in a devastated contemporary world in which the impact of the past on individuals nonetheless seems decisive. "A sled brocaded with history," she remarks in "Curriculum Vitae," "sweeps over me (I cannot stop it)." Elsewhere, a six-line poem pessimistically ends: "Our godhead, / history, has ordered for us a grave / from which there is no resurrection." Despite or because of this determinism, felt by so many other Europeans after the war and even today, Bachmann also constantly ponders the possibilities of liberation.

As it turns out, a second Bachmann wave has rolled up on our shores. Let me skip over the unfinished novels of the *Death Styles* cycle, namely *The Book of Franza* and *Requiem for Fanny Goldmann*, published together by Northwestern University Press in 1999. And let me only mention *Letters to Felician* (Green Integer, 2004), a series of letters that the late-adolescent author penned (but never mailed) to a lover at the end of the Second World War. These at once personal and literary love letters, and the two novelistic manuscripts, offer valuable retrospective insights into all of Bachmann's mature work.

Most importantly, Zephyr Press has produced an expanded edition of Filkins's earlier version of Bachman's collected poems, originally entitled *Songs in Flight*. The bilingual *Darkness Spoken* not only provides well-considered translations of all of Bachmann's poems, but also includes twenty-five manuscript drafts that Filkins discovered in the Bachmann Archive at the Austrian National Library in Vienna. These finds have never appeared in German. As rough drafts, they hardly equal Bachmann's finest pieces, which tend to be long and sometimes structured by meter and rhyme; and which also intricately and sometimes surrealistically—as critics often point out—weave together ideas and polysemous symbolism. (It occurs to me that it is not surrealism that encourages the collisions and unsettling juxtapositions of imagery in some of her verse, but rather her philosophical scrutiny of the borders, or lack thereof, defining different categories of mental, emotional, and sensate experience.) In any event, the oft-desperate poetic outcries of both her spontaneous and more polished drafts, as well as confessional pieces composed after her breakup with the Swiss writer Max Frisch in the fall of 1962, are impressive in their directness and emotional power.

It is sobering to reread *Malina*, with its intense triangular love story, after taking into account Bachmann's avowals about depression, psychiatric care ("They have smoked out / every feeling inside me, / I don't know what warm / or cold or blue / is"), electroshock therapy, a morphine addiction caused by a miscalculated medical prescription ("The blessing of morphine, / but not / the blessing of a word"), suicidal urges ("Is there no one there to tell me to step back from the window?"), pain, shattered love, and unaffectionate sex. A poem depicting oral sex is particularly striking and open to various interpretations. A telling leitmotiv in several rough drafts is "don't you see, my friends, don't you see!" In fact, the archival material reveals that Bachmann suffered from doubt and solitude throughout her career. An early manuscript page concedes: "The dark shadow / which I have followed from the start / leads me into the deep loneliness of winter." This is the darkness that Bachmann courageously "speaks," as the apt, homage-paying, title of Filkins's edition puts it.

Yet despite the pertinence of the posthumous papers for a more thorough understanding of Bachmann's life and work, one can surmise why she had not yet chosen to publish even the more advanced drafts dating from the earlier part of her career—though it is possible, had she not died so young, that she would have returned to some pieces and perfected them. It is not so much that she possessed the highest stylistic standards (though this was true), but rather that she entertained an original view of what literary language—as opposed to everyday speech—should aspire to. Attaining her goals demanded more than craft. I am once again alluding to the lectures, about a "utopia of language," given at the University of Frankfurt. It is essential to keep this notion in mind when reading her poems, and notably archival pieces in which she despairingly envisions this utopia as out of reach:

> Always to live among words, whether one wants to or not,
> always to be alive, full of words about life,
> as if words were alive, as if life meant words.
>
> But it's otherwise, believe me.
> Between a word and a thing
> you only encounter yourself,
> lying between each as if next to someone ill,
> never able to get to either,
> tasting a sound and a body,
> and relishing both.
>
> It tastes of death.

Filkins's edition refutes the critical myth that Bachmann gave up verse for fiction and playwriting after her second collection, *Anrufung des großen Bären* (Invocation of the Great Bear, 1956). Even if she chose not to publish other poems, Bachmann wrote verse until about 1967, when the *Death Styles* project took up all her energy. She always worked in various literary genres, sometimes simultaneously, a creative flexibility that can be perceived par excellence in *Malina* and even in single long poems. The best example is "A Monologue of Prince Myshkin," a "ballet pantomime" that was set to music by Bachmann's lifelong friend, the composer Hans Werner Henze. This dramatic poem concludes *Die gestundete Zeit* (Borrowed Time, 1953), a first collection published to acclaim only one year after the event that made her famous overnight: a reading in Munich with Celan and members of the Gruppe 47, a postwar association of major German writers. According to Filkins, "the German literary world was immediately swept away by the young blonde-haired poet reading her poems in a near whisper." (Take up the hint: read her poems in a whisper.)

Filkins's introduction is insightful. At the onset, he offers a deep-probing summary of Bachmann's originality, implicitly formulating reasons why engrained Anglo-American realism and empiricism have so much conceptual trouble accommodating her poetics:

> Bridging the poetry of experience and the poetry of ideas, Bachmann's vision is one continually fixed upon the terror she perceived within the quotidian, as well as the need to elicit the unspoken, primeval truth that lies just beyond the pale of the "unspeakable." In following this trajectory, Bachmann's poems conduct a journey *in* thought *towards* feeling, for hers is not a poetry of recollected experience, nor a poetry of ideas about experience, but rather a poetry that enacts *the experience of ideas* in order to evoke the nature of true feeling, despite the impediments that exist in cognitive speech.

Darkness Spoken can be accompanied by *Last Living Words: The Ingeborg Bachmann Reader* (Green Integer). Translated by Lilian M. Friedberg, the volume gathers eight key stories and fourteen of the best-known poems. As English poems, Friedberg's versions are occasionally livelier than Filkins's. When Bachmann evokes, in the all-important "Great Landscape Near Vienna," a "Lächeln Ja" and the "Lächeln Nein," literally a "smile of Yes and the smile of No" (Filkins), Friedberg interestingly construes the words as a "smirking yes and the smirking no." But in the distich introducing this image, Bachmann writes "unter den Pappeln am Römerstein grab ich / nach dem Schauplatz vielvölkriger Trauer." Filkins accurately translates the lines as "under the poplars I dig by a Roman stone, / searching for the theater of many peopled grief," whereas Friedberg characteristically interprets: "beneath the poplars at the Roman obelisk, I dig / for the buried arena of multi-national tragedy." Extrapolations like "multi-national" are debatable: Bachmann usually bases multiple meanings on a relatively concrete, physical, image ("peoples" as opposed to the more abstract "nations"); and these images are habitually expressed in phrasal contexts somewhat removed from immediate colloquial patterns. Moreover, I have difficulties imagining an "obelisk" beneath poplars, as opposed to the comparatively much smaller Roman steles, landmarks or engraved "stones," as Bachmann literally writes, that are frequently found in Europe.

Always closer to the German, Filkins is more attentive to the rhymes and meters of the original; and his English is surer. In "Night Flight," Friedberg renders "Nenn's den Status der Einsamen, / in dem sich das Stauen vollzieht" ungrammatically as "Call it the status of solitaries / where astonishment occurs." Filkins rightly proceeds: "Call it the status of the lonely / in whom wonder still occurs." And in "Wood and Shavings," Filkins correctly offers "But in wood, / as long as it is still green, and with bile, / as long as it is still bitter, I am / willing to write what happened at the start!" while Friedberg more ambiguously and incompletely proposes "But / as long as it is still green, and bitter gall, / I would write into the wood / what was in the beginning!" However, Friedberg's phrase "what was in the beginning" echoes Biblical phraseology, which is often conjured up in Bachmann's verse, not to mention in *Malina*. I cannot untangle why the latter translator begins "Great Landscape Near Vienna" with a quatrain that Filkins publishes separately (and correctly, I think) as "In the Storm of Roses." As to the reliable versions of *Darkness Spoken*, an oversight occurs in "The Tightened Lip," dedicated to the poet Nelly Sachs (1891-1970), who despite her 1966 Nobel Prize also remains mostly unknown to English readers. Filkins oddly renders "und wie du schweigst, wenn du mündig bist" by "and how silent one becomes when you come of age" instead of "and how silent you become."

* * *

With *The Night Begins with a Question*, Carcanet and the Scottish Poetry Library have co-published a pleasant anthology of twenty-five Austrian poems, written by as many poets. Memorable are an atmospheric prose text by Ilse Aichinger (b. 1921), which gives the title to the book, and a sensitive love poem by Evelyn Schlag (b. 1952). Schlag charts the progress of a privileged moment of self-awareness as she feels—but this we learn only at the end—"the resonance / Of your casual words / That I had been thinking over." The diction may appear simplistic, but it convincingly stages not only this delicate mental meeting of the woman and her seeming lover, but also an "apperception," in the sense that Kant, Leibniz, and Maine de Biran gave to the term. After the poet puts her "fingers to the shadows / under [her] eyes," her mind becomes aware of its own movements. It is as if the self also became an "other" during the kind of border-crossing experience that Bachmann also described. "My fingers belonged to a being / From a world with different measures," admits Schlag, "It was an often-performed / Gesture but relieved of its weight / Capable only of the echo of a pressure." The anthology also comprises pieces by three of Bachmann's contemporaries whose work is familiar to American "language poets": Friederike Mayröcker (b. 1924), Ernst Jandl (1925-2000), and H. C. Artmann (1921-2000). Austrian literature has long been marked not only by philosophical quests, but also by linguistic experimentation. Bachmann, however, was concerned less with language as a medium that could be boldly manipulated, than with the psychological and ontological implications of speech.

The anthology opens with her "Bohemia, a Country by the Sea." Iain Bamforth's version captures Bachmann's poetic music, which is forthright here, as well as its meanings. His translation reminds us that the lyric factor in her work must never be underestimated. Here, she wittily and also sadly evokes her exile from Austria, symbolically merged with her relentless poetic task of pushing language beyond limits:

If I'm not the one, then someone else will do just as well.

If a word here lies beside me, it'll be my borderline.
If Bohemia's still a country by the sea, I can believe in the sea again.
And still believing in the sea, I can hope for land.

(...)

Still I border on a word and on another country,
verging more closely, if never very much, on what exists,

a penniless Bohemian, a vagabond without ties,
my sole talent to be at sea at the sight of my chosen land.

In his introduction, Iain Galbraith recalls a discussion, in 1967, between Bachmann and the exiled Austrian poet Erich Fried (1921-1998), whose claustrophobic portrait of Georg Trakl is also included in *The Night Begins with a Question*. Fried wondered about the "Austrian elisions" that Bachmann had employed in this poem, in contrast to the standard German in which she usually wrote. Some two decades later, Thomas Bernhard had the main character of his novel *Extinction* (1986) define this same poem as "so Austrian, but at the same time so permeated by the whole world, and by the world surrounding this world." As you take Ingeborg Bachmann's complex and compelling poems in hand, remember this clue as well.

In Search of Presence
(Peter Handke)

Keep the title—*Absence*—in mind while reading this difficult yet strangely mesmerizing novel by the Austrian writer Peter Handke (b. 1942). Like the German word *Abwesenheit*, "absence" etymologically means "the state of being away," and the four characters (an old man, a woman, a soldier, and a gambler) indeed remain at a distance from "a center" that they can intuit but rarely attain. "Whenever in my life I have thought I arrived, at the summit, in the center," declares the old man, "it has been clear to me that I couldn't stay.... There is no permanence in fulfillment." Published in German in 1987, *Die Abwesenheit* has been translated with characteristic rigor and smoothness by Ralph Manheim.

Where this search for the lost center, for presence, takes place is not, however, obvious. Nor can it be. References are made to a "garden where time no longer matters," to "forbidden zones," to "oases of emptiness." As a plateau slopes gently to form an immense hollow," the reader may even imagine a "mental landscape" painted by Yves Tanguy. A natural catastrophe has in any case occurred, probably an earthquake, and "empty has become empty, dead dead, the past irrevocable, and there is nothing more to hand down." Sometimes telltale appurtenances of our civilization appear, such as a "Hotel Europa," or a table-soccer game" that stands upright among "scattered garden benches." Other details seem hallucinations, such as the cape that remains "puffed out" although "there is no wind." Incidentally, this philosophical novel has been provocatively classified by Handke as "a Märchen," a "fairy tale."

As in many of his writings, there are recurrent evocations of what he has elsewhere called the "inner world of the outer world of the inner world"; and of the interpenetration of the self and all that the self is not. In his notebook, for example, the old man makes "signs" that "are unrelated to what is going on outside"; riding in a bus, the soldier looks up from his book, "always longer than needed to digest what he has been reading"; the old man explains how when walking he "turns with the apples on a tree."

Puzzling signs (in the semiotic sense) pass constantly before the reader's eyes, and Handke tacitly inquires whether the world's bewildering surface can be accurately interpreted at all. Only when the "jolt" of presence passes through us, the author seems to conclude, do we truly smell the new-mown hay, hear the birds "calling" from the cedar tree, see the bell "hanging" in the cathedral tower, imagine the roots of the cedar tree "extending," the magma "blazing," the sea "surging," the cosmos "whirring."

One recalls Wim Wenders' film *Der Himmel über Berlin* (*Wings of Desire*, 1987), for which Handke wrote the scenario. In the film, angels walk invisibly among humans, secretly enlightening them. In *Absence*, a wind arises "as though from within us, and permeates all things: in a very different absence." Many such sentences—hermetic aphorisms or poetic fragments in themselves—take on a disquieting, supernatural radiance.

The quest for presence thus constitutes our sole chance to transcend the human condition, that of being mere perceivers. In this respect, *Absence* rehabilitates the metaphysics of Romanticism and Transcendentalism, and even holds out a certain hope against contemporary nihilism and despair. One also thinks of the theme of "presence" as it recurs in the work of contemporary French poets like Yves Bonnefoy and Philippe Jaccottet (whose especial influence on Handke is perceptible). Given an inner state of emptiness, there is a search for plenitude: even if found or attained, it remains an open question whether this plenitude belongs to an "other world" or is simply a highly concentrated moment of full (material) sensation.

The context of *Absence* is thoroughly modern, for the characters must first experience anguish and grief. "Now at least we were something," remarks the narrator when the "water-drawing fairy tale tree" is chopped up, "at least we were unhappy." "In our grief," he adds, "we acquired the eyes of all human races."

Who is this narrator, sometimes omniscient and apart, sometimes one of the soliloquizing characters, sometimes all of them at once? Narrative perspectives shift suddenly as the novel progresses, and when the last paragraph commences with the avowal "I could write a whole book about our quest," one surmises that Handke has been writing all along about himself, about a composite self made up of a writer, his four characters, and perhaps someone else, more secret and concealed. For *Absence* is also clearly about writing, that ever-elliptical way of arriving at the center of things and of attaining a few rare moments of "presence."

The Poetry of Thomas Bernhard

Thomas Bernhard (1931-1989) is so much better known as a novelist and playwright that few readers will have suspected a poetic debut for the author of *The Voice Imitator* (1978), *The Loser* (1983), *Woodcutters* (1984), and *Extinction* (1986). In a lively and probing preface to his translation of the Austrian writer's second and third volumes of poetry, James Reidel elucidates Bernhard's almost exclusive focus on poetry throughout the 1950s, which culminated in the publication of *Auf der Erde und in der Hölle* (*On Earth and in Hell*) in 1957 and then, the next year, of both *In Hora Mortis* and *Unter dem Eisen des Mondes*. It is a pity that Princeton University Press did not have Reidel translate the first volume as well. Both volumes rendered here are sequences of untitled poems and, with the initial book, form a trilogy.

Based on recurrent symbolic motifs and repetitions of key lines within individual poems, Bernhard's lyric outcries and prayer-like plaints draw on the stylistics and themes—physical pain, metaphysical groping, ontological solitude—of Austrian expressionism. His bitter, desperately yearning verse indeed sometimes echoes that of Georg Trakl (1887-1914), especially in *Under the Iron of the Moon*. More generally, although distinct personal sources are traceable in Bernhard's evocations of "a breast bursting with agony" (he received chest punctures when he was hospitalized with pleurisy and tuberculosis after the war) or rural life as opposed to "the fury of those cities never loved," his poems also recall the spiritual struggles of the Austrian poet Christine Lavant (1915-1973), a selection of whose poetry about deep suffering and Christian mystic exaltation he himself edited.

The latter influence underscores the most surprising aspect of *In Hora Mortis* and *Under the Iron of the Moon*: their blatant religiosity. Readers aware of Bernhard's violent novelistic and dramaturgical satire of Catholics and institutional Catholicism will have to ponder Psalm-like outpourings of ardent spiritual feeling. Is he really sincere when he exclaims "Where are You Lord and where / is my happiness"? Should the lines "God hears me / in every corner of the world" be taken seriously? Elsewhere, Job-like, Bernhard exhorts God:

> Wake up
> wake up
> and hear me
> I am inside You my God.

Reidel delves into whether Bernhard's spirituality is genuine or an ultimately comic *faux* pietism, "a send-up and critique of the tragic sense of life even as one ascribes to it." No conclusions can readily be drawn, and without Reidel's analysis the possibility of an overarching irony remains mostly hidden. Only rarely does a line, stanza, or passage suggest a *caveat lector*. Yet they do crop up. The burlesque, sexually suggestive finale of *In Hora Mortis* offers an illustration: "my thorn sticks / piercing / oh / piercing / oh / piercing / oh / oh / oh / my / Oh." A poem in *Under the Iron of the Moon* similarly mentions "lips of fire" flaming "into laughing flowers / of death," an initially conventional, positive, spring-like image that becomes—after the enjambment—a *memento mori* designating life as a farce that would presumably include fervent poem-prayers to (an absent) God. Taken on their own terms, several pieces are moving as crafted laments of despair, fear, anger, existential fatigue, or angst. Few if any, however, exhibit the kind of intricate intellectual or spiritual insights that compel prolonged meditation. The greatest mystery of these poems lies, not in their spiritual contents *per se*, but rather in their cumulative rhetorical intention. This intention defines their interest as well as their limitations.

The translation is nearly always accurate, though there are a few minor errors and odd departures from the original. Of these, "When we die closing the frosted windows" inverses the logic of "Wenn wir sterbend die milchigen Fenster schließen," which implies that we are dying as we close the window (yet not yet dead). In the same poem, "wird der Frühling / der uns entging im März" cannot be "the spring will / escape us in March" because the verb "entging" is in the simple past tense and not an infinitive; instead, the spring that escaped us in March comes back into being, as it were, when we close the window. Both poetic cycles are full of references to the four seasons, often with symbolic expectations reversed: spring is a "deathbed" in one piece; in another, summer is "dead, / on white pillows."

Finally, the important line "Wie schwer fällt mir ein Wort," which opens and closes an eighteen-line poem and is repeated three more times in the middle does not seem right as "how hard my word drops." Like other Austrian and German writers of his generation, Bernhard was forced to think through every word, indeed every phoneme, in light of the perversions inflicted on the German language (and thus on literature) by the Nazis. Here he conveys the difficulties of this struggle: how difficult it is for him to come up with a word, indeed with an authentic way of thinking, speaking, and writing. Moreover, he elsewhere declares that he "was chosen" ("war ich auserwählt")—not "I chose"—to speak "to the wind." Writing is designated as his calling in, once again, a quasi-religious sense, for the verb *auserwählen* has conspicuous Biblical connotations. With these early poems, had he already comprehended this calling as impossible to fulfill *unironically* in that, following upon the Nazi-engendered horror then his excruciating bout with tuberculosis, no sincere pursuit of truth, no common language, and thus no hope seemed possible anymore? Reidel cites a 1968 speech in which Bernhard maintained: "I speak the language that I alone understand, no one else, the same as anybody understands only his own language." In any event, this line about being chosen sums up well the strange and sometimes fascinating ambivalence of these poems, ostensibly addressed to the Christian God but perhaps, after all, to the wind, that is to No One, or to a sort of absurd, empty, unattainable Motion—a breezy Notion.

Intriguing Specimens of Humanity
(Veza Canetti)

It is incredible that *Yellow Street* took so long to be published. Written by Veza Canetti (1897-1963), the wife of the Nobel prizewinner Elias Canetti (1905-1994), the stories enjoyed great success when they first appeared in an important Austrian avant-garde newspaper of the 1920s and 1930s, the *Arbeiter-Zeitung*. These stunning evocations of Viennese life were rediscovered and collected into one volume only in 1989, the year of the first German edition of *Die gelbe Straße*. In subsequent years, most of Veza Canetti's work has fortunately been similarly recovered and republished: her play *Der Oger* (1991); her short-prose collection, *Geduld bringt Rosen* (1992); her novel about the Nazi invasion of Austria, *Die Schildkröten* (1999); and her collection of stories and plays, *Der Fund* (2001). *Die Schildkröten*, which Veza wrote in 1939 just after the Jewish couple had fled to London, has been translated as *The Tortoises*.

The "Yellow Street" in question is, as Canetti tells us, remarkable. "All sorts of people live there," she writes, "cripples, somnambulists, lunatics, the desperate and the smug." Canetti brilliantly caricatures the most eccentric members of this teeming microcosm, arranging a series of vivid vignettes into five main intersecting stories. The most peculiar of the characters is Herr Vlk, who, "every time he turned over a page of his newspaper, checked with a ruler to see that he was holding it at the right distance so as not to damage his eyesight."

The everyday routines of these intriguing specimens of humanity—some pitiable, several repulsive—crisscross at the Café Planet, the tobacconist's, and the soap boutique, the latter two shops owned by a redoubtably misanthropic cripple, Frieda Runkel. One day, while her faithful maid Rosa is guiding her across the street in a perambulator, Runkel decides to end her "wretched life." She makes confusing signs and shouts angrily, trying to get Rosa to push the perambulator in front of a speeding motorcycle. But it is the maid who is run over.

Underlying the behavior of many of the Yellow Street citizens is the merciless cruelty one associates with a novel by Balzac. Unlike the French master, however, Canetti never analyzes a character's psychology; letting acts and facts speak for themselves, the author alludes only offhandedly to details suddenly revelatory of human malevolence. In his foreword, Elias Canetti describes this "lateral method" as touching "only lightly upon the essentials in apparent haste, without giving it full expression." The initially sympathetic Herr Iger, for example, hands out money to all kinds of acquaintances and charities, but we later learn that he beats and starves his wife in their miserable one-room apartment. Frau Hatvany runs an agency for placing unfortunate girls in homes as maids, but more often than not she leads them into prostitution.

Often, as in Rosa's accident, a series of initially insignificant events ends in catastrophe. Emilie, one of Frau Hatvany's victims, resolves to drown herself in a canal. "She looked into the water and shuddered at the thought of the cold," writes Canetti, "but then doesn't a serving maid jump out of bed into the icy cold morning at five, that's almost the same as jumping into the water, and then it occurred to her that she didn't want to take off her jacket, she somehow had the vague idea that she would be warmer in the water with it on." As it turns out, the policeman who pulls the girl out of the water dies of pneumonia. "What a tragedy," cries the grocer's wife, indifferent to the maid's fate. "Now we've got no policeman no more!"

Canetti's lively, ironic style is an allegro-paced blend of spare syntax, sharp images, and folksy colloquial terms, an unusual German idiom that Ian Mitchell skillfully translates. Rarely has an author so concisely summed up the nastiness of man, who, of course, "walks erect," as Canetti acidly concludes, "lofty spiritual qualities etched into his countenance."

A Delicate Touch
(Peter Altenberg)

Well-known to the leading Austrian and German intellectuals, writers, and artists of his day—his acquaintances included Robert Musil, Thomas Mann, Hugo von Hofmannstahl, Sigmund Freud, Oskar Kokoschka, and Stefan Zweig—the Viennese prose poet Peter Altenberg (1859-1919) was then forgotten during the five decades following his death. During the late 1960s and 1970s, however, this "freest soul of the epoch," as satirist Karl Kraus defined him, suddenly reappeared in German-speaking countries. In 1968, Reclam issued a popular paperback selection (*Sonnenuntergang im Prater*) of his characteristic short prose texts, a form that he had perfected into a highly personal mode of expression. To this handy selection were added *Das große Peter Altenberg Buch* (1977) and a two-volume *Ausgewählte Werke* (1979). Finally, in 1984, the useful *Peter Altenberg: Leben und Werk in Texten und Bildern* was brought out by Altenberg's long-time publisher, Fischer. Focused on both the life and the writing, this album consists of illustrations, letters, contemporaneous critical commentary about Altenberg, and prose pieces that had previously been overlooked. Interestingly, during the same period, translations appeared in France and were widely discussed. Unfortunately, this unclassifiable writer whose stated ideals comprised "the adagios in the violin sonatas of Beethoven, speckled tulips, solo asparagus, new potatoes, Carolina rice, the blue pen 'Kuhn 201,' ketchup, money, and Hansy Klausecker (thirteen years old)," remained undiscovered in English-speaking countries.

For these and still other reasons, the publication of Peter Wortsman's selection, *Telegrams of the Soul* (Archipelago Books), is very welcome. No reader attracted to the "between the genres" types of prose that are practiced by numerous European authors yet that are too often scorned or misunderstood by their American counterparts can afford to ignore Altenberg, a innovator in this respect, little matter that he was inclined to dismiss himself, either too modestly or with false modesty (or both). In "A Letter to Arthur Schnitzler," for example—note that a letter or even a postcard jotting yields a prose text for Altenberg—he qualifies himself as "a kind of little pocket mirror, powder mirror, no world-mirror." (Contrast these images to Stendhal's "mirror that strolls down a wide road.") He adds that he never revises his texts, and gives the impression of being an idler more than a writer. Yet certainly he worked harder than he lets on. An off-hand comment in "The Private Tutor" about "two aguti, Dasyprocta aguti" suggests that he took notes on the spot; he was probably not as spontaneously inspired as he claimed. Altenberg in fact wrote two-thousand-odd prose pieces, not to mention other writings of various kinds. Twelve books appeared during his lifetime—no mean accomplishment. A posthumous volume came out in 1925. Although needing not the slightest exegesis to be enjoyed, his prose pieces constantly raise the two-in-one question: When does poetry "fall" into prose (as Gérard de Nerval put it), and when, inversely, does prose "fall" into poetry?

His studies, brief narratives, sketches, vignettes, reminiscences, and mini-essays are all situated somewhere between the prose poem and the short story. This "somewhere" defies exact definition. For the second edition (1898) of his first and still best-known book, *Wie ich es sehe* ("As I See It"), originally published in 1896, Altenberg uses as an epigraph a quotation from J.-K. Huysman's novel *À rebours* (1884). "Manipulated by an ingenious alchemist," declares Huysmans, the prose poem "should enclose in its tiny volume...the power of a novel in which the analytic lengths and descriptive superfluities have been suppressed." But as Hans Dieter Schäfer (who prefaces the aforementioned Reclam anthology) rightly observes, whereas "Baudelaire usually gives a symbolic interpretation at the end of his texts, Altenberg leaves everything in suspense." One senses that "prose poem" ill suits his stylistically less intense (though no less subtle) evocations; language *per se* does not call attention to itself, as it were. His frequent rejection of narrative closure, moreover, represents a valid aesthetic position and a sobering worldview: life can be reflected only in its transience and fluidity, a human being only in his unfulfilled yearnings; there is perhaps no essence of life to sum up or symbolize in the first place. This position has consequences for the primacy traditionally given to description in prose. Altenberg writes impressionistically of Viennese street and café scenes, of summer holiday resorts in the Austrian countryside, all the while providing glimpses of prostitutes, paramours, coffeehouse habitués, and other social marginals more or less like himself (whom he also portrays). "Extracts from life," he called his texts, "the life of the soul and what the day may bring, reduced to two or three pages." These reductions or distillations suggest much more than they affirm; the reader continues to look beyond or muse upon the words. The titles of some of his collections reveal aspects of this particular sensibility: *Was der Tag mir zuträgt* ("What the Day Holds in Store for Me," 1901), *Prodromos* ("Prodrome," 1906), *Märchen des Lebens* ("Fairytales of Life," 1908), *Bilderbögen des kleinen Lebens* ("Picture Book of the Petty Life," 1908), *Neues Altes* ("New Things from Old," 1911), and *Vita ipsa* (1918). The word "life" is conspicuous.

Altenberg conjures up a fin-de-siècle melancholy; it can have a certain charm. Yet just below the surface of this emotion lurks a persistent anxiety about fleeting time. At times this anxiety is exacerbated into still more powerful feelings, as when he relates (in "The Hotel Room") how he vainly tries to seduce "sweet Ms. J."—that "Ms." in Wortsman's translation is too contemporary—and in addition loses a benefactor's "modest monthly largesse." These strokes of bad fortune move him to remark: "The song of the birds in the treetops grows clearer with shreds of simple melody. Quiet storms disseminate the scent of meadows. It would be the perfect hour to hang myself from the window box - - -." By the way, those three hyphens at the end are typical of Altenberg's idiosyncratic punctuation, which often strives to avoid the definitive conclusions of periods and here, perhaps, the carrying out of his urge to kill himself.

Some moving pieces return to the death of his mother. He also wrote erotica about the treacherous beauty of under-age girls. Altenberg was famous in Vienna, not only as a regular of the Café Central and the Café Griensteidl, but also as a collector of postcards and photographs depicting girls of sundry nationalities and in various stages of undress. (*Peter Altenberg: Leben und Werk in Texten und Bildern* includes samples, some of which would today probably get the prose poet investigated for pedophilia, though no evidence of sexual abuse of minors has ever been recorded in his regard.) His first love, in 1878 (when he was nineteen), seems to have been the thirteen-year-old Bertha Lecher. In fact, Richard Engländer (his real name) chose his pseudonym because he had met Bertha, nicknamed "Peter" by her brothers, in the Danube River village of Altenberg an der Donau. Born the first child of the well-to-do Jewish merchant Moriz Engländer and his wife Pauline, the writer, after halfheartedly endeavoring to study law, then medicine, and failing at both, settled into a bohemian lifestyle and never worked, though he did review cabaret shows for the *Wiener Allgemeine Zeitung* when his father's firm went bankrupt in 1905. Until his death, when a fortune of 100,000 kronen was discovered in his possession, he was considered to be destitute. (He had arranged to have this sum bequeathed to a child protection charity.) On several occasions, his friends organized fund-raising campaigns on his behalf. Several texts mention impecuniousness with disdain or humorous resignation; in "Traveling," for instance, he relates his habit of taking holidays by studying train schedules "from mid-May on" instead of actually buying a ticket and hopping aboard. When he did travel, to Munich notably, he announced that he was "not interested in the things that were," but rather "in the things that are, that will be!" This desire for the present (or the future) is an essential trait of this prose poet who also wrote about his parents and lost childhood. Often he seeks to bring his writing ever closer to the here and now, to evoke details ever more tangibly. Yet yearning to bridge the gap separating consciousness from the brute facts of the world has its price to pay. Already diagnosed in 1882 as suffering from hypersensitivity, he spent time, particularly toward the end of his life, in psychiatric sanatoriums, a story that is recounted in *Widerhall des Herzens* ("Echo of the Heart") by Helga Malmberg, the author's companion from 1906 (when she was eighteen and he forty-seven) to 1911. Altenberg never married.

Besides as an admired if eccentric author, Altenberg was well-known in his day because of Arnold Schönberg's controversial directing, at the Wiener Grossen Musikvereinssaal on 31 March 1913, of two of Alban Berg's "Five Orchestral Songs after Picture Postcard Texts by Peter Altenberg" (Opus 4). The author of "On Smells" probably had a sharp musical ear as well. In any event, he kept a carbon print of Gustav Klimt's portrait of Schubert above his bed and elsewhere he relates his attempt, in a watchmaker's shop, to win over a young lady by having her favorite tune, Schubert's *The Trout*, played on the gramophone. With obsessive precision, he even notes the exact reference to the record: "Deutsche Grammaphonaktiengesellschaft C2-42531." Oddly enough, this precision is also part of his "poetry," here conceived as the art of forcing language and literature into little-frequented nooks. In this text about the gramophone, the narrator's seductive ploy fails, and he can only acknowledge that "autumn came, and the esplanade was lightly paved with scattered yellow leaves. And then they shelved the gramophone in the watchmaker's shop since it no longer paid to keep it." Tellingly, in another piece, the narrator walks every day past a ground floor window through which he notices a young woman sewing; eventually she, too, notices his regular appearances. One evening, he comes across her standing outside the house; they exchange a few words, but she announces that she has accepted a factory job in another town. They will not see each other again, but their glances and single conversation have nevertheless constituted the narrator's "one real true relationship," as he phrases it. Altenberg was acutely sensitive to the plight of the solitary urban individual.

It is a critical commonplace that his best book is his first one, *As I See It*, with which Thomas Mann claimed to have fallen in "love at the first sound" and whose "compressed style" was praised by Musil. Schäfer remarks that Altenberg's "subsequent books bring nothing new from the artistic viewpoint and show ever more frequent compositional weaknesses. Often the impressions are only offered in a gossipy narrative style and devaluated to the level of personal anecdotes. As the Belle Epoque fell into decline, Altenberg's prose style fell off proportionately. Poetry is still expressed in a few late pieces, in which no longer people, but rather things—postcards, walking sticks, cigarette packs, steel springs—make up the heart of the text."

These later thing-texts should not be underestimated. When Altenberg focuses on things, he is not only keeping in technological step with his times (by describing, for instance, riding in an elevator), but he is also helping to introduce into literature a major conceptual shift. He was certainly Husserl's and Rilke's contemporary in this respect. He is not being glib when he observes: "The significant things in life have absolutely no importance. They tell, they make known nothing more about being than we ourselves already know about it!... The important differences are only manifest in the details.... Little things in life supplant the 'great events.'" Franz Kafka likewise pinpointed the significance of the insignificant in Altenberg's writing. "In his small stories," remarked the author of *The Trial* and *The Castle* but also of numerous short prose texts (and notably those very short ones of his first book, *Betrachtung*, 1912), "his whole life is mirrored.... Peter Altenberg is a genius of mere nothings [*Nichtigkeiten*], a singular idealist who discovers the splendors of this world as he does cigarette butts in coffeehouse ashtrays." (When he cites this phrase, Wortsman interestingly translates "Nightigkeiten" as "nullifications," but the meaning of the term is closer to "trifles.")

As for Altenberg's German, which is often based on delicate understatement and fine irony, Wortsman's oft enthusiastic and engaging renderings are nonetheless sometimes too slangy. Brash effects like "I was wild, wild arggggggggh I was wild!" (p. 43), "Gee, Peter" (p. 56), "Our salesgirls wouldn't earn a dime like that. Got to be friendly, sweetheart, nobody's gonna bite you" (p. 70), "goddamn nut" (p. 73), "Ya know, Peter Altenberg. He's a slob, I mean, poor guy, he ain't got nothin'" (p. 75), or "I can't quite get the hang of it" (p. 80) evoke atmospheres, places, and epochs that are far removed from fin-de-siècle Vienna. More of Altenberg's erotic texts could have been included in an otherwise generous and stimulating selection. Some bring the prose of the Japanese novelist Junichiro Tanizaki (1886-1965) to mind, especially the coincidentally entitled "Japanese Vegetable-Fibered Toilet Paper," which is not comprised in *Telegrams of the Soul*. In this narrative, a presumably much older man has given a young girl whom he admires seemingly every gift, including some which "under other circumstances would have been considered too intimate, such as a parasol, a pair of gloves, a belt buckle, handkerchiefs, and so on and so on and so on - - - ." Now the man presents her with ten packs of "genuine Japanese toilet paper, made out of Japanese vegetable fibers, unbelievably tender and nonetheless strong in texture, toilet paper of which a pack of course costs a Krone eighty, whereas the best local brand goes for a Krone - - -." At first the girl was "revolted, offended, upset," explains the narrator, "but gradually more natural thoughts took the upper hand. And she simply wrote in reply: 'From now on, darling, you who have such a tender, delicate touch, it is going to be very difficult for you to come up with still another idea to give my life more ease and comfort - - -." Incidentally, in a text ("In Munich") having nothing to do with the preceding, Altenberg exclaims: "Learn from the Japanese!"

The Fertile "Crisis Years" of Rainer Maria Rilke

Edward Snow, the translator of Rainer Maria Rilke's *Uncollected Poems*, rightfully insists that readers who know the Prague-born German-language poet (1875-1926) only through the early work or the famous late *Sonnets to Orpheus* and the *Duino Elegies* (both 1923) are still missing much. Choosing a hundred samples from the over five-hundred poems and pocket-book jottings that Rilke accumulated during his so-called unfertile "crisis years," which began in 1908, Snow demonstrates that the author of the prose work, *The Notebooks of Malte Laurids Brigge* (1910), actually never ceased versifying, as legend would have it, and that these uncollected poems "stand over against" the "high vatic mode" of the better-known work in "necessary counterpoise."

If, comparatively, these poems do often "articulate a realm of pure occasion," as Snow puts it, admirers will nonetheless find much additional proof of Rilke's lifelong engagement with "inwardness," with an "outside world" from which we are separated, with "things-in-themselves" (like that tree rising before us "in the spell / of [our] renouncing" of self), and with death: "Somewhere the flower of farewell blooms and scatters / ceaselessly its pollen... / even in the winds that reach us first we breathe farewell." The word *Wesen* ("Being") recurs; indeed Rilke, like his predecessor Friedrich Hölderlin (to whom a fine poem is dedicated), is a precursor of several major European poets who, in our time, have similarly sought out "spaces" wherein Being may be sensed. He aspires not to be "cut off" by "a slight partition" from "the stars' measure"; elsewhere, he wishes to "cross over / and invest this world." Is such traversing possible? The tension of these pieces results from the ardor of his hopes and the unlikelihood of fulfilling them; the poet—and few have been more sensitive—must sacrifice his subjectivity to Being; the alternative is unending thirst and thus denial. Humankind is "meant for" this affirming renunciation, declares Rilke, and "not, in the rigid room, after a night of negation, / one more negation-filled day."

Snow translates the original closely and clearly, although a few Anglo-Saxon genitives (with abstract nouns) create ambiguities and one key rendering is questionable: Why is the first line of the ominous last poem translated "Come, you last thing," when the German "letzter," in "Komm du, du letzter," is in the masculine case (first perhaps suggesting *der Tod,* "death," then in any case syntactically linking up with "heilloser Schmerz," "unholy agony")? No "thing," an otherwise essential word in the poet's philosophy, is mentioned. Nor do the translations convey Rilke's rhyming or his metrical mastery, a formal strictness that in some cases reflects, ironically, the poet's aspiration to flee the self's rigid cage.

Snow's intelligent work on and contagious sympathy for this little-known corpus soars so far above Anita Barrows and Joanna Macy's misleading version of *Das Stundenbuch* (1905), published by Riverhead Books as *Rilke's Book of Hours: Love Poems to God,* that the latter would be unworthy of mention were it not an appalling example of disrespect that deserves to be denounced. The translators severely edit Rilke's original, reordering the poems, combining two poems into one poem, changing punctuation, ignoring line-breaks and enjambments, shortening lines, striking out passages where "the thread was lost" or the text was "unclear" or too "sentimental," intentionally mistranslating ("To avoid excessive piety, we changed... *frömmsten Gefühle*"...to "what waits within me"), and exhibiting in their self-regarding prefaces, their notes and their error-ridden translations a pretentious and shameless desire to manipulate Rilke's poetry for their own ideological purposes.

And How Hope is Violent
(Paul Celan)

When Paul Celan (1920-1970) committed suicide, he probably jumped off the Pont Mirabeau, the Parisian bridge to which one of his favorite poets, Apollinaire, had devoted a particularly melodious, melancholy love poem. "Et comme l'Espérance est violente," observes Apollinaire in "Le Pont Mirabeau," "And how Hope is violent." The line sums up Celan's own troubled life, his bleak, yearning poetry, perhaps also his desperate attempts to break out of his "masticated tristesse" and love others, notably his wife, the artist Gisèle Celan-Lestrange. Although his poetic oeuvre courageously engages with the Holocaust (in which his parents perished) and with the redoubtable task of writing German verse "after Auschwitz," much of his later, vertiginously polysemous work—with its multiple "you's"—also explores, cryptically, love's possibilities. As Celan despaired deeply, he also hoped violently.

Yet how to translate his thematically multi-layered, sometimes multilingually inspired German poems, whose philosophical implications extend into phenomenology, ontology, and Jewish mysticism? A gifted polyglot from his youth onward, the Rumanian-born Paul Antschel chose to write in the language through which his mother had inculcated in him a love of classical German literature. Later, adopting his pen name, Celan pushed German beyond what even experimental writers considered its farthest borders. No unshackled word-spinner, however, he ever scrutinized etymology and exhibited a logician's rigor with respect to language's ability to negate and affirm, to designate and suggest. He carefully structured his work around almost insupportably tense contradictions, paradoxes, and oxymorons. He twisted common images inside out, or tore them asunder, whereupon he could expose the hidden and hide the obvious. Probing the most concealed and harrowing existential truths, he forged astonishing neologisms that tap the wellsprings of the Germanic languages, especially as regards compounding and verbal prefixes. Faced with these intimidating profundities and entanglements, the reader and translator must depart upon an exhausting, but ultimately rewarding, "Bedeutungsjagd" or "meaning chase"—as Celan himself terms it.

Of three translations that appeared between 2000 and 2001, John Felstiner's *Selected Poems and Prose of Paul Celan* is the most reliable. Quite usefully, the author of *Paul Celan: Poet, Survivor, Jew* first gathers samples from the more conservatively structured *Early Poems* (1940-1943)—although the skeletal "Darkness," expressing Celan's insurmountable mourning for his murdered mother and growing fascination with morbidity ("Only dying / sparkles"), already announces the tortured forms and hermetic personal symbolism of his maturity. These initial efforts reveal that the later poems—veritable "woe-" or "distress-shards"—were fashioned by a man who could practice the most exacting prosody. Felstiner then chooses well-known poems from the famous collections, as they run from *Poppy and Memory* (1952) and *From Threshold to Threshold* (1955), through *Speech-Grille* (1959), *The No-One's Rose* (1963), *Breathturn* (1967), *Threadsuns* (1968) and *Light-Compulsion* (1970), to the posthumously-published *Snow-Part* (1971) and *Homestead of Time* (1976). Three speeches, which collectively form an *ars poetica*, round out the volume.

Of four uncollected poems from the *Nachlass*, which are also added, the long "Wolfsbean" is uncommonly explicit. "Mother," asks the poet, "whose / hand did I shake / when I went with / your words to / Germany?" Celan's German sojourns devastated him. His last trip, during which the philosopher Martin Heidegger attended one of his readings, occurred less than a month before his self-drowning. The encounters between the two men were momentous, at least for Celan, because their respective poetics intersected intimately. "Hear deep in / with your mouth," writes Celan, for instance, paralleling Heidegger's more abstract image of a "Logos" to which the poet must hearken. The poet memorably recalls his first meeting with Heidegger in "Todtnauberg" (1967), which evokes hopes of obtaining "a thinker's /...word / in the heart": an acknowledgement that the author of *Being and Time* had shamelessly consorted, even if briefly, with the Nazis. Celan never obtained this *Wort*.

Because revealing variants exist, and because the mature work can be densely intertextual, much more copious notes are needed than are provided in Felstiner's otherwise intelligently conceived selection. This is less true of the annotations accompanying some of the poems from *Threadsuns*, translated by Pierre Joris, although clarification for other poems should have been provided. As Celan encrypts, he confesses. His wife in fact disclosed (to Felstiner) that her husband's work was "one-hundred percent" based on his own experience—an essential guideline to keep in mind.

Felstiner is a careful, if sometimes over-cautious, translator. Although generally faithful, his versions do incite a few quibbles. "Winter," for example, is a heartbreaking poem devoted to Celan's mother, who was shot by Germans somewhere in the Ukraine, about a half-year after being deported from the family's hometown of Czernowitz, Rumania, in June 1942. (By chance, Celan was away from home when his parents were arrested.) In this poem, "Wachstum" means "growth," not "wakening," so the terrifying concluding question should read: "What would come, Mother: growth or wound— / if I too sank in snows of the Ukraine?" Although Celan's wrenched metaphors can prompt philosophical or theological speculation, they are often surprisingly concrete in construction. "Snow," with its ominous personal connotations, appears frequently; as does "eye," with an emphasis on the organ's materiality and physiological functions. "Wachstum," a common biological term, foretells Celan's increasing recourse to technical, scientific, and especially medical vocabularies, as well as to foreign terms (notably from Yiddish and Hebrew).

An arresting case of this latter stylistic trait occurs in an unusually serene poem from *Threadsuns*. A Hebrew word, "Ziw," crops up at the end. By repeating a soft short-"i" sound ("Ziw, jenes Licht"), Celan adroitly blends this mystical term (related to the Shechinah, the radiant presence of God in the world) gracefully into the line. Joris translates the concluding strophe this way:

> Quiet, in the coronary arteries,
> unconstricted:
> Ziv, that light.

This is what writing poetry "after Auschwitz" is all about: struggling, despite the unspeakable acts that have been committed, to speak again; seeking out sounds, syllables, or words that might heal the gaping wound between the Germanic and the Judaic. In the intensely claustrophobic "Stretto," a Beckett-like stutter initiates the rebuilding: Came, came. / Came a word, came, / came through the night, / would glisten, would glisten." And in "Whichever Stone you Lift," Celan points to the guilt ever corroding the pure creative energies he musters for this undertaking: "Whichever word you speak— / you owe to / destruction." Few post-Holocaust authors have delved as desperately as Celan into the fate of having survived.

Having lived through forced-labor camps, settled in Paris (in 1948), and married an exceptionally devoted, artistically gifted French woman, Celan nonetheless continued to suffer. The couple's first child, François, died shortly after birth. In an epitaph marked at the end by a solemn repetitive cadence, as well as by a hesitating pause, Celan concludes: "und [wir] tragen das ungewisse, / und tragen das Grün in dein Immer." The distich illustrates Celan's typical "multiple meanings," and Felstiner misconstrues German syntax by interpreting the adjective "ungewisse" as an adverb. He writes: "and [we] bear it uncertainly, / and bear this Green into your Ever." Yet the first line of the distich actually trails off, momentarily, as Celan—the parent-narrator—poignantly searches for something that can be qualified by "ungewisse" ("uncertain"). An ellipsis could almost be inserted, denoting the poet's painful mental groping: "and [we] bear the uncertain...." In other words, the epithet "uncertain" seeks to determine a neuter noun that fails to appear. As Celan ponders his son's death, the only "thing" that he can ultimately imagine, as a fitting metaphor for or memorial to this short life, is a color—which is no "thing" at all. Philosophers have long grappled with this paradox: colors need an objective "support" in order to exist. At first, Celan can conceive of no justifiable "support" for this annihilated life—so inconsolable is his sorrow, so emptied of content his imagining of any afterlife. The adjective "uncertain" is attached, literally, to nothing. By the second line of the distich, he can finally fill in the blank, as it were, with "Green," a neuter noun in German. So the "uncertain" of the preceding line finds at last, theoretically, its "support": the color "Green"—a phenomenon itself without a support. Yet "uncertain" can at least now qualify "something," silently, at one remove: "and [we] bear the [uncertain] Green into your Ever." Celan appeals to so many grammatical resources at once, that the poem attains the very limits of translatability.

This question of a "support" is fundamental. Celan's poems often narrate a vain search for an ontological or a theological foundation. His envisioning of, or acerbic taunting of, the traditional Godhead of his ancestors shifts, Job-like, from anger to doubt, from doubt to flickering hopes, then back to bitter unbelief. In "Psalm," he prays acidly:

> Blessèd art thou, No One.
> In thy sight would
> we bloom.
> In thy
> spite.
>
> A Nothing
> we were, are now, and ever
> shall be, blooming:
> the Nothing-, the
> No-One's Rose.

Yet for Celan, God's "being-over-there" ("Hinübersein") can be "fetched... back with words" as well as—the poet adds with frightening irony—when we contemplate the gruesome "whole[ness]" that He takes on "in the death / of all who've been reaped." Notions such as distance, trespassing, right-of-way, orientation, and direction—conveyed by those tricky German prepositions and verbal particles—are crucial.

Indeed, Celan's quest for consolation, peace of mind, ontological security, spiritual rebirth, and love (he even composed erotic poems), not only continually crisscrosses the realm of ideas but also meticulously explores the intricacies of grammar. Yet the "mother-tongue" whose grammar he dissects so minutely is also that of the enemy. For Celan's most famous poem, "Deathfugue," with its striking juxtaposition of a luminous Goethean Margareta and a death camp-doomed Shulamith (the Hebrew maiden of *The Song of Songs*), Felstiner fashions a provocative translation. By leaving "Deutschland" as "Deutschland" (as opposed to Germany) and by gradually re-introducing into the last part of the translation the original German for "Death is a Master from Deutschland" as well as for the refrain "your golden hair Margareta / your ashen hair Shulamith," the translator gives German an invading, sickening contagiousness. This tour de force re-creates what a German-language Jewish poet like Celan, after the war, felt when he wondered to which language—let alone, to what hope—he could turn. German was hopelessly diseased.

Joris translates *Fadensonnen* more or less word-for-word. At its best, his version makes English sound like Celan; and Joris rarely errs when interpreting German words, though he fails to perceive a few English homonyms that need to be channeled out of ambiguity. His methodology is otherwise profoundly ill-conceived. Coining neologisms by compounding or verbal-prefixing is, when compared even to English, a comparatively much greater strength of German. Even cognate particles—the German *ein*, the English "in"—do not necessarily function in the same way grammatically or exhibit exactly coinciding semantic spectra. Joris, who has also translated *Atemwende* (*Breathturn*), ignores the natural English tendency to post-position verbal particles with respect to the verb, a syntactic maneuver bringing out all their semantic force.

An exceedingly difficult translation exercise related to these problems occurs in an important poem beginning "Eingewohnt-entwohnt, // einentwohnt, // die gehorsame Finsternis." Joris renders these lines as "Inhabited, dishabited, // indishabited, // the obedient darkness." Rather like the "uncertain" of the lines quoted above, here the incipit is formed by three uninflected participles, each awaiting a support. Until "the obedient darkness" surges forth, it is unclear what grammatical subject(s) these participles might qualify. The poet-narrator? Perhaps a "you," which in fact appears farther down in the same poem? Moreover, Celan characteristically constructs a fascinating, yet ultimately comprehensible, etymological labyrinth that remains impenetrable—unless annotated, which it is not—in Joris's Latinate solution.

The verb *wohnen* means "to live, to dwell," whereas *einwohnen* means "to inhabit"; yet the compound verb still actively connotes "getting used to a place by living there," a nuance introduced by the particle *ein*. Strictly speaking, this latter sense also animates our English "inhabit." Yet we remain insensitive to this derivation, which is perhaps easier to feel if we separate the verbal particle from the verb and form neologisms: "habit (yourself) in," "live (yourself) in," "dwell (yourself) in." In German, Celan's meaning is doubly tangible, because the second word, the neologism *entwohnt*, is only an umlaut away from *entwöhnt*. The verb *entwöhnen* means "to get out of the habit of doing something," and specifically "to wean." Here, as elsewhere in Celan, getting back to non-Latinate English roots can enlighten our parallel comprehension of the German. Our "wean," it turns out, similarly derives from Old English and Old High German words meaning "to dwell, be used to." Our "wont" is also tied to these same roots. "Weaned," as one of the meanings of *entwöhnt*, subtly permeates the surmisable senses of *entwohnt*, a startling effect invoking other maternal images recurring in Celan's oeuvre. The most memorable of these is the "black milk" of "Deathfugue":

> Black milk of daybreak we drink it at evening
> we drink it at midday and morning we drink it at night...

And a poem from *Threadsuns,* seemingly set in a mental asylum, links "the excavated heart, / wherein they install feeling" with a "milksister / shovel" with which the digging is done.

The quasi-syllogistic logicality resulting from these opening words is not unusual in Celan, who is much more analytical, as a thinker, than is widely supposed. His heartfelt outcries are deeply thought through, syntactically and etymologically. Here, he first evokes a habit (of dwelling somewhere or in something); second, this habit is broken off (weaned); in a third stage, the "obedient darkness" has had to accustom itself to this state of weanedness, to that of being severed from a former dwelling place. Arguably, this former dwelling place is the poet's own mind and body; but depending on the stress given to *ein* or *ent* in the third compound participle (*einentwohnt*), the image might vary from reader to reader. A tantalizing indeterminacy or opacity of imagery in fact often accompanies Celan's maniacal ratiocinations—and this is a quality of truthfulness, not a weakness of style, because of his work's personal, historical, and philosophical concerns. The multifarious symbolic ramifications of this stark incipit are obvious. Above all, the terse triad sums up Celan's adulthood struggle to maintain an increasingly fragile equilibrium with respect to his multiple losses, multiple obscurities. He was ever wrestling with hope.

In comparison to Felstiner and Joris, Nikolai Popov and Heather McHugh have not printed the originals *en face* in *Glottal Stop: 101 Poems by Paul Celan,* justifying their decision by a reluctance "to encourage...too early a recourse to the kind of line-by-line comparison that fatally distracts attention from... a poem's coursing, cumulative power." Unfortunately, though many of their versions read well as English poems, their overall results are not always so "extraordinary" as they announce, once one "distracts" oneself by examining what Celan actually wrote.

To their credit, Popov and McHugh see more clearly than both Joris and Felstiner that the reputed strangeness of Celan's syntax and vocabulary must be relativized. Lacking a highly sensitive measuring device for Celan's stylistic innovations makes accurate translation impossible. Like any poet, he uses word order in a highly conscious way in order to sequence certain sounds, images, or ideas. Yet word order, in a given language, has its own peculiar rules, traditional oral patterns, stylistic felicities, relative freedoms. Syntactically, nothing odd occurs in an invocation like "Ihr mit dem / im Dunkelspiegel Geschauten," which Joris renders incomprehensibly as "You with the / in the darkglass gazed at." Several other like renderings could be listed. Felstiner is less guilty of convoluted literalism, but—to cite one example—his "It is / only the mouths / are saved," for a Noah's ark image ("Es sind / nur die Münder /

geborgen") is needlessly unwieldy when compared to Popov and McHugh's "Only / the mouths / were saved."

Similarly, in "Lyon, Les Archers," Popov and McHugh wisely paraphrase Celan's neologistic "fremdet sich ein" as "with- / drawing into its otherness," alongside Joris's "instranges itself." Moreover, their translation of the last two lines elegantly recovers the invocation to the bow implicit in the German ("das verschollene Ziel / strahlt, Bogen"): "Oh bow, the missing target / looms." Joris's version is duller and grammatically confused: "the missing target / radiates, bow." At their best, Popov and McHugh study, interrogate, then penetrate the meanings of the original and forge powerful, not-too-distant, English equivalents.

Yet not all in their selection (of mostly late poems) is successful. Their worst translating decision, in terms of stylistic taste, historical accuracy, and cultural sensitivity, occurs in a short poem evoking Leibniz. Even without the original at hand, readers should doubt that the philosopher had a "golfball" growth in his neck. Celan writes "das taubeneigrosse Gewächs." Joris, albeit with uncertain punctuation, accurately renders this as "the pigeon egg-size growth." In the same poem, Popov and McHugh then translate "Herzstich" (Joris, "heartstab") as "chest / pain," an anatomically vague euphemism that, furthermore, effaces "heart"—a key term here, as elsewhere. In their laudable attempt to make Celan as forcible in English as he is in German, Popov and McHugh sometimes drift away from simpler, more direct, solutions.

Likewise disappointing, in a relatively explicit poem about "re-education" (probably set at a psychiatric clinic), is Popov and McHugh's interpretation of the phrase "Hörreste, Sehreste" as "audio-visual vestiges." What can the comparatively abstract "audio-visual," usually associated with equipment, possibly mean here? And "vestiges" is too grandiose for "-reste," which concretely (and pejoratively) designates things that are "left over": the "remains" of a meal or a corpse. Felstiner renders the lines soberly, though unadventurously, as "remnants of hearing, of seeing, in / Ward one thousand and one." I envision left-behind "scraps" of hearing and seeing. Finally, the important last distich ("du wirst wieder / er") of this poem, with its ironic reversal of Goethe's well-known saying ("become what you are"), is rendered respectively by Felstiner and Popov-McHugh as "once more you are / him" and "you'll be / a him / again." The latter translators, who mention this poem's "much wider [politico-historical] resonance," justify their quirky "a him" thus:

> The poem's position at the head of [*Light-Compulsion*] suggests a philosophical program...which subsumes the twin coercions of political and psychiatric orthodoxy under the generalized coercive power of a light source or force. The latter tolerates only third-person public functionality, and so subjects the intimate but shifty *you* and its linguistic correlate, poetic speech, to forms of institutional control. We opted for the objective form of the third-person pronoun partly for vernacular naturalness... and partly to emphasize the third-person's subject-object split.

This interesting analysis notwithstanding (and the Popov-McHugh annotations are thorough, if at times too self-confidently interpretative), the problem remains that Celan did not write "a him" but rather "him." (German grammar requires the nominative *er*, "he.") This is not an isolated instance of where Popov and McHugh canalize their exegesis, and thus the translation, while Celan leaves all questions open. Much of his poetry is of course structured around his "habit" of dwelling amidst tormenting open questions.

Celan's tragic incapacity to resolve and move forward is especially highlighted by the six-liner with which Popov and McHugh conclude their gathering. Moving and candid, this short piece remained unpublished during the poet's lifetime. Astonishingly, the poem contradicts, or at least calls for an intense personal combat with, four of the most salient characteristics of Celan's work. Popov and McHugh write:

> Don't sign your name
> between worlds,
>
> surmount
> the manifold of meanings,
>
> trust the tearstain,
> learn to live.

Once again, Felstiner is closer on target when he comprehends the first distich ("Schreib dich nicht / zwischen die Welten") as "Don't write yourself / in between worlds." Here, at last, is a shrewd use of the English "in." There is nothing in the original about "signing a name." Less banally, these lines point to Celan's constant dilemma of finding himself (whence the idea of "writing himself") "between" inner and outer worlds, "between" the self and the other, "between" the present and the past, "between" an adopted country and his homeland, "between" the language of love (the French that he spoke to his wife) and the language of poetry (German), and so on. For Celan, this list of "betweens" can be extended greatly. Felstiner's "in" suggests "getting stuck" between opposing worlds, a nuance belonging to the original as well.

Seemingly speaking to himself (or perhaps to a disciple), Celan must also "surmount" or "rise up against" (as Felstiner more graphically renders "komm auf gegen") the multiple meanings that torment him, bog him down, in endlessly punning, polyglot, poetic puzzles. He now seeks more fundamental truths, whether eternal or immediately curative. He must learn to "trust" the "Tränenspur" (Felstiner, "trail of tears"); in other words, to trust feeling (as opposed to cogitation), to follow up on clues left behind by weeping, notably weeping for others. The poet pleas for an escape from perpetually wounding, and self-wounding, mental mazes. Celan may likewise be summoning himself to take up the abandoned strands of his earlier, more lyrical, poetry.

A manuscript variant of this same poem, however, calls for remaining on the "periphery" or "wayside" of the trail of tears and thereby suggests that feelings are threatening, that it is safer to keep away from them. Be this as it may, the poem concludes in a Rimbaud-like urge to re-unite with some deeply desired, vaguely perceived, *vraie vie* or "true life"—even if stumbling upon the hidden access to this intuitable Beyond (that is so close) implies forsaking that which gave birth to the intuitions in the first place: writing poetry. Such may also have been one of Paul Celan's "violent hopes." Learning to live in the world as it is, promised an end to all those "betweens."

Seeking the Self, Seeking Beyond the Self (Hans W. Cohn)

A tantalizing profundity characterizes the sparse verses of Hans W. Cohn (1916-2004), a remarkable, too-little-known German poet who escaped to England from the Nazi-infested Central Europe of the 1930s. No professional poet but rather, first, a bookseller, then a psychotherapist, Cohn produced a tiny, yet thoroughly essential lifework. His first book, *Gedichte* (Fortune Press, 1950), contains only seventeen poems. A second, but different, *Gedichte* was brought out in 1964 by Sigbert Mohn. A few subsequent pieces were published in reviews and anthologies during the following decade, including in Michael Hamburger's classic *German Poetry 1910-1975* (1977). Yet by Cohn's own admission, he stopped writing poetry at that point. The forty-one poems of *Mit allen fünf Sinnen* (Edition Memoria, 1994), composed at least twenty years before their publication and now limpidly translated in *With All Five Senses* (Menard Press) by the poet's brother, represent Cohn's third and final gathering.

Cohn's renunciation of poetry writing may well seem sad, even inconceivable, to the reader coming across these discrete but no less astonishing poems for the first time. Yet the exiled German poet's literary path, like Samuel Beckett's, seems aimed at attaining silence, or peace of mind, and this fundamental orientation must be kept in mind when we meditate on his gently metered existential paradoxes. In this respect the poem "Father," expressing the ironies of self-seeking, may be a key one. The Biblical Joseph is depicted as a "tireless tailor / of many-coloured coats / none of which fitted" and as a wanderer "lost in the streets / of [his] misinterpreted dreams." Finally, however, Joseph succeeds—"sometimes," Cohn specifies—in making "something real / rough / and tangible" when he mends his sons' shoes. The parable suggests that the poet, too, may ultimately acquire a deeper understanding of himself only by shunning his own anxieties, by concentrating on objective tasks, and by helping others; in short, by courageously turning his back on the self-alluring, self-bewitching, introversions of writing.

Another poem, "Doves and Toads," indicates a similar disappointment about the ability of poetry to convey love. At first, admits the poet, he imagined that his poems were "all doves / messengers of love / when he cradled them on his tongue." Yet now he must confess that he can only "squat / among the toads /

that sprang from his lips." Such lines are not the only places in the collection which conjure up, as a sort of conceptual backdrop to the entire volume, the philosopher Martin Buber's challenging paradigm of the "I" and the "Thou." In what ways, if at all, Cohn seems to ask implicitly, can poetry reach another human being? If poetry cannot in fact bridge the gap to the "Thou," what then is its justification? Sometimes, moreover, Cohn depicts poetry as being able to do little more than express a "sudden wish / to leave / the building site // the incomplete building / the pile of bricks / unused." In despair, the poet wants "to check the blueprints / the plans," but all he can ultimately acknowledge is that "all is building site / and the plans / nobody has seen." Even in parables borrowed from the Bible, Cohn focuses our attention on the Void, on God's absence, on human impossibility, and it is not poetry, he seemingly maintains, that can quench our spiritual thirst.

Such is the atmosphere of several poems, which is not the same as saying that recurrent themes of futility, relational failure, or metaphysical hopelessness sufficiently explain Cohn's abandoning of poetry. By no means do all poets obsessed with such themes give up poetry. Yet the problem of how to live a deep and full life is admirably ever-present in Cohn's work, and often—via his simple, deceptively calming diction—with a singular urgency. Cohn brings us face to face with the perhaps irresolvable dilemma of choosing either to help others, selflessly, or to concentrate on our own individuation and pressing spiritual questions. Other riddle-like poems point to the perils of losing oneself in worldly tasks and thereby suggest, on the contrary, that somehow more poetry should have been written; that the poet should not have gone "outward," but ever more "inward." In these cases, the self is often featured as double; what is neglected or "mislaid" is the most precious half—a "half" that could have been nourished, preserved, or protected if the poet had only paid more attention to it. Now it is too late; all that is left after the "disappearance" of this precious part of the soul is a hollow shell, and bewilderment. No fellow human has been helped, and the narrator's solitude is irremediable. "Disappearance" puts it this way:

> One morning
> he could not find himself any more…
>
> It did not come unexpected:
> for some time he had
> with growing concern
> noticed how each day he became
> smaller and smaller…
>
> He had taught himself
> to speak with a loud voice
> so that he could hear himself
> if the worst should happen.

He had pinned on himself
coloured ribbons
to keep an eye on himself
if the worst should happen.

For all that it has happened.

Quiet disasters occur often in these memorable verses. In "Loss," the genuine self is portrayed as a man whom "you put…into the small room" and "visited only rarely." Years later, you discover that the room is empty and you no longer "know… / whether you really put him / into that room." In fact, asks the poet, "Was there ever anybody / to put into a room?" In "Fall," the poet finds his face falling "from the mirror / into his hands." He lets it fall, and we are left to imagine what happens next. In several instances, this unstated "what happens next"—representing a decisive turning-point or coming-to-awareness—constitutes the most important element of the poem. The essential lies just beyond the final words.

Rather like Rimbaud (who likewise abandoned poetry, and for reasons that are still much debated), Cohn's deepest urge, when writing, may have been to relocate some truly authentic "reality" that he felt as being suddenly, brutally, "elsewhere" (though perhaps ensconced "inside" the self), a "reality" in any event hopelessly perverted by the Nazis, by their acts and by their discourse. The German philosopher Theodor Adorno famously remarked that it is impossible, in fact "barbarous to write poetry after Auschwitz." Yet as for other poet-survivors—one thinks immediately of Paul Celan—whose young adulthoods were changed radically by the Holocaust, it often seems that the exact opposite can be true, at least for a certain period of their lives.

One must not forget that Celan, a polyglot born in Rumania, committed suicide in 1970, after composing his linguistically difficult and to many critics apparently hermetic, yet in truth often autobiographically specific, poems in German, which was the native language of his deported parents as well as their concentration camp murderers. But Cohn, a miraculous escapee who was able to survive in Britain, was perhaps long left afterwards with *only words*—and at that, with many more questions than answers. Those fragile words, pieced together with great effort into skeletal poems that are admirable for their total absence of the slightest rhetorical ostentation, continued to be the vehicle of his asking, of his seeking. And those words, if not the unique then by far the most precious possession of this refugee, thus not only made surviving possible but also significantly remained German despite his several decades in an English-speaking country. He came to author important psychological studies in English, notably *Else Lasker-Schüler: The Broken World* (1974), *Existential Thought and Therapeutic Practice* (1997), and *Heidegger and the Roots of Existential Therapy* (2003). No poem of *With All Five Senses* blatantly refers to the Second World War, but "Border Crossing" and "Even Now Poland" reveal how long the suffering endured, even in more secure climes. In the latter poem, set during his flight from Prague (where he was a medical student) through northern Europe, Cohn confesses:

> Sometimes it seems
> as if he had
> never left Poland.
>
> The thirst for instance
> is almost the same
> unquenchable
> for there is no real
> water.

This being said, in contrast to much German postwar poetry, Cohn's allegories—however rooted in tragic history—are above all timeless and metaphysical. His poetry constantly searches for that "real water," which is of course the fresh water that the war- and hate-fleeing civilian needs desperately and cannot find, but also much more. This is made clear in the Cavafy-like "Tale of an Apostle":

> A chamberlain of the Queen of Ethiopia
> a eunuch
> drove through the desert and read the prophecy
> of the dumb lamb led to the slaughter.
>
> We know the tale, have also heard
> how Philip the apostle
> illuminated Isaiah's words.
>
> The story goes they came to some still water
> the eunuch said "look there is water",
> climbed off the wagon. Philip baptised him.
>
> This, more or less, is the cheerful tale
> of the chamberlain of the Queen of Ethiopia.
>
> Other eunuchs travel through the desert
> and maybe also read the prophet's words.
> Apostles also come this way
> and sometimes water brightens in the sand.
>
> Yet from wagon to water the road
> is very long
> much longer than the span
> of their castrated
> lives.

These transparent but no less troubling poems, with their occasional cryptic symbols (for example, a "tree" that a "mother" can perhaps "accept," after her death, when "the strong face" breaks "through the blurred mask") and with their poignant understated anguish, fill out a rare and compelling book. *With All Five Senses* is a volume to be treasured. Cohn stopped writing verse long before he died, but his oeuvre remains to be discovered fully. Early advocates of his originality and importance included the German poet Erich Fried and especially Michael Hamburger, who provides a sensitive foreword to this translation. In 2004, the Menard Press welcomely brought out *Landscapes and Other Poems*, a second volume of verse that includes versions of poems whose originals were comprised in the aforementioned Sigbert Mohn and Fortune Press editions. Let us hope that more readers will come to meditate on Cohn's profound and sure-crafted verses. Their cumulative effect is truly moving. One can substitute the lastingness of his contribution into lines that he himself uses to describe a sculpture by Joachim Karsh: "The feet are silent / but they stand."

A Radical Path to the Ordinary
(Elke Erb)

Midway through Elke Erb's *Mountains in Berlin*, an anthology of short prose translated by Rosmarie Waldrop and selected from *Gutachten* (1976), *Der Faden der Geduld* (1978), and *Vexierbild* (1983), appears a relatively long text devoted to Heinrich von Kleist (1777-1811). This text keystones Erb's collection for several reasons. Most importantly, Kleist, best known for his plays, was also the pioneering author of a series of "anecdotes" written for the *Berliner Abendblätter* during the winter of 1810-1811. Within the context of the classic German novella, Kleist's *Anekdoten* constituted early examples of brief narratives; in other words, prototypes of "short-shorts." Twenty years later, young Charles Dickens (1812-1870) would be producing similar pieces, eventually collected in *Sketches by Boz* (1836-1837); Chekhov (1860-1904), too, sharpened his pen by composing half-literary, half-journalistic stories based on humorous daily incidents; and by the end of the nineteenth century, the newspaper sketch had evolved into a major genre, perhaps best represented by the indefatigable American O. Henry (1862-1910). Yet it was paradoxically Kleist, otherwise a Romantic, who was among the first to provoke European authors into questioning the literary legitimacy of the "unheard-of event that has actually happened," as Goethe magisterially defined the sole subject matter appropriate for a full-fledged *Novelle*. Kleist's *Anekdoten* encouraged writers to focus instead on the most banal facts and routines of everyday life, and to disclose their unsuspected significance.

With Kleist's *Anekdoten* in mind, Erb (b. 1938) charts a radical path to the ordinary. She is fascinated by the gap between objects and our perceptions of them; and by the ways in which we designate objects with words. "What Could the Man Have in Mind" begins with a typically flat description of three car tires. Filled with earth and planted in the earth, the tires lie "on top of one another...largest, middle, smallest." Erb continues:

> Until fall, when flowers, stems, leaves will have filled out into a blunt cone with hardly any trace of terracing, the flower seeds come up in their ring of earth in the first, the second, the round earth of the third tire. Monument: rising to show that dead does not mean sunk? Monument of the survivor's sense of beauty, widowed last year? He stands at the window, thoughtful, says: "First you've got to cut the inner rim out of

the tires, that's not easy. The blade must be sharp and—lightly oiled. Then it'll work; otherwise, not…." But in his mind, even while he speaks, he is elsewhere.

Being "elsewhere" mentally and thus inattentive to the brute particulars of the present moment defines a salient characteristic of humankind: the ontological separation that we experience between our self and the physical world. "It is very difficult to accept something real as it is," writes Erb in "Staunch Friendship"; and her opening text, "Grimm's Fairytales," tellingly depicts a gray sow standing in a low pen "at the end of the world." Before arriving at Karl's farm and acknowledging the existence of this sow "at the end of the world," the poet and her companion(s) have taken "a long walk in muddy shoes," followed by an "endless ride in the local." Are we supposed to laugh at this mock pilgrim's progress, the sole reward for which is the sight of a sow? Probably, but in the sense that the French say "to laugh yellow," by which is meant an uneasy, forced chuckle because we actually find the tale quite depressing. Initially, the sow symbolizes those unattainable particulars that we strive for—a noble quest that has engaged philosophers ever since Antiquity. Ultimately, however, we must admit that the sow remains a sow, even as for Gertrude Stein a rose is a rose is a rose. There is no transcendence whatsoever, and it is our attitude to this inevitable conclusion that is at stake.

Several low-key texts—ranging from riddles and short narratives to diary-like jottings and dreams—indeed chronicle perceptions of the world "as it is" and implicitly communicate the sentiment of being "let down" after a long journey back to the "thing-in-itself." (Compare the exaltation and desperation conveyed by Rilke in his poetry on the same theme.) Being let down, permanently, by the world, is the point; or perhaps one should qualify these texts as attempts to attain a sort of emotionless acceptance of the material world "as it is." In Erb's text on Kleist, she first recounts a rather dramatic incident that someone had witnessed years before. She concludes by confessing: "After a Kleist anecdote nobody says: So what? I seem unable to write this text in such a way that nobody could say: So what?" In "Ruppiner Street," Erb seemingly announces ("I must write it down, I will") an extraordinary event in the Goethean sense, but the incident turns out to involve a dog sticking his neck "out over a window box with two / drooping old tulips, petals wide open, / in front of quiet Dederon drapes, / …on the third floor." Here we do say, as so often elsewhere in this volume: "So what." Only a few enigmas may stir one's curiosity, such as this oblique portrait, which nonetheless begins with disarmingly unemotional statements of extraordinary facts:

N.'s wife had, even before the war, left him and married somebody else. The destruction of Dresden turned his street into rubble and ashes, later into a field. A bombing of Nordhausen murdered N.'s parents. Both his sisters died fleeing, God knows where, they had no children. One friend was gassed, another was and remained missing. His brother fell in Holland. N. himself was a prisoner of war in England. He had helped build villas, not a single one remained standing. The only thing that, after the war, reminded us of N., was N.

Some readers may ascribe the drab "so-what-ness" of these narratives to the fact that they were written in Communist East Germany during the two decades preceding the fall of the Berlin Wall in 1989. A few pieces evoke poverty directly or reflect the understandable obsession with material goods that characterized East Germans after the end of the Second World War and during the Communist regime. "My Comfort My Trunk," for example, describes an inherited "wonderful, big, brown trunk" that turns out to be an illusion, "a mere trick." Yet even in such texts, it remains doubtful that the writer first and foremost alludes to man's economic relationship with things. Perhaps these narratives should be read as ironic—thus subversive?—factual counterpoints to the ideological abstractions of Marxist discourse and to the blunt aesthetics of Soviet Realism. In many cases, her writing is so bland and straightforward that one wonders whether it might be fundamentally, or secretly, ambiguous. One effect remains clear, however. Upon finishing this volume, we comprehend that a choice perpetually remains open for us, in every instant of our lives. Confronted with the scintillating surface of the world—which may surge forth in the form of a gray sow—we can choose to affirm a miracle or simply shrug our shoulders and say: "So what."

A Noble Brightness
(Peter Huchel)

There are moments in our experience of the world when the familiar becomes unfamiliar, when hard facts we thought we could perceive clearly and name accurately turn into omens or indecipherable signs. Attentiveness to these unsettling instants is one of the qualities admirably developed in the concise, sometimes cryptic, poetry of Peter Huchel (1903-1981), a major selection of which—*The Garden of Theophrastus*—has been translated, impeccably, by Michael Hamburger.

Associated with rural Brandenburg after the publication of his first collection, *Gedichte* (1948), Huchel became increasingly fascinated by both the opacity and potential hidden meanings—as opposed to the transparency—of reality. This evolution is all the more arresting in that the poet spent his childhood on his grandfather's farm, where he acquired an insider's knowledge enabling him to evoke a world in which there is "nothing to interpret":

> I walked through the village
> And saw what I expected.
> The shepherd held a ram
> Wedged between his knees.
> He pared the hoof,
> He tarred the stubble lameness.
> And women counted the pails,
> The day's milking.

Yet this poem, significantly entitled "The Sign" and included in Huchel's second collection, *Chausseen Chausseen* (Roads Roads, 1963), already announces more probing perceptions. After noticing the women and the pails, Huchel thinks of death. The permanence of this comforting rural world, with its routines and regularity, is an illusion; only the dead really know, he realizes, that "the icy shadow of earth / slid[ing] over the moon" is what will endure after humankind has vanished. This revelation of finitude thereafter affects his understanding of appearances; and when he comes across half-legible "warning words" on a signpost, he begins looking differently at well-known surroundings, indeed at the viper thicket which, "frozen / In the silence of snow / . . . / Blindly sle[eps]."

This new and uneasy scrutiny of appearances—these attempts to penetrate or get beyond them—often culminate nonetheless in avowals of defeat and impossibility. Yet an intimated strangeness persists in the poet's mind. Huchel's mature verse is compelling (and honest) because of this ultimate implied ambiguity. His poetry strives to attain, but cannot, the metaphysical; for all its sparseness and understatement, it overbrims with this yearning. In a poem from his fourth and final collection, *Die neunte Stunde* (The Ninth Hour, 1979), for example, he wonders (implicitly) if he can surpass the boundaries of physical sensation. He clutches at falling snowflakes, seizes "only coldness," then notices "snow scars on the rock." But where, he asks, do these seeming "trail markings" lead? His answer is terse: "Glyphs, / indecipherable." This does not mean that he rejects all response, simply that natural phenomena are like words written in an alphabet that remains indecipherable to the uninitiated. Huchel is a discoverer of Rosetta stones, not their Champollion.

In other poems, key details are less signs than symbols associated with enclosure and concealment. In "Elegy," a clay vessel breaks in which "life's title deed" has been sealed. In "Monterosso," a stonemason delicately wraps up his chisel in cloth after sculpting stones for a cathedral. Without this tool, there can be no beauty, let alone beauty inducing an emotion of transcendence. In "Thrace," Huchel similarly cautions the reader not to lift a stone that "stores up stillness" because beneath it "the millipede sleeps away / Time."

Silence is thus also associated with accesses to the essential. This is why poetry must remain rare, succinct, unrhetorical. In Huchel's third collection, *Gezählte Tage* (Days That Are Numbered, 1972), the poem "Opinions" characteristically assigns wisdom to silent cats "dozing / behind the door / on the landing, in halflight." More ominously, the same poem mentions a former Bautzen-camp prisoner who "goes to the window and reads" while "the [bar]room fills / with young and old voices, / with tobacco and ash, / with hope and doubt." What really matters, including hope, can be found only on the peripheries of dailiness, far from babble.

"Opinions" is not the only political or historical piece in *The Garden of Theophrastus*. Huchel believed for a while in Marxist dreams, as is attested by his early poem "The Polish Reaper." Beautiful word-pictures of the kind that he would later perfect (e.g., "At the rim of night / the stars glitter / like grain on the threshing-floor") appear alongside more facile political symbolism: the immigrant reaper goes "home to the eastern country, / into morning's red light." More gripping is the title poem of *Chauseen Chauseen*, with its evocation of war or the Shoah: "Corpses, / Flung over the rail tracks, / Their stifled cry / Like a stone on the palate." In a poem commemorating the Greek historian Polybius, Huchel similarly searches (in vain) for a tablet on which is inscribed a telling epitaph: "Here lies one / Who would not desist from singing / With a thistle in his mouth."

The allusion is autobiographical. Huchel suffered àt the hands of hard-line Communists. He lived in East Germany until 1971, when he was finally allowed to emigrate to the West. Beginning in 1949, he had been the editor of the literary review *Sinn und Form*, and had opened up the magazine to non-Communist writers, both German and foreign. This policy resulted in his being fired and publicly disgraced in 1962.

   This harsh political context must be taken into account when reading a few pieces. The garden of Theophrastus is conspicuously "dead" in the title poem, and its single remaining olive tree is destined to be felled and uprooted by an anonymous "they." Yet other interpretations of this poem are conceivable and, more generally, most of Huchel's poetry was written with timeless concerns in mind. His life was difficult and—like Polybius—he lived in an age of "ashes, bones and rubble." This is why it is so moving when he verifies, and in fact confirms, that poetry can still affirm. In this regard, one remarkable epiphany stands out. In "Behind the Brick Kilns," Huchel notably finds "noble brightness / …in the putrid light / Of stagnant water," and adds that "Here gold is washed / And poured over broken bricks."

The Poetry of W. G. Sebald

A three-part long-poem, *Nach der Natur* (1988) marked W. G. Sebald's debut in literature and, like his subsequent prose writings, it defies facile classification. The title itself is intriguing. "Nach der Natur" suggests "after (the end of) Nature" or even "after Nature's place (in a row)"; also "toward Nature"; and if the etymology of "nach" is taken into account, then "near Nature" is likewise imaginable. Considered as an expression, the title signifies "(painted) from life," and this additional sense crops up in an important passage of this unusual book. Regretfully, the obliquely provocative German subtitle, *Ein Elementargedicht*, is missing from this American edition of *After Nature* (as Michael Hamburger has rightly entitled his accurate and engaging version). With this subtitle, the author stresses the unity of his tripartite project and ironically likens it to a "primer."

All these notions inform *After Nature*, a "triptych" narrating scenes from the lives of the Renaissance painter Matthias Grünewald, the eighteenth-century botanist Georg Steller (who accompanied Vitus Bering on his Arctic exploration), and the poet himself (a self-portrait that includes glimpses of his grandparents and parents during the First and Second World Wars). Each section is thus also a "life study"; and Sebald's approach furthermore resembles the classical *Vita* in that a man's essence is distilled from a series of telling anecdotes. As in Sebald's prose works (*Vertigo*, 1990; *The Rings of Saturn*, 1992; *The Emigrants*, 1992; *Austerlitz*, 2001), rightly praised for their haunting existential inquiry and formal originality, this initially disarming, increasingly compelling, long-poem gives a fresh twist to several distinct literary genres.

While reflecting on these two German lives (then on his own), Sebald asks: "How far . . . must one go back / to find the beginning?" This is the question around which revolves an ultimately complex poetic meditation on nature and human nature, on art and destruction, on individuation and catastrophe. This central question, like its corollary (the beginning of what exactly?), moreover prefigures Sebald's later writings, with their focus on "emigrants" seeking—in the most unlikely places—their vanished origins or the sources of an indefinable malaise.

Sebald (1944-2001), who himself taught for three decades at an unlikely place (the University of East Anglia in Norwich, England), perceives Grünewald and Steller as instructive models, even alter egos. How not to think of his own masterful descriptions (a hallmark of his strangely digressive prose) when Steller, a student in the natural sciences, comes to "think of nothing other than / the shapes of the fauna and / flora" of the Arctic and "of the art and skill / required for their description"? Although the very nature of poetry induces Sebald to evoke more than describe in *After Nature*, an overarching "description of unhappiness"—as one of his essay collections is entitled—nevertheless characterizes one goal of this ambitious poetic project.

Sebald's search for "the beginning" of his own sentiment of *Unglück* thereby reaches back well before the twentieth century, with its wars, its Shoah ("a silent catastrophe that occurs / almost unperceived"), its inhumane technology, its monumental architecture, its ravaged nature—themes to which he alludes. Yet was there ever a Lost Paradise "after" which we are condemned to exist, and "toward" which we yearn? Looking back five hundred years teaches the poet that no less waste, destruction, and disease (phenomena that are no metaphors in his oft-graphic poetry) blight the social and ecological realities through which his brothers-in-arms followed their own wayward paths, pursuing the mastery of their art or science.

Like the poet, Grünewald and Steller—whose surnames affirm ideal "green woods" and "stars"—wander far and wide. They must overcome, or at least sidestep, various negative forces. These are summarized by Sebald, as he invokes a painting by Grünewald, as the "heritage of the ruining / of life that in the end will consume / even the stones." Being born implies receiving this ominous heritage. One is thrown, as it were, into the midst of "corrosion," a permanent life-destroying process visible both in the world-at-large (Grünewald's futuristic, if realistic, vision of our planet as "utterly strange, chalk-coloured") and in the inner landscapes that Sebald also charts (and self-charts). A "slow corrosion" notably eats away at Steller's soul after he embarks on the Siberian trek which, at the same time, fulfills his longtime aspiration. As to Bering, only when the snow-covered peaks of Alaska loom "resplendent," signaling the success of his mission, does he come aloft from his cabin, where he has been "staring / at the ceiling of beams above his head." Amidst the "incessant jubilation / of the crew," he contemplates "the scene / in a fit of deepest depression."

Yet even as *After Nature* is not about "the environment" in any banal contemporary sense, neither does the book simplistically depict "depression." The three protagonists escape from "quasi / sublunary state[s] of deep / melancholia," and renew their quests, when flashes of self-enlightenment emanate from fortuitous experiences. As in all of Sebald's books, chance fosters fleeting revelations, even brief joys. Another life-preserving force is "wonder." As Sebald rambles through Manchester, he "wonder[s] / at the work of destruction, the black / mills and shipping canals, / the disused viaducts and / warehouses, the many millions / of bricks, the traces of smoke, / of tar and sulphuric acid." By preserving this capacity to wonder, even when faced with ugliness or abjectness, Sebald seeks an ultimate compassion, not a vain disgust.

Imagine him "wondering" retrospectively. Why, as he composed *After Nature*, did this master of German prose scrutinize the ends of his lines and construct suspenseful enjambments? *After Nature* is no *Prosagedicht*, no "prose poem," as the back cover of the most recent German edition (2002) inaccurately defines the undeniable "prosaicness" of this oddly-styled poetry. More precisely, Sebald's carefully constructed free-verse narratives make bold use of some of the most typical "unpoetic" contents of pedestrian prose. He mixes dates, unwieldy foreign place-names, and scholarly facts into his chronicles. Miraculously, these details soon fascinate us, as does the lightly versified structure in which they are presented. This formal tour de force is impressive, as is the moral seriousness of this intricate, moving, eminently readable *exemplum*.

Facing Up to Unspeakableness
(Robert Walser)

It is regrettable that the Swiss writer Robert Walser (1878-1956) remains so scarcely known in the United States at a time when his arresting novels and short prose pieces are considered, not only in German-language countries but throughout continental Europe, to constitute a major *oeuvre*. For most American readers, the author of *Jakob von Gunten* (1908) and *The Robber* (written in 1925, published in 1972)—if he is acknowledged at all—is obscured by the long shadows cast by contemporaries who, in recent decades, have become more renowned: Hermann Hesse, Franz Kafka, Robert Musil. Yet in his day, Walser's work was admired by these and other pioneering modernists. Tellingly, when Musil reviewed Kafka's first collection of stories, he observed that the Prague author was "a special case of the Walser type."

However intriguing this remark now seems, when we can fully compare the two authors (who were at least equally fascinated by castles), it implies that Walser's accomplishments were already taken for valid touchstones. And if, having been championed by Kurt Wolff, who brought out three collections of Walser's short prose in 1913-1914, the writer later had to overcome greater obstacles when seeking publishers for his writing (which had gained in stylistic complexity and philosophical consequence), his books continued to be studied closely by exacting minds. He was never forgotten; perhaps only, as Elias Canetti put it, "camouflaged" for a while. Finally, two decades after Walser's death, as the Suhrkamp *Collected Works* began to appear and as two scholars, Bernhard Echte and Werner Morlang, brilliantly deciphered Walser's notorious "micrograms"—unpublished manuscripts composed in an infinitesimal shorthand—the Swiss author was enthusiastically rehabilitated, in Europe, as a stunning precursor of our own preoccupations.

The genres in which he excelled comprise hypersensitive reminiscences, sketches of banal yet "delightful"—a favorite epithet—everyday occurrences, oblique accounts of haphazard "strolls" through town and countryside, disturbing monologues constructed upon a conspicuous absence of conventional transitions, as well as sundry dreams, fantasies, parodies, fairytales, and ironic anti-*Bildungsromane* involving mediocre Everymen who "prefer believing they are nowhere" or who eventually "leave behind" all that they have toiled to achieve. (A recurrent phrase is "But, at last, I departed.") Long before the novelists associated with the French New Novel, Walser questions the epistemological validity of narrators and characters, and doubts that events can be described linearly or linked together causally. Above all, he wonders deeply about the "self." Provocatively, his *intimisme* self-affirms as it self-dismisses. "I feel how little it concerns me," he observes in *Jakob von Gunten* (translated by Christopher Middleton), "everything that's called 'the world,' and how grand and exciting what I privately call the world is to me." At the end, however, this "individual me is only a zero." (To comprehend this reductive process, so typical of Walser, try giving an infinite regress to Peter Handke's interesting title, indebted to Rilke: *The Inner World of the Outer World of the Inner World*....) Walser feels at any rate ominously, painfully, "separated" from all that he subsumes under the notion of "the world," as well as from all that which, as he vaguely yet tenaciously intuits, might compose his true self. "His head," he perceptively avows in *The Robber* (translated by Susan Bernofsky), "was constantly busied with something somehow very far distant." Truly astonishing can be the elaborate stylistic and narrative means mustered when he endeavors to span bridges to those distant horizons.

Reading Walser's prose on its own terms demands keeping in a proper perspective certain disturbing facts concerning the last third of his life, which was spent in two mental asylums. This troubling personal dimension can of course allure, even endear us, to his work, particularly to its ultimate stage, when his style tended to eschew the more immediate—if ever engagingly quirky—realism of his first, essentially autobiographical, provincial novels. By the 1920s Walser, although never abandoning his autobiographical inspiration and his search for self-lucidity, increasingly explores the tenuous relationship between language and perceived reality, between personal experience and the thought processes brought to bear on the narrative reconstruction of experience. The results can disconcert, with their abstruse perspectives and cogitative leaps. Walser himself describes *The Robber* as "one great huge gloss, ridiculous and unfathomable." What stands behind, we must ask, this "gloss"?

Clues are furnished by *The Robber*, a (self-)portrait and love-story narrated at playful removes. Paradoxes abound, the most striking of which concerns the first-person narrator—a writer of course created by another writer named Robert—who gradually merges with his protagonist, given the quasi-punning nickname of "der Raüber." Even at the beginning, this Robber "pilfers...landscape impressions" and "purloins affections." Later, the narrator—the Robber's "guardian"—worries that the impressions "crowding in" on him likewise pressure his character. By the end, we come full circle: the Robber is "ghostly pale from all his writing, for you can imagine how valiantly he's been assisting me in the composition of this book." Faced with this somehow contour-less personality (that is, faced with himself), the writer-narrator of *The Robber* announces: "On the basis of [the Robber's] extraordinary and yet also quite

ordinary existence, I am constructing here a commonsensical book from which
nothing at all can be learned."

This is not the only place in Walser's oeuvre where a painstakingly, even
frenetically, constructed edifice of language collapses like a castle of cards.
Walser's characteristic joy at coming across "charming" events or objects
is often similarly numbed. His writings devolve internally from proclaimed
wonder (or at least an odd, self-mocking, contentment) to the conclusion that
there exist no sure foundations for marveling at anything. "I like listening for
something that doesn't want to make a sound," he states in *Jakob von Gunten*.
"I pay attention, and that makes life more beautiful, for if we don't have to pay
attention there really is no life." This "no-life," however, always threatens the
writer's fragile, transitory, attentiveness. Often his delight, invoked by the will's
renewed energies, resembles pulling oneself up by one's own bootstraps.

Although Walser can concentrate on a given anecdote per se (thereby revealing his predilection for the singular event and the isolated instant, as opposed
to a world-view presupposing temporal continuity), the logic of coherent storytelling—in which several anecdotes must be woven together plausibly—can
become comically chaotic. The narrator of *The Robber* regularly declares his
desire "to narrate in an orderly fashion," yet he implies—without telling us
why—that his subject matter inherently resists rational structuring. Having
introduced a footbath into the story, he immediately laments: "To this footbath
we are most certain to return.... Oh, if only I could get to work on this footbath
right away! But, alas, deferred it must be." Walser often converses in this frantic,
if lighthearted, fashion with his reader; yet he also insists on mirroring his own
thought processes faithfully, preserving the exact order in which perceptions,
sentiments or reflections pop up in the mind, then vanish. The "gloss" that
ensues includes no graceful rhetoric, no fictional filler, no narrative smoothing
out of flighty associations:

> The swans there in the castle pond, the Renaissance façade. Where did I see this?
> Or rather, where did the Robber? Staircases led up the trunks of old trees. Entire
> tea parties could ascend so as to hold their gatherings beneath a roof of green. And
> that inn standing upon a lonely rise, that little forest of birches, or whatever sort of
> trees they were. And the pavilion on the hill, the house with its low wall, and, behind
> windowpanes, gazing out solemnly at the arriving guests, the proud lady. Pride is
> often our last refuge, but a refuge to which we should never take flightÉ.

A heartfelt plea included in *The Robber* sums up this tense ultimate approach
and points to an overriding concern of modernism: "How to conjoin these
disjunctions?"

Yet Walser's biography cannot fully be ignored when we read his work,
for his internment perhaps nonetheless remains linked to an important theme
already underlying his earliest work. The known facts, succinctly stated, run as
follows: In 1929, while he was suffering from depression and even had attempted

suicide, Walser allowed himself to be committed to the Waldau Sanatorium. He continued to write there until 1933, when he was transferred—probably against his will—to Herisau, a closed asylum. Classified (mistakenly) as a schizophrenic, the once-prolific Walser apparently stopped writing once he was locked up in Herisau—although recent testimony given by a former attendant claims that Walser continued to write there, even extensively, on tiny scraps of paper. Be this as it may, none of these jottings (whatever they were) have surfaced, and Walser seems to have spent his days mostly performing menial tasks, such as assembling paper bags. Rather portentously, Walser had, in an earlier text, described life itself as a "shaded dead-end."

The only respite from these routines came, once or twice a year, when his admiring *confrère*, Carl Seelig (1894-1962), dropped by for a visit. Seelig, who became the writer's guardian, would take Walser for a long hike in the surrounding mountains, then invite him to a sumptuous meal in some nearby inn. Seelig's necessarily repetitive yet touching memoirs, *Wanderungen mit Robert Walser* (1957), portray an author who had abandoned writing yet who enjoyed steep climbing, savory victuals, potent beer and wine, as well as pro-longed discussions about books (though not his own). Then the author of *Die Spaziergang* (*The Walk*, 1917), an essay-like novella heralding German and French "strolling literature," would be accompanied back to the asylum for another six months or so. In *The Walk*, Walser eerily recalls the 18th-century German writer Jakob Michael Reinhold Lenz who, "having fallen into madness and despair, learned how to make shoes and indeed made them."

Walser's literary destiny thus abruptly terminates—for complex psychological, familial, and perhaps even metaphysical, linguistic, or aesthetic reasons—in one of those awesome "silences" that we also associate with, say, Arthur Rimbaud, Jean Genet, or, more recently, Louis-René des Forêts. Walser's silence is particularly troubling because, from the beginning of his career through the mid-1920s, and despite increasing periods of abject poverty, self-reclusion, and nomadism, his productivity was impressive by any writer's standards. One of his best-known novels, *Geschwister Tanner* (*The Tanner Siblings*, 1906), a lightly fictionalized account of his own growing up, was completed in six weeks. His first book, *Fritz Kochers Aufsätze* (*Fritz Kocher's Essays*, 1904), as well as *Der Gehülfe* (*The Apprentice* [or *The Assistant*], 1908), which recounts time spent assisting an unsuccessful inventor, date from this same fruitful period. Walser's exalted creative spells also included the simultaneous production of stories, vignettes, reviews, and mini-essays for various periodicals. The man worked hard to earn his living as a freelance writer; he accepted dozens of part- or full-time jobs, even enrolling in a school for servants in Berlin, in 1905. Yet already in *Jakob von Gunten*, in which Walser memorializes this butler school (as a mysterious "Benjamenta Institute" in which hardly nothing happens, let alone is taught), the narrator can exclaim: "One thing I know for certain: in later life I shall be a charming, utterly spherical zero."

Whatever now-opaque reasons underlie Walser's real-life literary silence, his earliest prose manifestly anticipates it. Yet like des Forêts's classic novella, *Le Bavard* (1946), Walser's literary investigation of this theme soars beyond his own torment. Both writers envision "talking," indeed "babbling," as man's poignant, vain search for—or perhaps, rather, postponement of searching for—ontological or metaphysical roots in a hostile, God-less, cosmos. Already in *The Tanner Siblings*, the narrator experiences existential stability only when he is talking himself into a job. It is striking how the young Walser turned so many of his attempted occupations into, literally, "pretexts" for future texts; during the same period, he could movingly write: "I don't want a future, I want a present." "There is something unspeakably cool about me," the narrator of *Jakob von Gunten* pellucidly admits, "in spite of the excitements that can attack me." Robert Walser's prose, and perhaps his life as well, courageously point time and again to the hovering threat and significance of that harrowing qualifier, "unspeakably."

A French-Judeo-Spanish-Polish Interlude

Idioms of Remembering
(Marcel Cohen and Michał Głowiński)

The Peacock Emperor Moth (Burning Deck, 1995) and *Mirrors* (Green Integer, 1998) revealed to American readers that Marcel Cohen (b. 1937) was a subtle French stylist of a most unusual kind. The short prose narratives gathered in these and his other, untranslated, collections rely on understatement, oblique irony, and often—for subject matter—ordinary events whose harrowing psychological, social or historical depths the author unveils almost in passing.

It is a prose of daily life, for which Stendhal's remark about literature holding a mirror up to reality is unsettlingly apt; but it is also a prose that is fully aware of certain brutally acquired, now ingrained, cognitive factors hitherto structuring our experience of the contemporary world. Cohen, notably, often examines the aftermath of the Shoah, as it is traceable in the thoughts, emotions, and behavior not especially of extermination camp survivors, but rather his own generation; in other words, French Jewish children who, like himself, were hidden during the German Occupation, who against all odds escaped deportation, and who then, after the war, as they were coming of age, had to cope with the loss of their family and with the utter horror of the Holocaust as a systematic program of mass extinction. The countless tangible vestiges of the Shoah, as Cohen shows, can be as deceptively insignificant as the sight of a cow, the wisp of a certain eau de cologne, or a banal turn of phrase.

In "Notes," a self-revealing lecture given in 1998, Cohen defines his literary dilemma as "being able neither to speak nor to remain silent." He means that he cannot write about the Nazi extermination camps because he did not experience them, nor about his "crushed, annihilated" childhood because, "except for a few minor details," Jewish children like him "all have the same story to tell." He calls this state "being dispossessed of one's biography." All of Cohen's books revolve around this notion, although it is never stated forthrightly—a restraint that has its own literary, philosophical, and personal implications, and that, moreover, produces a troubling cumulative effect on the reader. Many of his anecdotes, vignettes, and succinct descriptions suddenly haunt, even shock, once one has grasped their connections with this theme. Cohen's recent collection of instructive "facts," *Faits: Lecture courante à l'usage des grands débutants* (2002), extends his purview to the ways "biographies are dispossessed" by barbaric economic practices on a global scale. (As this book goes to press, a sequel—*Faits, II*—has appeared.)

It is in this context that his delicate and moving memoir, *In Search of A Lost Ladino: Letter to Antonio Saura*, must be read. As the poet and art critic Raphael Rubinstein explains in his sensitive and probing introduction, this melancholy yet also gently humorous book—the original appeared in Madrid in 1985—is unique in Cohen's oeuvre because it was "composed in Judeo-Spanish, a language [that the author] heard all around him as a child, but never spoke" in the Parisian suburb of Asnières where he first grew up. This linguistic choice results from no whim, and Cohen's feat is not only impressive stylistically, but also thought-provoking and, once again, moving. For other Jewish writers and poets—Paul Celan, Edmond Jabès, Piotr Rawicz, Ghérasim Luca, Elias Canetti, Franz Kafka—the choice of a literary language was equally difficult, sometimes boldly unnatural; it was intimately and at times uneasily related to their Jewish heritage and quotidian, their mother tongue (literally speaking), their autobiographical (or anti-autobiographical) intentions, and their overall existential outlook, inasmuch as their deepest philosophical intuitions posited language as the fundamental ingredient in our perception of the world. "The mother tongue," reflects Cohen, "that's what we called what we spoke at home. Will this mother ever die, Antonio?... How could we imagine that we could one day become mousafires ['foreigners' or 'visitors' in Turkish] to ourselves in our own tongue?" Like Yiddish, Judeo-Spanish is in its "death agony," observes Cohen. "Agonizing in my language," he later specifies, "I let the mousafires express themselves while I write at their dictation. It's they who write, they who read me."

Cohen is thus as speculatively introspective as he is autobiographically factual, a narrative approach that contrasts with the (sometimes) fictionally imagined first-person and (sometimes) cryptically personal third-person viewpoints that he uses elsewhere. But these twenty-five finely crafted prose texts, which form a letter to his close friend, the Spanish painter Antonio Saura (1930-1998), are autobiographical in other original ways. (Cohen has also written five articles about Saura's painting; they are collected in *Quelques faces visibles du silence*, 2000.) The impetus for writing the letters was the author's eerie impression that he already knew the real subjects behind his friend's "imaginary portraits," many of which are half-abstract, half-figurative mask-like faces or totem-like bodies. (The elegant, bilingual, Ibis Editions volume reproduces drawings that Saura made for the author.) Cohen senses that the portraits go back to the Spain of his Sephardic ancestors, who were among the approximately two hundred thousand Jews driven out of the country in 1492, many of whom subsequently settled in Greece and Turkey. As Cohen examines the portraits, he feels Judeo-Spanish welling up inside him. "Strange, Antonio," he writes, "to speak to you for the first time in the name of the Sephardic Jew that I am, and also for the last time. In my bedroom, I close my eyes, lie in wait for the words of the past, feel them come back to me, little by little, flush them out as if with a fener ['lantern' in Turkish], and know that in these words there is no room for lying: it's in the music of these words that I feel most myself." It is thus through an absence, an emptiness, a lack, that the author—with his "dispossessed biography"—becomes present to himself, as it were. He can re-possess himself, briefly, only by closing his eyes, by sinking down into the abysmal ancestral past, by groping here and there, and then by restoring, through writing, a few recovered details—words at once foreign and familiar, and what they struggle to designate—to an irreparable loss. The reader will meditate long on this sobering truth, for it pertains—I would argue—to many of us who are not of Cohen's specific background.

The original title, *Letras a un pintor ke kreya azer retratos imaginarios*, is in the plural and literally means "Letters to a painter who believes he makes imaginary portraits." At one point, Cohen teases his friend about them: "'Imaginary portraits,' you call the faces that proliferate in your paintings. I don't think for even a moment that they are. For me, the 'imaginary' is simply what we have forgotten." Cohen remarks that artists' "memories are sometimes so vast that their works draw on knowledge they don't even know they possess. Jews are just the same: they've seen everything, or almost."

Snapshot-like fragments accordingly capture daily scenes set long ago in Istanbul, Toledo, and Salonica, as well as the writer's "aunt and uncle's little house on the outskirts of Paris, [where] you'd find David-the-good in his long underwear with two or three day's growth of beard, smoking his first cigarette in front of the window" and then carrying on "with another song from the fifteenth century" (whose lyrics Cohen cites). There can be no continuity in such reminiscence, and filling in the many empty narrative spaces with fiction or erudition would have destroyed the engaging genuineness of his approach, let alone its claim to a certain kind of truth about memory and the destruction of identity. Djudyo, as Judeo-Spanish is also called, acquired many terms from Greek and Turkish after the forced exile of the Sephardic Jews, and Rubinstein's fluid and touching English translation—which is based on Cohen's 1997 French version—retains the Turkish words that Cohen naturally employs.

In Search of a Lost Ladino can be read alongside Michał Głowiński's memoir, *The Black Seasons*, which has been translated by Marci Shore. Born in 1934, Głowiński, who is a well-known Polish literary critic, suffered through the same "crushed, annihilated" childhood as did Marcel Cohen. Interned in the Warsaw ghetto, the boy and his family escaped certain death in early January, 1943, thanks to a German soldier who, because his clients were not "too Jewish-looking," accepted money and sneaked them out in a car. After this miraculous escape, which might well have been a trap but was not, the boy and his parents hid out in various places, mostly separately; there were close calls; a particularly gripping scene takes place in a pastry shop, where the boy has to wait for a few minutes before being escorted to another hideout.

Głowiński's goal is not to chronicle his survival in any continuous manner. Acknowledging great gaps in his memory, he proceeds in fragments, each of them being, he declares, "a relation of an experience, emerging from flashes of memory, neither embracing the entirety of events nor encompassing all of [his] life and the history of how [he] survived." He concentrates only on what he remembers, adds "I don't know" whenever he no longer remembers, and refuses to fill out his tale with "fiction, conjectures, and...information drawn from other sources." This tale of how his book is composed—the tale of his memory in the aftermath of the Shoah—is also part of the story. It is essentially "the same story," as Cohen puts it, that all such Jewish children have to tell, but here, too, is a particularly compelling authenticity.

Poland

Questions of Fulfillment
(Czesław Miłosz)

Heterogeneousness and a certain ambivalence, by which I mean a deep skepticism about single overarching answers and solutions, have always characterized the poetry of Czesław Miłosz. *Facing the River* (1995), translated by the author and Robert Hass, is no exception to this rule. Here thirty-seven new poems and two texts combining prose and verse evoke the Polish writer's Parisian sojourns in the 1930s, his teaching experiences in the United States (where he lived, beginning in 1960), Christian themes (such as Hell, sin, and pity), Dutch realist painting, embattled Sarajevo, Allen Ginsberg, and above all his childhood in Szetejnie, Lithuania, where he was born in 1911. (He died in 2004.) An unexpected return visit to Szetejnie, after a fifty-two-year exile, inspires Miłosz to compose many of these poems as avowals, self-interrogations, and summings-up. As in the significantly entitled "One More Contradiction," they pivot around an exacting question: "Did I fulfill what I had to, here, on earth?" In Miłosz's case, this need to acknowledge unappeasable doubts, to determine whether his life has been fashioned by fate ("Early we receive a call, yet it remains incomprehensible, and only late do we discover how obedient we were") or by free will and thus perhaps self-delusion ("Out of self-delusion comes poetry and poetry confesses to its flaw"), is of course intensified by this homecoming which, for decades, because of political contingencies, remained inconceivable. This is not to say that any remarkable urgency or intensity informs the writing; these are meditative poems, prosaic in tone even when metered discreetly. Miłosz uses the aphoristic compactness of poetic language as a means of provoking, not so much our feelings, as our thoughts on artistic egocentrism, the mystery of coexisting with other human beings who see "the same but not the same thing," the unpredictable marvel of a "transubstantiated moment," and—in nearly the last line of this volume—the altruism of poetry. "All we know is that sin exists and punishment exists," he notes. "If only my work were of use to people and of more weight than is my evil."

As for many European poets of his generation, the uprootedness experienced in his person is as ontological as it is geographical, political, or cultural. However, unlike many of those same poets, he emphasizes no overarching single cause of the painful instability and solitude that results. Nor can this poet who takes individual responsibility so seriously—to the extent of blaming himself for "events" that are actually "stronger" than himself—give priority even to moral behavior, as in his account of an unnamed painter who surely needed "tenderness…to drive a brush with such attention / Along the eyelids of a sorrowing eye," yet who, as his biographers reveal, must have been aware of the "harm he did to others." The painter was "just not concerned," agrees Miłosz. "He promised his soul to Hell, / Provided that his work remained clear and pure." Miłosz examines what ensues for better or worse, in all fields of human endeavor, when we hear "the immense call of the Particular, despite the earthly law that sentences memory to extinction."

Is acquiescence the ultimate, or the only viable, response to these dilemmas? Confronted, in Szetejnie, with the disappearance of his family's manor and the devastation of the property—"the oldest trees have been cut down / And a thicket overgrows the traces of former alleys"—the aged wanderer spots a *sambucus nigra* that has survived "in the green of weeds and bushes." Yet this reminder of his youthful love for botany incites no undue bitterness or sentimentalism, for he realizes that life has carried on in other, moving ways. However "poorly," it has nonetheless "lasted," and fellow human beings have been able to eat "their noodles and potatoes / And at least had the use of all the old gardens / To cut wood for burning in our long winters."

This quest for serenity—with its detours through outrage, as in "Sarajevo," albeit a weak poem—time and again brings Miłosz face to face with death, a confrontation that first implies coming to terms with the mainstay of his adult existence: the seeming permanence taken on, in his mind, by his childhood. Examining Joseph Conrad's manuscripts (in "Pierson College"), he wonders whether he, now "an old professor with an accent," is "identical with a boy / Who, starting from Bouffalowa Hill / Would walk Louis home along Mala Pohulanka" and then go to "Tomasz Zan Library / To get a book of sea adventures." For today this boy has arrived, almost unbelievably, at "the very edge, just before falling." And while Miłosz admits, in the key final poem, that "wherever I wandered…my face was always turned to the River" (of his native valley), he knows that nostalgia offers only a deceptive security. The center of his life must now be seen for what it really is—subjectless. Rediscovering a beloved riverside meadow from his past, in which the same kinds of grasses and flowers still grow, he significantly half-closes his eyes and absorbs the "luminescence." "All knowing ceased," he observes. "Suddenly I felt I was disappearing and weeping with joy." Elsewhere, he calls this self-effacement "disappearing, in order to be, unpersonally."

Can "hope" thereby be invested in the cyclic renewability of Nature, or in the possibility of rejoining a state of being from which one is separated at birth (or during infancy), as is suggested by "Capri," a poem depicting a "pious boy" chasing after "disguises of the Lost Reality"? With more awe and inquisitiveness than despair—whence the challenge these poems put to twentieth-century nihilistic clichés— Miłosz leaves this essential question open. He in fact at times raises it within the context of Christian eschatology. His last lines indeed compellingly appeal to an intriguing, polysemous "you" who, "alone, wise and just, would know how to calm me, / explaining that I did as much as I could. / That the gate of the Black Garden closes, peace, peace, what is finished is finished."

Metaphysics and Lyric Factors
(Piotr Sommer, Krzysztof Kamil Baczyński, Tadeusz Różewicz, and others)

If you admire the poetry of Czesław Miłosz (1911-2004) and especially Wisława Szymborska (b. 1923), seek out Piotr Sommer (b. 1948). Based on *Continued*, the engaging versions of which have been made by Halina Janod working with co-translators (thirteen in all, including John Ashbery, Douglas Dunn, and D. J. Enright), Sommer deserves a place alongside these philosophically alert Polish poets. Let me add that he joins their company almost offhandedly. He is graced with an original kind of curiosity that scrutinizes at once the fine details of the quotidian and, at a gentle remove, its foibles. He obviously relishes common words and expressions for their own sake, all the while poking fun at poetic *gravitas* by wondering—in "Little Graves" notably—where he will be buried and commenting that "my thing is talking, / but in fact I like to listen, that is, to ask things"; or, inversely—in "Lighter, Darker"—that

> I ask questions
> when I should finally be giving some answers.
> I don't know who I'm directing them to
> or if I'm directing them to anyone at all.

More specifically and movingly, he avows in "Visibility" that he has not "figured out" who he is "saying" his poem "to, or even who / would care that through the leaves // you can see Halifax / and someone's life." I'll return to what observing Halifax just like this implies.

Such meta-poetic ruminations suggest that Sommer espouses the cynical contemporary view whereby the author is an arbitrary construct and interpersonal communication well nigh impossible. However, his poetics are more complex. A poet's interest can be perked in random fashion; conveying what has been perceived, imagined, or intuited can assuredly run up against the ineffable (or indifference); but there is more—as Sommer shows time and again—to this age-old literary dilemma. His poems unfold unexpectedly, always developing redeeming nuances that posit, then overturn, dogmas, including those associated with the aesthetics of post-structuralism and post-modernism; in other words, that open up fresh ways of feeling, and thinking about, life as we experience it.

"Indiscretions" bluntly asks "Where are we?" The query sums up the impetus of many poems. The poet first declares firmly that humankind is situated "in ironies / that no one will grasp, short-lived / and unmarked, in trivial points / which reduce metaphysics to absurd / detail." Yet in the final quatrain, he qualifies our predicament less trenchantly:

> And one also likes certain words and those—pardon me—
> syntaxes that pretend that something links them together.
> Between these intermeanings the whole man is contained,
> Squeezing in where he sees a little space.

Here, "pretend" sneers at the false pretensions of order and rationality, yet the word is attenuated by mankind's plucky "squeezing in," an image recalling that life is also made up of emotions, biological drives, spontaneous strategies, as well as forms of logic other than syntactic. Like the archetypal non-heroes of Central- and Eastern-European novels, individuals—poignantly, pathetically—may find temporary housing in an interstice, having simultaneously managed to lug into their burrow those unwieldy questions that Sommer likes to raise. Who but the far-seeing and reminiscing author of *A Subsequent World* and *What We're Remembered By* would wait until the twenty-first line of a thirty-two-line poem to wonder: "What would I write poems about? / I'd have to think, / because in fact I'm fed up with them." However, although Sommer's playful, vaguely disturbing, poems sometimes pull themselves up by their own bootstraps, they are hardly word games. They do not particularly solicit intellectual analysis or research (as do, after all, crossword puzzles), but rather something more precious: bemused yet concerned meditation on what it means to be alive and act in the world.

To wit, Sommer may point to an individual's ultimate solitude, but then, in arresting contrast, refocus on the individual among family members or friends, or even in society at large (whereby "we," not he, "live secluded under the smoke of steelworks"). The individual's existential plight is therefore depicted less starkly, even humorously, and relativized historically and geographically: the steelworks poem is adapted from lines by Wang Wei (701-761). Sommer is not claiming that life is untragic; he simply creates a perspective from which tragedy can be viewed with detachment. As to politics, he alludes once or twice to the Communist Poland in which his childhood and early adult life were spent. The spirited "Ode to the Carnival," dated 1985 and thus well after the onset of the Solidarnosc movement but four years before the major political changes began in Eastern Europe, predicts that

> ...we'll travel together one day,
> maybe not right now and not precisely where we had in mind,

> maybe somewhere else, it's hard to say where,
> but almost certainly this trip will work out
> not just for us obviously,
> all our loved ones will come along, kids,
> friends, I mean people you can even
> have a quarrel with, just a few, a fair chunk
> of the world...

Moreover, although the poet quips now and then about the absence of readers or the impossibilities of communication, he conjures up—communicates—reality in surprisingly tangible ways. When we peruse the aforementioned lines about Halifax, we cannot help but peek through the leaves, spot the town, and face up to anonymous lives like our own. And if we, too, necessarily belong to the "redundant people" whom the poet studies elsewhere, "each of them can do a lot and each can bear a lot." Sommer's poems culminate in ambivalences such as these. In a characteristic line such as "a maple leaf with the sun shining through it / at the end of summer is beautiful, but / not excessively so," images are intentionally cast out a bit too far, then reeled back in. These images represent no aspiration to classical "nothing in excess" aesthetics, but instead indicate doubts and an acute awareness of limits. As opposed to the certainties of the golden mean, Sommer's poems celebrate—with fitting modesty—tenuous, ephemeral, equilibriums.

As to poetic form, the author of *Lyric Factor* introduces storytelling qualities into his verse without, however, being a narrative poet. He describes daily acts and facts, and has penned short prose narratives that are neither prose poems nor short stories (nor even "short-shorts"). (By the way, more attention to these "in-between" genres, which are increasingly used by European poets and often misunderstood by American readers, needs to be drawn.) Analogously, one clever poem entitled "First Sentence" relates the circumstances surrounding Sommer's coming up with the opening sentence of a projected short story. The story does not get written ("I don't remember what came later / or if there was any later, probably not"), but the poet's telling, in verse, of this story about the unwritten story enables him to write a poem and, retrospectively, indeed the story about the unwritten story as well as, consequently, the original (unwritten) story itself, for in the meantime he has provided enough details for us to imagine it more or less; the unwritten story is written in our minds. A poem wittily invoking the sundry meanings of the word "line" likewise creates a bouquet of independent narrative fragments that the reader can fill out. Other poems, such as the oneiric "Prospects in Prose," are prose-like in orientation; as in the etymology of "prose" (from the Latin *provertere*), they "turn forward," seek to move on and see what happens, though where they end up is unpredictable. These haphazard progressions by means of a verse style which has forgotten neither prose nor storytelling and which in Polish—if we are to believe August Kleinzahler's insightful introduction—is "intensely musical," reflect another philosophical question of which Sommer occasionally reminds us: Is the world made up of continuities or is it, instead, a chaotic hodgepodge of discontinuities? Incidentally, the word "world" appears rather often; one poem begins "One day I'll open the world / and step inside as if coming home," then later ends with a conspicuous semicolon. (If the semicolon is a misprint, please leave it as it stands!)

As regards continuities and discontinuities, Sommer often imagines unusual links among the heterogeneous facts he comes across. "Station Lights" formulates this quest explicitly, provides six half amusing, half serious examples of links, then hands the poem back to the reader:

> Interesting how the world
> connects tomorrow and the day after that.
> If that's not it,
> maybe you'll tell me what is.

Speculation about hidden links also arises in "A Small Treatise on Non-Contradiction" (a telling title), which oddly associates human action, mechanical facts, and usefulness:

> Son goes out of the apartment block to get some air
> since the fall is still pretty, and why waste the weather.
> He goes to the pond to study bugs, returns
> and checks everything in books.
>
> From the kitchen window I watch the boys kick a ball.
> The door opens, and while the door's open
> you can hear that the elevator works today,
> clicks shut and moves on, to be useful.

Should one thus conclude that the world is composed of continuities, however hard it is to discern them? Once, Sommer insists that "nothing's / at odds with anything." But his very act of formulating such an axiom stems from initial, perhaps lasting, circumspection. Throughout *Continued*, the reader must ruminate on tantalizing ambiguities. Interestingly, the title poem best expresses this persistent uncertainty. Despite the reassuring title (for we fear both changes and closures), the text posits that "nothing will be the same as it was / and that too will be new somehow, since after all, / before, things could be similar: morning, / the rest of the day, evening and night, but not now." Our puzzling over continuities and discontinuities must continue.

* * *

The work of other important Polish poets has recently appeared in translation, including that of the meteoric Krzysztof Kamil Baczyński (1921-1944).

Baczyński volunteered for the Polish underground "Home Army" during the German Occupation and was killed in action. Bill Johnston's selection, *White Magic and Other Poems*, presents intricate verse that depends on bold metaphors, Baudelairean *correspondances*, and a heightened synaesthetic awareness. In an elegy on summer, Baczyński imagines avenues dreaming "in shade from broad baobabs of lindens," then adds:

> With a Bach fugue, the next-door balcony
> leads the landscape to the church
> and the wheels of the sky can be heard—the planet's creaking.
> What then is left?

His answer can be taken as emblematic of his entire oeuvre: small black roses that remain after poems have been burned to ashes.

A catalogue of Baczyński's similes should be made. Many are perturbing and somehow oppressive, such as when "dusk sinks like lead filings into the plush-upholstered furniture"; or, more simply but more eerily, "by night the woods grow like murmuring lakes." Yet beyond these formal qualities, Baczyński's poetry compels with its evocations of love for his wife—called "Basia" in his verse—or with his struggle to maintain his Catholic faith in the face of war and Nazi brutality.

* * *

Tadeusz Różewicz (b. 1921) is less complex than Sommer and Baczyński, but many of his poems—syntactically skeletal, based more often on juxtapositions of static noun-images than on verbal movement—offer brief ironies that give pause. Adam Czerniawski's earlier selections of Różewicz's work have now been revised and further enlarged into *They Came to See a Poet*.

Różewicz is famous for two poems set in the museum at Auschwitz, one of which unforgettably ends with "clouds of dry hair / of those suffocated / and a faded plait / a pigtail with a ribbon / pulled at school / by naughty boys." Often the impact of Różewicz's verse relies on images mentioned as if in passing. "I Closed my Hand," a love poem that begins tensely but rather abstractly (for it is not clear why the poet clenches his fist, nor why he quotes a sentence from one of Kafka's letters to Felice Bauer), tellingly concludes with a terse statement: "I tried to make you come / to sunny Italy / but last week you died / and were buried."

Although some of his earlier work is, like Bertolt Brecht's, facilely fabular or lightly paradoxical, other poems reveal a deeper poetics, such as when he observes that "from the crack / between me and the world / between me and the object / from the distance / between noun and pronoun / poetry struggles to emerge." Many modern European poets have stared intently at this fundamental fissure.

* * *

As for younger Polish poets, their acquaintance can be made in a stimulating anthology, *Carnivorous Boy, Carnivorous Bird*. Marcin Baran (b. 1963) has selected twenty-four poets, including himself, and my only regret is that his introduction is schematic and very short. Some of his own work is arresting, especially "Love. The Inimitable Variant," a "between-the-genres" prose text in the form of a couple's biographical résumé.

Amorous relationships come to the fore in other poets' work. The most subtle and sensitive poems are written by the only woman present, Marzanna Kielar (b. 1963), who knows how to create captivating atmospheres and suggest much more than she states. In "Nakedness," she focuses on herself and her lover only gradually, after first evoking natural surroundings:

> boughs thickset with white and dark pink
> with the hum of bees
> the wing of day spreads open in the sun,
> in gentle breeze, in a scent of fresh-mown
> meadow, tall camomiles on its southern edge.
> Sheltered, the darkening bank of the pond.
> Your hand in my hair, on my neck, gently,
> softly. All its fragility (its quiver?).
> The nakedness of opening leaves, thickening
> green, fingers slipping off the dress-strap.

(trans. Elżbieta Wójcik-Leese)

A similar confessional restraint obtains in "To Stefania P.," by Krzysztof Koehler (b. 1963). The yearning and religious introspection of this sonnet depends on a single image: "delicate hands, as if of marble, on tired bedsheets."

Other poems inherently pointing to something essential that is absent in the poem's wording itself, yet increasingly present in the mind of its reader, are written by Marcin Sendecki (b. 1967), who—like Sommer—also likes concluding semi-colons. One poem begins "Of course, it's impossible to know," then describes a woman walking down a street. The erotic allusions are several. But what is it that we do not know? The question is implicitly asked by the narrator-observer, probably by pedestrians and also, arguably, by the woman in regard to herself; not to mention by ourselves, who puzzle over the otherwise straightforward imagery. Yet if there is a mystery here, transcending the realm of desire and attraction, it remains unelucidated. Similarly, Eugeniusz Tkaczyszyn-Dycki (b. 1962) spins a striking first line: "when for years a dead man has been your home") and uses haunting repetitions to raise fundamental metaphysical issues. Some of these new Polish poets are promising. They brave the "infinite / rubicon of detail," as Mariusz Grzebalski (b. 1969) puts it nicely, and tend to see life as "nothing but riddles."

Brief Crystallizations of Plenitude
(Adam Zagajewski)

"Suddenly you see the world lit differently," writes the Polish poet Adam Zagajewski in *Mysticism for Beginners,* a collection mostly selected from *Ziemia Ognista* (*The Fiery Land,* 1994) and translated with characteristic smoothness by Clare Cavanagh. (Among other poetry books in English, *Tremor* and *Canvas* have previously appeared, and *Without End: New and Selected Poems* was brought out by Farrar, Straus, and Giroux in 2003.) This declaration sums up well the engaging movement of these meditative poems, which meander gently toward moments of enlightenment. Informed by exile and travel (Zagajewski long divided his time between Paris and Houston), as well as by respect for everyday life, his longer poems especially search not so much for severed Polish roots as for insight and wisdom—wherever he is. In "Letter from a Reader," which seemingly defines his own aims, he tells himself to attend to "the endless patience / of the light." Metaphors involving light and darkness (or shadow) indeed appear frequently, with the hope tendered that this miraculous light can sometimes—as he remarks apropos of Vermeer's "Little Girl"—inhabit a work of art.

Contemporary lives, suggests Zagajewski, are only rarely rooted, stable, spiritually secure, let alone illuminated. We experience "travel instead of remembrance"; we write "quick poem[s]" instead of "hymn[s]." Yet for all its sad tonalities, his verse shows that an existence marked by mobility and ontological doubt need not eventually bog down into anguish—the paralyzing predicament of many modern writers. Despair can depend on our view of our earliest years—from which we may be brutally separated. Yet "why is childhood," asks the poet, "our only origin, our only longing?"

Zagajewski grapples with this key question of "origin" in *Mysticism for Beginners*, in his absorbing and urbane essay collections, *Two Cities* (1995) and *A Defense of Ardor* (2002), as well as in *Another Beauty* (1998), his thoughtful collage-like memoir of Kraków, the town in which he studied at the university after being raised in Gliwice. (He was born in Lwów in 1945, but his family was displaced when this medieval Polish city, in accordance with the Yalta Agreements, was absorbed into the Soviet Union.) One easily imagines the weight of History on individuals in such a context; during the Communist regimes that ensued from the Second World War, any number of Eastern European writers and poets, often from their outposts in exile, delved into this predicament, sometimes most deeply in works that were not overtly or immediately political. As for Zagajewski, who was born into the generation following that of certain literary "titans," as he has called them, he is not truly (any more, at least) a political poet. His gazing back, when it occurs, is mostly familial or personal; and he is neither embittered nor nostalgic when he does so. In his discreet self-oriented pieces, he is essentially aiming beyond the self.

Mysticism for Beginners mostly examines the present and looks forward, though elegiac images from the past do arise and give pause. "It was a gray landscape," he solemnly recalls, "houses small / as Tartar ponies, concrete high-rises, / massive, stillborn; uniforms everywhere, rain, / drowsy rivers not knowing where to flow, / dust, Soviet gods with swollen eyelids." Another compelling poem likewise mourns his mother and meditates on memory. Yet moving away from the postwar Poland in which he grew up, he more often readies himself for encounters with uplifting transcendence, even amidst the flat dehumanizing drabness of modern societies, little matter the political regime. Near-prayers can result, such as is expressed by his wish to see "Tierra del Fuego, / …where the rivers / flow straight up."

Our lives can briefly crystallize, he movingly shows, in unexpected plenitude. After leaving a Romanesque church, for example, he marvels at how a mere moment miraculously enters "the timid grass," inhabits "stems and genes, / the pupils of our eyes" and conveys its "boundless, senseless, / silly joy." Tellingly, however, these moments "know something" we cannot grasp. Aspiring to such mysteries, Zagajewski realizes that he must eschew irony, become completely sincere, turn poetry into a means of exploration, not an end in itself. Some poems reflect his struggles to do so. A subtle craftsman, he avoids ostentatious effects, focuses on the deepest meanings. The title poem revealingly equates even our finest perceptions with only an "elementary course" in mysticism. The path to understanding necessarily remains untrodden; but its first turnings have been glimpsed by the attentive, self-effacing poet.

* * *

As this book was going to press, I was able to read the galley proofs of *Eternal Enemies* (2008), Zagajewski's latest collection, once again fluidly rendered by Cavanagh. Central elements from the poet's previous work, ranging from his Polish background to his inveterate traveling (Italy is particularly present), and from his focus on "ordinary life" and how it "desires" (as a simple yet significant poem puts it) to his intimations of the "unseen Lord," reappear here accompanied by the persistent questioning and gentle emotions that have become his hallmark. There are also homages, notably to Czesław Miłosz (whose ideas and poems he has frequently analyzed in essays), W. G.

286 Into the Heart of European Poetry

Sebald ("our world in his prose, / ...so calm—but / full of perfectly forgotten crimes"), Kathleen Ferrier, William Blake, Tadeusz Kantor, Aleksander Wat, Joseph Brodsky, and his own father. Even Karl Marx in old age is the subject of two pieces. Fourteen short poems tellingly summed up as "En Route" interestingly waver in genre between the haiku and the Greco-Roman epigram, while other pieces set in Mediterranean surroundings and sometimes in remote historical periods suggest the influence of C. P. Cavafy. It is a varied gathering, emphasizing in the process the discontinuities of the poet's life as well as his search for an overarching existential or even spiritual unity that, as he knows all too well, cannot be easily defined, let alone obtained. One unifying aesthetic element, however, is his unironic, almost ingenuous, quest of answers to that old question: the meaning of life. In unornamented, crystalline, intentionally almost prose-like poems, Zagajewski is as candid about this search as about his doubts of succeeding.

The tutelary figure of Miłosz is especially important because Zagajewski similarly seeks a second ideal that in our harried and cynical age has likewise become old fashioned: wisdom. Unsurprisingly, Miłosz's lifelong grappling with metaphysics and the possibilities of faith has also inspired the younger man, who on "life's path" with its "instants of astronomy"—a fine image of both our limitations and aspirations—seeks, with skepticism nonetheless, a glimpse or intimation of something greater than the mere dust of the cosmos and our bodies. A short poem about Francisco de Zurburán suggests that "objects / lying on heavy tables" can potentially be perceived as "holy," at least by a sensibility such as the Spanish painter's, yet in "Reading Miłosz," Zagajewski's occasional impression that "every day is sacred," thanks to his mentor's verse, ends abruptly in the "city's ordinary din," the sound of someone's cough, and then someone else's crying and cursing. Are these banal and disturbing noises also sacred? Time and again, Zagajewski implicitly asks if omnipresent ordinariness fully circumscribes, compresses, even inexorably crushes our lives, leaving us no hopes, or whether drab routines and the utter materiality of matter have boundaries that can be crossed, if only in singular privileged instants. If so, where are the boundaries located? How might they be spotted, let alone approached? Perhaps, as some of Zagajewski's poems seem to indicate, and notably the short piece about Zurburán, transcending ordinariness paradoxically implies delving into it with renewed attention and respect. Zagajewski is hardly the only European poet who not only sharply observes, but also and especially peers into dailiness because it is an unavoidable poetic and philosophical problem.

But even this desire for transcendence, plenitude, meaning, or sacredness can become complacent, mechanical, inauthentic. The poet is aware of this danger; in consequence, a few poems challenge self-illusions. One or two of these counter-poems, as they might be termed, flatly declare that the poet does not know who he is. The splendid "Wait for an Autumn Day," a poem based on verse by the Swedish poet Gunnar Ekelöf, expresses a desire for serenity and acceptance, but it also warns that "the bonfire's smoke" can contain "the heady taste of ungettable wisdom." And in a long poem entitled "Walk through this Town," the poet interrogates himself almost severely, in an ominous past tense:

> Could you voice the smallest fragment of the whole?
>
> Could you name baseness when you saw it?
>
> If you met someone who was truly living
> did you know it?
>
> Did you abuse high words?....

At the same time, an *ars poetica* is being sketched.

Zagajewski fundamentally remains an affirmative poet, which is not to say that he is optimistic. He is inclined to affirm, to open himself up, rather than reject or deny. His persistence in this general direction, which includes the numerous detours and backtrackings that I have indicated, gives his oeuvre a distinctive, and quite rare, sense of good-naturedness—albeit infused with lucidity and sometimes also melancholy. At the end of *Eternal Enemies*, he has placed a series of notebook-like sentences that he calls "Antennas in the Rain." Like a profusion of rooftop antennas in a contemporary cityscape, they can be imagined as receiving all kinds of disparate broadcasts: some are quips, while others resemble brief descriptions, questions, reminders, overheard phrases, images, or declarations. Of these, one stands out. "Poetry is," Zagajewski maintains, "joy hiding despair" But he adds as quickly: "under the despair—more joy."

Searching for the Materia Prima
(Marzanna Kielar)

Marzanna Kielar's poetry first caught my eye in *Carnivorous Boy, Carnivorous Bird*, an anthology of younger Polish poets that Zephyr brought out in 2004. Now this inquisitive and resourceful small press, focused on Russian and Eastern European literature, has published a first selection of Kielar's sensuous and deep-probing verse. As in the anthology, Elżbieta Wójcik-Leese has provided an engaging translation.

Salt Monody draws on Kielar's three Polish collections, *Sacra conversazione* (1992), *Materia prima* (1999), and *Monodia* (2006). These titles announce the philosophical range of her work, as well as its aspiration to an unusual kind of poetic, even musical, grace. Indeed, the musical sense of "monody" as a single solo line describes the structure of many poems, often composed of one, two, or just a few long sentences which, through colons, semi-colons, dashes, enjambments, stark juxtapositions, and lines of irregular length, gradually unfold their multiple meanings and implications.

Kielar's poems are set in the windy, woody, lake-speckled Baltic hinterland and seascapes of her native Mazuria, a region of northern Poland. (She was born in Gołdap in 1963.) She conjures up this particular geography and its climes extremely well, as the first lines of the first poem immediately show:

> enormous sea—as far as the dunes, with its lips
> ever against the skin of wind, as if against the other
> half of its being; steep,
> empty saddles of waves, touched by the light
> which already turns back, slips out leaving behind
> the dimming seam.

However, for all the beauty of her evocations, Kielar above all ventures behind natural phenomena and questions the perceiver's relationship to them. She charts subjectivity's grappling with that from which it is logically separated. In this regard, her poetry pinpoints impassable gaps, but also and especially searches for hidden unifying principles and unexpected intersections of Nature (or the Other) and individual experience. Sometimes descriptions of natural settings ("boughs thickset with white and dark pink, / with the hum of bees") strangely transmute into a human encounter. "Your hand in my hair, on my neck, gently, / softly," she continues, for instance. "All its fragility (and quiver?). / The nakedness of opening leaves, thickening / green, fingers slipping off the dress-strap." Characteristically, delicate eroticism blends here with movements within Nature, and vice versa. Other poems lament—another sense of monody—lost love, death, and various disunions. The nightmarish "Pre-existences," apparently about a miscarriage or a stillborn baby (but in fact about a terminated love affair), provides an unforgettable example.

Kielar's earlier title, *Materia prima*, is also telltale. Sometimes the "materia prima" that the poet senses in herself, or outside her body, resembles a vital energy, as in the lines "the silence inside me: not even a bird sings // only fire." In "The Hawk," she makes this explicit alignment: "blood, materia prima." Here and in other poems, she thus revolves around that elusive concept, "life," which as a "materia prima" has proven harder to define for philosophers than it may appear. In another important piece, this life-engendering, existence-revealing, or reunifying "materia prima" is ascribed to love. "When love comes back and reminds us of our true being," she exclaims, "When it pieces together the body of the world again, anew...."

A dialectic is thereby established between disintegration and wholeness. Moreover, her poems often evolve, through sharply focused but also semantically rich word pictures, toward a lost or invisible starting point; or more precisely: toward a fundamental dynamic principle that recalls the *arkhé* that ancient Greek poet-philosophers intuited. Not surprisingly, throughout *Salt Monody*, there is a sense of something ancient that must be recovered and renewed. Kielar particularly favors geology as a source for remarkable metaphors traversing vast stretches of time:

> As in the earth, the wing of the fault moved in me: fossil remains
> of love vows, your names,
> resurrected gestures—like damned-up ice—penetrated forests,
> clearings of dreams.
>
> Narrow blade of the moon's stake scratches the ice-sheet.
> Time splits like a hewn stone: along the brittle bright vein
> of that love.

Yet because she observes reality so closely and penetratingly, Kielar never clutters her verse with even a skillful juggling of concepts. Intense and groping, her crafted poems retain the on-the-spot urgency of note-taking. This freshness is reinforced because philosophical aims are usually expressed only through vivid imagery and offhand allusion. Even when deploying complex metaphors, her writing keeps atmospheric qualities in the forefront, underscoring the primacy of sense perceptions. The aforementioned first poem of *Salt Monody*

concludes, for example, with a vision of "clouds / at the wall of the horizon."
But then this sight, which might arguably have ended the poem, is qualified
in significant parentheses as "(prayer without words, / without a tomorrow)."
The poet-perceiver must contemplate the utter materiality of matter and the
utter presence of the present. Yet although both language and the future have
withdrawn from hope, the poet's yearning, to say the least, remains palpable;
this emotion, too, is implicitly posited as a "materia prima."

These poems often seem masterly fragments of an encompassing, though
unstated, whole; a whole that the poet is seeking to form or glimpse. This is also
somewhat suggested by Kielar's third Polish title, *Sacra conversazione*. The
Italian phrase can refer to a Renaissance genre in which the Virgin is depicted
as conversing with both the infant Jesus and various saints; the present and the
future are thus merged in the present of the painting. Yet in her homonymous
poem, Kielar offers no such explicit parallels. She simply mentions "your sudden presence" at her side, qualifying it as "trembling and trusting." As with
other tantalizing "you's" in these splendid, mysterious poems, the interpretation—despite a concluding "shut lips"—typically remains open:

> The soft hollyhock of touch, as before a journey
> with its inevitability, why?
> Like a scent, close,
> the tempting concave of the palm, when out of all
> things, good and bad,
> from their refined, impermanent profusion
> you deliberately choose one: a handful of blackberries,
> and my lips are shut
> by berries.

Russia and the Former Soviet Union

Anna Akhmatova and Her Magic Choir
(Dmitry Bobyshev, Joseph Brodsky, Anatoly Naiman, Evgeny Rein)

She was the "bridge between Not and Was in a wail of torments and rapture." This arresting line, written by the Russian poet Anatoly Naiman (b. 1936), evokes the legendary Anna Akhmatova (1889-1966), one of the seminal poets of the twentieth century and the mentor, not only of Naiman, but also of Joseph Brodsky (1940-1996), Dmitry Bobyshev (b. 1936), and Evgeny Rein (b. 1935). Beginning in 1959, in Leningrad (now Saint Petersburg), these four aspiring poets—who were friends—sought out the ailing, impoverished, ever transient, and oft publicly denounced Akhmatova, the author of the poetic sequences *Requiem*, *Poem without a Hero*, and *The Way of All the Earth*. The young men recited their poems to her, helped her out in daily chores, and Naiman served as her secretary from 1962 to her death. Some of the one-to-one friendships in the foursome eventually soured; the reasons are suggested in Rein's poem "In Pavlovsk Park." Let's avoid that topic. "Life is like a letter," he rightly observes in "Signature for a Torn Portrait," "with blotches on the page."

Naiman, Brodsky, Bobyshev, and Rein were writing more or less secretly (their verse circulating in handwritten copies and through private readings), for they rejected the Socialist realism that was promoted—with all too tangible threats for dissenters—by Communist politicians and cultural watchdogs. Brodsky termed Socialist Realism "recycled garbage," a quip not to be confused with Akhmatova's famous remark about poets being "born of rubbish." The latter signifies, in Brodsky's gloss (and in regard to Rein):

> ...everything that a person comes up against, turns away from, to which he pays attention. This rubbish is not only his physical—visual, cognitive, olfactory and acoustic—experience; it is also the experience of everything lived, superfluous, unreceived, taken on faith, forgotten, devoted to, known only by rumor; it is also the experience of what has been read.

In other words: vital, radiant, resonant rubbish. Back then, among the four men's contemporaries, the only Russian poet well known abroad was the politically more ambiguous, poetically more facile, Yevgeny Yevtushenko (b. 1933), who even became the darling of some American politicians and intellectuals.

Yevtushenko's case is more complicated than that, but it is important to know that a technically more elaborate, philosophically more ambitious, Russian poetry was being composed at the time by these four men whom Akhmatova had nicknamed her "magic choir." Eventually, translations of poems by Brodsky, who had involuntarily emigrated to the United States in 1972, began appearing, culminating in the Penguin *Selected Poems* of 1973. Brodsky went on to international fame and the 1987 Nobel Prize, while the poetry of his three former sidekicks remained little available in English. This is why the publication of Naiman's *Lions and Acrobats*, a gathering of recent work, as well as Rein's *Selected Poems*, is welcome news. Only missing, alas, is a selection of the work of Bobyshev, who emigrated to the United States in 1979 and teaches at the University of Illinois (Urbana). Samplings are available in *Contemporary Russian Poetry*, *In the Grip of Strange Thoughts*, and *Modern Poetry in Translation* (No. 10, Winter 1996). These men were the "outcasts and custodians of the age," to paraphrase Rein's untitled poem beginning "You walk across a frozen stream in a field lost in snow drifts."

Streams, rivers, and bridges—as metaphors—are common to these poets. Naiman, whose *Remembering Anna Akhmatova* (1989) vividly evokes their formative years, was thinking in his aforementioned poem about how the frail woman, as a sturdy literary bridge, was the last survivor from among the great Russian poets of the first half of the twentieth century. Neither the term "survivor" nor the "Was" of Naiman's poem are to be taken lightly. Most of Akhmatova's literary peers and family had disappeared decades earlier in tragic, violent circumstances. Indeed, "how many ways the poet could meet death," she aptly laments in *Poem without a Hero*. The symbolist Alexander Blok (1880-1921), the "music" of whose verse fascinated her, had long before become discouraged with the Revolution, lost his will to live, fallen ill, and died. Marina Tsvetaeva (1892-1941) had fled the Soviet Union in 1922, then returned in 1939, only to commit suicide. Akhmatova's close friend, Osip Mandelstam (1891-1938), had been arrested, then left to perish in a transit camp. Her first husband, Nikolai Gumilyov, had been executed in 1921; and at about the same time as Mandelstam's death, Akhmatova's son Lev was caught and sent away to a prison, then to the Gulag. These victims constituted a mere handful of the millions who, in Naiman's words, "hung like smoke above labor camp stacks / or [fell] like carrion on long forced marches, / or rotted, crushed to death in hard-labor barges."

With "three hundred women ahead of you," as she phrases it, Akhmatova waited in lines outside jails and camps in the hopes of passing on warm clothing to her son. If the prison guards accepted the package, this meant that the convict inside was still alive. "Can you describe *this*?" asked a woman who recognized her. "I can," Akhmatova answered, affirming against the starkest odds that poetry can grapple with the most horrific realities. The repartee simultaneously gives birth, it seems to me, to the particular individualism and intricate metaphorical realism that one later finds in the work of her magic choir. In any event, this challenge, cited "instead of a foreword," motivated *Requiem*, of which a rhymed version is provided by Nancy K. Anderson in *The Word That Causes Death's Defeat*. Anderson also offers compelling translations of, and extensive commentaries on, the other two sequences. This is a path-breaking book in what seemed to be a well-traveled forest. Anderson begins with a biography, which includes a sensitive and judicious account of Akhmatova's daily struggles, writing, and political behavior during the regimes of Stalin and Khrushchev. Then, in her translations, she convincingly interprets the "music" of the Russian poems, an important achievement in that Akhmatova contended that a true poet possessed a unique "song." Do not we Americans tend to speak of a poet's "voice," which is something else again? Reading the verse of Akhmatova and her magic choir obliges one to face up to telling differences between two essential "modernisms."

Akhmatova's presence, let alone her poems (some of which she was still revising), gave the four poets access to the recent Russian literary past: the "Was"—the Silver Age—that had been walled off by the Russian Revolution. Moreover, thanks to her vast learning, poetic passion, and sharp ear, the young men had a vital, not just bookish, link to classical European poetry, from Virgil to Petrarch, from Dante to Shakespeare. And because Akhmatova maintained such high standards, her example must have encouraged them to persist in the individual-negating "Not" of the present. Naiman, Rein, and Bobyshev waited for decades before most of their respective oeuvres could be published. Rein seems to evoke this in his lines "life slipped away: forty or fifty years / were needed to conclude / the most vexing of all vexations."

Akhmatova's tutelary role is the immediate meaning of Naiman's bridge metaphor, which crops up again in a poem dedicated to Bobyshev. "How strange," notes Naiman, "to walk half your life over bridges spanning a river." The poet refers to travel after "half a lifetime" spent "nowhere," during which he could cross only the Neva. Now he finds himself on a Hudson River bridge that "is as like as two drops to the first one." "How strange," he repeats, expressing a self-ironic, good-natured bewilderment that recurs often elsewhere. The poet characteristically concludes his poem by meditating on his growing "confusion…at the world not lying, / as [he] just catch[es] the sound of life latching metaphor's lock." Implicitly, the bridge metaphor thus also points to the poet's task of constructing a credible walkway between poetry and life in all its chaotic spontaneity. This is a realism, ever questioning and re-examining its postulates, of the most serious order.

This movement from a central object to existential or metaphysical concerns is typical of Naiman. The metaphorical bridge also spans an "eternal river." Teleology is never far from his thoughts. But even more, he seeks a wisdom superseding his own qualms. His focus on details is precise, but it is rarely a bitter squint; he simultaneously searches for equilibrium, proportion. In fact,

Naiman more frequently questions life, not death—what it means to be alive, what it feels like to be alive, a phenomenological enigma that is more difficult to work out in words than it may seem. Attempt to feel yourself feeling, to catch yourself looking, to sense yourself thinking....

Naiman endeavors precisely this when he gazes starward—a favorite pastime. "Whoever has [so] gazed," he posits, "is alive. / Without doubt. No breath-fogged mirror is needed, no proof, / no flutter of eyelids." And yet the poet's initial confidence about his aliveness is, characteristically, called into question by the second strophe:

> Still, some sign would be good. A cough. Some such trivial thing.
> An answer to whether that's Schumann or Schubert outside,
> from the window. That we look at the sky and the one who is looking—
> you or me.

Finally he accepts his initial proposition, which could perhaps be described as "I sense myself gazing, therefore I am." This self-reflexive apperception, reinforcing his belief in his own existence, enables him to deduce stunningly that "optics, not mercury, show / that what came to life was no mere inanimate cosmos."

Other poems (like the engaging "Fuga et vita") similarly enter into, or imply, paradoxes about our experience of time: the future cannot be known; the present moment is fleeting, ungraspable; only the past exists, but in memory, and in fragments perhaps accessible through reminiscence yet otherwise beyond all possibilities of re-experience. Although allusions to Russia's somber past are made in *Lions and Acrobats* (notably in "A Wake for Our Time"), Naiman tends to pursue apolitical themes with philosophical ramifications such as these. A chemical engineer by training, he deftly brings science into his poems as well. This motivates an even greater wonder at existence per se. "Of what is known," he writes, "—a pitiful amount, / [but] no pity is required—it only makes / a handful, but a handful holding all." Our knowledge is scant, but sufficient enough to give us intimations into underlying or overriding unities.

Scientific and philosophical metaphors are crucial to Naiman and Brodsky. Because of his metaphorical propensities, the latter, especially in his English poems, sometimes irritated American critics. In the more circumspect Naiman, the heterogeneous elements going into a metaphor can also be striking. In "Alone on a Hill," an almost childlike question ("What's a tree made of?") leads to this heady answer:

> ...Holes and deep recesses
> like a swarming spring of midges hovering in space,
> a violinist's bowed designs, figure 8's and passes,
> the fiddler like a matador cocooned in swathes of cape.

Like Brodsky, Naiman is fully aware of those "quirky fascinations and nervous flights of feeling," as he puts it in a different context, that define modern man's unstable, anxiety-ridden relationship to nature and his fellow man. His more characteristic tone, however, is one of inquiry and reconciliation. He often renews one's feeling for human fragility, ephemeralness. In "Early Berry-Picking," whose title perhaps nods to Robert Frost (whom Akhmatova met when the American poet visited the Soviet Union in 1962), Naiman writes of "rush[ing] to pick cranberries, head looming over the lunar moss / and together with the falling dew, I let an eyelash drop." Never overbearing, he evokes himself discreetly: we sense him more in the eyelash than in his "rushing." The overall atmosphere is very different in Akhmatova's elegies (not to mention Rein's truculent verse tales), but it is probably not unrelated to Naiman's development that she pioneered an autobiographical poetry that takes off from everyday experience (very grim, in her case) and strives for an unromantic, classically restrained, yet fully empathic and universal, narrative viewpoint. Her approach was not always understood. Even Alexander Solzhenitsyn missed the point. When Akhmatova recited her *Requiem* to him in 1962, shortly before the first *Novy Mir* publication of *One Day in the Life of Ivan Denisovich*, he praised the "beauty" and "sonority" yet told her that "it's a poem about an individual case, about one mother and son.... The duty of a Russian poet is to...rise above personal grief and speak of the nation's grief." She was doing no less.

Naiman can also be funny, which is remarkable in light of the hardships he himself suffered and eyewitnessed. There's "sense and nonsense mixed" into several pieces, and they counterbalance the darker implications of others. Addressing a series of lighthearted poems to his granddaughter, Sophie, he counsels: "Don't rush to grow up; grown ups are dumb; / they don't put their baby teeth out for the fairy to come / but blurt out 'calcium.'" Expectedly, these light verses have a more serious side. Sophie is growing up. And who can forget that "Sophia" is an archetypal figure in Russian literature for "wisdom"?

In contrast, Rein plunges into a half-century of dismal Soviet dailiness with a sort of robust acrimony. Memorable poems recall his camaraderie with Brodsky. The graphic "Ararat" recounts how Brodsky, drinking cognac with Rein in a raucous Armenian restaurant, is suddenly "transfigured": "On his face miraculously appears / all that had been hidden within it: genius / and the future.... All around us—an Armenian uproar." A Rabelaisian vitality runs through such verse, which owes as much to Rein's wide reading as to popular songs and an intimacy with urban life. Melancholy, bitterness, erudition, and bits of drollery are refined by sophisticated rhymes and meters. The penultimate poem in the selection is a homage to Rein's deceased pal. Rein first recalls staying with Brodsky long ago, in a "provincial hotel-cum-drinking-den." Disparate historical periods are superposed, before Rein again finds himself with his friend, this time in New York. He asks Brodsky if he will return to Russia. The answer is a resounding "Why should I? No way!" Another flash of memory transports

Rein to a Venetian canal, where he asks Brodsky the same question. This time, the author of *A Part of Speech* (1980), *To Urania* (1988) and *So Forth* (1996) says nothing. Remembering the days of Akhmatova's magic circle, Rein can only conclude:

> ...A bell chimed
> And told me, *Nevermore. You two, you four,*
> *Will never meet again.* The night receded.
> Venice flowered, decayed, and seemed to drown
> In violet darkness, like a painting by Vrubel.

On the Ledge
(*Joseph Brodsky*)

In his birthday poem entitled "May 24, 1980," Joseph Brodsky (1940-1996) evokes hardships that he has encountered during forty years of living, then he concludes stunningly: "Yet until brown clay has been crammed down my larynx, / only gratitude will be gushing from it." "Gratitude"—this is a fine word with which to remember him. Despite exile and a faulty heart, as well as personal disappointments to which a few poems (such as "On Love" or "Six Years Later") discreetly allude, the Russian poet invigoratingly, and contagiously, expresses gratitude for a cosmos in which, as philosophers phrase it, there seems to be "something instead of nothing"—a cosmos full of beautiful, funny, or puzzling "things" in which we can delight. And not just delight, it must be added, but also, potentially, the welling-up of that rare and, as Brodsky sometimes terms it, "higher" sentiment created in us when we read evocations of and thus envision—see anew—the same things, yet this time as they are passed through the revivifying perceptual and linguistic filters of a gifted poet. However onto-logically separate they remain from us, cobblestones, for Brodsky, are not just wet, they "glisten like bream in a net." And the frigidness of the North (and of the Communist era during which he grew up and suffered) is experienced as a polysemous "cold that, to warm my palm, / gathered my fingers around a pen." This ultimately optimistic—or more precisely, *affirming*—outlook does not mean that Brodsky's poetry is naive, self-deluding, or facilely joyous. On the contrary, his writing can be melancholy, even bitterly clear-sighted. It can also be tantalizingly mysterious, akin in this respect to the ungraspable cognitive processes of thinking and especially versifying:

> Man broods over his life like night above a lamp.
> At certain moments a thought takes leave of one
> of the brain's hemispheres, and slips, as a bedsheet might,
> from under the restless sleeper's body clamp,
> revealing who-knows-what-under-the-sun.

Instead of succumbing, in incurable despair, to "the queer, vertiginous thought of Nothingness," a notion nonetheless backdropping and surely often catalyzing his inspiration, Brodsky is more inclined to praise these "who-knows-what-under-the sun." He hails butterflies, for instance, for being "frail and shifting buffer[s] / dividing [Nothingness] from me." He is deeply grateful for these comforting "buffers," for the miracle of existing in an unpredictable, bewildering cosmos (and even in our "wholly new / but doleful world"), for being gifted with a sensitivity ever-attuned to the plenitude and intricacy of a moment of being alive, and above all for what he considered to be man's noblest response to the human condition: poetry. With characteristic modesty (yet not a little pride), he proclaims an admirable commitment to his craft in his poem "1972":

> Listen, my boon brethren and my enemies!
> What I've done, I've done not for fame or memories
> in this era of radio waves and cinemas,
> but for the sake of my native tongue and letters.
> For which sort of devotion, of a zealous bent
> ("Heal thyself, doctor," as the saying went),
> denied a chalice at the feast of the fatherland,
> now I stand in a strange place. The name hardly matters.

The name of the country? The name of the poet? The ambivalence is telling, as well as moving. The very title of his welcome posthumous gathering, *Collected Poems in English* (2000), underscores Brodsky's intimate relationship with the English language—the initial attraction to which occurred long before his forced emigration to the United States in 1972. In *Less than One* (1986), he recounts his first exposure to English poetry, and notably to that of W. H. Auden, who would become his generous friend. As regards Brodsky's own translations and original compositions in English, this special relationship has of course been impugned by some critics and fellow poets; and I admit to having myself been occasionally estranged, literally, by Brodsky's linguistic "xenity": his quirky uses of American slang; his sometimes troublesome syntax with our uninflected language; his unidiomatic juxtapositions (whereby cuckoos and magpies "chirp"); or his not-quite-natural verbal tenses, such as the confusing simple past—as opposed to a pluperfect—in the second of the first two lines of his magnificent sequence, "Vertumnus": "I met you the first time ever in latitudes you'd call foreign. / Your foot never trod that loam; your fame, though, had reached those quarters."

This being said, it is important to recall that the poet, in the same essay on Auden, justifies his initial attempts to write in English as a desire to communicate, as it were, with his deceased mentor. This is a characteristically self-dismissing, half-superstitious, though (I think) sincere, confession; and listening carefully to its deepest implications should move us to reread English poems (and translations) of which a word here or there perturbs. After all, he forthrightly claims (in a brief note included in the first edition of *A Part of Speech*) to "rework" translations made by other hands, "to bring [the versions] closer to the original, though perhaps at the expense of their smoothness." It has been my experience that bilinguals, let alone polyglots, are rarely pedantically over-concerned with "smoothness"; and they often even appreciate a certain "xenity," because it can reinforce the fidelity of a translation. Is not this critical position as tenable as the more widespread rule that the host language should remain, at all costs, without nicks and smudges? In this essay, I'll keep coming back to this issue, which in Brodsky's poetry is particularly thorny.

We must also remember that he remained a Russian poet (despite his increasing forays into English) and that only a third of his Russian poems were translated during his lifetime—an arrestingly small amount of work that is available to us. The two main French collections of Brodsky's verse, *Collines et autres poèmes* (Seuil, 1966) and *Poèmes 1961-1987* (Gallimard, 1987), reveal the importance of earlier, pre-immigration, poems that we still lack in English, a lacuna that will hopefully be filled by the upcoming, expanded, edition of George L. Kline's *Joseph Brodsky: Selected Poems* (1973). A bilingual complete works is thankfully in preparation.

In the meantime, *Collected Poems in English* reprints *A Part of Speech* (1980), *To Urania* (1988), and *So Forth* (1996), and it includes twenty-six previously uncollected poems as well as five translations (two poems by Marina Tsvetaeva, and one each by Osip Mandelstam, Zbigniew Herbert, and Wisława Szymborska). Disappointingly, no genuine surprises crop up among the previously uncollected poems; most of them are light verse or political satire. Yet the translations include Mandelstam's most famous poem, "Tristia" (1916), which evokes Ovid's exile. This translation thus represents a double homage: first, to the Roman poet with whom Brodsky most deeply empathized and about whom he himself wrote several poems, sometimes in the same epistolary forms favored by the author of *Tristia* and the *Epistulae Ex Ponto*; second, to a fellow countryman whom he considered to be the greatest Russian poet of the twentieth century.

This key translation, moreover, acts as a corrective. For Americans who are impressed by the disarming "surrealism" of Brodsky's startling similes (which yoke together heterogeneous images or, with only obscure transitions, combine sense impressions and ideas), it cannot be emphasized enough how much he learned from Mandelstam's densely textured, tightly crafted, symbolism, and, more generally, from the aesthetics of the Russian Acmeist movement. Brodsky praises the way poetry "accelerates thought," in other words its ability to compress into a remarkably stimulating handful of words a bundle of ideas, sensations and sentiments, and thereby to reveal their unsuspected, esoteric, interconnections. The poem helps us to leap ahead, cognitively, along paths that discursive prose can never parallel. In "Elegy: for Robert Lowell," one encounters this extremely dense image-idea-question: "What is Salvation, since / a tear magnifies like glass / a future perfect tense?" In "Lithuanian Nocturne," to cite another example, Brodsky writes, both concisely and synaesthetically:

"A sequence of face / blots the dark windowpane / like the slap of a downpour."
In his great sequence "Lullaby of Cape Cod," he similarly compares formally
spaced "streetlamps glisten[ing] in stifling weather" to "white shirt buttons
open to the waist." One hears echoes of Mandelstam in such lines or at least
imagines that the elder Russian poet—who, having been arrested by the Soviet
police, perished in a transit camp two years before Brodsky was born—would
have appreciated them. Like Brodsky after him, Mandelstam also abruptly
shifts perspectives or seemingly transmutes configurations of matter into other
existential states. Brodsky's two other Russian models were Tsvetaeva and
especially Anna Akhmatova, who called attention to his poetry when he was
only eighteen years old.

Brodsky's earlier "Elegy on John Donne," which is not included in this
comprehensive gathering, likewise suggests that he attentively read the English
Metaphysicals. From the Metaphysicals he presumably gained confidence in
his own natural inclination to mix metaphysics and whimsy, cosmology and
love, religion and zoology, travel and mathematics. Geometric allusions crop
up conspicuously in Brodsky, who is obsessed—whenever contemplating the
cosmos and intuiting its hidden inner structures—with the possibility of chaos
as opposed to coherence, irrationality as opposed to logic. In "Homage to Yalta,"
he denounces the way "we have been trained to treat [life] as if it were / the
object of our logical deductions." "I wish I knew no astronomy," he similarly
sighs in the partly whimsical "A Song," "when stars appear, / when the moon
skims the water." His poetics thus privilege perceptual immediacy and sudden
insight, but they also toy with strict logical inference. Besides dauntlessly
extrapolating metaphysical conclusions from Euclid's mathematical presup-
positions ("the zer- / o Euclid thought the vanishing point became / wasn't
math — it was the nothingness of Time") or concocting fantastical geometric
self-portraits ("Draw an empty circle on your yellow pad. / This will be me:
no insides in thrall. / Stare at it a while, then erase the scrawl"), Brodsky also
occasionally conjures up the specter of Nikolai Lobachevsky (1792-1856), the
Russian mathematician who founded non-Euclidean geometry by imagining
parallel lines converging in infinity. This theoretical conjecture haunts Brodsky,
who derives from it a model of his own personal history:

> The change of Empires is intimately tied
> to the hum of words, the soft, fricative spray
> of spittle in the act of speech, the whole
> sum of Lobachevsky's angles, the strange way
> that parallels may unwittingly collide
> by casual chance someday
> as longitudes contrive to meet at the pole.

Some of those "unwittingly colliding" parallels involve similarities between
Brodsky's life and the biographies of Roman poets such as Martial and Ovid.

He is naturally sensitive to their courageous stances with respect to society and the State, as well as to the emotions induced in them by exile. (Martial was born in Bilbilis, in the northeastern part of Spain, and considered himself a "Spaniard" though he long lived and worked in Rome.) A close reader of the classics (who quips in a versified letter that his own poetry resembles "Roman writ *cum* Cyrillic"), Brodsky is likewise a "loyal subject," as he defines himself in "I Sit by the Window," of our contemporary "second-rate years." Yet he is not a genuine satirist, and he regards "tyrants" (as he terms, using a vivid anachronism, the evildoers of our times) with a cold-blooded detachment brilliantly reminiscent of that practiced by the poets of the Roman decadence. Singled out by the Soviet police for "parasitism," he was sent to a hard-labor camp not for writing dissident poetry, but rather because his poems lacked an easily definable political ideology. Rarely indeed does he portray people, let alone himself, in a social context that can be adequately described. For him, the "essence of self-portraiture" is, moreover, a kind of "suicide"; and it demands a special awareness of one's future "absence." In "At Carel Willink's Exhibition," he observes that "mastery" is the "ability / to not take fright at the procedure of / nonbeing—as another form of one's / own absence, having drawn it straight from life."

The poet ever inserts the daily vicissitudes of human life into larger cosmic perspectives comprising the certainty of our inevitable non-existence. Even a touching, late, love poem like "Porta San Pancrazio" makes this point:

> Life without us is, darling, thinkable. It exists as
> honeybees, horsemen, bars, habitués, columns, vistas,
> and clouds over this battlefield whose every standing statue
> triumphs, with its physique, over a chance to touch you.

These English, classical, and philosophical influences all inform Brodsky's eventual use of two languages. Because of his specifically Russian poetic background (which involves not only the sophisticated Acmeist poetry of the preceding generation but also the rigorously metered forms beloved by nearly all Russian poets), he cannot be compared in every detail to bi- or tri-lingual writers like Joseph Conrad, C. P. Cavafy, or Samuel Beckett (who themselves are not strictly comparable). Long years in a foreign country can diminish the spontaneity with which the expatriate conjures up his mother tongue, as well as strip a native vocabulary of its deposit of slang; yet no writer or poet experiences this evolution in the same ways. As soon as Brodsky was deported from the Soviet Union, he became cognizant of the linguistic enfeeblement potentially threatening him. In a poem dated the year of his exile, and thus referring to the United States, he states: "here I'll live out my days, losing gradually / hair, teeth, consonants, verbs, and suffixes." By 1988, as he is co-translating the first of the "Twenty Sonnets to Mary Queen of Scots," he notes: "I'll stuff the old gun full of classic grape- / shot, squandering what remains of Russian speech / on your pale shoulders and your paler nape." (This is by no means the unique line where Brodsky, who puns as much with words as with entire poetic forms, divides a end-word into an enjambment and makes, not only a wisecrack, but also a rhyme.)

In contrast to other exiled writers who lock themselves up inside their mother tongue so as to protect their creativity, Brodsky delved headlong into the enticements of his second language, all while continuing to write in Russian. Expatriates who, like him, embrace an adopted language with less anxiety, sometimes learn to pass back and forth, without inhibition, between literary and "low" levels of the second language (most notably when swearing or making declarations of love), all the while remaining linguistic puritans or purists in their native tongues. An irrepressible rebel from his adolescence onwards, Brodsky probably precociously seized such extensive poetic freedom, in Russian, that he did not really need this supplementary boost. At any rate, as an English-language poet and self-translator, Brodsky dared to wander farther, into American slang and even regionalisms, than nearly all other foreign writers who have adopted our language. He was perhaps a victim of this intrepidity from time to time. A telling example is his recurrent, not always euphonic, use of the verb "to ape," meaning "to imitate." In his defense, it is true that he often uses animal and, even more often, fish metaphors, usually while poking fun at a mankind hardly evolved, in manners, from our primate ancestors. In "Lullaby of Cape Cod," he notably remarks that "man survives like a fish, / stranded, beached, but intent / on adapting itself to some deep, cellular wish, / wriggling toward bushes, forming hinged leg-struts, then / to depart (leaving a track like the scrawl of a pen) / for the interior, the heart of the continent."

A glimpse into the poet's private life is in fact given in this allegorical scene, as occasionally elsewhere in a poetry otherwise eschewing direct confession (though remaining idiosyncratically personal in its tonalities and diction). "Odysseus to Telemachus" provides another instance of concealed avowal. That poem and a few others allude metaphorically to the long-lost son, from a failed marriage, whom Brodsky left behind in Russia when he emigrated. Such verse offers unexpected poignant moments in an oeuvre often leaping between philosophical high seriousness, melancholic lucidity, joking, celebrations of serendipity, and more discreet acknowledgements of good fortune. "It's strange to think of surviving," he admits almost in passing in one poem, "but that's what happened." Yet whereas few poets have so adamantly championed individual liberty and free will, there are nevertheless a surprising number of references to destiny in Brodsky; and they arise in settings not necessarily associated with Greeks and Romans, or their fatalistic philosophies. Also curiously, sometimes the Jewish-born poet addresses a Roman god, and there are remarkable Christmas poems based on the New Testament.

As an undeceived observer of two empires, as a prophetic chronicler of the end of one world and the onset of another (though some passages—in a key poem, "Fin de Siècle," and elsewhere—suggest we face only an ending), Brodsky is fascinated by how the past and the future interpenetrate. At first, his remarks about "the future that came" or the "different sort of fate...the one that you missed" seem to position his meditations on Time within an autobiographical context; leitmotivs of exile and travel support this impression. Yet the many trips abroad that Brodsky began taking after he had settled in the United States—not to mention his sojourns in Ann Arbor, New York City, and rural Massachusetts—inspire not traditional descriptive poetry set in a specific locality but rather far-ranging ruminations in which local details appear alongside other, disparate, perceptions, memories, insights, or speculations. Brodsky is unconcerned with viewing himself (or any "place") "as the hub of even a negligible universe"; even when he mentions "binoculars" and "gendarmes," his scope tends to encompass the supra-human.

As the focus of these poems shifts from past to future, then back again, the importance of the present is greatly relativized. One might say that Brodsky considers the present to be a point as defined by mathematical theory. Whereas other poets celebrate this point as it swells with what they intimate to be "fullness"—a "significance-beyond-appearances" presumed to linger despite the present's ever-fleeting nature—Brodsky views man's potentialities more circumspectly and more comically. The "socks and neckties" sold in a boutique on the Via Funari, for example, are "more indispensable" than he is—"from any standpoint," he adds, in case we thought he was joking. "Axiom," with its astrophysical allusions, harshens the message: "In shrieking beaks, in cumulus, in blazing pulsars none see, / the ear makes out a nagging 'No vacancy'." Other near-maxims about man's ephemerality and cosmic insignificance drive this point home. In "North of Delphi," to live is to be caught up in the process of vanishing: "To man, every perspective empties / itself of his silhouette, echo, smell."

Whereas much (especially European) poetry written since the Second World War has dealt with self-effacement, few writers attain the naturalness, even insouciance, of Brodsky's baroque detachment. "As I lie dying / here," he admits in "Törnfallet," "I'm eyeing / stars. Here's Venus; / no one between us." A poem like "A Photograph" combines vivid pictures of the poet's childhood ("We lived in a city tinted the color of frozen vodka") with a sobering appraisal of the lasting value of all these memories: "It's strange and not very pleasant / to think... / ...that life has been spent for the sake of an apotheosis / of the Kodak company, with its faith in prints / and jettisoning of the negatives." Such observations would be chilling in cynical poets, but in Brodsky—who can be funny, even giddy—communing with "absence" does not induce nihilism. This is why his poems seem to constitute, paradoxically, a new way of considering humanism.

* * *

Let us look at the language question from still another angle. Brodsky famously read American slang dictionaries, hunting for eccentric images and possible rhymes. The results are sometimes words, or juxtapositions of words, that test the limits of poetic license. This is the albeit vague criterion that has made some of us wrinkle our brows: when does the foreign poet, writing in English, trespass boundaries of legitimate linguistic inventiveness? For which lines, for which exact words, should Brodsky perhaps have heeded the (presumable) doubts of his co-translators or first Anglophone readers? In "May 24, 1980," translated by the author, Brodsky seemingly recalls his open-heart surgery: "Twice have drowned, thrice let knives rake my nitty-gritty." Note the proximity of the literary "thrice" and the slang "nitty-gritty." Note the knives that "rake." Note the way "nitty-gritty" has become, in Brodsky's mind, a synonym of, say, "guts." Of course, the poet is making a philosophical point: "nitty-gritty," in the meaning the term takes on in the expression "getting down to the nitty-gritty," posits the body—in general, matter—as the ultimate horizon or dead end of existence.

Brodsky's final collection, *So Forth,* again displays questionable verbal tenses, strange mixtures of high and low vocabularies, and other oddities—some charming or incisive, others irksome. Brodsky was an experimenter with meter and rhyme, in both Russian and English. What might be termed his cognitive exuberance justify some of these lapses and extravagances. Yet what about the "it blew" in "Star of Nativity," where even a preceding semi-colon cannot keep us from trying to attach—in vain—the pronoun to a noun in the previous line? Rereading the quatrain establishes "wind" as the phenomenon referred to by "it," and the confusion also stems from Brodsky's neglect (recurring elsewhere) of the past continuous tense. Did the perfective-imperfective dichotomy of the Russian verb system interfere with his apprehension of time in English? What about the cases where the exact meaning of the polysemous "one" is not rigorously delimited? Or where the boundaries of meaning marked out by certain words are trespassed? Should, moreover, a rhyme scheme permit Brodsky to treat English as it were an inflected language, as in a troublesome line, "at rites for our friends or acquaintances, now continuous," from the otherwise compelling "Brise Marine"? Brodsky's mature poetry, whether written directly in English or translated by himself from Russian originals, sometimes raises these stylistic and lexical questions. At times the questions become barriers, however slight or surmountable, to a full appreciation of a poem. This is much less true of his prose.

As has amply been seen, Brodsky was as conscious of his linguistic vulnerability in English as intrepid in his will to bend his second language to his poetic purposes. His awareness of the problem is also revealed, ironically, by the first line of "Infinitive," the opening poem of this final collection of twenty-one English poems and forty-three others translated from the Russian either by himself or with accomplices. Although set at a time when Europeans were first encountering Native Americans, "Infinitive" sums up the poet's two decades of living, as an exile, in the United States: "Dear savages," he begins, "though I've never mastered your tongue..., / I've learned to bake mackerel wrapped in palm leaves and favor raw turtle legs, / with their flavor of slowness." That "flavor of slowness" of course points up Brodsky's immense talent for surprising us with complex perceptions, dazzling juxtapositions, and profound aphorisms. "Everything leaves a spoor, / time especially," he notes for example in "Vertumnus." "Our rings are / those of fat trees with their prospective stump, / not the ones of a rustic round dance in the dooryard, / let along of a hug." In brief, we miss much if we refuse to accept Brodsky's language on its own terms: an occasionally eccentric, nonetheless powerful tool for exploring the human condition.

Of course, this dissonant, jubilant, linguistic provocativeness is pure Brodsky. His Marxist censors quite rightfully designated him as a glaring tumor infesting the cruelly policed, self-censoring, drabness of socialist realism. He obviously aims at teasing readers with words or images that are out of kilter; once again, one suspects the gratitude and glee with which he must have welcomed oddities into his lines. "Letters to a Roman Friend" is a free adaptation of (or evocation of) verse by Martial. Here the translator, George L. Kline, surely working with Brodsky's approval, writes:

> Pontus drones past a black fence of pine trees.
> > Someone's boat braves gusts out by the promontory.
> On the garden bench a book of Pliny rustles.
> > Thrushes chirp within the hairdo of the cypress.

Given the classical setting, the colloquial "hairdo" amuses, as it jars, the ear—a lively twist reminiscent of Martial's own Latin poetry. Even more exuberantly grating is this wacky pastiche, translated by the author, of both children's fables and Homer's "rose-fingered dawn": "Like the mouse creeping out of the scarlet crack, / the sunset gnaws hungrily the electric / cheese of the outskirts."

What is at stake, philosophically, in such a style? What is the underlying implication of Brodsky's typical alignments of disparate perceptions? In what way do his poems, frequently commemorating a specific date or occasion and rigorously modeled on a classical poetic form, cohere in detail? Are the details linked to one another? Why do separate perceptions so often, in Brodsky, tend to remain closed off, or almost, from others in the same poem? Here is an example from "Lullaby of Cape Cod":

> It's stifling. And the thick leaves' rasping sound
> is enough all by itself to make you sweat.
> What seems to be a small dot in the dark
> could only be one thing—a star. On the deserted ground

of a basketball court a vagrant bird has set
its fragile egg in the steel hoop's raveled net.
There's a smell of mint now, and of mignonette.

Countless similar passages gather sundry sense perceptions around a single moment of passing time—a moment thereby revealed in all its frenetic complexity. Yet what lies beyond this complexity? Between the lines, between these acute and compact "accelerations," lurks the void. Each highly crafted line, combining images, thoughts, and sensations, acts as a butterfly-like "buffer" preserving us from nothingness; yet the remarkable lack of transitions, in much of Brodsky's poetry, can slowly but surely make us aware of an ominous, interpenetrating, emptiness traversing the entire oeuvre. The poem "Nature morte" explicitly confirms this:

Summing their angles up
as a surprise to us,
things drop away from man's
world—a world made up with words.

Things do not move, or stand.
That's our delirium.
Each thing's a space, beyond
which there can be no thing.

For all the pleasure that we derive from Brodsky's poems, these glimpses into the abysm can leave us with lasting tremors. In a relatively late poem, "An Admonition," he confronts this troubling fundamental dichotomy, in which he eventually discerns a justification for writing:

when you shudder at how infinitesimally small you are,
remember: space that appears to need nothing does
crave, as a matter of fact, an outside gaze,
a criterion of emptiness—of its depth and scope.
And it's only you who can do the job.

Such a responsibility demands great courage. It is no easy thing to adopt this "criterion of emptiness" as one's poetics, indeed as one's raison d'être. For Brodsky, his ability to imagine his own permanent absence, his self-effacement, all while feeling the deepest gratitude for existing, was probably the rich personal and philosophical quality that made all the difference in what must have been, at times, an excruciating inner duel. It is to his honor that his affirming propensities were finally able to overcome, in nearly every poem, a no less compelling attraction to nothingness—even as one who is dizzy, admiring the landscape, strives not to be drawn over the ledge, into the chasm.

Subjective Realism and Lyrical Urgency
(Tatiana Shcherbina)

The arresting title—*Life Without*—encompassing the Bloodaxe selection of poems and mini-essays by the Russian poet Tatiana Shcherbina (b. 1954) essentially refers to the theme of lost love running movingly through several pieces in the first, and most substantial, section of the book. "Life without you is neglected, ramshackle, / cheap and simply unapproachable," begins the title poem, "nightmarish like a provincial grocer's shack, / frozen through in a light summer mac, / without feeling, without right of appeal, / and judgment day, every second signed and sealed." But it is never clear what has caused the amorous destruction, estrangement, or disappearance. A narrative mystery prevails as the poet, faced with her lover's absence, writes with an effusiveness that may surprise readers used to more arch evocations of contemporary liaisons. A neo-Romantic exaltation rises from several pages of *Life Without*, and an aesthetics rooted in the most personal manifestations of European lyric poetry. Shcherbina is unafraid of penning lines like: "I want to be with you till the very last day / and afterwards. Afterwards, if it's allowed."

This is not to say that her verse is mere declaration, exclamation, longing, or lament. In the preceding quotation, skepticism already qualifies and restrains, like an afterthought, her erotic and eschatological *élan*. A line like "I'm complete when I kiss, otherwise a spit / threaded with meat and given to thought" is similarly characteristic of her simultaneous predilection for well-targeted wit, audacious images, lucid self-portraiture, and sharply detailed metaphors drawing on the objects or surfaces of the outside world. These objects and surfaces—what is suddenly and acutely perceived *over there*, beyond emotional turmoil—often become compelling correlatives of that turmoil. "The whole town is lit by my desire," she writes for instance, "all the streets are my traces." And we see the houses, flowers, and shrubs, before being reminded of their (and thus her) "misery / and other senselessness." Self-observation belongs to these dialectics of the innermost self and objective reality, for to apperceive oneself is to perceive the self as another person who is both inside and outside, in the past and in the present. "I drank some coffee," avows the narrator, "ate a biscuit, swallowed down / a gulp, even managed to get pissed, / changed the locks, moved the furniture around, / (. . .) / all to no avail—the pain won't go."

This blend of strong present feelings and banal yet personally significant everyday details is certainly far removed from the Marxism and Soviet Realism in which Shcherbina's formative years must have steeped. In one of her mini-essays, she claims to be a follower of "subjective realism," and the phrase instructively sums up what often goes on here. (Her short prose is less striking and explicitly autobiographical than the poems, but it delineates the political and cultural contexts in which she has worked.) Elsewhere, she notes that "in outward feelings acquisition prevails, in inward feelings loss does." The unresolved struggle of extroversion, desire, and hope against introversion and despair correspondingly adds tension and ambivalence to certain pieces. Tellingly, a "marathon" in which Shcherbina runs actually involves sitting at a table and drinking Cointreau. The metaphor of a group race is poignantly restored in the final strophe when "in the night's dark desert / a vowel stands out in front— / 'I' refuse to run like this— / quite alone in the world." By the way, Shcherbina is one of the Russian translators of Mallarmé, and she shares with the Frenchman a hypersensitivity to the fundamental elements of language, notably sound and the letters of the alphabet. The preceding lines are hardly the only ones where language per se is given a special focus, almost as if it were an independent, disincarnated entity, a "pure" Mallarméan concept.

These more abstract notions concerning the philosophy of language can be spotted in Shcherbina's work, but they do not distract from the authenticity of the unelucidated love story or stories at stake, which convince from the onset. Moreover, the poet expresses her yearning ("Passion is always more urgent," she confesses) in graphic contemporary settings that include, not only Russia, but also France, where she lived between 1992 and 1997, before returning to "the land where only curses are heard." (She also sojourned in Munich.) Her recent poems are boldly up-to-date (with "packets of hankies" and computer "kilobytes"), provocative in diction (a "Holy shit" here, a "fuck-all" there), and thus world-wise as well as sometimes world-weary. Shcherbina writes from the perspective of a Russian who grew up during the Cold War of the 1960s, suffered through the artistic "inner emigration" of the 1970s, experienced the cultural and democratic breakthroughs of Gorbachev's Perestroika, then traveled and lived abroad before resettling in her hometown, Moscow, with which she necessarily entertains a sort of intimate relationship at one remove.

At any rate, conspicuous in her poems are unringing telephones, answering machines, and distant or broken-off dialogues. The vicissitudes of love are of course often at the source of anguished solitude ("I waited out eternity in the entrance hall— / tormented by the telephone"), but the dates at the bottom of her poems suggest a growing, less self-oriented, concern not only with "the past's speech" which the poet hears "intravenously" (a stunning synaesthetic image), but also now with an ugly, depressing, and robotic present in which "Russia is no more—only Ru.net is left." Perhaps more readily than many European poets of her generation, the individualistic Shcherbina—in her recent verse—has taken up the challenge put forth by globalization (and globalized English) to traditional (specifically Russian) poetic topics and time-tested norms of stylistic beauty.

Other kinds of "withoutness," such as moral emptiness and contemporary vacuity, indeed crop up increasingly. So also do silence, ennui, asphyxiation, "dead ends and compromises." She asks whether "every passed day [is] a plus or a minus" and perceives that "life has caved in, / has started to resemble a sine-wave graph, / a wearying numbness, a hunched back."

Though there are a couple of misprints and one or two obscurities, Sasha Dugdale's translation in the Bloodaxe selection is generally vivid. As is usually the case with Russian poetry, the rhyme schemes defy a full rendering, but this British version does not shy away from them entirely. Skillful rhymes, half-rhymes, and other formal prosodic features enable us to obtain a good sense of the oft-passionate, ever-engaging originals. Though quite distinct from the dissident prose and poetry of her predecessors, Shcherbina's writings have been considered subversive in her homeland.

* * *

J. Kates's vigorous and resourceful translation of Shcherbina's *Null Null* (1991) and several other poems has now appeared as *The Score of the Game* (Zephyr). The volume includes a translator's introduction that usefully explains the evolution of Russian poetry since Joseph Brodsky, whom Shcherbina in fact met and to whom she has dedicated at least one poem. (Moreover, he is mentioned in one other poem here and probably discreetly alluded to in others.) It is impossible for me to judge which English translation is better. I learned more about Shcherbina's formal structures from Dugdale; perhaps sensed her force and spontaneity more in Kates. But I can give counterexamples for both propensities. Kates, for example, cleverly provides an equivalent of the Russian rhyme scheme in this twelve-line piece:

> What about the branching nervous system
> Of the world's overwhelming swagger-itch,
> At the borderline of skillful coitus—
> Life remains incomparably rich.
>
> Pussycat-scat! Sweet names in little flocks
> Follow along like a handful of tykes.
> O most trivial of human habits—
> The dehumanization of decent folks.
>
> All love is a notorious specific
> Against its own particular life of crime:
> Membership in an otherworldly species
> Speaks in gestures of an earlier time.

As to the "Life Without You" poem that Dugdale also renders (see above), Kates has: "Life without you is neglected and wretched, / cheap and as much as untouchable / nightmarish like a general store in Podunk, / chilled to the bone in a cold little coat, / hard-hitting and pitiless, / a terrible judgment, handed down every minute." The inventive "Podunk" (as opposed to "provincial grocer's shack") is impressive, but Dugdale staunchily rhymes "shack" and "mac," skillfully alliterates "every second signed and sealed," all the while agreeably half-rhyming "appeal" and "sealed." It's a toss-up.

As is evident here, the poems of *The Score of the Game* once again brilliantly reveal Shcherbina's rich vocabulary, which draws on numerous lexical sources and levels of diction. Kates has enthusiastically rendered the ambience of liberty and unbridledness, rapidly changing perspectives, flashing imagery, leaps of thought, and departures—or, more appropriately, exiles—as linguistic, emotional, and existential as they are geographical. Yet as in the mature verse of that preeminent master of departures, Rimbaud, close inspection reveals that Shcherbina's kaleidoscopic effects are often highly—that is, musically—controlled. They can obtain even when there are firm rhymes (in the original), as in this excerpt:

> No need for bullets, the heart explodes on its own.
> It thinks about dragging itself into voluntary
> exile. Take Anacin? No, on its own.
> Ocean is it into you I stick my fork,
> Or into a schnitzel, into cottage cheese?
> October swimming past in the Milky Way,
> An organism chilled to the bone
> And untouched.

Both Kates and Dugdale show very well how Shcherbina's language is so heightened that it defies reality to be so intrepid.

* * *

Readers of French but not Russian can gain even more access to her poetry by procuring *Parmi les alphabets* (1992), *L'Âme déroutée* (1995), and *Antivirus* (2005). The first and third titles, published respectively by Le Castor Astral and L'Idée bleue, gather Christine Zeytounian-Beloüs's fine translations of verse originally written in Russian by the poet, whereas *L'Âme déroutée* (also L'Idée bleue) is a collection of twenty-four poems and prose poems written by Shcherbina in French.

Parmi les alphabets opens with a cry remotely recalling the spirit of famous opening lines of Allen Ginsberg's *Howl*. "What's happening?" asks Shcherbina, "An epoch is ending. / Everyone dear to me is in danger and faraway, / while the earth is about to collapse / beneath evil, misfortune, delirium. / Everyday a messenger speaks to us / of corrosion, of loss, / every day is the end / of bread, the air, and our kin / whose blood is spilled, / who lose their minds, / everything ends, the light and the water, / slowly but surely but also suddenly."

This book also comprises a poem dedicated to Brodsky. This rather obvious genealogical affiliation is thus officially acknowledged, and signs of it recur elsewhere, in different ways. Brodsky and the author of *Natiurmort s prevrashcheniiami* (Still Life with Transformations, 1985) possess a common love for whimsy, the classical (especially Greco-Roman) heritage, philosophical allusion, multi-layered metaphors, and formal patterns. The mentor could have signed his student's claim: "I play my typewriter like a legendary dulcimer." But Shcherbina, whom the avant-garde critic Boris Yukananov has nicknamed "the Phythian priestess of entire generation," also, of course, stands firmly in a here and now quite different from the one in which Brodsky—who was forced to emigrate to the United States in 1972—lived during his most productive adult years. In the long poem "Eastern Koan," translated by Kates, these lines, among several others, echo Brodsky all the while emphasizing a contemporary harshness: "everything welled up from my gullet spewed on the railroad quay, / and howls through this throat as through an Aeolian pipe." (Compare Brodsky's "Yet until brown clay has been crammed down my larynx, / only gratitude will be gushing from it.") The other French collection, *Antivirus*, includes several astute poems involving computers and virtual reality, notably in the context of love. The following lines from "Enlacement" ("Embrace" in English) read: "What joy to turn off her computer. / It's better than embracing an idiot. / (…) / The computer tenderly caresses you with its keys, / it closes its eyes and moans languishingly / as if you were already stripping. / (…) / I send it / bouquets of letters in Times New Roman, / its compresses them, sticks them in files / and its screen radiates with satisfaction" (my translation).

Apropos, the title of Shcherbina's *Lazurnaya Skrizhal'* (2003), a collection from which poems have been selected for *Life Without*, has several connotations, ranging from the Ancient World to our *monde informatique*. Depending on the context, the word "skrizhal'" means "tablet of stone" (like Moses's), "scroll," "annals," even "chronicles." It is a place (usually stone) where sacred letters are written. "Azure," "sea-blue," or "sky blue" are possible translations of "lazurnyi," but Shcherbina also refers here to a computer screen. A paraphrase of the title might thus be: *The Sky-Blue Computer Screen Tablet*.

Shcherbina's poems are often built out of bursts of images, thoughts, and exclamations, more than long interconnected arguments. Puns, prosody and sometimes rhyme tie strands together, more than single coherent narratives, transitions, or logical sequencings. Among her several other talents, Shcherbina has an aphoristic turn of mind. "Language is as exiguous as the body," she notes in "The Garden," for instance, "which is enough to make you want to hang yourself, to flee language." "The times are hard, nervous, and political," she remarks elsewhere, "whatever the conclusion, it's not practical." When she evokes "thallus" in her homonymous poem, even defining the botanical term in an epigraph, she probably self-describes or at least hints at her own poetics, especially as regards her more effusive long poems: "the undifferentiated stemless, rootless, leafless plant body characteristic of thallophytes." That's the definition, from the *American Heritage Dictionary*, quoted by Kates, who also renders this poem. "To speak someone else's tongue in syntactical ignorance," it begins, "collecting words for the joy of connection and sense / Poesy! Mesopotamia! Archipidèx!"

With these lines, the reader is ready for Shcherbina's French poems. They exhibit the characteristic themes of her oeuvre and, impressively, the same provocative verve. When one dares to write in a foreign language, one can be cautious or audacious. Shcherbina is very audacious. Sometimes even more than her Russian verse, the French poems illustrate her love for *jeux de mots*, consonance, assonance, and half-whimsical, half-serious (and sometimes half-ominous) juxtapositions. Popping up in the middle of her long poem "À vue d'oiseau," for example, are these typical lines: "Et la nuit donne des mirages, / "irages (aller au future, rages, âges) — / le chant du cygne se termine toujours en echo." This perception involves a coined word, "irages," which is based on the future tense of the verb "aller" ("j'irai" means "I will go") and also suggests "errance," "wandering." Four words echo, as "mirages" passes to "irages," and then on to "rages" and "âges," before the poet adds that "the swan's song also ends in an echo." This is not the only piece in which Shcherbina at once describes and struggles, indeed rages, against self-imprisoning cycles, repetitions, permutations—here, "echoes."

An even more complex series of puns concludes the prose text "Point," the simple yet immediately polysemous title of which already announces certain variations to come. Here is the final passage, explainable but surely untranslatable:

> Les "e" muets, les oeufs muets. La différence: la liaison. Elle passe entre. Elle entre, elle passe. Je la suis. C'est ma chasse, ma passion. Et mes fruits de la passion ne sont point fruits pressés. Point. Point—le trompe-l'oeil le plus répandu.

Evoking one of the most important elements of French prosody, the mute "e," Shcherbina first juxtaposes the plural "les 'e' muets" with "les oeufs muets," literally "mute eggs" but also almost "les oeufs mollets" ("soft-boiled eggs"). She adds this equivalence: "The difference: the liaison." This alludes to the phonetic and prosodic sense of "liaison," but also already to the amorous connotation of the term. (And "les oeufs muets" now perhaps retrospectively takes on such connotations as well.) After this, Shcherbina writes: "It (the liaison, but also now "she," a woman) passes between." In the next sentence, "entre" as "between" is turned into the verb "entre": "It / she enters, it / she passes." The next two sentences announce: "I follow it / her. It's my hunt, my passion." The final three sentences play with the various meanings of "point." The first sense or function is that of a grammatical negation element: "And my passion fruits are not (at all) pressed fruits," where "pressed fruits"—besides as an obvious sexual image—also connotes "fruit juices," as in "orange pressé" or "citron pressé," and where "passion fruits" can arguably also be read, not as a particular tropical fruit, but rather as "fruits of passion." This is because of the preceding paragraph, which begins: "When I pick the fruits of reason, they are black mushrooms or red currants." The second, single, "point" then echoes the reinforced negation of the passion fruit image and also means "period." To these two meanings of "point," the final sentence then adds that of a mathematical point, noting that "(a) point" is "the most frequent trompe-l'oeil." This quip offers an apt way of thinking of Shcherbina: a strong-willed poet who considers any final point to be an illusion, ever aspires to freedom and infinity, and seeks to peer through sham. *Life Without, The Score of the Game*, and the three French volumes comprise work published as late as 2004, with *Antivirus* including some recent work that is not yet available in English. One senses a sensitive, quick-minded, and evolving poet, and it will be interesting to see where she goes from here.

Estonia

Of Home and Hereness
(Jaan Kaplinski)

Evening Brings Everything Back is a splendid volume generously selecting work from three books by Jaan Kaplinski (b. 1941), an important Estonian poet and essayist. The touching, thought-provoking poems and short prose texts often masterfully reveal the mysteries underlying simple phenomena, both household and natural. Blooming wood sorrel, for example, characteristically induces him to wonder why "something primeval and strange / …occasionally — but furtively, evasively — / touches you."

Not just evoking, but indeed meditating upon this sentiment of strangeness defines Kaplinski's poetics. He chances upon, say, "a birch leaf / lying on the sauna floor" or "light refracted / sideways through my wife's iris" and seeks out the hidden implications. Stylistically limpid, his poems ask deep questions and emphasize enigmas. Getting off a bus and gazing up at "the stars / and the sickle of the new moon," for instance, remind the poet of a former fleeting love and make him ponder why it is easier to remember a certain "blue" of the night sky than "names, titles or faces, / even the faces of those you once loved."

The simplicity of such verse, translated by the poet and Fiona Sampson, is deceiving. Many poems are informed by extremely precise scientific knowledge. Kaplinski knows languages, has traveled widely, and is curious about different cultures, including that of the Saamis dwelling above the Arctic Circle. As he reflects on his and others' daily riddles, notably the possibility that "heaven actually begins / here at this very place," he searches for an ever-greater ecological and spiritual understanding of this "hereness," of this "simply what is," as he puts it. This ultimately self-relativizing quest is especially engaging. It is no easy trick to develop ideas in poems, without belaboring an ideology. A student of Eastern religion and Western science, as well as of world poetry, Kaplinski accomplishes this feat admirably, as he investigates what "home" on this earth might more profoundly mean.

Peeling Back the Veneer
(Jaan Kross)

Armchair diplomats and exacting connoisseurs of that all-too-rare delicacy, the subtle historical novel, will be delighted by *Professor Martens' Departure* (1984), the second book by the Estonian poet and novelist Jaan Kross (1920-2007) to be translated into English. Following *The Czar's Madman* (1978), which was published in 1993 in an equally vivid translation by Anselm Hollo, this new, often dreamlike novel, set in the first decade of the twentieth century but sometimes reaching back long before those years, traces the fears and fantasies of a foreign affairs expert, Professor Friedrich Fromhold Martens, who is taking a very long train ride through Czarist Russia.

Removed from pressing cares and thus obtaining a detached perspective on himself and the world, Martens takes stock, muses over past achievements and failings, worries about his cardiac arrhythmia, and eventually imparts his introspections to a total stranger, a "rosy oval face like a cameo against the purple velvet of the headrest." This lovely face notwithstanding, Professor Martens remains alone for most of his trip, so that his avowals are made mentally mainly to his absent wife, Kati, to whom he is traveling. "Have I not been candid with you until now?" he asks, repeatedly conjuring up her specter to his troubled mind.

Gripped by what he first calls merely an "*ordinary* fear of death," the professor, near retirement, plunges into his deepest feelings, concealed by decades of success as a famously "neutral" arbitrator of international disputes. As he peels back his professional veneer, he discovers frustrations, sentiments of insecurity and inferiority, even doubts about his identity as an Estonian. A recent encyclopedia article questioning his intellectual honesty further embitters him. The author of the article, a colleague named Vodozov, blossoms into a redoubtable mental nemesis as the train chugs onward.

Martens must also own up to a few adulteries, one of which (with Yvette, a young art student met in Brussels while he is participating in a congress against slavery) inspires two beautiful chapters full of discreet, sensual images. A few days after an excursion to a beach, described with gentle, touching modesty, the couple make love in Yvette's garret studio, "the thin alcove curtain softening the gaslight." Yet once he has returned to Russia, Martens loses contact with her. A few years later, he learns that he had fathered her child. In the meantime Yvette has married a young man, also named Martens, and departed, without otherwise leaving a trace, to the Congo.

Kross knits his web of plots and parallel plots even more intricately by christening the child "Frédéric," a coincidence that can only further disturb the professor. Martens has indeed long been obsessed with a "double" named Georg Friedrich Martens, a German specialist in international law who died in 1821. Events in the two men's lives, although separated by 89 years, display uncanny similarities, to the extent that the professor anxiously wonders whether he might be a "reincarnation," a "shadowy variant of [his] predecessor." Hallucinated scenes from his deceased doppelgänger's life naturally oblige him to count up the exact amount of time presumably left for him to live.

This refined, complex, thoroughly engaging novel is not without political allusions to the Soviet Union of the early 1980s; the author himself spent nine years in exile and labor camps after his arrest by the Soviets in 1946. More pertinent to the plot of *Professor Martens' Departure*, however, is how the main character's casual, urbane retrospections are artfully transformed, by the final chapters, into intense visions of finality. One even wonders: Did he actually take the trip? The novel concludes with an ambiguous scene, which leaves one with the impression that the professor, like a drowning man, has dreamt his entire existence in a single, at once terrifying and reassuring, moment. These qualities, moreover, perk one's curiosity about Kross's poetry from the 1960s, never translated into English and highly regarded in his homeland.

Finland

Finnish Poets and their Greek Dichotomies (Pentti Saarikoski, Tua Forsström, Paavo Haavikko, and others)

It is an apt coincidence that a translation of Pentti Saarikoski's quirkily erudite, soul-searching, yet also frank and down-to-earth *Trilogy* (1996), penned in Finnish on the chilly Swedish island of Tjörn, has been finely produced in hot, sandy New Mexico by La Alameda Press. This geographical paradox sums up amusingly the ultimately endearing (if sometimes irritating) Saarikoski (1937-1983), who traveled far and wide during his too short lifetime and had a marked predilection for the "topsy-turvy." He was also—to cite another warm and dusty spot—the foremost Finnish translator of ancient Greek literature. He rendered Aristotle's *Poetics*, Sappho's poems, epigrams from *The Greek Anthology*, some of Euripides's plays (and Plato's dialogues), and especially fragments of his beloved Heraclitus, whom he appointed "a staff member of [his] poetry." "What I'm after are the dead," he revealingly remarks, "and unborn gods / Nothing very problematic about the era of angels / in which we now live." Besides Greek, which deeply informed the directness and essence-seeking qualities of his verse, he translated from Italian (notably Italo Calvino), Norwegian, Swedish, German (Bertolt Brecht), and extensively from English. From our literature, his renderings comprised books by Henry Miller, Saul Bellow, J. D. Salinger, Philip Roth, John Barth, Anais Nin, and Allen Ginsberg. He put John Lennon into Finnish and—as tellingly—James Thurber.

Astonishingly, the only translator in the world to have rendered both *The Odyssey* and James Joyce's *Ulysses* still found time to be a prolific, maliciously provocative poet. In the *Trilogy*, he likens writing to being "in the woods looking for mushrooms" and not just taking "the cap," but also "the stalk and the volva / even the mycelium." He believes that "the writer of a book needs to be interrupted / or it'll be a bad book." Whence his awareness that some of his poems might seem pleasant (or trenchant) hodgepodges of ideas, allusions, quotations, musings, little narratives, sensations, and facts—each of these rhetorical figures "interrupting" the logic established by its predecessor.

Yet to the reader of *Trilogy*, it becomes clear that Saarikoski carefully crafts these heterogeneous elements into valid mirrors of his thinking processes, moods, yearnings, and perceptions; and links the poems together into coherent narrative sequences. He is concerned about exploring different levels of consciousness, notably as the mind passes from visions, memories, or ruminations to more objective appraisals of the outside world. Hence, lines describing Ulysses ("who had himself tied to the mast") induce political questions ("He saved his country / but from what / and for what / do means sanctify the end?"), and then abruptly terminate in the factual: "Birds appear in the air / this fine evening."

Trilogy is his last and most absorbing volume. Some of Saarikoski's early poems are simplistic, now dated (in their too narrow espousing of the 1960s Zeitgeist), and misguided—especially his Communist verse. However, he later distanced himself from his initial allegiances, which were not that rigid, after all. He eventually got into trouble with Communist hardliners, because what he clearly loved most of all were writing, thinking, learning languages, feeling aliveness, and—as is well known—occasionally drinking himself away from these strong sensations. One of his virtues was the ability to call himself into question, and evolve. As Anselm Hollo explains in a thoughtful foreword to his engaging translation, Saarikoski's initial work (*Out Loud, The Red Flags, I Look Out over Stalin's Head, Walking Wherever, Letter to My Wife, The Time in Prague*, and especially *What is Really Going On*) need to be understood in a much deeper context. Hollo shows how these books relate to the intricately structured and semantically rich *Trilogy*, which brings together *The Dance Floor on the Mountain* (1977), *Invitation to the Dance* (1980), and *The Dark One's Dances* (1983).

Conspicuously, a labyrinth appears and reappears. Sometimes the Minotaur, its intimidating occupant, suggests an existential anxiety at the heart of Saarikoski's project. But at the same time, the poet already aims at getting though the maze—the three books form a sort of initiation rite—and thereby attaining liberation: a "dance" that has several imaginable metaphorical senses. He mentions "a tetrahedron made out of sticks / a landmark for me to find my way / to the dance floor / and through the labyrinth / home." The key reference occurs when the poet walks down to the seashore. "The birds leave a tree / suddenly, as if it were shedding leaves," he writes, "and I feel cold / I simplify the world / into a labyrinth / in whose heart dwells the panting minotaur / (...) // Only when the minotaur has been destroyed / and the labyrinth transformed into dance / polity, politics / will be possible again." The Minotaur is much greater than the dangers threatening a single self.

A sensibility is thus taking stock of humankind as well as himself. Saarikoski is more of a philosopher (and even a theologian) than one might suspect. (Interestingly, he also translated the Gospel of Matthew.) "Grief without content / is hard to bear," he confesses, for instance, "but I still, still want to see / everything in another light, the sea's light." Elsewhere he notes: "the harmony of the evening / equals the balance of terror within me / but the peace of the mountains." I have added a period here, but there is no period in the original—the thought breaks off without even an ellipsis. This struggle between affirmation and negation—so characteristic of postwar European poets even of distinct poetic, philosophical, or spiritual orientations—is an underlying theme of *Trilogy*, which touches upon pantheism, Christianity, philosophical materialism, and even gnosticism. Did Saarikoski resolve the dialectic? He wavers between devastating truths like "Heaven humbles itself // and thought // leads nowhere // we are forever // lost" and—on the very next page—"I believe it is possible to find a way out of these woods." The last poem ("Post Scriptum"), which begins "and so I have made the Dark One / dance / and so I have driven him into anguish / his cave," can long be pondered.

* * *

Not every Finnish poet writes in Finnish. The mother tongue of five percent of the population is Swedish, which is also the second official language. (Russian was also once an important language.) Moreover, as Anni Sumari explains in *How to Address the Fog: XXV Finnish Poems*, modernism began earlier in Finland-Swedish poetry than in its Finnish counterpart. Sumari recalls the role of Edith Södergran (1892-1923), who began writing in German—to add still another language to the Finnish Tower of Babel—and then switched to Swedish. (Bloodaxe brought out her *Complete Poems*, translated by David McDuff, in 1984.) "In her poetry," notes Sumari, "the voice of modern lyricism was heard for the first time in Finland."

Tua Forsström (b. 1947) is a leading representative of this Finland-Swedish tradition. Her *I Studied Once at a Wonderful Faculty* (2003), now translated by McDuff and Stina Katchadourian, includes a new sequence plus three previous books: *Snow Leopard* (1987), *The Parks* (1992), and *After Spending a Night among Horses* (1998). The volume amply presents a poet who situates her pensive poems amidst daily life yet who often narrates them from oblique or abstract angles. This effect emphasizes estrangement. The opening lines of a poem that eventually mentions benches, barking dogs, "a summer kitchen // with radio news for blowing curtains," and her mother's empty bedroom, is typical:

> There is a certain kind of loss
> and September's objectivity
>
> Something is released imperceptibly,
> and is displaced: it does not
>
> matter. There is a coolness
> that has settled on surfaces...

Whether dealing with loss, love, or landscape, Forsström focuses on quiet moments concealing intense struggles between despair and a re-mustering of one's will to live or one's faith in the possibilities of genuine amorous union. One poem pictures despair bluntly as "so great that it cannot be seen: a smoke / in our breath on cold days." And the same piece concludes with despair as enclosure, entrapment, "as inescapable / as ice, the fishes' white-shimmering sky." Like Saarikoski, the dichotomy of affirmation and negation, of hope and illusion (the beautiful and promising white-shimmering sky that is actually an impenetrable roof of ice) characterizes Forsström's poems. Most of them are untitled, which underscores the openness of ultimate meanings.

Another telltale piece relates a taxi ride during which the poet suddenly sees the young driver's cheeks as stating: "it really exists." This "it" becomes a "nocturnal music" that "flows along the ice-cold road"; in other words, a love- and life-asserting melody that persists despite the negating night of intractable solitude; hope has gained the advantage. Forsström then envisions "rags and masks [falling]," an indication that two human beings can sincerely encounter each other. Yet this is not all. Her poetry often ends with a complex image that adds ambiguity or uncertainty. "There we are eye against eye," she observes, before defining herself and the driver as "ashes against rain."

This same unfolding of unexpected positive and negative facets occurs in a subtle poem that lends a line to the title of the entire collection. The poem sets the "wonderful faculty" at which the poet studied "long ago" (a pall is already cast here) and "a lake that makes the passer-by / giddy" against the arresting line "It is painful not to remember / with pain anymore" as well as a sight of "terrified / . . . hunters at the edge of the night." Once again, Forsström keeps the angst ominous by not naming it. Yet she shows elsewhere that one must surpass this existential dilemma; getting beyond it, which demands acceptance of one's finitude, is the noble challenge of living. "There's a door into the / dark," she declares, as if remembering a vanquished childhood fear: "one gets used to it." And in lines conjuring up the same "Dark One" that haunted Saarikoski, she offers a compelling summary of the perpetual conflict:

> It's easy to get attached to anything: a few
> knick-knacks and poor shoes, a horse.
> The Dark Companion follows us
> The sense of defeat follows us
> But on clear days I see the shore through
> a pattern cut in tissue paper!
> On clear days I don't see anything!

* * *

How to Address the Fog is an originally conceived gathering of lively po- ems—one per poet and variously translated by McDuff, Donald Adamson, and Robin Fulton. Sumari's introduction charts the development of Finnish poetry, from the age-old oral folklore collected in *The Kalevala* (first published in 1849), through the subjectivity and toned-down diction of modernist free verse, and from there to the today's rebellious underground scene. In contrast to other anthologies of European poetry, Sumari has made the excellent decision to include both verse and "poetic prose"—such as the varied pieces written by Sirkka Turkka (b. 1939), Mirkka Rekola (b. 1931), Markku Paasonen (b. 1967), and especially the grimly hilarious monologue about noisy apartment building neighbors that is composed by Arto Melleri (b. 1956). In contemporary European literature, "poetry" hardly consists exclusively of work with line breaks; "short prose" no longer necessarily implies "fiction" or "short story."

Sumari notes that the prose poem "is one of the central trends in contemporary Finnish poetry." "One main reason for [its] strength," she explains, "may be the nature of the Finnish language: the words are relatively long, and numerous inflections are added.... On the other hand, Finnish is adept at yielding neologisms whose associative and auditory qualities seem natural to the reader and are easily understood." I must add that in French, a language that also hosts much "prose poetry," the opposite is true: words are relatively short, inflections few, and neologisms difficult to form. The prosodic, phonetic, and narrative questions raised by "poetic prose," whose roots are in fact ancient and multilingual, continue to defy critical responses.

Saarikoski and Forsström are present in the anthology, alongside twenty-three poets writing in Finnish or Finland-Swedish. The title comes from the important modernist Paavo Haavikko (b. 1931), who writes in a characteristically aphoristic poem:

> War is time that has marched through the mind, and is later presented in
>   such a way that boots are the be-all and end-all.
> Thus it is important to teach the soldier exactly how to treat the ghosts, how
>   to address the fog, or
> how time and space appear on paper to describe absolutely everything.
> Do not say that was true in antiquity, as there the same sentence changed
>   many times, petrified into mountains,
> precisely where it was open...

Haavikko's indebtedness to ancient Greek literature can be contrasted not only with Saarikoski's, but also with the latter's own aphoristic style and concern for the polis. Judging from their writings, their sensibilities (and perhaps their politics) stand at antipodes; yet in vivid ways, both Finns mingle exceedingly well with ancient Greek poets and thinkers in the agora. Haavikko's *Selected Poems* are available from Carcanet in Hollo's fine versions. Combining insights into history and politics, meditations on love and death, and reflections about the *raisons d'être* of writing, the poems reveal a lucid and ironic skepticism about living, war, peace, sexual attraction, and death.

Otherwise, the anthology includes "The Orange Glow," by Lassi Nummi (b. 1928). The poem impresses with its multi-chromatic reflections on death and its leitmotiv of a mysterious "great orange light" that synaesthetically

> ...peals through everything.
> As I walk down the slope
> I see greenness that soon will thin to grey, see
> the forest opposite, as utterly black
> as the caves of sleep. How thin are the lines that draw death's silhouette
> where blue-eyed lamps peer out, the eyes of life.
> Thus abide these two—the arc of our incandescence,
> the self
> that owns the world, and the eye, prisoner of the world, free
> in the flash of an eye-blink.

Creating a different metaphysical atmosphere is a collage-like poem by Anne Hänninen (b. 1958). She asks this riveting question about and gratitude for being alive while we are alive: "Do you go entirely when you go? No one can go on your behalf. Though on your behalf the whole world existed." Also noteworthy is a touching piece by the widely translated Finland-Swedish poet Bo Carpelan (b. 1926), who describes meeting, in Monterey, an old Finn who had settled long ago in the United States. The man has forgotten his native Swedish and now speaks only a little Russian. He wants to know if there are still oak forests in his homeland, for "when the wind moves through an oak forest, you remember that, always."

Because several languages have already been cited, let me conclude by mentioning Juhani Koskinen (b. 1972), who writes in a Northern Finnish dialect. This linguistic choice may seem quaint, but it is not. Are there American poets, aged thirty-five, who work in some sort of equivalent patois and express contemporary disgust, cynicism, and insouciance? Adamson has carried off the feat of rendering "Irvikuva kreikkalaisesta korkokuvasta"—I cannot resist quoting those long Finnish words—into Scots. I hasten to add that Koskinen, too, has discovered Greece; he pens a "caricature" of a Greek relief. Here are the concluding lines, which evoke ominous "nicht-birds"—once again, those negative forces—singing "maist bonnily":

> A'm stretcht oot on ma ain mattress in cool darkness, under a reindeer skin
> and A ken how folk in thir loneliness cease tae care.
> How in the end it disnae maitter.
> ...
> A see the void. And intae the void A piss a map o the warld
> For aa the dugs tae sniff at.

Norway

A Poetry of Acceptance
(Rolf Jacobsen)

Sensitive to the natural world, to everyday city life, and metaphysically inclined, Rolf Jacobsen (1907-1994) was one of Norway's premier modernists. He does not so much announce or bewail the solitude of Urban Man and the loss of traditional spiritual beliefs, as attempt to come to terms with them in a gently persistent, inquisitive manner. Jacobsen himself wrote that "the age of the great symphonies / is over." His concise, sometimes slightly surreal imagery takes off from this historical fatality—which he seems to accept with a sort of melancholy stoicism. "Acceptance" is in fact a key notion. Other poems concern "accepting" fleeting time and death. Syntactically, his poems are crystal clear; the characteristic mystery enveloping their meaning is not that of hazy writing but rather that of life itself—our anxiety and bewilderment at being "far from home," as the poet observes, attributing these words to a street lamp "glacially alone in the night."

Jacobsen indeed explores existential exile and solitude, wondering about the possibility—nonetheless—of God's presence in earthly lives. In "Haydn," he praises a harpist's fingers for creating a "dance of butterflies" that—here's the rub—flutters "at a large window that never opens." In other words, art, however beautifully executed, cannot pass over into transcendent realms. The remarkable uplifting movements in his poetry—he evokes clouds, constellations and galaxies—inevitably stop short on our perishable side of matter. However, in one poem he admits that though "we don't know God's heart / ... we see / something that showers down around us / like rain over our hands." This open-mindedness to the invisible and the conceivable is thoroughly engaging. Warm and thought-provoking, he is also often moving, especially when mourning his wife's death.

The above quotations are taken from Robert Bly, Roger Greenwald, and Robert Hedin's translation, *The Roads Have Come to an End Now*, which Copper Canyon brought out in 2001. The next year, Greenwald singly produced an impressive, even larger selection, *North in the World*, published by the University of Chicago Press. This is the authoritative translation to which readers should now turn. As Jacobsen thinks back on the river Glama (or Glomma), "north in the world," alongside which he grew up, his last published poem sums up the self-knowledge *cum* self-detachment, and above all the acceptance, that he consistently sought through writing. The poem concludes:

> My childhood was here—barefoot-days.
> Now I'm old and look back
> —the beach at Lauta. Happy times
> close to the flashing blue mirror of water.
>
> Sandbars, and still water in deep pools.
> River of Ages that reflects the stars,
> Gray-weather skies and sun-steered clouds.
> Behind our thoughts, we know you are with us.

The Netherlands

Discovering "The Dutch Fiftiers"

Living Space: Poems of the Dutch Fiftiers is one of the most exciting anthologies that I have ever read. It is full of compelling, funny, unsettling, challenging, and formally innovative poems that should deeply impress English readers, though for the Dutch this provocative writing indeed springs from over a half-century ago. De Vijftigersbeweging—"the Fiftiers' Movement"—was made up of Dutchmen and Flemish-writing Belgians who were born just after the First World War or in the 1920s and who burst onto the literary scene after the Second World War, that is during "the grand spree of / Liberation" when, in the words of the ever-frank Remco Campert (b. 1929), "water turned into whisky" and "everybody boozed and fucked, / all Europe was one big mattress / and the sky the ceiling / of a third-rate hotel."

Such describes some of the ambience—rowdy, Bruegelesque, inebriating both physically and intellectually—in which the nine poets featured in *Living Space* came of age, though Campert also mentions a "year of the strike" whose "consequences still / are with us." Several poems by the Fiftiers accordingly point to hardships, uncertainties, and false illusions, while others celebrate sudden freedoms, pleasures, and possibilities, namely that of writing an "other" poetry, as the philosophically alert Gerrit Kouwenaar (b. 1923) phrases it. For him, new-found literary liberties motivate a quest of the "poem as object," of which he gives this, among other quiet, vivid examples: "a glass revolving door and the chinese waiter / returning steadily with other dishes." Other samples of his lexically straightforward, gently bizarre, and thought-provoking poems reveal his suspicions about "naming," "experience," and "reality"—which he declares is "no island," an intriguing transformation of John Donne's famous apophthegm. Like Kouwenaar, all Fiftiers are occasional philosophers in poet's clothing (though their outfits differ significantly from one to another), and they specifically dabble in philosophical anthropology. "Man hardly knows what man is," remarks Jan G. Elburg (1919-1992), "the poet knows all about nothing." In another epistemological piece, entitled "knowledge of what is," he sums up our plight as "more absence than what is called existence / is man."

Alongside their shattering of comfortable moral, social, and existential concepts, it is crucial to remember what marked the adolescence or young manhood of each Fiftier: the German Occupation, the dirty work of Dutch and

Belgian collaborators, the deportation of the Jews, sabotage acts and survival in the Underground, illness, hunger, and poverty. Or, as Campert details it:

> Imagine: we were snowed in.
> We were running out of food,
> Radio was out of order, shoes split,
> We stoked the fire with notebooks
> Filled with memories to gain bleak heat
>
> And the flag, that we ought to have
> Planted somewhere, we used
> For a blanket of course. There was
> Absolutely no hope left at all,
> Not even hope for hope…

This unpredictable poet then veers his next strophe toward an amorous memory still spiced with a few erotic details, characteristically teasing in the process our own expectations. He is not alone among Fiftiers when he sets personal narratives within a context of social concerns, though this by no means implies blind allegiances. For probably all Fiftiers, the experience of the Occupation destroyed their illusions forever. Campert simply announces: "Poetry is an act / of affirmation. I affirm / I live, I do not live alone." In this dual acknowledgment is underscored his and presumably most Fiftiers' simultaneous staunch individualism and uncompromising scrutiny of others, be they siblings, sex partners, deceitful upstanding citizens, or retired people in the south of France waiting "for death in parked cars / a newspaper folded over their faces // burp[ing] on their food over tables in restaurants" (Campert, once again).

The Fiftiers' Movement coalesced in Amsterdam, where it was associated with COBRA ("COpenhagen-BRussels-Amsterdam"), a group of painters who stayed friends and worked together for only three years (1948-1951) yet whose impact on European culture is still felt today. Some of the founding members of COBRA, such as Asger Jorn, Constant, and Christian Dotremont, were later linked, closely or remotely, to the International Situationists (1957-1972), an aesthetically intense, anarchistically and nihilistically inclined group of writers and artists—the French essayist Guy Debord was their mastermind—who called attention to themselves through their provocative writings, art, and films, as well as through their scandalous antics and vociferous internal squabbles. Other members of COBRA, such as Karel Appel and Pierre Alechinsky, have since gone on to wider individual fame. Fascinated by primitive art, prehistoric art, folk art, children's art, and the *art brut* produced by psychotics and the mentally handicapped, these painters all emphasized spontaneity, "natural creative urges," and—as Peter Glassgold puts it in his informative introduction to *Living Space*—a "complete overturning of received aesthetic, social, and intellectual standards, with a special stress on the very physicality of art."

Hugo Claus (1929-2008) and Lucebert (1924-1994), who are included in *Living Space*, are likewise artists who belonged to COBRA.

It is enlightening to keep this artistic ferment in mind when reading the anthology (which is welcomely bilingual), not least because the COBRA group denied that there was a valid opposition, in art, between abstraction and figuration. This specific dichotomy, or rather lack of dichotomy, is instructive. COBRA's refusal to accept a key critical distinction established and defended by other, contemporaneous, generally America-based "avant-gardes" has analogies in the overall poetics of the Fifties. For all their vigor, anger, cynicism, and rebelliousness, the Fifties do not really discard, reject, eschew; they above all stake out broader claims for poetry, explore uncharted territories of subject matter, relativize the canons of ugliness and beauty, and mine little-tapped rhetorical resources; that is, they do not systematically refuse what had been accomplished by their European predecessors: Romantics with their focus on extreme feeling and use of hybrid poetic and narrative forms, Realists with their sharp social eye, and especially Modernists who probed profoundly into the relationship between language and the many inner and outer levels of reality. This kind of assimilation is visible in the heady writings of Bert Schierbeek (1918-1996), who wrote experimental poems as well as "poetic prose" so expansive that it grew into what he called "compositional novels." Such works smear distinctions between poetry, prose poetry, and prose. As Schierbeek creates unusual poetic and narrative structures (which convincingly mirror his thought and feeling patterns), he also reflects on or simply reflects "what man has formed on earth, what he's performed and deformed"—an essentially backward-looking project with forward-looking techniques. It is remarkable how he moves, in the long-poem *Shapes of the Voice*, from "the shape of [his own] voice" and his "left hand hold[ing] a hearing aid" to an epic perspective on voice, sound, music, and creativity, that is extends his own perishable self to any self amid teeming humanity—past, present and future:

> I set my heart out into the groping spaces
> my mouth upon the lattice of distress
> my lips kissing the dark passage of this life
> in the breakthrough of the eyes the light
> of the voice's architecture
> which enters the tongue's generations
> through the frame of the streams of representations
> in the marvelous crystal formed by the sweat of our hands
> along the imaginary wall
> with the portals of passage in and out
> across the threshold of the seventh solitude man
> who builds with the architecture of voice
> which rests as the roof over words
> the black sea and the covered wagon of love
> the magnifichord of the scriptures of extinct peoples
> and the truss for the rupture of the deafened ear
> the architectonic passage of the voice upon earth....

COBRA's and consequently the Fiftiers' "overturning of...standards" there-fore implies not so much a rigorous *exclusion* of so-called traditional formal ele-ments (rhyme, meter, and especially permutational schemes) as an ever greater appropriation of potential stylistic techniques and an ever broader *inclusion* or poeticization of neglected, avoided, scorned, scandalous, or "prosaic" subject matter: scientific facts, banal objects, anti-patriotic sentiment, brute eroticism, existential rootlessness, loss of faith in language—the latter theme, for instance, as it is bluntly stated by Simon Vinkenoog (b. 1928): "don't know the words / of the language I speak." To these losses, doubts, suspicions, and failures can be added, for some Fiftiers, the poet's anxiety about remaining permanently apart from reality, the present, others, and nature. In the same poem by Vinkenoog, despite his linguistic bewilderment, he claims to "follow [his] thoughts." How-ever, these are then defined as ontologically disconnected from his "beloved's hands," from the "swans on the water," indeed from "the world in which [he perishes]." Against this apperception of himself as a sort of absurdly cogitating phantom who can at best chase, not literally pin down, his thoughts, he can only adopt new strategies for momentarily grasping the ungraspable present moment. In a long-poem, "Oosterpark," he attempts to arrest the fleetingness of the passing time by "just sitting" in a public garden:

> I smell the fresh grass
> and the smell of the first falling leaves.
>
> Easing a bit,
> resting a bit,
> doing a bit,
> but doing it:
> with conviction,
> because there is nothing else
> but what you're doing *now*.

The poem is dated 1976, and despite the relative insouciance of the 1970s in Europe, one senses that the over-brimming sensuality of the postwar period, when hope sprouted and even flourished, is now far in the past. Doubts have crept into the poet's body and mind; he has to force himself to get back to the present and minor pleasures like smelling fresh grass; he makes the effort "with conviction." (Let's not turn to *our* present, where the relative insouciance of just sitting and smelling fresh grass, even "with conviction," seems desperately compromised.)

The stock market, collective labor contracts, and the like also enter the poetry of the Fiftiers, especially through the playful Sybren Polet (b. 1924), who otherwise draws on technology and physics. His punning "We Matter" begins abruptly:

> I say. Say nothing, I say nothing but: We. It often
> fissions but is, for it has a sp. gravity

of 34.3, atomic number 2 : 2 protons (you
and I), 2 neutrons (?), and a very small neutrino.
While emitting a λ particle
we develop so much erotic heat
—the equal of six complete married couples in their first degree
of acquaintanceship—that we matter-mystics dissolve
in light....

Even such abstruseness shows that one common denominator of the Fiftiers, so otherwise disparate in many ways, is their effort to take a new look at the role of the emotions in poetry. The looks, roles, and emotions vary greatly, yet each Fiftier gives Dutch poetry unexpected battery charges, and above all reconnects writing to "primitive" (as COBRA members might formulate it) or fundamental phenomena of thinking, feeling, sensing, and simply "living" as an individual surrounded by others. While venturing into emotion as an insufficiently explored literary (and phenomenological) frontier, some Fiftiers—Claus and Campert come to mind—seem "spontaneous" (in COBRA's sense) on the page, however painstaking their labors may have been in the study, while others—Polet, Kouwenaar, Schierbeek—display control, calculation, and careful construction. Some Fiftiers bring out feeling and sense impressions—like Polet's "erotic heat"!—with a sort of exuberant, Mallarmé-like, cerebralism. Kouwenaar, for example, has penned an oblique love poem comprising references to a city council meeting and Wittgenstein's "whereof one cannot speak, thereof one must be silent," yet ultimately his point about "love that without much talking / flattens the world like grass" is effectively made. "Robot Poetry," by Paul Rodenko (1920-1976), is a sort of *ars poetica* and mock prayer all-in-one that provides still another take on the use of emotion in poetry:

Teach us with pincering words
To squeeze off the fingers of bleating emotion
Teach us with taut rustling words
To break through the manyvoiced barrier of the soul:
Teach us to live in the deadly vacuum
The pure and faceless pain, the poem.

Claus is much cruder. He serves up "roasted vowels, scorched phrases." He is the most vigorous and compelling of the Fiftiers, and the earthy, sometimes harrowing verse gathered in *Living Space* can profitably be read alongside his powerful novel, *The Sorrow of Belgium* (1983), brought out in translation by Pantheon in 1990. Besides Claus's seventeen poems anthologized in *Living Spaces*, a selection of fifty-eight pieces has been brought out by Harcourt as *Greetings*. John Irons's versions read well, and he has often rendered rhymes with success, but it is a pity that his publishers have not produced a bilingual edition with a suitable introduction and exact bibliographical references.

Otherwise, the choices are excellent. Every poem paints gruesome, haunting, or grotesque—yet profoundly human—scenes. Claus evokes gratuitous
violence ("the child strangles a little crow"), the fragmentation of individual
and collective memory ("a story can only survive in ashes"), dehumanization
("we lived in an age of using / and being usable"), and especially ardent, oft-
jubilatory, sexuality juxtaposed with graphic *memento mori*.

Death becomes the "Destroyer" in his gripping sequence of twenty-eight
erotic poems, "Still Now," whose language in translation, and presumably in
the original, distantly echoes Shakespeare's verse and the narratives of the Old
Testament. Shakespearean at least in sensibility is Claus's way of combining
sensual physical materialism and a sense of pervasive finitude with a lofty
overview of human endeavors and their incorrigible vanity. For all his precise
evocations of human acts and facts, he always situates his poems against "the
heavens, hell, or the void" (to paraphrase a line from "Without Form of Process"); amid much that seems pagan and, once again, "primitive," a Christian
heritage is also sometimes involved, even if negatively, as in "His Notes for
'Genesis I.1.'" In other words, beneath the exact and startling imagery, there is
much precise thinking. His terse philosophical quips always give pause, such
as when he qualifies "nature" as having "edges and loose ends." Dire and dark,
sometimes bitter and always moving, Claus's masterful poetic oeuvre formulates
a deep and rare compassion. Note the conclusion of a long-poem significantly
entitled—for this was one of the Fiftiers' dilemmas—"What to speak about":

> …honor the flowering
> of the shadows that inhabit us,
> the shadows begging for consolation.
> And still stroke her shoulder blade.
> Like the back of a hunchback
> hankering for a ferocious happiness.

*   *   *

A second recent, though much less extensive, bilingual volume devoted to
Dutch poetry is likewise welcome, despite its limitations. The 2003 Nobel prizewinner J. M. Coetzee, who has edited, translated, and introduced *Landscape with
Rowers: Poetry from the Netherlands*, provides engaging, yet too small, samples
of the work of six key Dutch-langauge poets. To Polet and Claus, included in
Living Space, he adds Gerrit Achterberg (1905-1962), Cees Nooteboom (b.
1933), Hans Faverey (1933-1990), and Rutger Kopland (b. 1934).

Despite the brevity of the work presented, Coetzee has astutely rendered
poetic sequences, rather than individual poems. His choice highlights what
unites, not separates, distinct literary sensibilities. Achterberg's fourteen-part
sonnet sequence "Ballad of the Gasfitter," Polet's at once playful and grim

"Self-Repeating Poem," Claus's witty "Ten Ways of Looking at P. B. Shelley," Nooteboom's four-part homage to "Basho," Faverey's five-part suite "Chrysanthemums, rowers," and Kopland's at once touching and philosophically inquisitive "Descent in Broad Daylight" (a five-part series accompanied by Co Westerik's haunting illustrations) often permute words, phrases or themes and employ formal schemes sometimes broaching upon the mathematical. In such ways, these poets—in these pieces—represent an experimental branch of contemporary European poetry, as it has evolved from early twentieth-century Modernism. Yet there are other kinds of experimentalism—much less formalized and structural, much more stylistic and philosophical—which are practiced by some of these same writers and which more deeply underlie the genuine innovations and explorations of European poetry.

Besides Kopland's limpid, profound verse, the contributions by Claus and Nooteboom notably call for attentive rereading. Interestingly, the latter are better known as novelists. Coetzee should have penned a much more detailed introduction, not just a frustratingly succinct summary of Dutch-language literary history, followed by brief bios for each poet. The reader of this volume will want more, especially from the poets not closely associated with the Fiftiers.

$$* \quad * \quad *$$

With the resurgence of anti-Semitism and right-wing extremism in Europe—I am writing in 1990; the situation has worsened considerably—Arnold J. Pomerans's translation of Hugo Claus's *Het Verdriet van Belgie* (1983) as *The Sorrow of Belgium* is not only an important literary event but also a timely political one. Set just before, during, and after the German Occupation of Belgium and concerning one Louis Seynaeve's coming of age, this widely and rightfully praised provocative novel brilliantly explores how "average" human beings conduct themselves evilly in evil times.

Not that *The Sorrow of Belgium* exemplifies the literature of political commitment. On the contrary, the novel illuminates our understanding of moral turpitude by only indirectly addressing the ethical issues raised by the Second World War. By evoking only the surface or outer core of seemingly trivial events and refusing to expatiate upon them or even link them together into a facile linear plot, Claus probes deeply into the cruelest, most consequential human acts. Keeping to the phenomenological level of behavior, he provides few, if any, generalizations—but countless acute perceptions. Few other European novels so memorably and accurately evoke how life went on in an occupied country. "The only thing you went through," remarks a disillusioned Louis at the end of the war, "was making sure you got enough food and clothes and coal."

Alluding only occasionally to the suffering or the deaths of the Jews and of the rare resisters living in Louis's small town of Walle, Claus immerses the reader in the mediocrity of common citizens: their indifference, pusillanimity, unscrupulousness. Most members of Louis's family passively—and a few actively—collaborate with the Nazis. The boy's mother becomes the mistress of a Nazi officer; his father helps the Germans with their propaganda. We follow Louis from his Catholic boarding school, through his brief stint with the local chapter of the collaborationist Nationaal Socialistische Jeugd Vlaanderen, through his increasing awareness of his own identity and of the despicable moral climate enveloping him, and finally to his decision to become a writer and record what he has seen.

We are given a supersaturated solution of history. No ordinary *Bildungsroman*, *The Sorrow of Belgium* (sometimes reminiscent of James Joyce's *Portrait of the Artist as a Young Man* and even *Ulysses*) also employs dreams, daydreams, hallucinations, and fantasies—besides realistic storytelling—to capture the complexities of a sensitive, rapidly changing, hardly unblemished adolescent soul. The narrative is dense, meticulously composed, sometimes exhausting, and intentionally confusing as it shifts rapidly between first and third persons. This risky artifice, however, successfully reflects Louis's attempts to find himself amid the variously domineering, wishy-washy, or lascivious adult personalities still ruling over him: his grandfather, his father, his mother, several nearby relatives, and one singular priest. Nicknamed "The Rock," the latter is the most vivid character in the novel. Before being deported to a concentration camp, he teaches Louis to read ancient Greek and to start thinking for himself. Louis eventually sees people for what they are, and in the process comes to see himself clearly. This book about Louis, we learn at the end, has been written by Louis. Beyond its historical concerns, *The Sorrow of Belgium* is a gripping study of how one young man becomes a writer.

If this novel is already considered a classic in Europe, it is also because of its purely literary qualities, which masterfully convey Claus's vision of the war. Leitmotifs, from "curdling mayonnaise" to the French expression "toujours sourire" ("keep smiling"), from Belgian "chicory coffee" to lines from "Thirteen Ways of Looking at a Blackbird," give the book an intriguing musical structure. Claus is a master of transitions; the most horrific scenes are often subsumed into banal or even comic ones, such as when Louis imagines Bekka hitting "her mouth against the edge of the metal tank (...), her teeth rolling over the floor like misshapen white peas" and then, in the next sentence, he orders rolls at a bakery. In other words, "humankind cannot bear very much reality," as T. S. Eliot observes in "Burnt Norton." This perennial lesson is profoundly and unceasingly illustrated in *The Sorrow of Belgium*.

Back to France

A French Stage Costume for the Matter of Britain: Florence Delay and Jacques Roubaud's Graal Théâtre

Overlooked by French critics, despite the literary reputations of the "scribes" (as Florence Delay and Jacques Roubaud define themselves in a *postscriptum*), *Graal Théâtre* is an original dramatic re-creation of "la matière de Bretagne," that is the tales and epic poems that are more familiarly, if too narrowly, known in English as the Arthurian legends. Drawing on a rich medieval corpus of texts in German, Spanish, Portuguese, Italian, Welsh, English (notably *Sir Gawain and the Green Knight*), and of course French (in which the *Lancelot en prose* and Chrétien de Troyes's verse narratives stand out among anonymous fragmentary variants of the same stories of love, quest, battle, death, and miracle), Delay and Roubaud have produced vivid theatrical equivalents of the best-known tales as well as many little-known ones. If you read French and, like myself, are rather put off by the Arthurian stories—perhaps because of their fantastical denouements or imposing symbolism—then *Graal Théâtre* offers an excellent opportunity to give this medieval subject matter a new try. As far as I know, so much of the Matter of Britain has never appeared, in any language, in a dramatic form such as Delay and Roubaud have wittily and artfully forged for their *Graal Théâtre*.

Now republished in France in a revised and substantially augmented edition of the initial two-volume set (1977/1981), *Graal Théâtre* is thus much more than an adroitly conceived and eminently readable translation. The authors transpose prose and especially poetry into dramatic dialogues and scenes, and specifically into sequences of interrelated tableaux that beckon to be staged or at least recited. A coherent play results from each sequence. Linked in turn by the centralizing symbols of the Round Table and the Holy Grail, the ten plays of *Graal Théâtre*—the first edition comprised six—recount the feats, failures, and aspirations of two knightly orders, a "celestial" one, as the authors put it, which is founded by the saintly Joseph of Arimathy "who collected Christ's blood when He was on the cross and buried His human body" and who is thereby given, in a key opening scene, the Grail cup by the Holy Ghost; and a "terrestrial" one that is spirited by the sharp-minded Merlin who, first a prophet, increasingly becomes a wizard. Revolving around Uter Pendragon, Gawain,

Perceval, Lancelot, Morgan, Guinevere, Galahad, King Arthur, and a host of minor characters, the plays constitute a "Breton novel"—to again cite the translators, who thereby appropriate still another literary genre. This cyclical, multifaceted, dramatized "novel" concludes when the Holy Grail, followed by a sword, a lance, and Galahad, soars up to heaven and when King Arthur, wrapped in a great white sail, leaves his steed ashore and is borne out to sea in a boat carrying several ladies and his sister Morgan.

The striking horizontal and vertical imagery of the two concluding scenes already suggests that the rejuvenated Matter of Britain unfolding from these ten French plays is narratively more intricate and philosophically more resonant than a mere chronicle of events, however charming, amazing, or deeply moving they each can be. In an allusion to the very book that they are writing, Delay and Roubaud have one character, Blaise, give a nod to Jorge Luis Borges and refer to "les Graal fictions." As the etymology of "fiction" (ultimately from the Latin *fingere*) suggests, now and then the reader almost glimpses the translator-authors molding, shaping, devising, inventing, and even ironically "feigning" while literally re-forming the Matter of Britain into plays. In such nods and winks, one easily imagines how much fun Delay and Roubaud are having. When reading medieval texts, do we not similarly sense the presence of poet-translator-storytellers, who also sometimes participate in the events recounted? Establishing an animated nexus of narrators, sub-narrators, and narrator-participants—even God is accused by Merlin, at one point, of being a "conteur"—also belongs to Delay and Roubaud's art of translating and meta-translating.

Needless to say, Chrétien de Troyes, Robert de Boron, Wolfram von Eschenbach, Gottfried von Strassburg, and especially Sir Thomas Malory, who attempted to unify all the Matter of Britain into a coherent cycle called *Le Morte Darthur* (ca. 1469), would have understood Delay and Roubaud's project and its challenges. Essentially, Delay and Roubaud's task recalls Malory's: they must hunt down, collate, edit, translate, and fill in the details of dispersed, sometimes incomplete, stories that are penned in various languages and give coherence to the entire corpus by channeling it into an appropriate narrative form. By choosing drama as their target literary genre, the translators do more than retell stories in a modern idiom, and in fact more than merely enabling them to be acted out on a contemporary stage. Their translation methodology also includes reestablishing the settings of the Matter of Britain, which Delay and Roubaud define as ranging from a "Place of Secular Words," through sundry water bodies, a forest, a prairie, a castle, and a "room of love" to King Arthur's Court, the Grail Castle and a "Place of Sacred Words." These natural, historical, intimate, and sacred *lieux* also become the settings of our own intellectual and spiritual quests (and foibles). Certain characters, and especially Merlin, occasionally formulate philosophical quips or even conundrums, based on our contemporary notions of Time, Space, Wholeness, Plurality, or the Godhead. In one passage, for instance, Bron states that "the Multiple is still the One because it is the succession of the Unique," to which a character called Disciple 2 retorts by positing another paradox, this one also cryptically mathematical because it alludes to continuity, discontinuity, and the definition of "points": "Why is there between Bron and Joseph a space so large that I could sit down in it whereas we are actually crowded together?" The Voice of the Holy Ghost then interjects this answer: "The space represents the place where Our Lord was sitting at the Last Supper. It must remain empty because it awaits He whom we will send to occupy it." Finally, Disciple 2 again: "Oh really? Let's see what will happen when I have sat down in the space!" In the otherwise remote context of medieval romance, these philosophical, theological, and mathematical jokes (as well as more solemn statements) greatly liven this free-spirited rendering.

On still another narrative level, *Graal Théâtre* charts the gradual victory of Christianity over Paganism in Europe and specifically in Britain, a process commenced when Joseph of Arimathy crosses the English Channel—a scene dramatized in the book. Natural law is notably pitted against emerging Christian ethical or eschatological values, a dichotomy that increases the dramatic tension of certain tableaux. In an early scene, moreover, Joseph of Arimathy addresses a character called Memory and significantly exclaims: "Night is falling and I no longer know how to contemplate it. Why Memory are you turning so and drawing me back into the shadows of natural law?" Here, as elsewhere, Delay and Roubaud not only provide metaphors or allegories for the evolving history (and intellectual history) of Europe but also simultaneously stage the inner turmoil of a single personality caught up in a quickly changing world—our world, *mutatis mutandis*. Joseph's spiritual aspirations struggle with (his own) Memory, as well as with characters named Volonté (Will) and Entendement (Understanding), who are evidently part of his personal makeup as well. Similarly, fate and chance (or coincidence, a thematic element often used by Delay in her own alert novels) also wrestle with each other throughout *Graal Théâtre*.

These are not the only innovations and penetrating insights of the translators with respect to the first interpreters of the Matter of Britain. Like Delay and Roubaud, the latter were obliged not only to translate all or parts of whatever hodgepodge of legend, folktale, fable, doggerel, and highly crafted verse was available to them, but also to create an appealing stylistic tone. In the target language, many-told tales have to sound fresh, never-told, unheard-of. Lexically and syntactically, Delay and Roubaud opt for a natural-sounding oral French that can be recited publicly with ease. At the same time, their crafted language makes no concessions to rhetorical facility, emotional blandness, or trite colloquialisms. Interestingly, as can be spotted in the above quotation concerning Joseph of Arimathy and Memory, not a single comma appears in nearly six hundred pages of text, which comprise countless sentences that would normally be punctuated for rhythmical or logical reasons. (Only the translators' italicized two-sentence *postscriptum* uses commas.) This audacious decision gives great interpretative freedom to the actors who will one day stage these plays, as well as, in the process, to readers, who must turn themselves into actors, as it were, while reading the unpunctuated French sentences. Indeed, the temptation to read aloud is great. Each reader must find, or found, his or her own rhythm, a stimulating and not unpleasant exercise that in addition encourages a deeper engagement with the text, with a Matter of Britain that, until *Graal Théâtre*, may well have seemed impersonal, hopelessly anachronistic. By eschewing rhythmical and logical markers, except for periods at the end of sentences, the translators bring to the fore possibilities of sense and sound and even comprehension and readerly identification that are hidden beneath customary typographical norms. And the lack of punctuation gives a timeless quality to a contemporary French that also, seemingly, pays homage to the much earlier stages of French and other European languages.

Besides this at once provocative and playful tour de force, Delay and Roubaud's vocabulary can suddenly surprise with its quirky drollness. Eruptions or interruptions—moments of comic relief, literally—occur on the otherwise smooth yet, as has been seen, malleable stylistic surface of the dialogues. Now and then the translators notably add, usually through the character of Merlin, jocular references to such contemporary objects or concepts as signifiers, antibiotics, serial music, radar, Riemann surfaces, Welsh rugby matches, even e-mail. Yet Delay and Roubaud never make overuse of these pleasantries.

These funny asides also rush the Matter of Britain into our here and now, albeit so incongruously that they resemble the unpredictable events studied by chaos theory. I have already mentioned the presence of mathematics in *Graal Théâtre*. This comes as no surprise. Besides his literary activities, Roubaud long taught mathematics at the university level. The reader discovers mathematical jokes as early as page four, when these stage directions are provided: "The great hall of the Palace of Emperor Vespasian in Rome is a cube whose dimensions obey the principles that Pythagoras received directly from Moses during his stay in Egypt. The shortest dimension of the hall is three cubed, the medium dimension is four cubed, and the longest dimension is five cubed. The sum of these dimensions is 216, which is the third perfect number. This great hall is supported by both visible and invisible columns." The reader is then invited to ponder the numerological significance, if any, of Veronica's "large piece of cloth," which is described as being 4.36 meters in length and 1.10 meters in width.

In a later scene, the character Merlin taunts his protagonists (Tintagel, Ygerne, Nu, and Lot) with a "logical and topological problem" involving Saint Columcille's climb to the top of a mountain in order to pray. "He left at dawn walked all day," reports Merlin. "As he arrived higher and higher he sometimes stopped to contemplate from different angles as the poet says the shifting scene below. He arrived at the end of the day passed the night in prayer alongside a heron pilgrim and the next day at dawn he walked back down the same path toward his monastery which he reached at nightfall. Here is the problem. Show that there exists on the path walked by Saint Columcille a place that he passed at the same time of day both when ascending and descending the mountain." In another tableau, in which Merlin also "invents the picnic," the wizard challenges Morgan, Arthur, Gawain, Guenevere, and others to solve the "enigma of the adulterous wives of Baghdad." Similar detours and divagations resemble the digressions of embedded storytellers in many other medieval narratives, such as those composed by Chaucer and Boccaccio. The idiosyncratic passages remind the reader that the original medieval texts were hardly chronologically consistent, nor devoid of humor, indeed ribaldry. By the way, there are sensitive erotic scenes in *Graal Théâtre*.

Readers familiar with the personal oeuvres of Delay and Roubaud will expect no less than wittiness, deft erudition, inventiveness, and storytelling prowess. Besides writing clever and absorbing novels that are set in a variety of historical periods and are often about the mysteries of amorous attraction, Delay is an eminent translator of Spanish authors, ranging from the playwrights Lucas Fernández and Pedro Calderón de la Barca to Ramón Gómez de la Serna, Federico García Lorca, and especially her own mentor, José Bergamín. Her stylistic range, which includes not only theatrical dialogues but also what she calls "imitations," is vast. Among the prolific output of the Oulipean and Anglophile Roubaud are (partly medieval) mystery novels (the "Hortense" series), as well as seminal book-length essays on and edited collections of Troubadour poems and European sonnets from several languages. *Graal Théâtre* brilliantly puts the translators' many talents to work.

The Gold of Ripe Fruit
(Yves Bonnefoy)

Always hardworking, Yves Bonnefoy, who was born in 1923, has become even more prolific in his mid-eighties. Several book-length essays and collections of essays, plus the translations of, respectively, his commentaries on Shakespeare and his most recent collection of poems, have appeared since 2003. Of course, some volumes originated as public lectures, and repetitions occur in distinct texts on Mallarmé, Baudelaire, and Goya; but this is not to suggest that any of these books has been hastily prepared. Bonnefoy has amended, polished, and often expanded his talks, all the while maintaining the conversational tone and implicit openness to dialogue that have become the hallmark of his criticism. His expansive style never blurs his close reading, sensitive observations of fine details, and sure knowledge of biographical, philological, or historical research on his subject.

Importantly, Bonnefoy clarifies the ideas and intuitions that have informed his criticism ever since such seminal studies as *Arthur Rimbaud* (1961) and *Rome, 1630* (1970). While probing deeply into the creative work of others, he refines what he means by, indeed, "the other," "presence," "absence," "finitude," "reality," "image," "concept," "truth," "being," "incarnation," "excarnation," and—increasingly—"compassion," not to forget that key term that is so difficult to translate: "parole." Let me add the deceptively simple "lumière" as it appears in the captivating essay "Aut lux nata est aut capta hic libera regnat," which focuses on the phenomenon of light in Saint Sophia in Istanbul and then, after a surprising twist, on a simple chapel in Ravenna. Both the latter piece and the title essay stand out in *L'Imaginaire métaphysique* (2006), alongside other thoughtful texts about architecture, Mallarmé (the odd "ptyx" of his "Sonnet in -yx"), medieval Breton novels, and the poet's own *Récits en rêve* (1987) in its Italian translation. These and other essays are unified by Bonnefoy's focus on how human beings fail to turn away from an alluring "background" of myths, tales, "gnostic dreams," fantasies, intellectual "concepts" or religious credences, and toward "what exists here, now, in our essential finitude."

As regards poetry, he adds that each poet "is divided, torn, between a vow of incarnation and dreams of excarnation." The essays about Baudelaire and Nerval in *Le Poète et "le flot mouvant des multitudes"* (2003) and elsewhere, about Mallarmé (in several books), about Piero della Francesca in the subtly argued *La Stratégie de l'énigme* (2006), which offers a stunning interpretation of "The Flagellation of Christ," about Goya (in a rich exegesis of the Spaniard's "Pinturas negras" series), and about Rilke (in *Le Sommeil de personne*, 2004) all apply this touchstone to the poets and artists in question. When it comes to the Bard, the results are equally provocative. As the preeminent French translator of Shakespeare's poems and plays (eleven to date), Bonnefoy is in an extraordinary position to elucidate "the opposing metaphysics that govern and, sometimes, tyrannize the French and English languages." This he does brilliantly in five of the twelve essays of *Shakespeare and the French Poet* (2004), which should become required reading for translators and foreign critics of French poetry: there is no better explanation of how ideas and images function in a poetry notoriously reputed to be abstract. In other essays, he brings his critical acumen to bear on Shakespeare's characters (notably women), world-view, and poetic language. With respect to Othello, for instance, Bonnefoy posits that

> poetry is not the crystallization that occurs in a poem; it is a questioning which, by observing writing from within lived existence, deconstructs its images, disperses its dreams, and desires a new beginning—a more vigorous one—to the search for truth that the finest writings start but abandon. Poetry is critical of poetry, and it is only by making demands that it can fully be what it is. Othello has the misfortune of being only partly a poet.

In some passages, Bonnefoy is perhaps ultimately Racinean (to recall the contrast that has engaged countless French thinkers) in his emphasis on the language and "truth"—a daunting word—of Shakespeare's plays as poetry, in contrast to their dramaturgical qualities as tragedies and comedies that can be acted out on the stage in certain (particularly Anglo-American) ways. However, if this bias obtains, it is constantly stimulating. (Bonnefoy's versions are often used on the French stage, by the way.) All along, he keeps an eye on his own "excarnations." He is perfectly capable of objective criticism; he has an acute ear, a translator's love of dictionaries, and a trained mathematician's taste for syntactic and semantic analysis. Yet one senses Bonnefoy silently testing his own evolution by scrutinizing, as if they constituted plausible mirrors, revealing ideas inherent in key poems or prose poems by Baudelaire, Nerval, Rimbaud, and Mallarmé—his four considerable predecessors (if I may adapt the latter's quip about the "considerable passer-by" who wrote *A Season in Hell*). Bonnefoy measures their successes and shortcomings in regard to their "genuine re-affirmation of the fact of being," as he puts it in *Le poète et "le flot mouvant des multitudes"*, a volume of five essays devoted—the cited phrase is from Baudelaire's *Artificial Paradises*—to the ontological dilemmas facing the modern poet amid the anonymous urban crowd. This is not the only case where Bonnefoy assays poetry's or art's ability to respond deeply to dire social and ecological transformations.

Bonnefoy has been well served by small publishers. *Le Sommeil de personne*, a meditation on Rilke's epitaph ("Rose, oh reiner Widerspruch, Lust, / Niemandes Schlaf zu sein unter soviel Lidern"; "Rose, oh pure contradiction, desire / to be no-one's sleep under so many eyelids"), is perfectly illustrated by Farhad Ostovani's twenty-four grey-toned pastel variants of Le Grammont, the mountain facing the poet's grave in Raron, Switzerland; and these pastels enter into Bonnefoy's compelling conjectures about Rilke's ultimate views of symbolism, reality, personality, and death. *Goya, les peintures noires* (2006) reappraises the significance of the artist's gruesome series, placing it very high in the history of Western art; the book is also abundantly illustrated and can be enhanced by an amicable public debate between Bonnefoy and the critic Jean Starobinski, as transcribed in *Goya, Baudelaire et la poésie* (2004). In *Feuillées* (2004), which reproduces charcoal drawings and acrylic paintings by Gérard Titus-Carmel, Bonnefoy casts light on the artist's "leafages" (*feuillées*) by appealing to Shakespeare, Rimbaud and, once again, Mallarmé. He ties Titus-Carmel's accomplishment to "the great experience shared by some of the best minds of the twentieth century: the sentiment of merely being, as regards language, distraught visitors in a deserted house whose furniture appears empty, whose pictures are meaningless, whose gaping doors open out onto wind and night."

The author of *Divigations* has absorbed Bonnefoy of late. Mallarmé's strange prose poem "Le Démon de l'analogie" is at the heart of *Le Secret de la pénultième* (2005). Mallarmé was a teacher of English and, like Baudelaire, a translator of Poe, about whom Bonnefoy also has much to say, both here and in *Le Poète et "le flot mouvant des multitudes"*—reminders of how the American's writings continue to inspire French literary thinking. In the prose poem, Mallarmé leaves his apartment on the (unmentioned) rue de Rome, the Paris street where musical instruments are traditionally made, and declares that his sensation of being "a wing gliding across the cords of an instrument" has replaced a voice pronouncing the phrase "the penultimate [accent] is dead." Taking off from the bilingualism behind Mallarmé's obscure text (which demands knowing that French is not a heavily accentuated language) and referring to Poe's "Annabel Lee," Bonnefoy formulates thought-provoking hypotheses, one of which is that iambic pentameter ever "draws [English-language poets] beyond constraints . . . and doubts, giving them the impression that a 'genuine life' is possible." (This recalls Beckett's remark to the effect that he chose to write in French because it was too tempting to write English "poetically.") The illusions held out by a "vraie vie"—as in Rimbaud's perception that it is "elsewhere"—are in the foreground of Bonnefoy's thinking in all these books.

When I co-edited the October 2000 French issue of *Poetry*, I published a submission by Hoyt Rogers, who had translated six "stones"—as the author of *Pierre écrite* (1965) calls a kind of short poem intimately related to his poetic and philosophical outlook. Bonnefoy has observed: "I cannot consider stone without acknowledging that it is unfathomable, and this abyss of full-ness, this night sheathed by eternal light, for me exemplifies the real." The new "stones" from Yves Bonnefoy that Rogers had rendered for that issue of *Poetry* characteristically concerned finitude and death (as the epitaphic connotations suggest), but also love and memory; they belonged to a series called "La Pluie d'été." The originals of these and other "Summer Rain" poems—some of them not "stones"—were then included in *Les Planches courbes* (2001), which was Bonnefoy's first major collection of verse since *Ce qui fut sans lumière* (*In the Shadow's Light*, 1987) and *Début et fin de la neige* (*Beginning and End of the Snow*, 1991). It is arguably his most personal volume: dreamlike poems and the title (prose) piece evoke the poet's "maison natale" in Tours, his mother and, more unexpectedly, his father (who died when the poet was thirteen years old and who has rarely appeared in previous work). I have rarely seen such ac-complished versions of French poetry as those given by Rogers in *The Curved Planks*, published by Farrar, Straus and Giroux in 2006.

Rogers has appended a far-reaching afterword and "Translator's Note" to his bilingual edition. The first essay, "Water from Stone," charts Bonnefoy's poetic evolution, beginning with the little-known chapbook *Le Coeur-espace* (1945) and *Du mouvement et de l'immobilité de Douve* (*On the Motion and Immobility of Douve*, 1953). Taking into account the watery imagery in *The Curved Planks* and examining the boat as a central metaphor, the translator spots a telltale dichotomy in Bonnefoy's oeuvre and shows how "the unyield-ing rock of the real is vivified by the living water of the poetic awareness." Rogers illustrates Bonnefoy's aspiration to "hope"; how, for the poet, "it is poetry not philosophy that teaches us to die." "Our acceptance of death saves us from 'excarnation,'" continues Rogers with reference to the beautiful se-quence "The Farewell Voice," "from closing our hearts to the here and now of our earth, the 'house' into which we were born. This is [Bonnefoy's] daring answer to Hölderlin's question in 'Bread and Wine': 'What good are poets in times of dearth?'" In Bonnefoy, a mere "stone," let alone a sequence of poems, inevitably raises such issues.

Rogers's second essay discusses translation—Bonnefoy has also rendered Keats and Yeats—and outlines the challenges put forth by the French poet's "supple prosody." It's possible that some of us, who have long read this anti-conceptual poet par excellence, tend to seek out concepts in his verse, remaining deaf to its sheer phonetic beauty. Rogers counters this negligence with precise remarks about Bonnefoy's care for sounds (the word "barque" is exemplary), and he instructively explains the poet's views of the "mute *e*," an unavoidable question for all French poets. "Versatile, inventive," concludes the translator, "[Bonnefoy's prosody] wrenches and rends such historic French meters as the decasyllable and the Alexandrine, yet without wholly abjuring their fullness of contour." Such comments pin down why Bonnefoy's poetic voice gives an impression of roundness, of being at once frank and gentle, melodious and authoritative. If short poems can be soft-spoken and intimate, a sequence like "Let this World Endure" possesses a declamatory solemnity. Part III begins:

> Let this world endure,
> Let absence and word
> Fuse forever
> In simple things.
>
> Let word be to absence
> As color is to shadow,
> Gold of ripe fruit
> To gold of dry leaves.

Such pared-down yet moving lines underscore the fundamental austerity of Bonnefoy's poetics. He proposes profound responsibilities for poetry, such as "restoring to what is its full and immediate presence" (*Goya, les peintures noires*, 2006) or genuinely telling us "how we live" (*The Curved Planks*). Yet he makes these endeavors only after much has been cast aside, renounced, rejected. If his vantage point were Christian, which it is not (and it is blatantly anti-Christian in its rejection of salvatory archetypes), one might compare his poetics to a Puritanism. In any event, there is more iconoclasm in Bonnefoy than his warm-hearted tone sometimes let on. "The books: he tore them all apart", he reports in a "stone" condensing several of his themes:

> He went out. Torn, the visage of the world
> Took on another beauty, seemed more human now.
> In shadow play, the sky's hand reached for his.
> The stone where you see his weathered name
> Was opening, forming a word.

Notes

Exalting What Is (Jacques Réda)

The title *Aller aux mirabelles* refers to the cherry plums grown in the Lorraine. In this memoir, Réda describes the plums as "big, blond, shiny, smooth pearls spotted with a few reddish freckles, and underneath their shininess the pulp is dense like a chunk of mashed sun." *Le Citadin* means "The City Dweller." Note also that there are "five," not four points of the compass in Réda's world; and that "Xélos" is an anagram of Solex."

The *Yale Review* (January 2007). For an introduction to Réda's oeuvre, see the essay "From Serendipity to Metaphysics" in the first volume of *Paths to Contemporary French literature* (Transaction Publishers, 2004).

The Chromatic Prose of Josep Pla's *Gray Notebook*

Context, No. 21, Spring 2008.

The Pursuit of Shimmering Instants (Luis Cernuda)

Chelsea (No. 80, Summer 2006).

A Spanish Penelope (Francisca Aguirre)

Chelsea (No. 79, Winter 2005).

Haunting Absence, Intense Presence (Eugenio Montale)

The first section was published in *Poetry* (March 2000), the second section in the *Yale Review* (July 2002).

Songs of a Life (Umberto Saba)

The first section was published in *Poetry* (June 1999), the second section in the *Times Literary Supplement* (February 3, 2006).

Childhood as Sacrifice and Annihilation (Alberto Savinio)

Expanded from a review that originally appeared in the *San Francisco Chronicle* (March 8, 1992).

A Dark Degree of Suffering: Livia Svevo's Memoir of her Husband

Expanded from a review that originally appeared in the *San Francisco Chronicle* (December 30, 1990).

The Solitude of a Master Empathizer (Cesare Pavese)

The first section was published in *Context* (No. 10, Winter 2001-2002), the second section in *The Yale Review* (January 2004).

Appearance, Apparition, Aspiration (Giorgio Caproni and Giuseppe Ungaretti)

Antioch Review, "Poetry Today" (Spring 2005).

A Cornucopia of Italian Poetry (Camillo Sbarbaro, Vittorio Sereni, Andrea Zanzotto, Luciano Erba, Bartolo Cattafi, Lucio Mariani, Luigi Fontanella)

Zanzotto's translators are Patrick Barron, Thomas J. Harrison, Brian Swann, John P. Welke, and Elizabeth A. Wilkins. Fontanella's translators are Carol Lettieri, Irene Marchegiani, W. S. Di Piero, Michael Palma, and Emanuel di Pasquale.

The Yale Review (April 2008). In the passage about Luciano Erba, I have incorporated a review of Ann Snodgrass's translation, that originally appeared in *Chelsea* (No. 76, Fall 2004).

Between the Horizon and the Leap (Alfredo de Palchi)

When this essay was published in *Symposium* (Vol. 60, No. 2, Summer 2006), all quotations were in Italian and based on de Palchi's *Paradigma: tutte le poesie 1947-2005*. Here, I have used English translations for each Italian quotation and have drawn on the American editions that are listed in the bibliography; in certain cases, to avoid ambiguity, I have cited translators. See also the *Antioch Review* (Summer 1998). This essay was reprinted in *Alfredo de Palchi-La Potenza della poesia*, Alessandria, Italy: Edizioni dell'Orso, 2008.

A Quest for Continuity and Communion (Mario Luzi)

Of the untranslated titles, *La Barca* means "The Boat," *Avvento notturno* "Nocturnal Advent," *Nel magma* "In the Magma" and *Dottrina dell'estremo principiante* "Doctrine of an Absolute Beginner."

Gradiva, No. 33, Spring 2007.

The Nexus of Contradictory Verities (Roberto Bertoldo)

Chelsea (No. 76, Fall 2004).

Unresolved Betweenness (Milo De Angelis)

The *Antioch Review* (Fall 2004).

How We Would Live (Giovanna Sicari)

Chelsea (No. 78, Fall 2005).

A Generous and Courageous Lucidity (Edvard Kocbek)
The *Antioch Review*, "Poetry Today" (Winter 2005).

A Much Delayed Letter from Ljubljana (Veno Taufer, Aleš Debeljak, and others)
This *Letter* first appeared in *Dialogi* (Autumn 2007), in a Slovene translation by Jana Unuk. I am indebted to Jana Unuk for several precise remarks enabling me to improve my initial analysis of Veno Taufer's poem.

A Letter from Sarajevo (Miljenko Jergović, Vidosav Stevanović, Aleksandar Hemon, Velibor Čolić, and Svetislav Basara)
Context (No. 18, Winter 2005-2006).

Pleasure and the Deeper Ambivalence (Radmila Lazić)
The *Antioch Review* (Summer 2004).

Intricacies of Exile (Georgios Vizyenos)
Times Literary Supplement (February 17-23, 1989).

Invoking Saint Alexandros Papadiamantis
This essay combines two long reviews, the first published in the *Times Literary Supplement* (December 18-24, 1987), the second in the *International Fiction Review* (Vol. 15, No. 1, 1988).

A Bayeux Tapestry à la grecque (Stratis Myrivilis)
Expanded from an article that originally appeared in the *International Fiction Review* (Vol. 16, No. 1, 1989).

The Innate Passion and the Apotheosis (Odysseus Elytis)
Poetry (August 1998).

From Sorrow to Celebration (Andonis Decavalles)
Expanded from a short review that appeared in the *Times Literary Supplement* (July 10, 1987).

A Chromatic, Obsessional Poetics (Miltos Sachtouris)
Absinthe: New European Writing (No. 9, Spring 2008). See also the *Times Literary Supplement* (July 10, 1987) for my review of Stathatos's translation.

Erotic Knowledge and Self-Knowledge (Dinos Christianopoulos)
This essay is a greatly revised and expanded version of articles that initially appeared in *The Cabirion/Gay Books Bulletin* (No. 12, Spring-Summer 1985) and the *International Fiction Review* (Vol. 14, No. 1, 1987). In the first section,

all translated poems are by Kimon Friar. In the second section, specifically deal-ing with Christianopoulos's prose, I have translated from various texts. For the etymology of the word *rebetis*, see Stathis Gauntlett, *"Rebetiko Tragoudi* as a Generic Term," *Byzantine and Modern Greek Studies* (Vol. VIII, 1982-1983). See also Elias Petropoulos's *Rebetika: Songs from the Old Greek Underworld*, translated by John Taylor, London: Alcyon, 1992.

Poetry, Anti-Poetry, and Disgust (Elias Petropoulos)

This essay is the original English text of my preface to Petropoulos's col-lection of poems, *Pote kai tipota* (*Never and Nothing*, Athens: Nefeli, 1993); the Greek translation of this preface was made by Elias Papadimitrakopoulos. During the years 1978-1993, when I was regularly working with Petropoulos as his translator, I published eight articles about his writings:

1. "Elias Petropoulos: The *Mounópsira*," *Maledicta* (Vol. 5, Nos. 1-2, 1981); Greek translation: *Ihneftis* (October 1985);

2. "Elias Petropoulos: A Presentation," *Journal of the Hellenic Diaspora* (Vol. 8, No. 4, Winter 1981);

3. "Elias Petropoulos: Folklorist-in-Exile," *Greek Accent* (Vol. 3, No. 9, May-June 1983);

4. "L'architecture: mémoire populaire," *Le Fou Parle* (No. 24, May-June 1983);

5. "Benávis ta kaliardá?", *Gay Books Bulletin* No. 9, Spring-Summer 1983); ·

6. "Un album de souvenir [*Les Juifs de Salonique: In Memoriam*, par Elias Petropoulos]," *Les Nouveaux Cahiers* (No. 74, Autumn 1983);

7. "Kaliarda Revisited," *The Cabirion* (No. 11, Fall-Winter 1984);

8. *"The Jews of Salonica: In Memoriam*, by Elias Petropoulos," *Jewish Cur-rents* (Vol. 39, No. 1 [425], January 1985).

The Mentor of Pyrgos (Elias Papadimitrakopoulos)

The first section is revised and slightly expanded from my introduction to *Toothpaste with Chlorophyll/Maritime Hot Baths* (Asylum Arts, 1992), which I translated. It is used here by permission of Leaping Dog Press/Asylum Arts Press (P. O. Box 90473, Raleigh, North Carolina 27675-0473, www.leaping-dogpress.com.) This introduction first appeared, in a shorter version, in the *International Fiction Review* (Vol. XIII, No. 2, 1986); a few passages from a book review first printed in *The Review of Contemporary Fiction* (Vol. X, No. 2, 1990) were also incorporated. The second section is the original English text of "The Mentor of Pyrgos," which was first published in a Greek translation by Spyros Tsaknias in a special Papadimitrakopoulos issue of *Alpheios* (No. 11, Autumn 1996). See also the special Papadimitrakopoulos issue of *Oropedio*, No. 3, Summer 2007.

Eros and Other Spiritual Voyages (Veroniki Dalakoura)
Unpublished, except for the passage about *The Game of the End*, reviewed in the *Review of Contemporary Fiction* (Spring 1989). All translations are mine, except for those by Yannis Goumas that are quoted from *26 Poems*.

My Life as Someone Else's (Kapka Kassabova)
Much expanded from a short review (only about *Someone Else's Life*) that appeared in the *Antioch Review* (Spring 2004).

Milk Teeth Biting Granite (Attila József)
A shorter version of this article, focused only on Ozsváth and Turner's translation, appeared in the *Antioch Review* (Fall 2000).

The No-Man's Land of the Nameless (Ágnes Nemes Nagy)
The *Antioch Review*, "Poetry Today" (Fall 2005).

Holding Hungary's Broken Peony (Sándor Csoóri)
Chelsea (No. 77, Spring 2005).

Good-Bye Mother (Péter Esterházy)
The *San Francisco Chronicle* (April 14, 1991).

Dark Struggles for a Utopia of Language (Ingeborg Bachmann)
The first part was published in *Context* (No. 13, 2003). See also the *San Francisco Chronicle* (May 12, 1991). The second part was published as a "Poetry Today" column in the *Antioch Review* (Fall 2007).

In Search of Presence (Peter Handke)
The *San Francisco Chronicle* (July 1, 1990).

The Poetry of Thomas Bernhard
Absinthe: New European Writing (No. 9, Spring 2008).

Intriguing Specimens of Humanity (Veza Canetti)
The titles *Der Oger*, *Geduld brint Rosen*, and *Der Fund* can be rendered literally as "The Monster," "Patience Brings Roses, "and "The Find." The *San Francisco Chronicle* (June 30, 1991).

A Delicate Touch (Peter Altenberg)
The title *Sonnenuntergang im Prater* evokes the sun setting in the famous Prater Park of Vienna. Kafka's *Betrachtung* can be rendered as "Observation." A much shorter version of this essay appeared in *Chelsea* (No. 82, Fall 2007).

The Fertile "Crisis Years" of Rainer Maria Rilke
The *Antioch Review* (Winter 1998).

And How Hope is Violent (Paul Celan)
Poetry (September 2001).

Seeking the Self, Seeking beyond the Self (Hans W. Cohn)
Poetry (March 2001).

A Radical Path to the Ordinary (Elke Erb)
The untranslated titles can be given these equivalents: *Gutachten* ("An Expert's Report"), *Der Faden der Geduld* ("The Thread of Patience"), and *Vexierbild* ("Picture Puzzle").
The Prose Poem (Vol. 7, 1998).

A Noble Brightness (Peter Huchel)
Chelsea (No. 79, Winter 2005).

The Poetry of W. G. Sebald
Chelsea (No. 75, Spring 2004).

Facing Up to Unspeakableness (Robert Walser)
Context (No. 7, Spring 2001).

Idioms of Remembering (Marcel Cohen and Michał Głowiński)
For an introduction to Cohen's oeuvre, see the essay "Ever-Present Absence" in the first volume of *Paths to Contemporary French Literature* (Transaction Publishers, 2004). There is also a passage about his short prose in "From Aristotle's Quandary to French and American Prose Poems," the final essay of the second volume of *Paths to Contemporary French Literature* (Transaction Publishers, 2007).
Packington Review (No. 1, Fall 2008).

Questions of Fulfillment (Czesław Miłosz)
Poetry (February 1997).

Metaphysics and Lyric Factors (Piotr Sommer, Krzysztof Kamil Baczyński, Tadeusz Różewicz, and others)
It is impossible to mention all the translators in the body of the essay. In the passage about Piotr Sommer, the quotation from "Little Graves" was translated by Jarosław Anders; the quatrain from "Lighter, Darker," by Halina Janod and Michael Kasper; the lines from "Visibility," by Halina Janod, Michael Kasper, and Mark Slobin; the quoted lines from "Indiscretions," by Halina Janod and

D. J. Enright; the lines "What would I write poems about?," etc., from "Sometimes, Yes," by Halina Janod and Michael Kasper; the lines from "Ode to the
Carnival," by Halina Janod and Tadeusz Pióro; the line "each of them can do
a lot," etc., from "Space," by Halina Janod, Ed Adams, and Edward Carey; the
line "a maple leaf with the sun shining through it," etc., from "A Maple Leaf,"
by Halina Janod and John Ashbery; the lines from "First Sentence," by Halina
Janod, Douglas Dunn, and Michael Kasper; the line "one day I'll open the
world," from "One Day," by Halina Janod and Michael Kasper; the quatrain
from "Station Lights," by Halina Janod and D. J. Enright; the two quatrains
from "A Small Treatise on Non-Contradiction," by Halina Janod and Michael
Kasper; the line "nothing's / at odds with anything," from ""Morning on Earth,"
by Halina Janod, Mark Slobin, and W. Martin; and the lines from the title poem,
by Halina Janod and Michael Kasper. In the final passage about the anthology
Carnivorous Boy, Carnivorous Bird, unmentioned translators are Bill Johnston
(the lines respectively by Krzysztof Koehler and Mariusz Grzebalski), W.
Martin (the line by Marcin Sendecki), Ewa Elżbieta Nowakowska (the line by
Eugeniusz Tkaczyszyn-Dycki).

The *Antioch Review*, "Poetry Today" (Fall 2006).

Brief Crystallizations of Plenitude (Adam Zagajewski)
The first part is expanded from a review that originally appeared in *Poetry*
(December 1998); the second part is unpublished.

Searching for the *Materia Prima* (Marzanna Kielar)
Absinthe: New European Writing (No. 8, Fall 2007).

Anna Akhmatova and her Magic Choir (Dmitry Bobyshev, Joseph Brodsky, Anatoly Naiman, Evgeny Rein)
The *Antioch Review*, "Poetry Today" (Spring 2006).

On the Ledge (Joseph Brodsky)
This essay combines two articles, the first published in *Poetry* (June 1997),
the second in the *Michigan Quarterly Review* (Summer 2001).

Subjective Realism and Lyrical Urgency (Tatiana Shcherbina)
I am indebted to Sasha Dugdale and Tatiana Shcherbina for explaining the
several connotations of the title *Lazurnaya Skrizhal'*.

The review of *Life Without* appeared in *Chelsea* (No. 79, Winter 2005);
the two passages about *The Score of the Game* and the French translations are
unpublished.

Of Home and Hereness (Jaan Kaplinksi)
The *Antioch Review* (Winter 2005).

Peeling Back the Veneer (Jaan Kross)
The *San Francisco Chronicle* (July 10, 1994).

Finnish Poets and their Greek Dichotomies (Pentti Saarikoski, Tua Forsström, Paavi Haavikko, and others)
The *Antioch Review*, "Poetry Today" (Summer 2007).

A Poetry of Acceptance (Rolf Jacobsen)
A shorter version of this article, focused only on *The Roads Have Come to an End Now*, appeared in the *Antioch Review* (Summer 2002).

Discovering the Dutch Fiftiers
The *Antioch Review*, "Poetry Today" (Winter 2007) for the first section, *Antioch Review* (Fall 2004) for the second. The third section is expanded from a review in the *San Francisco Chronicle* (July 22, 1990).

A French Stage Costume for the Matter of Britain: Florence Delay and Jacques Roubaud's *Graal Théâtre*
Calque (Spring-Summer 2008).

The Gold of Ripe Fruit (Yves Bonnefoy)
The *Times Literary Supplement* (March 16, 2007). For a much longer presentation of Bonnefoy's ideas about Shakespeare, see the essay "Bonnefoy and Shakespeare" in volume two of *Paths to Contemporary French Literature* (Transaction Publishers, 2007). See also the essay "Elusive Presence" in volume one of *Paths to Contemporary French Literature* (Transaction Publishers, 2004).

Bibliography

Aguirre, Francisca
Ithaca, translated by Ana Valverde Osan, New York: Boa Editions, 2004.
Ensayo General: poesia completa 1966-2000, Madrid: Calumbur, 2000.

Akhmatova, Anna
Forty-Seven Love Poems, translated by Natalie Duddington, London: Jonathan Cape, 1927.
Selected Poems, translated by Richard McKane, Harmondsworth, England: Penguin, 1969/London: Bloodaxe, 1989.
Poems of Akhmatova, translated by Stanley Kunitz with Max Hayward, Boston: Little, Brown, 1973.
Tale Without a Hero and Twenty-Two Poems, translated by Jeanne van der Eng-Liedmeier and Kees Verheul, The Hague: Mouton (Dutch Studies in Russian Literature, 3), 1973.
A Poem Without a Hero, translated by Carl S. Proffer and Assya Humesky, Ann Arbor, Michigan: Ardis Press, 1973.
Requiem and Poem Without a Hero, translated by D. M. Thomas, London: Paul Elek, 1976/Athens, Ohio: Ohio University Press, 1976.
Selected Poems, edited and translated by Walter Arndt, with *Requiem* translated by Robin Kemball and *A Poem Without a Hero* translated by Carl. R. Proffer, Ann Arbor, Michigan: Ardis, 1976.
Way of All the Earth, translated by D. M. Thomas, London: Secker and Warburg, 1979/Athens, Ohio: Ohio University Press, 1979.
Poems, translated by Lyn Coffin, New York: Norton, 1983.
You Will Hear Thunder, translated by D. M. Thomas, Athens, Ohio: Ohio University Press, 1985.
Selected Poems, translated by D. M. Thomas, London/New York: Penguin, 1988.
The Complete Poems of Anna Akhmatova, translated by Judith Hemschemeyer, Boston: Zephyr Press, 1997.
The Word That Causes Death's Defeat: Poems of Memory, translated, with an introductory biography, critical essays, and commentary by Nancy K. Anderson, New Haven and London: Yale University Press, 2004.
Stikhotvoreniya i poemy, edited by V. M. Zhirmunsky; Biblioteka poeta, bolshaya seriya, 2nd edition, Leningrad: Leningradskoe otdelenie, 1979.

Sochineniya, volumes 1 and 2 edited by G. P. Struve and B. A. Filipoff, Munich: Inter-Language Literary Associates, 1967-1968; volume 3 edited by G. P. Struve, N. A. Struve, and B. A. Filipoff, Paris: YMCA Press, 1983.

Altenberg, Peter
Telegrams of the Soul: Selected Prose of Peter Altenberg, translated by Peter Wortsman, New York: Archipelago Books, 2005.
Esquisses viennoises, translated into French by Miguel Couffon, Aix-en-Provence: Pandora, 1982.
Nouvelles esquisses viennoises, translated into French by Miguel Couffin, Arles: Actes Sud, 1984.
Das Altenberg-Buch, edited by Egon Friedell, Vienna/Leipzig: Verlag der Wiener Graphischen Werkstätte, 1922.
Das große Peter Altenberg Buch, edited by Werner J. Schweiger, Vienna/Hamburg: Paul Zsolnay Verlag, 1977.
Ausgewählte Werke, Munich: Hanser, 1979.
Sonnenuntergang im Prater, edited by Hans Dieter Schäfer, Stuttgart: Reclam, 1983.
Peter Altenberg: Leben und Werk in Texten und Bildern, edited by Hans Christian Kosler, Frankfurt-am-Main: Fischer, 1984.
Expedition in den Alltag: Gesammelte Skizzen (1895-1898), edited by Werner J. Schweiger, Vienna/Frankfurt-am-Main, 1987.
Extrakte des Lebens: Gesammelte Skizzen (1898-1919), edited by Werner J. Schweiger, Vienna/Frankfurt-am-Main, 1987.
Wiener Geschichten, edited by Burkhard Spinnen, Frankfurt-am-Main: Schöffling, 1995.
Peter Altenberg: Auswahl aus seinen Büchern von Karl Kraus, edited by Christian Wagenknecht. Frankfurt-am-Main/Leipzig: Insel, 1997.
Sommerabend in Gmunden: Szenen und Skizzen zwischen Semmering und Salzkammergut, edited by Burkhard Spinnen, Frankfurt-am-Main: Schöffling, 1997.
Wiener Nachtleben, edited by Burkhard Spinnen, Frankfurt-am-Main: Schöffling, 2001.

Anderson, Nancy K.
Anna Akhmatova: The Word That Causes Death's Defeat: Poems of Memory, translated, with an introductory biography, critical essays, and commentary, by Nancy K. Anderson, New Haven/London: Yale University Press, 2004.

Bachmann, Ingeborg
Malina, translated by Philip Boehm, New York and London: Holmes & Meier, 1990.
Three Paths to the Lake, translated by Mary Fran Gilbert, New York and London: Holmes & Meier, 1989.
The Thirtieth Year, translated by Michael Bullock, New York and London: Holmes & Meier, 1987.

In the Storm of Roses, translated by Mark Anderson, Princeton, New Jersey: Princeton University Press, 1986.

The Book of Franza & Requiem for Fanny Goldmann, translated by Peter Filkins, Evanston, Illinois: Northwestern University Press, 1999.

Letters to Felician, translated by Damion Searls, Los Angeles and Copenhagen: Green Integer, 2004.

Ingeborg Bachmann and Christa Wolf: Selected Prose and Drama, edited by Patricia Herminghouse, New York: Continuum, 1998.

Three Radio Plays: A Deal in Dreams, The Cicadas, The Good God of Manhattan, translated by Lilian M. Friedberg, Riverside, California: Adriane Press, 1999.

Last Living Words: The Ingeborg Bachmann Reader, translated by Lilian M. Friedberg, Copenhagen and Los Angeles: Green Integer, 2005.

Darkness Spoken: The Collected Poems, translated by Peter Filkins, Brookline, Massachusetts: Zephyr Press, 2006.

Werke, four volumes, edited by Christine Koschel, Inge von Weidenbaum, and Clemens Münster, Munich/Zürich: Piper, 1978 (1993).

Frankfurter Vorlesungen: Probleme zeitgenössischer Dichtung, Munich: Piper, 1980.

Die Wahrheit ist dem Menschen zumutbar: Essays, Reden, Kleinere Schriften, Munich: Piper, 1981.

Wir müssen wahre Sätze finden: Gespräche und Interviews, edited by Christine Koschel and Inge von Weidenbaum, Munich: Piper, 1983.

"Todesarten"—Projekt, four volumes, edited by Monika Albrecht and Dirk Göttsche, Munich: Piper, 1995.

Letzte, unveröffentliche Gedichte: Entwürfe und Fassungen, edited by Hans Höller, Frankfurt-am-Main: Suhrkamp, 1998.

Ich weiß keine bessere Welt: Unveröffentliche Gedichte, edited by Isolde Moser, Heinz Bachmann, and Christian Moser, Munich: Piper, 2000.

Baczyński, Krysztof Kamil

White Magic and Other Poems, translated by Bill Johnston, Los Angeles and Copenhagen: Green Integer, 2005.

Utworfy wybrane, edited by Kazimierz Wyka, Kraków: Wydawnictwo Literackie, 1979.

Poezje, edited by Jerzy Swiech, Lublin: Wydawn Lubelskie, 1992.

Baran, Marcin

Carnivorous Boy, Carnivorous Bird: Poetry from Poland, selected by Marcin Baran, edited by Anna Skucińska and Elżbieta Wójcik-Leese, translated by Elżbieta Wójcik-Leese and others, Brookline, Massachusetts: Zephyr Press, 2004.

Basara, Svetislav

Chinese Letter, translated by Ana Lučić, Normal, Illinois: Dalkey Archive, 2004.

Kinesko pismo, Belgrade: Vidici, 1984.

Bergamín, José
La Décadence de l'analphabétisme, translated into French by Florence Delay, Paris: La Délirante, 1988.
La Solitude sonore du toreo, translated into French by Florence Delay, Paris: Seuil, 1989.
Beauténébreux, translated into French by Florence Delay, Paris: La Délirante, 1999.

Bernhard, Thomas
Woodcutters, translated by David McLintock, Chicago: University of Chicago Press, 1987.
Extinction, translated by David McLintock, Chicago: University of Chicago Press, 1995.
The Loser, translated by Jack Dawson, Chicago: University of Chicago Press, 1996.
The Voice Imitator, translated by Kenneth J. Northcott, Chicago: University of Chicago Press, 1998.
In Hora Mortis/Under the Iron of the Moon, translated by James Reidel, Princeton, New Jersey: Princeton University Press, 2006.
Werke, twenty-two volumes, edited by Martin Huber and Wendelin Schmidt-Pengler, Frankfurt-am-Main: Suhrkamp, 2003.

Bertoldo, Roberto
The Calvary of the Cranes, translated by Emanuel di Pasquale, Boca Raton, Florida: Bordighera, 2003.
Nuvole in agonia, Torino, privately printed, 1981.
Il pan-demonio, Torino, privately printed, 1993.
Il rododendro, Torino, privately printed, 1995.
Il calvario delle gru, Milan: La Vita Felice, 2000.
L'archivio delle bestemmie, Milan: Mimesis, 2006.

Bobyshev, Dmitry
Poems in *Contemporary Russian Poetry: A Bilingual Anthology*, edited and translated by Gerald S. Smith, Bloomington, Indiana: Indiana University Press, 1993.
Poems in *Modern Poetry in Translation*, edited by Daniel Weissbort (No. 10, Winter 1996).
Poems in *In the Grip of Strange Thoughts: Russian Poetry in a New Era*, translated by Judith Hemschemeyer, edited by J. Kates, Brookline, Massachusetts: Zephyr Press/ Highgreen, Tarset, Northumberland (U. K.): Bloodaxe Books, 1999.

Bonnefoy, Yves
Selected Poems, translated by Anthony Rudolf, London: Jonathan Cape, 1968.
Words in Stone: Pierre écrite, translated by Susanna Lang, Amherst, Massachusetts: University of Massachusetts Press, 1976.

The Origin of Language and Other Poems, translated by Susanna Lang, Montauk, New York: Monument Press, 1979.

Things Dying, Things New Born: Selected Poems, translated by Anthony Rudolf, London: The Menard Press, 1985.

Poems 1959-1975, translated by Richard Pevear, New York: Random House, 1985.

The Grapes of Zeuxis and Other Fables, translated by Richard Stamelman, Montauk, New York: Monument Press, 1987.

The Act and the Place of Poetry: Selected Essays, edited by John Naughton, translated by John Naughton and others, Chicago/London: University of Chicago Press, 1989.

Once More the Grapes of Zeuxis, translated by Richard Stamelman, Montauk, New York: Monument Press, 1990.

Early Poems 1947-1959, translated by Richard Pevear and Galway Kinnell, Athens, Ohio: Ohio University Press, 1991.

In the Shadow's Light, translated by John Naughton, Chicago/London: University of Chicago Press, 1991.

On the Motion and the Immobility of Douve, translated by Galway Kinnell, Newcastle upon Tyne, Great Britain: Bloodaxe, 1992.

The Last Grapes of Zeuxis, translated by Richard Stamelman, New York: Monument Press, 1993.

New and Selected Poems, translated by Anthony Rudolf and John Naughton, Chicago: University of Chicago Press, 1996.

Yesterday's Wilderness Kingdom, translated by Anthony Rudolf, London: Modern Poets in Translation, 2000.

The Horizon, translated by Michael Bishop, Halifax, Nova Scotia, Canada: Editions VVV Editions, 2003.

In the Lure of Language, translated by Michael Bishop, Halifax, Nova Scotia, Canada: Editions VVV Editions, 2003.

Shakespeare and the French Poet, edited by John Naughton, translated by John Naughton and others, Chicago and London: University of Chicago Press, 2004.

The Curved Planks, translated by Hoyt Rogers, New York: Farrar, Straus and Giroux, 2006.

Arthur Rimbaud (1961), Paris: Seuil, 1994.

Rome, 1630 (1970), Paris: Flammarion, 2000.

Poèmes, Paris: Mercure de France, 1978 (Gallimard, 1997—edition including *Du mouvement et de l'immobilité de Douve*, *Hier régnant désert*, *Pierre écrite* and *Dans le leurre du seuil*).

Shakespeare et Yeats, Paris: Mercure de France, 1998.

Les Planches courbes, Paris: Mercure de France, 2001.

Sous l'horizon du langage, Paris: Mercure de France, 2002.

Henry IV (I); Jules César; Hamlet; Le Conte d'hiver; Vénus et Adonis; Le Viol de Lucrèce, Paris: Club Français du Livre, 1957-1960.

Jules César, Paris: Mercure de France, 1960 (Gallimard, 1995).

Hamlet, followed by "Une idée de la traduction," Paris: Mercure de France, 1965 (1988).

Le Roi Lear, new edition preceded by "Comment traduire Shakespeare," Paris: Mercure de France, 1965 (new edition with essay, 1991).

Hamlet/Le Roi Lear, preceded by "Readiness, Ripeness: *Hamlet, Lear,*" Paris: Gallimard, 1978 (1988).

Macbeth, Paris: Mercure de France, 1983 (new edition with *Roméo et Juliette* and the essay "L'Inquiétude de Shakespeare," Paris: Gallimard, 1985).

Les Poèmes de Shakespeare, preceded by "Traduire en vers ou en prose," Paris: Mercure de France, 1993.

Le Conte d'hiver, preceded by "Art et Nature: l'arrière-plan du *Conte d'hiver,*" Paris: Mercure de France, 1994 (Gallimard, 1996).

La Tempête, preceded by "Une journée dans la vie de Prospéro," Paris: Gallimard, 1997.

Antoine et Cléopâtre, preceded by "La noblesse de Cléopâtre," Paris: Gallimard, 1999.

Othello, preceded by "La tête penchée de Desdémone," Paris: Gallimard, 2001.

Comme il vous plaira, preceded by "La décision de Shakespeare," Paris: Livre de Poche, 2003.

Le Poète et "le flot mouvant des multitudes": Paris pour Nerval et pour Baudelaire, Paris: Bibliothèque Nationale de France, 2003.

Goya, Baudelaire et la poésie, Geneva: La Dogana, 2004.

Le Sommeil de personne, Bordeaux: William Blake & Co., 2004.

Feuillées, Cognac: Le Temps Qu'il Fait, 2004.

Le Secret de la pénultième, Paris: Abstème & Bobance, 2005.

La Stratégie de l'énigme, Paris: Galilée, 2006.

L'Imaginaire métaphysique, Paris: Seuil, 2006.

Goya, les peintures noires, Bordeaux: William Blake & Co., 2006.

Brodsky, Joseph

Joseph Brodsky: Selected Poems, translated by George L. Kline, London: Penguin, 1973/New York: Harper & Row, 1974.

So Forth, New York: Farrar, Straus and Giroux, 1996.

Collected Poems in English, New York: Farrar, Straus and Giroux, 2000.

Collines et autres poèmes, translated into French by Jean-Jacques Marie, Paris: Seuil, 1966.

Poèmes 1961-1987, translated into French by Michel Aucouturier and others, Paris: Gallimard, 1987.

Sochineniia Iosifa Brodskogo, volumes I-IV, Saint Petersburg: Pushkin Fund, 1992-1996; revised edition, volumes I-IV, 1997-1998; volume V, 1999; volume VI, 2000.

Calderón de La Barca, Pedro

Le Grand Théâtre du Monde and *Procès en séparation de l'âme et du corps,* translated into French by Florence Delay, Paris: L'Avant-scène théâtre, no. 1159, 2004.

Campert, Remco
In the Year of the Strike, translated by John Scott and Graham Martin, London: Rapp & Whiting, 1968/Chicago: Swallow Press, 1968.
This Happened Everywhere: The Selected Poems of Remco Campert, translated by Manfred Wolf, San Francisco: Androgyne Books, 1997.

Canetti, Veza
Yellow Street, translated by Ian Mitchell, New York: New Directions, 1991.
The Tortoises, translated by Ian Mitchell, New York: New Directions, 2001.
Die gelbe Straße, Munich: Carl Hanser, 1989.
Der Oger: ein Stück, Munich: Carl Hanser, 1991.
Geduld bringt Rosen (1992), Munich: dtv, 2003.
Die Schildkröten (1999), Munich: dtv, 2002.
Der Fund: Erzählungen und Stücke (2001): Munich: dtv, 2004.

Caproni, Giorgio
The Earth's Wall: Selected Poems 1932-1986, translated by Ned Condini, New York: Chelsea, 2004.
Le Mur de la terre, translated into French by André Frénaud, Philippe Renard, and Bernard Simeone, Paris: Maurice Nadeau, 1985.
Le Comte de Kevenhüller, translated into French by Philippe Renard and Bernard Simeone, Paris: Maurice Nadeau, 1986.
L'ultimo borgo: poesie 1932-1978, edited by Giovanni Raboni, Milan: Rizzoli, 1980.
Il franco cacciatore, Milan: Garzanti, 1982.
Il Conte di Kevenhüller, Milan: Garzanti, 1986.
Poesie (1932-1986), Milan: Garzanti, 1989.
Res amissa, edited by Giorgio Agamben, Milan: Garzanti, 1991.
L'opera in versi, edited by Luca Zuliani, Milan: Mondadori, 1998.
Tutte le poesie, Milan: Garzanti, 1999.

Carpelan, Bo
Room without Walls: Selected Poems, translated by Anne Born, London: Forest Books, 1987.
Homecoming, translated by David McDuff, Manchester (U.K.): Carcanet, 1993.
Urwind, translated by David McDuff, Evanston, Illinois: Northwestern University Press, 1998.
Dehors, suivi de Credo de novembre, translated into French by Pierre Grouix, Paris: Arfuyen, 2007.

Cattafi, Bartolo
The Dry Air of Fire, translated by Brian Swann and Ruth Feldman, Ann Arbor: Translation Press, 1981.
Winter Fragments: Selected Poems 1945-1979, translated by Rina Ferrarelli, New York: Chelsea, 2006.

Le Mosche del meriggio, Milan: Mondadori, 1958.
L'Osso, l'anima, Milan: Mondadori, 1964.
L'Aria secca del fuoco, Milan: Mondadori, 1972.
La Discesa al trono, Milan: Mondadori, 1975.
Poesie scelte (1946-1973), edited by Giovanni Raboni, Milan: Mondadori, 1978.
L'Allodola ottobrina, Milan: Mondadori, 1979.
Chiromanzia d'inverno, Milan: Mondadori, 1983.
Segni, Milan: Scheiwiller, 1986.
Poesie 1943-1979, edited by Giovanni Raboni and Vincenzo Leotta, Milan: Mondadori, 1990.

Celan, Paul
Selected Poems and Prose of Paul Celan, translated by John Felstiner, New York and London: W. W. Norton, 2001.
Threadsuns, translated by Pierre Joris, Los Angeles: Sun & Moon Press, 2000.
Glottal Stop: 101 Poems by Paul Celan, translated by Nikolai Popov and Heather McHugh, Hanover and London: Wesleyan University Press, 2000.
Breathturn, translated by Pierre Joris, Copenhagen/Los Angeles: Green Integer, 2006.
Gesammelte Werke, Frankfurt-am-Main: Suhrkamp, 2000.

Cernuda, Luis
The Poetry of Luis Cernuda, translated by Anthony Edkins and Derek Harris, New York: New York University Press, 1977.
Selected Poems, translated by Reginald Gibbons, Riverdale, New York: Sheep Meadow Press, 1999.
Written in Water: The Prose Poems of Luis Cernuda, translated by Stephen Kessler, San Francisco: City Lights Books, 2004.
Ocnos/Variaciones sobre tema Mexicano, edited by Jaime Gil de Biedma, Madrid: Taurus, 1977 (second edition, 1979).
Ocnos, edited by D. Musacchio, Barcelona: Seix Barral, 1989.
La realidad y el deseo (1924-1962), Madrid: Alianza, 1991.
Poesía completa, edited by Derek Harris and Luis Maristany, Madrid: Siruela, 1993.
Prosa, edited by Derek Harris and Luis Maristany, Madrid: Siruela, 1994.

Christianopoulos, Dinos
"Five poems by Dinos Christianopoulos," translated by Kimon Friar, *Modern European Poetry: French/German/Greek/Italian/Russian/Spanish*, edited by Willis Barnstone, Patricia Terry, Arthur S. Wensinger, Kimon Friar, Sonia Raiziss, Alfredo de Palchi, George Reavey, and Angel Flores, New York/Toronto/London: Bantam Books, 1966.
"They are Tracking Down Everything Picturesque," translated by Kimon Friar, *The Second Century Anthologies of Verse*, Book 2, edited by R. A. Charlesworth and D. Lee, Toronto: Oxford University Press, 1967.

"Thirteen Poets of Salonika: An Anthology of Selections and Translations," including "Five poems by Dinos Christianopoulos," translated by Kimon Friar, *Charioteer*, No. 10, 1968.

"Five Poems by Dinos Christianopoulos," translated by Kimon Friar, *Café* (The Solo Press), Summer 1969.

"Eighteen Post-War Greek Poets," translated by Kimon Friar, *Chicago Review*, Vol. 21, No. 2, August 1969.

"Ithaca," translated by Kimon Friar, *Literary Review*, Vol. XVI, No. 3, Spring 1973.

"The Poetry of Dinos Christianopoulos: An Introduction and A Selection," twenty-one poems translated by Kimon Friar, *Journal of the Hellenic Diaspora*, Vol. VI, No. 1, Spring 1979.

The Downward Turn: Fourteen Stories, translated by Michael Vitopoulos, Toronto: National Heritage, 1994.

Poems, translated by Nicholas Kostis, Athens: Odysseas Publications, 1995.

The Naked Piazza, translated by Nicholas Kostis, Peania, 2000.

Istoriki kai aisthitiki diamorphosi tou rebetikou tragoudiou, Thessaloniki: Diagonios, 1961.

I kato bolta, Thessaloniki: Diagonios, 1980.

Mikra poiimata, Thessaloniki: Diagonios, 1982.

Nekri piatsa, Thessaloniki: Diagonios, 1984.

Poiimata, Thessaloniki: Diagonios, 1985.

Oi rebetes tou dounia, Thessaloniki: Diagonios, 1986.

Claus, Hugo

Selected Poems 1953-1973, translated by Paul Brown, Theo Hermans, and Peter Nijmeijer, Isle of Skye, Scotland: Aquila, 1986.

The Sorrow of Belgium, translated by Arnold J. Pomerans, New York: Pantheon, 1990.

Greetings: Selected Poems, translated by John Irons, New York: Harcourt, 2005.

Het Verdriet van België, Amsterdam/Antwerpen: De Bezige Bij/Contact NV, 1983.

Gedichten 1948-1993, Amsterdam: De Bezige Bij, 1994.

Gedichten 1969-1978, Amsterdam: De Bezige Bij, 2004.

Coetzee, J. M.

Landscape *with Rowers: Poetry from the Netherlands*, translated by J. M. Coetzee, Princeton, New Jersey: Princeton University Press, 2004.

Cohen, Marcel

The Peacock Emperor Moth, translated by Cid Corman, Providence, Rhode Island: Burning Deck, 1995.

Mirrors, translated by Jason Weiss, Copenhagen/Los Angeles: Green Integer, 1998.

"Notes," *World Literature Today*, Summer-Autumn 2001.

In Search of a Lost Ladino: Letter to Antonio Saura, translated by Raphael Rubinstein, Jerusalem: Ibis Editions, 2006.
Miroirs, Paris: Gallimard, 1980.
Letras a un pintor ke kreya azer retratos imaginarios, Madrid: Almarabu, 1985.
Le Grand Paon-de-nuit, Paris: Gallimard, 1990.
Lettre à Antonio Saura, bilingual edition, Paris: L'Échoppe, 1997.
Quelques faces visibles du silence (Antonio Saura), Paris: L'Échoppe, 2000.
Faits: lecture courante à l'usage des grands débutants, Paris: Gallimard, 2002.
"Notes" (1998), *À propos de Marcel Cohen*, special issue, *Le Préau des collines*, No. 7, 2005.
Faits, II, Paris: Gallimard, 2007.

Cohn, Hans W.
Gedichte, London: Fortune Press, 1950.
Gedichte, Gütersloh, Germany: Sigbert Mohn Verlag, 1964.
Existential Thought and Therapeutic Practice, London: Sage, 1997.
Else Lasker-Schüler: The Broken World, Cambridge: Cambridge University Press, Anglica-Germanica Series No. 2, 1974.
With All Five Senses, translated by Frederick G. Cohn. London: Menard Press, 1999.
Heidegger and the Roots of Existential Therapy, London: Sage, 2003.
Landscapes and Other Poems, translated by Frederick G. Cohn, London: Menard Press, 2004.
Mit allen fünf Sinnen, Hürth bei Köln: Edition Memoria, 1994.

Čolić, Velibor
Les Bosniaques (1993), translated into French by Mireille Robin, Paris: Le Serpent à Plumes, 1994.
Chronique des oubliés (1994), translated into French by Mireille Robin, Paris: Le Serpent à Plumes, 1996.

Connolly, David
Angelic & Black: Contemporary Greek Short Stories, edited and translated by David Connolly, Athens: Cosmos Publishing, 2006.

Csoóri, Sándor
Memory of Snow, translated by Nicholas Kolumban, Great Barrington, Massachusetts: Penmaen Press, 1983.
Selected Poems of Sándor Csoóri, translated by Len Roberts, Port Townsend, Washington: Copper Canyon, 1992.
Barbarian Prayer: Selected Poems of Sándor Csoóri, translated by George Szirtes and Edwin Morgan, London: Forest Books, 1996.
Before and After the Fall, translated by Len Roberts, Rochester, New York: Boa Editions, 2004.

Dalakoura, Veroniki
"December," "Let me Twist the Blade," "Mysterious Barricades," and "Excessive
    Aestheticism," translated by Nikos Spanias, *Coffeehouse*, No. 3, 1976.
"Excessive Aestheticism," "Mysterious Barricades," "Let me Twist the Blade"
    (translated by Nikos Spanias), "Demeter" (translated by Thanassis Maska-
    lieris), and "December" (translated by Dinos Siotis)," *Coffeehouse*, Nos. 7-8
    (Twenty Contemporary Greek Poets), San Francisco: Wire Press, 1979.
"Let me Twist the Blade," "Mysterious Barricades," and "Excessive Aestheti-
    cism" (translated by Nikos Spanias), "December," "Love that went Crazy,"
    "Demeter," and "Epilogue" (translated by Dinos Siotis), *Coffeehouse*, Nos.
    11-12 (Ten Women Poets of Greece), San Francisco: Wire Press, 1982.
"Last Text," translated by Edward Phinney, *The Amaranth* (Bulletin of the Mod-
    ern Greek Studies Program at the University of Toronto), No. 6, 1983.
"What Verefon Said to Pegasus" (from *Sleep*), translated by John Taylor, *Sphinx*
    (Paris), Volume 1, No. 1, Winter 1984, p. 45.
"My Answer to the Question," "And these Poets," "My Little Brother on the
    Stairs," "My Final Love will be with You," and "Mal de vivre," translated
    by Rae Dalven, *Daughters of Sappho: Contemporary Greek Women Poets*,
    Associated University Presses, 1994.
"The Other One" (from *Sleep*), translated by John Taylor, *Hellenic Quarterly*,
    No. 4, Spring 2000, pp. 64-65.
"Song," "How Many Pains," "Dimitra," "Your Sailing is Difficult" (translated
    by Allegro Shartz), "Excessive Aesthetics," "The Love that went Mad (I,
    IV)," "Epilogue," "Eternal Roebuck" (translated by Allegro Shartz and Nanos
    Valaoritis), *An Anthology of Modern Greek Poetry*, edited by Nanos Valaoritis
    and Thanasis Maskaleris, Jersey City, New Jersey: Talisman House, 2003.
"Demeter," translated by Yannis Goumas, *The Ancient Country of Poems: Modern
    Greek Poets on Ancient Greece*, edited by Elias Gris, Metaichmio, 2004.
"What Verefon Said to Pegasus" and "The Final Text" (from *Sleep*), translated
    by John Taylor, *Greek Writers Today: An Anthology*, Volume 1, Athens:
    Hellenic Authors' Society, 2004, pp. 42-43.
"Laughter" and "Landscape," translated by Yannis Goumas, *Bilieto*, Nos. 7-8,
    2006.
Several poems from *26 Poems*, translated by Yannis Goumas, *Poeticanet.
    com.*
Poiisi '67-'72 (Poetry 1967-1972), Athens, privately printed, 1972.
I parakmi tou erota, Athens: Diogenis, 1976.
O hypnos, Athens: Nefeli, 1982.
To paihnidi tou telous, Athens: Nefeli, 1988.
Meres idonis, Athens: Forma, 1991.
Agria angeliki photia, Athens: Agra, 1997.
O pinakas tou Hodler, Athens: Agra, 2001.
26 Poiimata, Athens: Agra, 2004.

De Angelis, Milo
Finite Intuition: Selected Poetry and Prose, translated by Lawrence Venuti, Los
    Angeles: Sun and Moon, 1995.

Between the Blast Furnaces and the Dizziness: A Selection of Poems: 1970-1999, translated by Emanuel di Pasquale, New York: Chelsea Editions, 2003.
Somiglianze, Parma: Guanda, 1976, 1990.
Millimetri, Turin: Einaudi, 1983.
Terra del viso, Milan: Mondadori, 1985.
Distante un padre, Milan: Mondadori, 1989.
Biografia sommaria, Milan: Mondadori, 1999.
Dove eravamo già stati (poesie 1970-1999), Rome: Donzelli, 2001.
Tema dell'addio, Milan: Mondadori, 2005.

Debeljak, Aleš
The Chronicle of Melancholy, translated by Michael Biggins, Chattanooga, Tennessee: Poetry Miscellany, 1989.
Anxious Moments, translated by Christopher Merrill and Aleš Debeljak, Fredonia, New York: White Pine Press, 1994.
The Dictionary of Silence, translated by Sonja Kravanja, Santa Fe, New Mexico: Lumen Press, 1999.
The City and the Child, translated by Christopher Merrill and Aleš Debeljak, Buffalo, New York: White Pine Press, 1999.
Zamenjave, zamenjave, Ljubljana: Mladinska Knjiga, 1982.
Imena smrti, Ljubljana: Mladinska Knjiga, 1985.
Slovar tišine, Ljubljana: Aleph Press, 1987.
Minute strahu, Ljubljana: Mladinska Knjiga, 1990.
Mesto in otrok, Ljubljana: Mladinska Knjiga, 1996.

Decavalles, Andonis
Ransom to Time: Selected Poems, translated by Kimon Friar, London and Toronto: Associated University Presses, 1984.
Nimule-Gondokoro, Athens: privately printed, 1949.
Akís, Athens: privately printed, 1950.
Okeanides, Athens: Ikaros, 1970.
Armoi Karavia Lutra, Athens: Ekdoseis ton Philon, 1976.

Delay, Florence
Le Aïe Aïe de la corne de brume (1975), Paris: Gallimard, 1999.
L'Insuccès de la fête (1980), Paris: Gallimard, 1990.
Riche et légère (1983), Paris: Gallimard, 1990.
Course d'amour pendant le deuil, Paris: Gallimard, 1986.
Petites formes en prose après Edison, Paris: Hachette/Fayard, 1987.
Partition rouge: Poèmes et chants des Indiens d'Amérique du Nord (1988), co-translated with Jacques Roubaud, Paris: Seuil, 1995.
Etxemendi (1990), Paris: Gallimard, 1992.
Catalina, Paris: Seuil, 1994.
La Fin des temps ordinaires, Paris: Gallimard, 1996.
Dit Nerval, Paris: Gallimard, 1999.
Trois désobéissances, Paris: Gallimard, 2004.

Graal Théâtre, co-written with Jacques Roubaud, Paris: Gallimard, 2005.

de Palchi, Alfredo
Sessions with My Analyst (Sessioni con l'analista), bilingual edition, translated by I. L. Salomon, New York. October House, 1970.
The Scorpion's Dark Dance/La buia danza di scorpione, bilingual edition, translated by Sonia Raiziss, Riverside, California: Xenos Books, 1993.
Anonymous Constellation/Costellazione anonima, bilingual edition, translated by Sonia Raiziss, Riverside, California: Xenos Books, 1997.
Addictive Aversions/Le viziose avversioni, bilingual edition, translated by Michael Palma, Sonia Raiziss, I. L. Salomon, and Alethea Gail Segal, Riverside, California: Xenos Books, 1999.
"Eight New Poems," translated by Barbara Carle, *Gradiva*, No. 19, Spring 2001, pp. 10-25.
Essenza carnale: quattordici poesie musicali su testi di Alfredo de Palchi. CD, music composed by Carlo Galante and recorded by the group "Sonata Islands." Translated by Barbara Carle. Produced by the Sonia Raiziss Giop Charitable Foundation, 2003.
Scritti sulla poesia di Alfredo De Palchi, special supplement to issue No. 6 of the Italian review *Hebenon*, October 2000.
Sessioni con l'analista, Milano: Mondadori, 1967.
Mutazioni, Udine: Campanotto Editore, 1988.
Costellazione anonima, Marina di Minturno: Carmanica Editore, 1998.
Paradigma, Marina di Minturno: Carmanica Editore, 2000.
Paradigma: Tutte le poesie: 1947-2005, Milano: Mimesis/Hebenon, 2006.

des Forêts, Louis-René
Le Bavard, Paris: Gallimard, 1946.

Dimaras, C. Th.
A History of Modern Greek Literature, translated by Mary Gianos, Albany: State University of New York Press, 1972.

Elburg, Jan G.
Gedichten 1950-1975, Amsterdam: De Bezige Bij, 1975.

Elytis, Odysseus
The Axion Esti, translated by Edmund Keeley and George Savidis, Pittsburgh: University of Pittsburgh Press, 1974/London: Anvil Press, 1980.
The Sovereign Sun, translated by Kimon Friar, Philadelphia: Temple University Press, 1974/Newcastle Upon Tyne (U. K.): Bloodaxe Books, 1990.
Selected Poems, translated by Edmund Keeley, Philip Sherrard, George Savidis, John Stathatos, and Nanos Valaoritis, New York: Penguin/The Viking Press, 1981.
Maria Nephele, translated by Athan Anagnostopoulos, Boston: Houghton Mifflin, 1981.

Analogies of Light, edited by Ivar Ivask, Norman, Oklahoma: University of Oklahoma Press, 1981.
Six and One Remorses for the Sky and Other Poems, translated by Jeffrey Carson, Helsinki: Eurographica, 1985.
What I Love, translated by Olga Broumas, Port Townsend, Washington: Copper Canyon, 1986.
The Little Mariner, translated by Olga Broumas, Port Townsend, Washington: Copper Canyon, 1988.
Open Papers, translated by Olga Broumas and T. Begley, Port Townsend, Washington: Copper Canyon, 1995.
The Collected Poems of Odysseus Elytis, translated by Jeffrey Carson and Nikos Sarris. Baltimore and London: The Johns Hopkins University Press, 1997 (revised and expanded edition, 2004).
Poiisi, Athens: Ikaros, 2002.

Erb, Elke
Mountains in Berlin, translated by Rosmarie Waldrop, Providence, Rhode Island: Burning Deck Press, 1995.
Gutachten, Berlin: Aufbau-Verlag, 1976.
Der Faden der Geduld, Berlin: Aufbau-Verlag, 1978.
Vexierbild, Berlin: Aufbau-Verlag, 1983.

Erba, Luciano
The Hippopotamus, translated from the Italian by Ann Snodgrass, Toronto/Buffalo: Guernica, 2003.
The Greener Meadow, translated by Peter Robinson, Princeton/Oxford: Princeton University Press, 2006.
Il male minore, Milan: Mondadori, 1960.
Il prato più verde, Milan: Guanda, 1977.
Il nastro di Moebius, Milan: Mondadori, 1980.
L'ippopotamo, Turin: Einaudi, 1989.
L'ipotesi circense, Milan: Garzanti, 1995.
Nella terra di mezzo, Milan: Mondadori, 2000.
Poesie 1951-2001, Milan: Mondadori, 2002.
L'altra metà, Genoa: San Marco dei Giustiniani 2004.

Esterházy, Péter
Helping Verbs of the Heart, translated by Michael Henry Heim, New York: Grove Weidenfeld, 1990.
A szív segédigéi, Budapest: Magvetö, 1985.

Feldman, Jennie
The Lost Notebook, London: Anvil, 2005.

Fernández, Lucas
Acte de la Passion, Théâtre espagnol du XVIe siècle, translated into French by Florence Delay, Paris: Gallimard-Pléiade, 1983.

Fontanella, Luigi
The Transparent Life and Other Poems, translated by Michael Palma, New York: Gradiva, 2000.
Angels of Youth, translated by Carol Lettieri and Irene Marchegiani, Riverside, California: Xenos Books, 2001.
Land of Time: Selected Poems 1972-2003, translated by W. S. Di Piero, Carol Lettieri, Irene Marchegiani, Michael Palma, Emanuel di Pasquale, New York: Chelsea, 2006.
La verifica incerta, Rome: De Luca, 1972;
La vita trasparente, Venice: Rebellato, 1978.
Simulazione di reato, Maduria: Lacaita, 1979.
Stella saturnina, Rome: Il Ventaglio, 1989.
Round Trip, Udine: Campanotto, 1991.
Ceres, Formia: Caramanica, 1996.
Azul, Milan: Archinto, 2001.

Forsström, Tua
I Studied Once at a Wonderful Faculty, translated by David McDuff and Stina Katchadourian, Highgreen, Tarset, Northumberland (U. K.): Bloodaxe, 2006.
Jag studerade en gång vid en underbar fakultet, Helsinki: Söderströms, 2003.

Friar, Kimon
Modern European Poetry: French/German/Greek/Italian/Russian/Spanish, edited by Willis Barnstone, Patricia Terry, Arthur S. Wensinger, Kimon Friar, Sonia Raiziss, Alfredo de Palchi, George Reavey, and Angel Flores, New York/Toronto/London: Bantam Books, 1966.
"They are Tracking Down Everything Picturesque" (by Dinos Christianopoulos)," translated by Kimon Friar, *The Second Century Anthologies of Verse*, Book 2, edited by R. A. Charlesworth and D. Lee, Toronto: Oxford University Press, 1967.
"Thirteen Poets of Salonika: An Anthology of Selections and Translations," translated by Kimon Friar, *Charioteer*, No. 10, 1968.
"Five Poems by Dinos Christianopoulos," translated by Kimon Friar, *Café* (The Solo Press), Summer 1969.
"Eighteen Post-War Greek Poets," translated by Kimon Friar, *Chicago Review*, Vol. 21, No. 2, August 1969.
"Ithaca" (by Dinos Christianopoulos)," translated by Kimon Friar, *Literary Review*, Vol. XVI, No. 3, Spring 1973.
"The Poetry of Dinos Christianopoulos: An Introduction and A Selection," translated by Kimon Friar, *Journal of the Hellenic Diaspora*, Vol. VI, No. 1, Spring 1979.

Galbraith, Iain
The Night Begins with a Question: XXV Austrian Poems 1978-2002, edited by Iain Galbraith. Manchester: Carcanet/Edinburgh: Scottish Poetry Library, 2007.

García Lorca, Federico
Six Poèmes galiciens, translated into French by Florence Delay, Paris: Raina Lupa, 1998.

Glassgold, Peter
Living Space: Poems of the Dutch Fiftiers, The PIP Anthology of World Poetry of the Twentieth Century, Volume 6, edited with an introduction by Peter Glassgold; revised and expanded, with a note, by Douglas Messerli. Los Angeles and Copenhagen: Green Integer, 2005.

Głowiński, Michał
The Black Seasons, translated by Marci Shore, Evanston: Northwestern University Press, 2005.
Czarne sezony, Warsaw: Open, 1999.

Gómez de la Serna, Ramón
Les Moitiés, translated into French by Florence Delay and Pierre Lartigue, Paris: Christian Bourgois, 1991.

Gracq, Julien
La littérature à l'estomac, Paris: José Corti, 1950.
Oeuvres complètes, volume 1, Paris: Gallimard, 1989.
Oeuvres complètes, volume 2, Paris: Gallimard, 1995.

Haavikko, Paavo
Selected Poems, translated by Anselm Hollo, Manchester (U. K.): Carcanet, 1991.

Hamburger, Michael
German Poetry 1910-1975, London: Carcanet, 1977.

Handke, Peter
Absence, translated by Ralph Manheim, New York: Farrar, Straus and Giroux, 1990.
Die Abwesenheit, Frankfurt-am-Main: Suhrkamp, 1987.
Die Innenwelt der Außenwelt der Innenwelt, Frankfurt-am-Main: Suhrkamp, 1974.

Hemon, Aleksandar
The Question of Bruno, London: Picador, 2000.

Huchel, Peter
A Thistle in His Mouth, translated by Henry Beissel, Dunvegan, Ontario, Canada: Cormorant Books, 1987.
The Garden of Theophrastus: Selected Poems, translated by Michael Hamburger, London: Anvil Press Poetry, 2004.
Gedichte, Berlin: Aufbau Verlag, 1948.

Chausseen Chausseen, Frankfurt-am-Main: Fischer, 1963.
Gezählte Tage, Frankfurt-am-Main: Suhrkamp, 1972.
Ausgewählte Gedichte, Frankfurt-am-Main: Suhrkamp, 1973.
Die neunte Stunde, Frankfurt-am-Main: Suhrkamp, 1979.
Die Sternenreuse (Gedichte 1925-1947), Munich: Piper, 1967, 1981.
Gesammelte Werke in zwei Bänden, edited by Axel Vieregg, Frankfurt-am-Main: Suhrkamp, 1984.

Ioannou, Yorgos
Good Friday Vigil, translated by Peter Mackridge and Jackie Willcox, Athens: Kedros, 1995.
Refugee Chronicles: Thessaloniki Chronicles, translated by Fred A. Reed, Athens: Kedros, 1997.

Jaccottet, Philippe
Après beaucoup d'années, Paris: Gallimard, 1994.
D'une lyre à cinq cordes: traductions de Philippe Jaccottet 1946-1995, Paris: Gallimard, 1997.

Jacobsen, Rolf
The Roads Have Come to an End Now: Selected and Last Poems of Rolf Jacobsen, translated by Robert Bly, Roger Greenwald, and Robert Hedin. Port Townsend, Washington: Copper Canyon, 2001.
North in the World: Selected Poems of Rolf Jacobsen, translated by Roger Greenwald, Chicago and London: University of Chicago Press, 2002.
Samlede dikt, Oslo: Gyldendal Norsk Forlag, 1999.

Jergović, Miljenko
Sarajevo Marlboro (1994), translated by Stela Tomašević, New York: Archipelago, 2004/London: Penguin, 1997.
Sarajevski Marlboro, Zagreb: Durieux, 1994.

József, Attila
The Iron-Blue Vault: Selected Poems, translated by Z. Ozsváth and F. Turner, Newcastle upon Tyne: Bloodaxe, 1999.
Perched on Nothing's Branch: Selected Poems, translated by Peter Hargitai, Buffalo: White Pine, 1999.
A Transparent Lion: Selected Poems, translated by Michael Castro and Gábor G. Gyukics, Copenhagen/Los Angeles: Green Integer, 2006.
Aimez-moi: L'Oeuvre poétique, edited by Georges Kassai, several translators, Paris: Phébus, 2004.
Összes versei, Budapest: Osiris, 2000.

Kaplinski, Jaan
Evening Brings Everything Back, translated by the author with Fiona Sampson, Highgreen, Northumberland (U. K.): Bloodaxe, 2004.

Õhtu toob tagasi kõik, Tallin: Eesti Raamat, 1984.
Jää ja kanarbik, Tallin: Looming, 1989.
Mitu suve ja kevadet, Tallin: Vagabund, 1995.

Kassabova, Kapka
All Roads Lead to the Sea, Auckland: Auckland University Press, 1997.
Dismemberment, Auckland: Auckland University Press, 1998.
Reconnaissance, Auckland: Penguin, 1999.
Love in the Land of Midas, Auckland: Penguin, 2000.
Someone Else's Life, Highgreen, Northumberland (U.K.): Bloodaxe, 2003.
Geography for the Lost, Highgreen, Northumberland (U.K.): Bloodaxe, 2007.

Kates, J.
In the Grip of Strange Thoughts: Russian Poetry in a New Era, edited by J. Kates, translated by Judith Hemschemeyer, Brookline, Massachusetts: Zephyr Press/Highgreen, Tarset, Northumberland (U. K.): Bloodaxe Books, 1999.

Kielar, Marzanna
Salt Monody, translated by Elżbieta Wójcik-Leese, Brookline, Massachusetts: Zephyr, 2006.
Sacra conversazione, Suwałki: Suwalskie Towarzystwo Kultury, 1992.
Materia prima, Poznań: Obserwator, 1999.
Monodia, Kraków: Znak, 2006.

Kocbek, Edvard
At the Door of Evening, translated by Tom Lozar, Ljubljana: Aleph, 1990.
Edvard Kocbek, translated by Michael Biggins, Ljubljana: Slovene Writers' Association, 1995.
Embers in the House of Night, translated by Sonja Kravanja, Santa Fe, New Mexico: Lumen Books, 1999.
Nothing is Lost: Selected Poems, translated by Michael Scammell and Veno Taufer, Princeton and Oxford: Princeton University Press, 2004.
Zbrane pesmi, two volumes, Ljubljana: Cankarjeva založba, 1977.

Kouwenaar, Gerrit
décor/stills, translated by Peter Nijmeijer, Deal, Kent (UK): Actual Size Press, 1975.
gedichten 1948-1977, Amsterdam: Querido, 1982.
helder maar grijzer: gedichten 1978-1996, Amsterdam: Querido, 1998.

Kross, Jaan
The Czar's Madman, translated by Anselm Hollo, New York: Pantheon, 1993.
Professor Martens' Departure, translated by Anselm Hollo, New York: The New Press, 1994.

Kreisri hull, Tallin: Eesti Raamat, 1978.
Professor Martensi Ärasōit, Tallin: Eesti, Raamat, 1984.

Kušar, Meta
La Voix dans le corps/The Voice in the Body/Glas v Telesu: Three Slovenian Women Poets (Erika Vouk, Meta Kušar, Maja Vidmar), various translators, Ljubljana: Slovene Writers' Association, 2005.
Ljubljana, Ljubljana: Cankarjeva založba, 2004.

Lazić, Radmila
A Wake for the Living, translated by Charles Simic, Saint Paul: Graywolf, 2003.
Price I Druge Pesme, Belgrade: KOV, 1998.
Iz Anamneze, Belgrade: RAD, 2000.
Doroti Parker—Bluz, Belgrade: Prosveta, 2003.

Limonov, Edward
It's Me, Eddie (1979), New York: Random House, 1983.

Lucebert
The Tired Lovers They Are Machines, translated by Peter Nijmeijer, London: Transgravity Press, 1974.
Weapons in the Grass: Selected Poems, translated by Peter Nijmeijer, James S. Holmes, Scott Rollins, and others, Los Angeles: Green Integer, 2006.
verzamelde gedichten, Amsterdam: De Bezige Bij, 2002.

Luzi, Mario
In the Dark Body of Metamorphosis and Other Poems, translated by I. L. Solomon, New York: W. W. Norton, 1975.
After So Many Years: Selected Poems, translated by Catherine O'Brien, Dublin, Ireland: Dedalus, 1990.
For the Baptism of our Fragments, translated by Luigi Bonaffini, Toronto/Montreal/Tonawanda, New York: Guernica, 1992.
Phrases and Passages of a Salutary Song, translated by Luigi Bonaffini, Toronto/Montreal/Tonawanda, New York: Guernica, 1999.
Earthly and Heavenly Journey of Simone Martini, translated by Luigi Bonaffini, Copenhagen/Los Angeles: Green Integer, 2003.
Trames, translated into French by Philippe Renard and Bernard Simeone, Lagrasse/Paris: Verdier, 1986.
Livre d'Hypatie, translated into French by Bernard Simeone, Lagrasse/Paris: Verdier, 1994.
La Barca, Modena: Guanda, 1935/2nd edition: Florence: Parenti, 1942.
Avvento notturno, Florence: Vallecchi, 1940.
Studio su Mallarmé, Florence: Sansoni, 1952.
Nel magma, Milan: All'Insegna del Pesce d'Oro, 1963/2nd edition: Milan: Garzanti, 1966.

Trame, Milan: Rizzoli, 1982.
Per il battesimo dei nostri frammenti, Milan: Garzanti, 1985.
Frasi et incisi di un canto salutare, Milan: Garzanti, 1990.
Libro di Ipazia, Teatro, Milan: Garzanti, 1993.
Viaggio terrestre e celeste di Simone Martini, Milan: Garzanti, 1994.
Tutte le poesie, two volumes, Milan: Garzanti, 1998.
L'Opera poetica, edited by Stefano Verdino, Milan: Mondadori ("I Meridiani"), 1998.
Sotto specie umana, Milan: Garzanti, 1999.
Dottrino dell'estremo principiante, Milan: Garzanti, 2004.

Malmberg, Helga
Widerhall des Herzens: ein Peter-Altenberg-Buch, Munich: Albert Langen/ Georg Müller, 1961.

Marchese, Angelo
Visiting angel: Interpretazione semiologica della poesia di Montale, Turin: Società editrice internazionale, 1977.

Mariani, Lucio
Echoes of Memory: Selected Poems of Lucio Mariani, translated by Anthony Molino, Middletown, Connecticut: Wesleyan University Press, 2003.
Antropino, Padova: Rebellato, 1974.
Ombudsman ed altro, Milan: Guanda, 1976.
Panni e bandiere, Rome: Il Pruno, 1980.
Dispersi gli alleati, Milan: Crocetti, 1990.
Pandemia, Rome: Edizioni dell'Elefante, 1990.
Il torto della preda: versi scelti 1974-1994, Milan: Crocetti, 1995.
Del tempo, Rome: Edizioni dell'Elefante, 1998.
Qualche notizia del tempo, Milan: Crocetti, 2001.

Matajc, Vanesa
Fragments from Slovene Literature: An Anthology of Slovene Literature, edited by Vanesa Matajc, various translators, Ljubljana: Slovene Writers' Association, 2005.

Messerli, Douglas
Living Space: Poems of the Dutch Fiftiers, The PIP Anthology of World Poetry of the Twentieth Century, Volume 6, edited with an introduction by Peter Glassgold; revised and expanded, with a note, by Douglas Messerli. Los Angeles and Copenhagen: Green Integer, 2005.

Miłosz, Czesław
Facing the River, translated by the author and Robert Haas, Hopewell, New Jersey: The Ecco Press, 1995.
Na brzegu rzeki, Kraków: Znak, 1994.

Montale, Eugenio
Satura 1962-1970, translated by William Arrowsmith, New York and London: Norton, 1998.
Collected Poems 1920-1954, translated by Jonathan Galassi, New York: Farrar, Straus and Giroux, 1998.
Posthumous Diary, translated by Jonathan Galassi, New York: Turtle Point Press, 2001.
L'opera in versi, Milan: Einaudi, 1980.
Tutte le poesie, Milan: Mondadori, 1991.
Diario postumo: 66 poesie e altre, Milan: Mondadori, 1996.

Myrivilis, Stratis
Vassilis Arvanitis/Pan/The Goblins and Other Short Stories, translated by Abbott Rick, New York: The American Library, 1959.
The Mermaid Madonna, translated by Abbot Rick, New York: Crowell, 1959/ Athens: Efstathiadis, 1998.
The Schoolmistress with the Golden Eyes, translated by Philip Sherrard, London: Hutchinson, 1964/Athens: Efstathiadis, 1998.
Vassilis Arvanitis, translated by Pavlos Andronikos, Armidale, N. S. W. (Australia): The University of New England Publishing Unit, 1977.
Life in the Tomb, translated by Peter Bien, Hanover/London: University Press of New England, 1987 (River Vale, New Jersey: Cosmos Publishing, 2004).

Naiman, Anatoly
Remembering Anna Akhmatova, translated by Wendy Rosslyn, New York: Henry Holt, 1991.
Lions and Acrobats: Selected Poetry, translated by Margo Shohl Rosen and F. D. Reeve, Brookline, Massachusetts: Zephyr Press, 2005.

Nemes Nagy, Ágnes
Ágnes Nemes Nagy: Selected Poems, translated by Bruce Berlind, Iowa City: Iowa Translations, International Writing Program, School of Letters, University of Iowa, 1980.
Between: Selected Poems of Ágnes Nemes Nagy, translated by Hugh Maxton, Dublin: Dedalus Press/Budapest: Corvina, 1988.
The Night of Akhenaton: Selected Poems, translated by George Szirtes, Highgreen, Northumberland (U. K.): Bloodaxe, 2004.
Között, Budapest: Magvetö, 1981.
Összegyüjtött versek és kiadatlan versek, Budapest: Osiris-Századvég, 1995.

Papadiamantis, Alexandros
Un rêve sur les flots, suivi de *L'Amour dans les neiges*, translated into French by Jean Dargos, Paris/Athens: Monde Hellénique, 1908.
The Murderess, translated by Anne Farmakides, Montreal: McGill Companions to Modern Greek Studies, 1975.

The Murderess, translated by George X. Xanthopoulides, London/Athens: Doric/Kathimerini Publications, 1977.

Tales from a Greek Island, translated by Elizabeth Constantinides, Baltimore/London: Johns Hopkins University Press, 1987/reprint 1994.

The Murderess, translated by Peter Levi, London: Writers and Readers, 1983 (London: Loizou, 1995).

Love in the Snow, translated by J. Coggin and Z. Lorenzatos, Athens: Domos, 1993.

Apanta, edited by N. D. Triantaphyllopoulos, five volumes, Athens: Domos, 1981-1988.

Alexandros Papadimantis, edited by N. D. Triantaphyllopoulos, Athens: Ekdoseis ton philon, 1979.

Phota Olophota, edited by N. D. Triantaphyllopoulos, Athens: Helliniko Logotehniko kai Istoriko Arheio, 1981.

Papadimitrakopoulos, Elias

Toothpaste with Chlorophyll/Maritime Hot Baths, translated by John Taylor, Santa Maria, California: Asylum Arts, 1992 (now distributed by Leaping Dog Press).

"Rosamund," *Angelic & Black: Contemporary Greek Short Stories*, translated by David Connolly, Athens: Cosmos Publishing, 2006.

Odontokrema me khlorophylli (1973), Athens: Typographeio Keimena, 1984/Athens: Nefeli, 1995.

Anaphores sto ergo tou pezographou Nikou Kachtitsi, Athens: privately printed, 1974.

Therma thalassia loutra (1980), Athens: Typographeio Keimena, 1985/Athens: Nefeli, 1995.

Epistolai pros mnistin (1980), co-written with Elias Petropoulos, Athens: Nefeli, 1998.

Parakimena, Athens: Kedros, 1983.

Voustrophidon, Athens: Ypsilon, 1987.

O Genikos Arkhiothetis, Athens: Keimena, 1989/Athens: Nefeli, 1995.

Epi ptilon avras nykterinis, Athens: Nefeli, 1992.

Rozamoundi (1995), Athens: Nefeli, 1999.

Apokimena, Athens: Nefeli, 2000.

Topoi tessereis syn treis, Athens: Stigmi, 2001.

Andreas Karkavitsas, Athens: Savvalas, 2004.

O Ovolos kai alla diiyimata, Athens: Nefeli, 2004.

Pavese, Cesare

Stories, translated by A. E. Murch, New York: The Ecco Press, 1987.

Travailler fatigue/La Mort viendra et elle aura tes yeux, translated into French by Gilles de Van, Paris: Gallimard, 1969.

American Literature: Essays and Opinions, translated by Edwin Fussell, Berkeley: University of California Press, 1970.

Hard Labor, translated by William Arrowsmith, New York: The Ecco Press, 1976.

Selected Letters 1934-1950, translated by A. E. Murch, London: Perter Owen, 1969.
The Burning Brand: Diaries 1935-1950, translated by A. E. Murch, New York: Walker, 1961.
This Business of Living: Diaries 1935-1950, translated by D. D. Paige, London: Quartet Books, 1980.
Dialogues with Leuco, translated by William Arrowsmith, Boston: Eridanos Library, 1990.
The Selected Works of Cesare Pavese, translated by R. W. Flint, New York: New York Review Books, 2001.
The Moon and the Bonfires, translated by R. W. Flint, New York: New York Review Books, 2002.
Disaffections: Complete Poems 1930-1950, translated by Geoffrey Brock, Port Townsend, Washington: Copper Canyon Press, 2002.
La letteratura americana e altri saggi, Turin: Einaudi, 1951.
Lettere, Turin: Einaudi, 1966.
Tutte le opere, Turin: Einaudi, 1968.
La poesie, Turin: Einaudi, 1998.
Tutti i romanzi, Turin: Einaudi, 2000.
Il mestiere di vivere: Diario 1935-1950, Turin: Einaudi, 2006.

Petrarch (Petrarca, Francesco)
De otio religioso/Le Repos religieux, translated into French by Christophe Carraud, Grenoble: Éditions Jérome Millon, 2000.

Petropoulos, Elias
The Graves of Greece, translated by John Taylor, Paris: Digamma, 1979.
Old Salonica, translated by John Taylor, Athens: Kedros, 1980.
Balconies in Greece, translated by John Taylor, Athens: Hatzinikolis, 1981.
Wooden Doors/Iron Doors in Greece, translated by John Taylor, Athens: Kedros, 1982.
Tsoclis's Tree, translated by John Taylor, New York: Jackson Gallery, 1982.
"Turkish Coffee in Greece,translated by John Taylor, *Journal of the Hellenic Diaspora*, Vol. 9, No. 4, Winter 1982, pp. 53-61.
"Les tombes bogomiles en Grèce?," translated by John Taylor and Françoise Daviet into French, *Le Fou Parle*, Nos. 21-22, November-December 1982, pp. 53-54.
Mirror for You, translated by John Taylor, Paris: Digamma, 1983.
The Jews of Salonica/Les Juifs de Salonique, translated by John Taylor and Françoise Daviet, Paris: Digamma, 1983.
Courtyards in Greece, translated by John Taylor, Athens: Phorkys, 1983.
"The Ubiquitous Kiosk," translated by John Taylor, *Greek Accent*, Vol. 5, No. 5, March-April 1985, pp. 22-27.
A Macabre Song, translated by John Taylor, Paris: Digamma, 1985.
"The Jewish Wooden Chests of Salonica," translated by John Taylor, *Newsletter of the Jewish Museum of Greece*, No. 16, December 1985, pp. 5-6.

In Berlin: Notebook 1983-1984, translated by John Taylor, Paris: Digamma, 1987.
Rebetika: Songs from the Old Greek Underworld, translated by John Taylor, London: Alcyon, 1992.
Nikos Gabriel Pentzikis (1958), Athens: Nefeli, 1980.
Elytis Moralis Tsarouhis (1966), Athens: Nefeli, 1980
Rebetika tragoudia (1968), Athens: Kedros, 1979.
Corps (1969), Paris: Moments, 1976 (French translation).
Suicide (1973), Paris: Moments, 1976 (French translation).
Poiimata, Athens: Nefeli, 1980.
Pote kai tipota, Athens: Nefeli, 1993.
Apanta, Athens: Nefeli.

Pla, Josep
Le Cahier gris: un journal, translated into French by Pascale Bardoulaud, Nîmes: Jacqueline Chambon, 1992.
El quadern gris: un dietari, volume I, *Obra completa*, Barcelona: Destino, 1983 (4th edition).
Les escales de Llevant, volume XIII, *Obra completa*, Barcelona: Destino, 1969.
Viaje en autobús, Barcelona: Destino, 1942/1980 (Madrid: Fundación Wellington, 2003).

Polet, Sybren
Gedichten 1948-1998, Amsterdam: De Bezige Bij, 2001.

Réda, Jacques
Récitatif/The Party is Over, translated by Dorothy Brown Aspinwall, Troy, Michigan: International Book Publishers, 1983.
The Ruins of Paris, translated by Mark Treharne, London: Reaktion Books, 1996.
Treading Lightly: Selected Poems 1961-1975, translated by Jennie Feldman, London: Anvil Press, 2005.
Return to Calm, translated by Aaron Prevots, Austin, Texas: Host, 2007.
Amen/Récitatif/La Tourne, Paris: Gallimard, 1988.
Le Sens de la marche, Paris: Gallimard, 1990.
Aller aux mirabelles, Paris: Gallimard, 1991.
Lettre sur l'univers et autres discours en vers français, Paris: Gallimard, 1991.
L'Incorrigible, Paris: Gallimard, 1995.
Le Citadin, Paris: Gallimard, 1998.
Moyens de transport, Fontfroide-le-Haut/Saint-Clément-la-Rivière: Fata Morgana, 2003.
Les Cinq Points cardinaux, Fontfroide-le-Haut/Saint-Clément-la-Rivière: Fata Morgana, 2003.
Nouvelles Aventures de Pelby, Paris: Gallimard, 2003.

L'affaire du Ramsès III, Lagrasse: Verdier, 2004.
L'adoption du système métrique: poèmes 1999-2003, Paris: Gallimard, 2004.
La Vingtième me fatigue, Geneva: La Dogana, 2004.
Cléona et autres voyageurs solitaires, Castelnau-le-Lez: Climats, 2005.
Europes, Fontfroide-le-Haut/Saint-Clément-la-Rivière: Fata Morgana, 2005.
Ponts flottants, Paris: Gallimard, 2006.

Rein, Evgeny
Selected Poems, translated by Daniel Weissbort, Robert Reid, Paul Partington, and Carol Rumens/Yuri Drobyshev, Highgreen, Northumberland (U. K.): Bloodaxe, 2001.

Rilke, Rainer Maria
Uncollected Poems, translated by Edward Snow, New York : North Point Press/ Farrar, Straus and Giroux, 1996.
Rilke's Book of Hours: Love Poems to God, translated by Anita Barrows and Joanna Macy, New York: Riverhead Books, 1996.
Sämtliche Werke, Frankfurt-am-Main: Insel, 1955-1966.
Gesammelte Werke in fünf Bänden, Frankfurt-am-Main: Insel, 2003.

Rodenko, Paul
Fire beside the Sea, translated by James S. Holmes and Hans van Marle, IJmuiden, Netherlands: Hoogovens, 1961.
Orensnijder tulpensnijder: verzamelde gedichten, Amsterdam: Harmonie, 1975.

Roubaud, Jacques
La Vieillesse d'Alexandre: Essai sur quelques états récents du vers français (1978), Paris: Ivrea, 2000.
Le Roi Arthur: Au temps des chevaliers et des enchanteurs, Paris: Hachette, 1983.
La Belle Hortense (1985), Paris: Seghers, 1990/Paris: Seuil, 1996.
La Fleur inverse: Essai sur l'art formel des troubadours (1986), Paris: Les Belles Lettres, 1994.
L'Enlèvement d'Hortense (1987), Paris: Seghers, 1991/Paris: Seuil, 1996.
Partition rouge: Poèmes et chants des Indiens d'Amérique du Nord (1988), co-translated with Florence Delay, Paris: Seuil, 1995.
Soleil du Soleil: Anthologie du sonnet français de Marot à Malherbe (1990), Paris: Gallimard, 1999.
L'Exil d'Hortense, Paris: Seghers, 1990/Paris: Seuil, 1996.
Graal Théâtre, co-written with Florence Delay, Paris: Gallimard, 2005.
Our Beautiful Heroine, New York: Overlook Press, 1987.
Hortense is Abducted, Normal, Illinois: Dalkey Archive Press, 2000.
Hortense in Exile, Normal, Illinois: Dalkey Archive Press, 2001.

Różewicz, Tadeusz
They Came to See a Poet, translated by Adam Czerniawski. London: Anvil Press, 2004.

Saarikoski, Pentti
Selected Poems of Pentti Saarikoski, translated by Anselm Hollo, London: Rapp and Carroll, 1967
Poems 1958-1980, translated by Anselm Hollo, West Branch, Iowa: Toothpaste Press, 1983.
Trilogy, translated by Anselm Hollo, Albuquerque: La Alameda Press, 2003.
Tiarnia-sarja ja muut ruotsin kauden runot, edited by H. K. Riikonen, Helsinki: Otava, 1996.

Saba, Umberto
Thirty-One Poems, translated by Felix Stefanile, Manchester: Carcanet, 1980.
Ernesto, translated by Mark Thompson, Manchester: Carcanet, 1987 (London: Paladin, 1989/New York: HarperCollins, 1989).
The Stories and Recollections of Umberto Saba, translated by Estelle Gilson, Manchester: Carcanet, 1993 (Riverdale-on-Hudson: Sheep Meadow Press, 1993).
Songbook: Selected Poems, translated by Stephen Sartarelli, Riverdale-on-Hudson: Sheep Meadow Press, 1998.
History and Chronicle of the Songbook, translated by Stephen Sartarelli, Riverdale-on-Hudson: Sheep Meadow Press, 1998.
Poetry and Prose, translated by Vincent Moleta, Bridgetown, Australia: Aeolian Press, 2004.
Trieste et autres poèmes, translated into French by Georges Haldas, Lausanne, Switzerland: L'Age d'Homme, 1982.
Couleur du temps, translated into French by René de Ceccatty, Paris/Marseille: Rivages, 1986.
Il Canzoniere 1921, Milan: Fondazione Arnoldo e Alberto Mondadori, 1981.
La spada d'amore: lettere scelte 1902-1957, Milan: Mondadori, 1983.
Atroce paese che amo: lettere famigliari 1945-1953, Milan: Bompiani, 1987.
Tutte le poesie, Milan: Mondadori, 1988.
Tutte le prose, Milan: Mondadori, 2001.

Sachtouris, Miltos
With Face to the Wall: Selected Poems, translated by Kimon Friar, Washington, D. C.: The Charioteer Press, 1968.
Quicklime, translated by John Stathatos, London: Oasis Books, 1974.
Selected Poems, translated by Kimon Friar, Old Chatham, New York: Sachem Press, 1982.
Strange Sunday: Selected Poems 1952-1971, translated by John Stathatos, Frome, Somerset (U. K.): Bran's Head Books, 1984.
Poems (1945-1971), translated by Karen Emmerich, New York: Archipelago Books, 2006.

Savinio, Alberto
Speaking to Clio, translated by John Shepley, Marlboro: The Marlboro Press, 1987.
Operatic Lives, translated by John Shepley, Marlboro: The Marlboro Press, 1988.
Capri, translated by John Shepley, Marlboro: The Marlboro Press, 1989.
The Childhood of Nivasio Dolcemare, translated by Richard Pevear, Boston: Eridanos Press, 1988.
Tragedy of Childhood, translated by John Shepley, Marlboro: The Marlboro Press, 1991.
The Lives of the Gods, translated by James Brook and Susan Etlinger, London: Atlas Press, 1991.
Dico a te, Clio, Milan: Adelphi, 1992.
Hermaphrodito e altri romanzi, Milan: Adelphi, 1995.
Capri, Milan: Adelphi, 1998.
Infanzia di Nivasio Dolcemare, Milan: Adelphi, 1998.
Casa "La Vita" e altri racconti, Milan: Adelphi, 1999.
Tragedia dell'infanzia, Turin: Einaudi, 2001.

Sbarbaro, Camillo
Shavings: Selected Prose Poems 1914-1940, translated by Gayle Ridinger, New York: Chelsea, 2005.
L'Opera in versi e in prose, edited by Gina Lagorio and Vanni Scheiwiller, Milan: Garzanti, 1999.

Schierbeek, Bert
The Fall, translated by Charles McGeehan, London: Transgravity Press/Dublin: Dedalus Press, 1973.
Shapes of the Voice, translated by Charles McGeehan, Boston: Twayne, 1977.
Cross Roads, translated by Charles McGeehan, Rochester, Michigan, Katydid Books, 1988.
Formentera/The Gardens of Suzhou, translated by Charles McGeehan, Montreal: Guernica, 1989.
Keeping It Up: The Countryside, translated by Charles McGeehan, Rochester, Michigan: Katydid Books, 1990.
Het boek Ik, Amsterdam: De Bezige Bij, 1951.
De andere namen, Amsterdam: De Bezige Bij, 1952.
De derde persoon, Amsterdam: De Bezige Bij, 1955.
De gestalte der stem, Amsterdam: De Bezige Bij, 1957.
Het dier heeft een mens getekend, Amsterdam: De Bezige Bij, 1960.
Ezel mijn bewoner, Amsterdam: De Bezige, 1964.
Een broek voor een octopus, Amsterdam: De Bezige Bij, 1965.
De deur, Amsterdam: De Bezige Bij, 1972.

Sebald, W. G.
The Emigrants, translated by Michael Hulse, New York: New Directions, 1996.
Vertigo, translated by Michael Hulse, New York: New Directions, 1999.
The Rings of Saturn, translated by Michael Hulse, New York: New Directions, 1999.
Austerlitz, translated by Anthea Bell, New York: Random House, 2001.
After Nature, translated by Michael Hamburger, New York: Random House, 2002.
Nach der Natur: Ein Elementargedicht, Frankfurt-am-Main: Fischer, 1995 (2002).
Austerlitz, Munich/Vienna: Carl Hanser, 2001.
Die Ausgewanderten, Frankfurt-am-Main: Fischer, 1994 (2002).
Die Ringe des Saturn, Frankfurt-am-Main: Fischer, 1997 (2001).
Schwindel. Gefühle, Frankfurt-am-Main: Fischer, 1994 (2000).

Seelig, Carl
Wanderungen mit Robert Walser, Frankfurt-am-Main: Suhrkamp, 2001.

Selimović, Meša
Death and the Dervish (1966), translated by Bogdan Rakić and Stephen M. Dickey, Evanston, Illinois: Northwestern University Press, 1996.
The Fortress (1970), translated by E. D. Goy and Jasna Levinger, Evanston, Illinois: Northwestern University Press, 1999.

Sereni, Vittorio
The Disease of the Elm and Other Poems, translated by Marcus Perryman and Peter Robinson, London: Many Press, 1983.
Selected Poems of Vittorio Sereni, translated by Marcus Perryman and Peter Robinson, London: Anvil Press, 1990.
Sixteen Poems, translated by Paul Vangelisti, Fairfax, California: Red Hill Press, 1971.
Variable Star, translated by Luigi Bonaffini, Toronto: Guernica, 1999.
The Selected Poetry and Prose of Vittorio Sereni, translated by Marcus Perryman and Peter Robinson, Chicago/London: University of Chicago Press, 2006.
Frontiera, Milan: Corrente, 1941/Milan: Scheiwiller, 1966.
Diario d'Algeria, Florence: Vallechi, 1947/Milan: Mondadori, 1965 (1979)/Turin: Einaudi, 1998.
Gli immediati dintorni: primi e secondi, Milan: Il Saggiatore, 1962 (1983).
L'Opzione e allegati, Milan: Scheiwiller, 1964.
Gli strumenti umani, Turin: Einaudi, 1965 (1975).
Stella variabile, Verona: Almici dei libri, 1979/Milan: Garzanti, 1981.
Senza l'onore delle armi, Milan: Scheiwiller, 1986.
Tutte le poesie, edited by M. T. Sereni, Milan: Mondadori, 1986.
Il grande amico: poesie 1935-1981, Milan: Rizzoli, 1990.
Un posto di vacanza e altre poesie, edited by Z. Birolli, Milan: Scheiwiller, 1994.

Poesie, edited by Dante Isella, Milan: Mondadori, 1995 (2004).
La tentazione della prosa, edited by G. Raboni, Milan: Mondadori, 1998.
Poesie, edited by Dante Isella, Turin: Einaudi, 2005.

Shcherbina (or Chtcherbina), Tatiana
The Score of the Game, translated by J. Kates, Brookline: Zephyr Press, 2003.
Life Without: Selected Poetry and Prose 1992-2003, translated by Sasha Dugdale. Highgreen, Northumberland (U. K.): Bloodaxe, 2004.
Parmi les alphabets, translated into French by Christine Zeytounian-Beloüs, Pantin, France: Le Castor Astral/Trois Rivières, Québec-Canada: Les Écrits des Forges, 1992.
L'Âme déroutée (texts written in French), Chaillé-sous-Ormeaux, France: Le Dé Bleu/Trois Rivières, Québec-Canada: Les Écrits des Forges, 1995.
Antivirus, translated into French by Christine Zeytounian-Beloüs, Chaillé-sous-Ormeaux, France: L'Idée Bleu/Trois Rivières, Québec-Canada: Les Écrits des Forges, 2005.
Natiurmort s prevrashcheniiami, Moscow, self-published, 1985.
Nol' Nol', Moscow: R. Elinine, 1991.
Zhizn' Bez, Moscow: Bibliotheka Zhurnala "Zolotoi Vek", 1997.
Kniga o. . . , Prague/Tver: Mitin Zhurnal (Kolonna Editions), 2001.
Lazurnaya Skrizhal', Moscow, O.G.I., 2003.

Sicari, Giovanna
Naked Humanity: Poems 1981-2003, translated by Emanuel di Pasquale, Stony Brook, New York: Gradiva Publications, 2004.
Decisioni, Sienna: Quaderni di barbablù, 1986.
Ponte d'ingresso, Rome: Rossi & Spera, 1988.
Sigillo, Milan: Crocetti, 1989.
Uno stadio del respiro, Milan: Scheiwiller, 1995.
Nudo e misero trionfi l'umano, Rome: Empiria, 1998.
Roma della vigilia, Rome: Ed. Il Labirinto, 1999.
Epoca immobile, Milan: Jaca Book, 2003.

Skucinska, Anna
Carnivorous Boy, Carnivorous Bird: Poetry from Poland, Selected by Marcin Baran, edited by Anna Skucinska and Elżbieta Wójcik-Leese. Brookline, Massachusetts: Zephyr Press, 2004.

Smith, Gerald S.
Contemporary Russian Poetry: A Bilingual Anthology, edited and translated by Gerald S. Smith, Bloomington, Indiana: Indiana University Press, 1993.

Södergran, Edith
Complete Poems, translated by David McDuff, Highgreen, Tarset, Northumberland (U.K.): Bloodaxe, 1984.

Solzhenitsyn, Alexander
One Day in the Life of Ivan Denisovich, New York: Signet Classics, 1998
   (reprint).

Sommer, Piotr
Continued, translated by Halina Janod and others. Middletown, Connecticut:
   Wesleyan University Press, 2005.
Pamiątki po nas, Kraków: Wydawnictwo Literackie, 1980.
Kolejny Świat, Warsaw: Czytelnik, 1983.
Czynnik liryczny i inne wiersze, London: Aneks, 1988.
Nowe stosunki wyrazów, Poznań: Wydawnictwo a5, 1997.
Piosenka pasterska, Legnica: Centrum Sztuki/Teatr Dramatyczny, 1999.

Stevanović, Vidosav
Voleurs de leur propre liberté, translated into French by Mauricette Begic and
   Nicole Dizdarevic, Paris: L'Esprit des Péninsules, 2003.
Abel et Lise, translated into French by Mauricette Begic and Nicole Dizdarevic,
   Paris: L'Esprit des Péninsules, 2003.

Sumari, Anni
How to Address the Fog: XXV Finnish Poems 1978-2002, edited by Anni
   Sumari, translated by Donald Adamson, Robin Fulton, and David McDuff,
   Manchester (U. K.): Carcanet/Edinburgh, Scotland (U.K.): Scottish Poetry
   Library, 2005.

Svevo, Italo
As a Man Grows Older, translated by Beryl de Zoete, New York: New York
   Review Books, 2001.
Zeno's Conscience, translated by William Weaver, New York: Vintage, 2003.
A Life, translated by Archibald Colquhoun, London: Pushkin Press, 2006.
Tutte le opere, Milan: Mondadori, 2004.

Svevo, Livia Veneziani
Memoir of Italo Svevo, translated by Isabel Quigly, Marlboro: The Marlboro
   Press, 1990.
Vita di mio marito, Trieste: Zibaldone, 1950/Milan: Dall'Oglio, 1976.

Taktsis, Kostas
The Third Wedding, translated by Leslie Finer, London: Alan Ross Ltd., 1967/
   New York: Red Dust, 1971.
The Third Wedding Wreath, translated by John Chioles, Athens: Hermes,
   1985.
To trito stephani (1963), Athens: Ermis, 1970 (1983).
I yiayia mou i Athena kai alla kimena, Athens: Ermes, 1979 (1982).
Ta resta, Athens: Ermes, 1972 (1982).

Taufer, Veno
New Music, translated by Michael Scammell, and Michael Biggins, Chatta-
nooga: Poetry Miscellany Chapbook (University of Tennessee), 1991.
Tongues of the Waterlings and Other Poems, translated by Michael Scammell
and others, Chattanooga: Poetry Miscellany Chapbook (University of Ten-
nessee), 1996.
Poems, translations into English, French, German, Italian, Spanish, and Swedish
by various hands, Ljubljana: Litterae Slovenicae, 1999.
Waterlings, translated by Milne Holton and the author, Evanston, Illinois:
Northwestern University Press, 2000.
Veno Taufer, translations into English, French, and German by various hands,
Ljubljana: Društvo slovenskih pisateljev (20th Vilenica International Liter-
ary Festival), 2005.
Svinčene zvezde, Ljubljana: privately printed, 1958.
Jetnik prostosti, Ljubljana: Cankarjeva založba, 1963.
Vaje in naloge, Maribor: Obzorja, 1969.
Podatki, Maribor: Obzorja, 1972.
Prigode, Ljubljana: Cankarjeva založba, 1973.
Pesmarica rabljenih besed, Ljubljana: Državna založba Slovenije, 1975.
Ravanje žebljev in druge pesmi, Ljubljana: Državna založba Slovenije, 1979.
Sonetje, Ljubljana: Mladinska Knjiga, 1979.
Pesmi, Ljubljana: Državna založba Slovenije, 1980.
Tercine za obtolčeno trobento, Ljubljana: Mladinska knjiga, 1985.
Vodenjaki, Ljubljana: Državna založba Slovenije, 1986.
Črepinje pesmi, Maribor: Obzorja, 1989.
Nihanje molka, Ljubljana: Mladinska knjiga, 1994.
Še ode, Ljubljana: Cankarjeva založba, 1996.
Kosmi in druge kratke pesmi, Ljubljana: Mladinska knjiga, 2000.
Rotive, Ljubljana: Cankarjeva založba, 2003.
Pismo v steklenici, Ljubljana: Nova Revija, 2006.

Thaniel, George
Homage to Byzantium: The Life and Work of Nikos Gabriel Pentzikis, Min-
neapolis: North Central Publishing Company, 1983.

Ungaretti, Giuseppe
Selected Poems, translated by Andrew Frisardi, New York: Farrar, Straus and
Giroux, 2002.
Opere, 4 volumes, Milan: Mondadori, 2000.

Vassilikos, Vassilis
Z, translated by Marilyn Calmann, New York: Farrar, Straus and Giroux,
1968.
Z, translated into French by Pierre Comberousse, Paris Gallimard, 1967.
Z, Athens: Themelion, 1966.

Vidmar, Maja
La Voix dans le corps/The Voice in the Body/Glas v Telesu: Three Slovenian Women Poets (Erika Vouk, Meta Kušar, Maja Vidmar), various translators, Ljubljana: Slovene Writers' Association, 2005.
Razdalje telesa, Ljubljana: Mladinska knjiga, 1984.
Ob vznožju, Ljubljana: Nova revija, 1998.
Prisotnost, Ljubljana: Aleph: Center za slovensko književnost, 2005.

Vinkenoog, Simon
And the Eye Became a Rainbow, translated by Cornelis Vleeskens, Melbourne: Fling Poetry, 1990.

Vizyenos, Georgios
My Mother's Sin and Other Stories, translated by William F. Wyatt, Hanover and London: Brown University Press/University Press of New England, 1988.
Vizyenou, ta Apanta, Athens: Biblos, 1967.
Vizyenos, Neollinika diiyimata, Athens: Ermis, 1980.
Georgios Vizyenos, Athens: Aetos, 1954.

Vouk, Erika
La Voix dans le corps/The Voice in the Body/Glas v Telesu: Three Slovenian Women Poets (Erika Vouk, Meta Kušar, Maja Vidmar), various translators, Ljubljana: Slovene Writers' Association, 2005.
Opis slike, Maribor: Litera, 2002.
Valovanje, Maribor: Litera, 2003.

Walser, Robert
Selected Stories, translated by Christopher Middleton and others, New York: Farrar, Straus & Giroux, 1983 (Vintage Books, 1983)/New York: New York Review Books, 2002.
Robert Walser Rediscovered: Stories, Fairy Tale Plays and Critical Responses, translated by Walter Arndt, Mark Harman, and others, Hanover: University Press of New England, 1985.
Masquerade and Other Stories, translated by Susan Bernofsky and Tom Whalen, Baltimore: Johns Hopkins University Press, 1990.
Robert Walser Number, *The Review of Contemporary Fiction*, Volume 12, No. 1, Spring 1992.
The Walk and Other Stories, translated by Christopher Middleton, London: John Calder, 1957/London: Serpent's Tail, 1993.
Institute Benjamenta, translated by Christopher Middleton, London: Serpent's Tail, 1995.
Jakob von Gunten, translated by Christopher Middleton, Austin: The University of Texas Press, 1969/New York: Vintage Books, 1983/New York: New York Review Books, 1999.
The Robber, translated by Susan Bernofsky, Lincoln and London: University of Nebraska Press, 2000.

The Nimble and the Lazy, translated by Tom Whalen and Annette Wiesner, Black River Falls, Wisconsin: Obscure Publications, 2000.
Speaking to the Rose: Writings 1912-1932, translated by Christopher Middleton, Lincoln, Nebraska: University of Nebraska Press (Bison Books), 2005.
The Assistant, translated by Susan Bernofsky, New York: New Directions, 2007.
Sämtliche Werke in 20 Bänden, Zurich/Frankfurt-am-Main: Suhrkamp, 2002.
Aus dem Bleistiftgebiet, 6 volumes, Zurich/Frankfurt-am-Main: Suhrkamp, 1985-2000.

Weissbort, Daniel
Modern Poetry in Translation, edited by Daniel Weissbort, (No. 10, Winter 1996).

Wójcik-Leese, Elżbieta
Carnivorous Boy, Carnivorous Bird: Poetry from Poland, Selected by Marcin Baran, edited by Anna Skucinska and Elżbieta Wójcik-Leese. Brookline, Massachusetts: Zephyr Press, 2004.

Zagajewski, Adam
Tremor: Selected Poems, translated by Renata Gorczyñski, New York: Farrar, Straus, and Giroux, 1985.
Solidarity, Solitude: Essays, translated by Lillian Vallee, New York: The Ecco Press, 1990.
Canvas, translated by Renata Gorczyñski, Benjamin Ivry, and C. K. Williams, New York: Farrar, Straus, and Giroux, 1991.
Two Cities: On Exile, History, and the Imagination, translated by Lillian Vallee, New York: Farrrar, Straus, and Giroux, 1995.
Mysticism for Beginners, translated by Clare Cavanagh, New York: Farrar, Straus and Giroux, 1997.
Another Beauty, translated by Clare Cavanagh, New York: Farrar, Straus, and Giroux, 2000/Athens, Georgia: University of Georgia Press, 2002.
Without End: New and Selected Poems, translated by Clare Cavanagh, New York: Farrar, Straus, and Giroux, 2002.
A Defense of Ardor, translated by Clare Cavanagh, New York: Farrar, Straus, and Giroux, 2004.
Eternal Enemies, translated by Clare Cavanagh, New York: Farrar, Straus, and Giroux, 2008.
Komunikat, Kraków: Wydawnicktwo Literacki, 1972.
Sklepy Mięsne, Kraków: Wydawnictwo Literacki, 1975.
List: Oda do wielości, Paris: Instytut Literacki, 1983.
Jechac do Lwowa, London: Aneks, 1985.
Solidarność i samotność, Paris: Zeszyty Literackie, 1986.
Płótno, Paris: Zeszyty Literackie, 1990.
Dwa miasta, Paris-Kraków: Zeszyty Literackie/Oficyna Literacka, 1991.
Ziemia Ognista, Poznań: Wydawnictwo a5, 1994.
W cudzym pięknie, Poznań: Wydawnictwo a5, 1998.

Pragnienie, Kraków: Wydawnictwo a5, 1999.
Obrona żarliwości, Kraków: Wydawnictwo a5, 2002.
Powrót, Kraków: Znak, 2003.
Anteny, Kraków: Wydawnictwo a5, 2005.
Poeta rozmawia z filozofem, Warsaw: Zeszyty Literackie, 2007.

Zanzotto, Andrea
Peasants Wake for Fellini's Casanova *and Other Poems*, translated by John P. Welle and Ruth Feldman, Champaign, Illinois: University of Illinois Press, 1997.
The Selected Poetry and Prose of Andrea Zanzotto, translated by Patrick Barron, with additional translations by Thomas J. Harrison, Brian Swann, John P. Welle, and Elizabeth A. Wilkins, Chicago/London: University of Chicago Press, 2007.
Dietro il paesaggio, Milan: Mondadori, 1951.
Elegia e altri versi, Milan: Gramigna, 1954.
Vocativo, Milan: Mondadori, 1957.
IX Ecloghe, Milan: Mondadori, 1962.
La Beltà, Milan: Mondadori, 1968.
Gli Sguardi i fatti e senhal, Pievo di Soligo: Bernardi, 1969/Milan: Mondadori, 1990.
Pasque, Milan: Mondadori, 1973.
Filò: Per il Casanova *di Fellini*, Milan: Mondadori, 1976.
Il Galateo in Bosco, Milan: Mondadori, 1978.
Fosfeni, Milan: Mondadori, 1983.
Idioma, Milan: Mondadori, 1986.
Racconti e prose, Milan: Mondadori, 1990.
Poesie (1938-1986), edited by Stefano Agosti, Milan: Mondadori, 1993.
Sull'Altopiano e prose varie, Vicenza: Neri Pozza, 1995.
Meteo, Rome: Donzelli, 1996.
Le poesie e prose scelte, edited by Stefano Dal Bianco and Gian Mario Villata, Milan: Mondadori, 1999.
Sovrimpressioni, Milan: Mondadori, 2001.

Index